ARISTOTLE: *ON GENERATION AND CORRUPTION*
BOOK I

SYMPOSIUM ARISTOTELICUM

Aristotle: *On Generation and Corruption*, Book I

Symposium Aristotelicum

edited by

FRANS DE HAAS

And

JAAP MANSFELD

CLARENDON PRESS · OXFORD

OXFORD

UNIVERSITY PRESS

Great Clarendon Street, Oxford OX2 6DP

Oxford University Press is a department of the University of Oxford.
It furthers the University's objective of excellence in research, scholarship, and education by
publishing worldwide in

Oxford New York

Auckland Bangkok Buenos Aires Cape Town Chennai
Dar es Salaam Delhi Hong Kong Istanbul Karachi Kolkata
Kuala Lumpur Madrid Melbourne Mexico City Mumbai Nairobi
São Paulo Shanghai Taipei Tokyo Toronto

Oxford is a registered trade mark of Oxford University Press
in the UK and in certain other countries

Published in the United States
by Oxford University Press Inc. New York

British Library Cataloguing in Publication Data
Data available

Library of Congress Cataloging in Publication Data
Data available

ISBN 0-19-924292-5

1 3 5 7 9 10 8 6 4 2

Typeset by Kolam Information Services Pvt. Ltd, Pondicherry, India.
Printed in Great Britain
on acid-free paper by
Biddles Ltd,
King's Lynn, Norfolk

PREFACE

The XVth Symposium Aristotelicum met from 21 to 28 August 1999 in Deurne, the Netherlands. We stayed at the Missiehuis St Willebrord, just outside town. We enjoyed the quiet atmosphere and spacious grounds of the Missiehuis, with their little lake, the weather being exceptionally favourable.

We followed the tradition of the Symposium by bringing together colleagues from various countries to study and discuss a topic of major interest in Aristotelian studies. We took the individual chapters of the first book of the foundational *De generatione et corruptione* as the theme of (at least) one presentation and discussion, and left one session for discussion of this book as a whole. In this way the tendency of the more recent meetings of the Symposium to devote special attention to (a substantial part) of an Aristotelian treatise was continued.

The chapters of the present collection do not form, and are not intended to form, a commentary on the treatise, though individual sections and passages are of course commented on. Instead, we want to focus on specific issues and controversial points, hoping that this inquiry will bring some measure of enlightenment to our readers, though disagreements on particular questions are unavoidably included. As always, the final versions of the papers differ from the drafts read at the Symposium, the authors having profited from the discussions, and from the comments they happened to receive while revising their text. The paper presented by Jaap Mansfeld has been integrated to some extent in that of Keimpe Algra.

Apart from the persons who read papers, the other participants were Enrico Berti, David Charles, Andrea Falcon, Michael Frede, Frans de Haas, Paul Kalligas, Geoffrey Lloyd, Mario Mignucci, Jan van Ophuijsen, Marwan Rashed, Bertus de Rijk, David Runia, Theodore Scaltsas, Malcolm Schofield, and Gerhard Seel.

The Symposium was financed by a generous grant from the Department of Philosophy, Utrecht University for which we are grateful. Our stay at the Missiehuis was made most pleasant by the unforgettable hospitality of Ms Nora Hendriks and Father Koos van Dijk, and the assistance of Marnix Hoekstra, who studies ancient philosophy at Utrecht.

CONTENTS

Contents

LIST OF CONTRIBUTORS

KEIMPE ALGRA, Professor of Ancient and Medieval Philosophy, Utrecht University

SARAH BROADIE, Professor of Philosophy, St Andrews

JACQUES BRUNSCHWIG, Emeritus Professor of Philosophy, Paris I, Sorbonne

MYLES BURNYEAT, Fellow of All Souls College, Oxford

DAVID CHARLES, Fellow of Oriel College, Oxford

ALAN CODE, Professor of Philosophy, University of California at Berkeley

JOHN COOPER, Stuart Professor of Philosophy, Princeton University

MICHEL CRUBELLIER, Professor of Philosophy, Université Charles de Gaulle, Lille

DOROTHEA FREDE, Professor of Philosophy, Hamburg University

EDWARD HUSSEY, Fellow of All Souls College, Oxford

CARLO NATALI, Associate Professor of Ancient Philosophy, Venice University

DAVID SEDLEY, Lawrence Professor of Ancient Philosophy and Fellow of Christ's College, Cambridge

CHRISTIAN WILDBERG, Professor of Classics, Princeton University

Editor's Introduction

Frans A. J. de Haas

The first book of Aristotle's *De generatione et corruptione* is a difficult text which deals with a number of key notions in Aristotle's physics, and does so at a high level of abstraction. These characteristics may serve to explain the choice of the Symposiasts for *GC* I: it is indispensable because it deals with key notions of Aristotle's physics in a way they are not dealt with anywhere else in the Aristotelian corpus. Moreover, because it is notoriously difficult, there is room for improvement on existing scholarship.

In this book Aristotle seeks to establish the differences between generation and corruption, alteration, and growth, three of his four kinds of change (locomotion is discussed in the *Physics* and *De caelo*). Furthermore, Aristotle argues that it is necessary to have a clear grasp of the concepts of touch, action and passion, and mixture before one can properly understand any of these kinds of change. More particularly, these concepts are required to understand the processes described in more detail in *GC* II and *Meteorology* IV, respectively: the transformation of the four sublunary elements, and the constitution of homogeneous materials, such as flesh, blood, and bone, out of these elements.

The contributors to this volume have aimed at clarifying the structure of Aristotle's text, revealing the strategy of his argument, and tracing its implications for his natural philosophy as a whole. By way of introduction, we here provide an outline of each contribution to facilitate access to the volume. It will be seen that most contributions cover a single chapter of *GC* I, with the exception of the contributions by Charles and Cooper. Moreover, three series of chapters constitute thematic units. Chapters 3–5 all concern the vexed issue of prime matter in Aristotle, Chapters 8–10 cover Aristotle's sustained discussion of action and passion in *GC* I. 7–9, and Chapters 11–12 both deal with mixture. The crucial role of the Presocratics, esp. Empedocles and the atomists, in Aristotle's argument is a theme that runs through this entire volume, with emphasis on Chapters 2–3 and 7–10.

In his introductory chapter *Myles Burnyeat* provides *GC* I with its proper setting in Aristotle's philosophy of nature. We learn that the chapters on action and passion, and mixture point forward to more refined applications in Aristotle's theory of perception and thought, as well as to the metaphysical notion of 'subject' (*hupokeimenon*). These considerations dislodge a traditional line of interpretation which regarded *GC* I as preparing only the discussion, in *GC* II, of the four elements, their transformations, and the homoeomerous mixtures which they make up. Although *GC* I is indeed concerned with these physical foundations, its references to the order of argument and exposition of the physical works as a whole, show its role in laying the conceptual foundations of Aristotle's philosophy of nature. Finally, *Meteorology* I. 1 reveals that *GC* I also provides the teleological foundations of Aristotle's physics: together the *Physics, GC*, and *De caelo* point to what is best: the cyclic transformation of the elements, which in its turn serves the eternal life cycles of the biological species to which Aristotle has devoted his most scrupulous attention.

In his discussion of *GC* I. 1 *Jacques Brunschwig* carefully considers the relationships between *GC* and other parts of the Aristotelian corpus, and between the treatises that now constitute *GC*. He identifies the question whether and how generation and alteration are to be distinguished as the central issue of his chapter. It dominates Aristotle's discussion of the Presocratics, which is modelled on the more primitive division between monism and pluralism. Monism lacks the distinction between generation and alteration, whereas pluralist theories require separate treatment in this respect because they are so different from each other. After a skirmish against Anaxagoras, Aristotle devotes *GC* I. 1 to Empedocles, leaving Democritus, whom he considers a far better physicist than Plato, for *GC* I. 2. Brunschwig's detailed analysis exploits the peculiarities of Aristotle's reception of Empedocles' text and shows how Aristotle's argument proceeds as if deepening, step by step, the distance between what theory leads to expect and what history seems to show. In the end even the initial distinction between monism and pluralism turns out to be problematic in the case of Empedocles. For this and other reasons Brunschwig offers the suggestion to read *GC* I. 1 as a false start, to be replaced in this respect by *GC* I. 2.

Aristotle devoted *GC* I. 2 to atomism as the strongest form of the thesis that generation and corruption reduce to aggregation and disintegration of indivisibles. *David Sedley* proposes a novel reading of the chapter's argument, which entails a transposition of lines 316^b 9–14. After the introduction of arguments supporting atomism in Democritean terms, Sedley suggests, Aristotle first grants the atomists a reply to the Aristotelian objection that infinite division is infinite only in potentiality.

With the actuality–potentiality distinction taken on board, the atomist position can be enhanced by arguing that potential division at least implies the *possibility* of actual division. Only then does Aristotle show that even the upgraded atomist argument for indivisibles cannot be sustained, and along with it the atomist view of generation and corruption falls.

Keimpe Algra's discussion of *GC* I. 3 introduces the theme of prime matter, which links Chapters 3–5 of this volume. According to Algra the notion of prime matter does not play a role in *GC* I. 3, either at the level of the description of substantial transformation, or in the more robust sense he believes a physical theory may well require. More particularly, Algra argues that Aristotle did not have prime matter in mind as the referent of 'not-being *simpliciter*' in *GC* I. 3. From an analysis of Aristotle's usage of the qualifier *simpliciter* (*haplôs*) it follows, against Williams, that no inconsistency exists between Aristotle's discussions of not-being *simpliciter* in *GC* I. 3 and *Physics* I. 8 respectively.

Sarah Broadie considers the issue of prime matter in dealing with *GC* I. 4, where Aristotle addresses the difference between substantial change and alteration, and refines the position he outlined in *Physics* I. 6–7. Broadie discusses two main interpretations of *GC* I. 4: If alteration is an exchange of *pathê* in a persistent *hupokeimenon*, substantial change is exchange of perceptible *hupokeimena*. Alternatively, if both types of change presuppose a persisting *hupokeimenon*, in alteration this is an empirical substance, whereas in substantial change it is non-empirical matter. She argues, unlike Algra, that Aristotle did not have any philosophical motivation to posit prime matter as a persisting *hupokeimenon*. In addition, Broadie defends an interpretation of *GC* II. 1. $329^a24^{-b}1$ as showing that the phrase 'Aristotelian first matter' picks out one or all of the four elements, presenting each as what changes into another simple body, or as that out of which another one comes to be. A number of problematic texts prove harmless when she shows how the substantial transformations of the simple bodies can also be regarded as a single change with a single common matter, differentiated only in so far as different agents cause them.

David Charles addresses the same issues as Algra and Broadie but reaches different conclusions. He also takes his starting point from Aristotle's hints in *GC* I. 3 that the matter of earth and the matter of fire are in some way the same and in some way different. However, he develops Aristotle's view in terms of a so-called logical or abstract object, with Aristotle's discussion of the now in *Physics* IV. 11 as an instructive parallel. Thus matter, understood as the one thing in virtue of being which all specific instances of matter underlie, will be the same in all cases of basic elemental change. In this way, Charles argues, Aristotle found a mid-course between the Scylla of monism and the Charybdis of pluralism, both of which we have seen him rejecting in previous chapters.

In *GC* I. 5 Aristotle distinguishes growth from both alteration and substantial change by a careful analysis of its nature. *Alan Code* unravels Aristotle's intricate argument and attributes to Aristotle a line of thought that is more coherent and more complete than what existing commentaries—both ancient and modern—have to offer. Growth comes out as a complex process involving locomotion of the acceding matter and of the matter in the growing thing which makes room for it, while the acceding matter is informed by, e.g., the form of flesh already present in the growing organism so as to start performing the function of flesh. The efficient cause of this process is the soul.

Carlo Natali deals with *GC* I. 6 by comparing the commentaries on *GC* by Philoponus (*c.* AD 490–570), Pseudo-Thomas Aquinas, and Zabarella (AD 1533–1589) with their modern counterparts. *GC* I. 6 divides into two sections: a methodological section on the need to define a number of preliminary notions, and a section devoted to the first of these notions, 'contact'. Natali shows how Aristotle's definition of 'contact', which is required by both monist and pluralist theories alike, is fundamental to 'action and passion', and to 'mixture'. The notion of 'contact' that is required in this physical context, i.e. contact properly speaking, turns out to be reciprocal touching accompanied by reciprocal movement. These conditions exclude, e.g., the touching of mathematical entities (without movement), unmoved movers (one-way movement), and psychological affections (one-way contact, one-way movement).

Christian Wildberg focuses on *GC* I. 7, the first of three chapters devoted to the theme of 'action and passion', or rather 'qualitative affection'. He shows how Aristotle here continues the project of understanding the properties, functions, and powers of the elements he started in *De caelo* III, and took up again in *Meteorology* IV. Wildberg's analysis of *GC* I. 7 gives us an Aristotle craftily designing a dialectical clash of opinion between his predecessors with the aim of clarifying the problems he himself is confronted with. For him qualitative affection cannot be based on *either* similarity *or* dissimilarity without jeopardizing key tenets of his physics. In this way Aristotle prepares the reader for his own solution: qualitative affection occurs among contrary qualities, flavours, colours, and the like, involving both identity in genus and difference in species. Aristotle then focuses on the relation between motion and qualitative affection, and claims that the first efficient cause of a series of reciprocal qualitative affections itself remains unaffected. Wildberg suggests that Aristotle's hints point to the sun as this first efficient cause rather than to the prime mover of the *Physics* and the *Metaphysics*.

In *GC* I. 8–9 Aristotle addresses the question how it is possible for the process of qualitative alteration to come about, both by reviewing his predecessors, and, in the first few lines of *GC* I. 9, by putting forward his own account. Following Aristotle's text closely, *Edward Hussey* shows how Aristotle reaches the conclusion that Empedocles' theory of pores is either false or useless. The atomists seem to fare better because of their coherent attempt to do justice both to the arguments of the Eleatics, and to the senses, from which we derive our concepts of generation and corruption, alteration, and growth. Hussey's analysis of Aristotle's dense argument shows that for Aristotle the weakness of the atomist theory consists in its failure to account for qualitative affection on the level of individual atoms because of their indivisibility. Aristotle adds more general criticisms of atomic theory, perhaps taken from what was originally another treatise, but he does not straightforwardly reject the atomist account of qualitative affection, or their notion of the void, until *GC* I. 9.

Michel Crubellier identifies the aim of *GC* I. 9 to deal with the problem of maintaining, against the Eleatics, the reality of qualitative alteration, without being committed to the atomist assumption of the discontinuity of matter. Aristotle focuses on the question whether affection occurs in part only, or through and through—and it is clear he argues for the latter option by reference to his own actuality–potentiality distinction. If actualized qualitative states of a physical body are present in all its parts, the corresponding possibility of such states must be present in all its parts, too. This requires the thesis, already familiar from *GC* I. 2 as well as I. 8, that physical magnitudes are divisible everywhere. At the same time Aristotle argues against affection in part(s) only, by rejecting it in all its historical varieties. In this light Empedocles, the atomists, and Plato turn out to exemplify a single *type* of theory, which understands qualitative alteration as a process that is located in some places of the affected body and not in others. Crubellier offers a tentative elaboration of how in Aristotle's universe the continuity of physical bodies entails susceptibility to qualitative affection through and through.

The last two contributions to this volume deal with Aristotle's concept of mixture, which accounts, as Aristotle's own inorganic and organic chemistry, for the generation of homogeneous stuffs from the four sublunary elements. *Dorothea Frede* first offers a seemingly straightforward account of the argument of *GC* I. 10. Against the atomists, Empedocles, and Anaxagoras alike Aristotle holds that mixture does not depend on aggregation beneath the level of perception. 'Mixing is the union of the things mixed after they have been altered' ($328^{b}22$). In a mixture the ingredients retain their own nature potentially—and are therefore potentially separable—but no longer display it. They reach this remarkable state as the result of reciprocal qualitative affection in which an overall equality of their powers obtains. Frede lists numerous problems that haunt this account of mixture: What kind of union is meant? Does the process really require alteration of qualities only? What does it mean to retain one's nature potentially, or to have equal powers? If the earlier chapters of *GC* I offer little help, Aristotle's discussion of elementary changes in *GC* II, as well as his study of homogeneous stuffs in *Meteorology* IV, are more informative and indeed provide most of the answers. Among other things we learn that the four so-called elements consist only of the four basic qualities (hot, cold, moist, dry), so that mixture can be regarded as incomplete substantial change between elements in which one quality is not completely replaced but only 'toned down' by its contrary.

John Cooper, in the final contribution of this volume, poses the question whether commentators since Philoponus have been right to attribute to Aristotle the belief that even the smallest part of, e.g., flesh contains (in potentiality) all four elements in the required ratio, or whether it only displays the ranges of hot, cold, moist, and dry which are specific to flesh. This is important since the first claim does not follow from Aristotle's account of mixture in *GC* I. 10. Cooper shows that, indeed, Aristotle should not be burdened with this view. Cooper's arguments are drawn from an original reading of Aristotle's discussion of the view that mixture is aggregation beneath the level of sense perception. Given that matter is indefinitely divisible it is impossible to envisage a situation in which any bit of an original ingredient will *not* be alongside other bits of the same ingredient. What is more, since mixture is based on reciprocal qualitative affection *throughout*, it is perfectly possible that parts of the mixture derive from a single ingredient only.

Introduction: Aristotle on the Foundations of Sublunary Physics

M. F. BURNYEAT

1. Generality

The first book of Aristotle's *De Generatione et Corruptione* is hardly a work for beginners. The second book is a straightforward exposition of his theory of the four elements and their transformations, together with an account of why coming to be and passing away never fail. But 'straightforward' is the last adjective one would apply to the knotty, abstract, dialectical argumentation of book I. Our difficulties begin at the very first sentence, which announces a programme that goes far beyond earth, air, fire, and water.

We are to study (i) the causes and definitions[1] of the coming to be and passing away of things which come to be and pass away by nature—*all* of them *alike* (I. 1. 314ª2, ὁμοίως κατὰ πάντων). We are also to learn (ii) what growth and alteration are, and (iii) whether alteration differs from coming to be *simpliciter*. Now coming to be and passing away, alteration, and growth are very general concepts, with a wide range of application. We might expect examples from all over the world of nature. But when we read on, already in book I we find an overwhelming concentration on the four elements and mixtures of them. Where are the plants and animals that would verify Aristotle's claim to be explaining the coming to be and passing away of *all* sublunary natural bodies *alike*? Even in chapter 5, a remarkably abstract discussion of growth, the examples cited are animal *parts* (flesh and bone, leg and hand) rather than whole creatures, and Aristotle makes no mention of a doctrine he states elsewhere (*de An.* II. 4. 415ᵇ23–8, 416ᵇ9–11), that growth involves soul because only living things can take in nourishment and grow; he merely speaks, quite indeterminately, of an internal principle of growth (*GC* I. 5. 321ᵇ6–7, 322ª12).

---

[1] Since Aristotle requires a scientific definition to specify the cause(s) of the phenomenon defined, 'causes' and 'definitions' are not separate objects of enquiry.

Joachim's response to this puzzle is to say that a close look at the contents of the treatise reveals that Aristotle is *primarily* concerned with the coming to be and passing away of mixtures of the elemental bodies. His references to the coming to be and passing away of living things are 'quite general and vague'. But since living things are constituted out of elemental mixtures, their birth and death involves the birth and death of the mixed stuffs from which they are composed; *to this limited extent,* Aristotle's treatment of the questions he discusses will apply to plants and animals as well.[2]

When I think back to the generation that produced *The Oxford Translation of Aristotle into English*, my respect for Joachim (1868–1938), both as an Aristotelian scholar and as a philosopher in his own right (he became Wykeham Professor of Logic), is second only to my respect for Sir David Ross (1877–1971), who was also a philosopher in his own right as well as a great scholar.[3] But Joachim's restrictive judgement on the treatise he so splendidly edited will not do. For it implies that *GC*'s theory of coming to be and passing away is not (meant to be) true of plants and animals, only of their homoeomerous parts. And this plainly contradicts not only the first sentence of I. 1 but also the first sentence of I. 2:

We must deal *in general* (ὅλως) *both* with unqualified coming to be and passing away—Do they exist or not, and how do they take place?—and with the other kinds of change, such as growth and alteration. (315^{a}26–8)[4]

Joachim goes so far as to say that *in the last resort* every genesis of a composite natural body is the coming to be of one or more new homoeomerous parts, each of which is a chemical compound whose constituents are earth, air, fire, and water.[5] If that reductive account were true, Aristotle would have no need of substantial forms.

The corrective I propose is to look into the way Aristotle's other writings refer to the treatise before us. These cross-references tell us something of how he conceived what he was doing in *GC* I.

---

[2] Joachim (1922), pp. xxxvi–xxxvii and note ad 314^{a}2.

[3] In the English-speaking world Ross is still read for his work on ethics: *The Right and the Good* (1930), *The Foundations of Ethics* (1939). Joachim is now undeservedly neglected. Anyone interested in the origins of the school of 'Oxford philosophy' will find in Joachim's *The Nature of Truth* (1906) and *Logical Studies* (1948) significant anticipations of J. L. Austin.

[4] My translations are from E. S. Forster's Loeb edition (1955), with modifications. On the particle pair τε δή I follow (against the majority of translators) Denniston (1934), 259–60: τε means 'both' and δή emphasizes either ὅλως or τε (Migliori (1976) alone allows the chapter to begin without a connective). Note the echo of Pl. *Phd.* 95 e: ὅλως γὰρ δεῖ περὶ γενέσεως καὶ φθορᾶς τὴν αἰτίαν διαπραγματεύσασθαι.

[5] Note ad 322^{b}1–26.

(1) *De Sensu* 3. 440^{a}31–^{b}4 and 13 cites *GC* I. 10 as his theory of mixture *in general* (ἐν τοῖς περὶ μίξεως εἴρηται καθόλου περὶ πάντων). That was where he gave his account of the difference between the juxtaposition of minute amounts of different ingredients and a genuine mixture of them, where the result is not just phenomenally, but physically, different from any of its components. The type of example at issue in *GC* I. 10 was the mixture of wine and water, as served at every Greek symposium. The examples in *De Sensu* are colour mixtures such as orange, which is a mixture of red and yellow.[6] But Aristotle is not speaking just of what happens when a painter mixes yellow pigment with red, nor even about laying yellow paint over red to produce (from a suitable distance) the appearance of orange. This last he mentions, but only to get clear about the *phenomenal* orange that is permanently visible, however close you get, on the surface of a piece of fruit. He was not to know that a decisive step for mankind was the co-evolution of sensitivity to orange in certain primates and the orange colour of the fruit of a particular species of tropical tree, as a result of which those primates scattered the seeds of that tree and humans have a more varied colour vision than most colour-seeing animals. But from a modern point of view it is still an extraordinary thing for Aristotle to be saying: If you want to understand how the orange colour of those fruits is a mixture of red and yellow, go read my account of what happens when wine is mixed with water.

Now in *GC* I. 7, on action and passion, we find this:

Body is by nature adapted so as to be affected by body, flavour by flavour, *colour by colour*, and in general that which is of the same kind by something else of the same kind. (323^{b}33–324^{a}1; emphasis added)

Reciprocal action and passion are a crucial factor in Aristotle's account of mixture in *GC* I. 10. The examples there are all of *bodies* interacting with bodies. There is no hint that the theory extends to certain sensible *qualities* as well, which get mixed when the bodies they qualify are mixed (*Sens.* 3. 440^{b}13–14).[7] That hint came earlier, in *GC* I. 7, which is Aristotle's account of action and passion as such. It anticipates his application of the general theory of mixture to the limiting case, so to speak, of colour.

---

[6] I switch to a modern example, because of the difficulty of matching Greek colour terms to ours. Aristotle's theory is that white or light (λευκόν) mixes with black or dark (μέλαν) to produce the intermediate colours; for elucidation and discussion see Sorabji (1972).

[7] The word 'mixture' is not used idly of the qualities as well as the bodies, because the mixed colours are a *ratio* (rational or irrational) of light and dark. This presupposes a unit and goes beyond standard interactions like that between hot water and cold, which results in a mixture with intermediate temperature. Flavours are similarly a ratio of sweet and bitter (*Sens.* 4. 442^{a}12–29).

(2) *De Anima* II. 5. $417^a1–2$ refers to *GC* I. 7 as the *general* discussion of action and passion (ἐν τοῖς <u>καθόλου</u> λόγοις περὶ τοῦ ποιεῖν καὶ πάσχειν). Perception is another limiting case, to be subsumed under *GC*'s general theory of alteration, according to which alteration occurs when an agent *A* assimilates a patient *P* to itself: *P* takes on the quality (form) that *A* already has. For example, a fire heats the air near by. Likewise, in perception an agent *A* makes a perceiver *P* take on the sensible form that *A* already has. But in *de Anima* II. 5, unlike *De Sensu*, Aristotle does not merely apply what he said in *GC* to a new and surprising case. He refines what he said in *GC* by introducing the distinction between first and second potentiality. This makes an important difference to our understanding of *P*'s taking on the quality (form) of *A*, as that notion is used first in the theory of perception and later in the theory of intellect.[8]

Now in *GC* I. 8, against the atomists' theory of pores, we read this:

Some people hold that each patient is acted upon when the last agent—the agent in the strictest sense—enters in through certain pores, and they say that it is also in this way that we see and hear and employ our other senses. ($324^b25–9$)

Just as Aristotle's theory of perception is adapted from his general account of alteration, so his refutation of a wrong theory of action and passion brings down with it the corresponding account of perception. He recurs to the topic of perception near the end of the chapter (326^b10 ff.), so the link between the general account of action and passion and the specific account of perception remains in his mind.

Not only that, but one of the *arguments* in *de Anima* II. 5 is a special case of an argument couched in general terms at *GC* I. 7. $323^b21–4$: if like acts on like, everything will constantly act on itself and nothing will be unchanging or indestructible. Move on to *de Anima* II. 5 and we find the like–like principle of causation invoked at 416^b35 to produce a puzzle about why the senses do not constantly cause themselves to perceive themselves ($417^a2–6$), from which Aristotle can infer that the senses are potentialities rather than actualities—they need an external cause to set them going ($417^a6–13$).

The opposite principle of causation, that unlike acts on unlike, also has a role in *de Anima*. At *de Anima* I. 5. $410^a23–6$ it makes trouble for the traditional idea that like perceives like and knows like by virtue of being like it. As in *GC* I. 7, so in *de Anima*, neither principle of causation will do as it stands, but each captures one part of a larger truth. What happens in *GC* I. 7 is a dialectical confrontation between the two inadequate

---

[8] For a detailed account of the refinement and its bearing on current controversies about Aristotle's theory of perception, see Burnyeat (2002).

principles of causation. The outcome is that the assimilation thesis is established in the most general form possible. For an agent *A* to affect a patient *P*, *A* must *assimilate P* to itself, as when fire makes a cold thing hot or warmer than it was before. *A* and *P* start off characterized by contrary predicates from the same range; they are thus generically alike, specifically unlike. When they meet, *A* is bound to act on *P*, and *P* is bound to be acted upon by *A*, just because they are contrary to each other; that is the nature of contrariety. So *A* and *P* end up with the same or closer predicates of the range. What happens in *de Anima* II. 5 is the application of that general thesis to the special case of perception: for *P* to perceive *A*, *P* and *A* must be unlike to begin with, so that *A* can affect *P* (because of the unlikeness between them) and make *P* like itself. The perceiving is an assimilation (on a refined understanding of that term) in which *P becomes* like *A*.

Here, then, is a second example where Aristotle refers to *GC* I for patterns of explanation which can be applied, with suitable adaptations and refinements, to phenomena in psychology. This gives a nice strong sense in which Aristotelian psychology is part of physics, as of course *de Anima* says it is (I. 1. 402^{a}4–7). If we have not studied *GC* I carefully, we will not understand colours and we will not understand perceptual or intellectual cognition. Nor will we understand the account of growth and nutrition in *de Anima* II. 4, where the dialectic of *GC* I. 7 is silently presupposed (416^{a}29–^{b}9).[9]

(3) My third example is *Metaphysics H* 1. 1042^{b}7–8. After a brief discussion of the role of substantial being as subject to the four categorially different types of change, Aristotle refers to the physical works (ἐν τοῖς φυσικοῖς εἴρηται) for an account of the difference between unqualified coming to be (τοῦ ἁπλῶς γίγνεσθαι) and coming to be *F*, where *F* is some predicate in the category of quantity, quality, or place. The first question to consider is which physical work is the most appropriate target for the reference.[10]

Bonitz answered: *Physics* V. 1. 224^{b}35 ff., and possibly also *GC* I. 3.[11] But the *Physics* passage is unsuitable. It operates at a more abstract level than Aristotle's standard classifications of the four types of change, and uses the word 'subject' (ὑποκείμενον) to cover the positive terminus in *any* change, including the white which is the terminus of alteration.

---

[9] Growth is another topic where the atomists invoke pores: *GC* I. 8. 325^{b}4–5.

[10] Bonitz (1870) 102^{b}9–13 shows that the title τὰ φυσικά can refer to physical works other than the *Physics*.

[11] Bonitz (1870) 101^{a}21–3. Eleven years earlier, in his *Metaphysics* commentary ad loc., he had added not *GC* I. 3 but the impossible I. 7. Presumably a misprint. But, sadly, the misprint lives on in the apparatus criticus of Jaeger's OCT edition (1957) of the *Metaphysics*.

More important, it nowhere mentions matter, which is the *raison d'être* of the *H*1 argument that prompts the cross-reference: an argument to show that, as just stated (1042^{a}27–8), the matter of a substantial being is itself substantial being, in the sense that, while it is not actually a so and so (τόδε τι), it is potentially one. We ought to be able to do better.

Accordingly Ross, while retaining the reference to *Physics* V. 1 (from piety towards Bonitz?), adds *GC* I. 2. 317^{a}17–31.[12] This is no doubt inspired by the introduction at 317^{a}21–2 of the idea that substantial change is changing from this to that *as a whole*. But that is merely the lead-in to *GC* I. 3–4, and it is especially in I. 4 that we find a match for the two subjects (ὑποκείμενα) of *H* I. 1042^{b}2–3. Not only is it especially in *GC* I. 4 that we get this, but we do not find more than one such subject in two other central passages we might think to go to: *Physics* I. 7–8 and III. 1–3. They stay with the less sophisticated triadic model of matter, form, and privation. Further, it is in *GC* I. 4 that the difference between substantial and non-substantial change is fully analysed.[13] So I propose that the cross-reference is to *GC* I. 2–4 as a continuous, unitary discussion.

My next point is that *H* 1 is not talking about the elemental transformations discussed in *GC* I. 2–4, but about the coming to be of metaphysically uncontroversial substantial beings like plants and animals: the sort of item which, once it has come to be, can change from healthy to sick (1042^{a}36–7). From the perspective of first philosophy, earth, air, fire and water are mere potentialities, not proper substantial beings (*Z* 16. 1040^{b}7–10). Yet Aristotle still sees his *GC* account of elemental transformations as a general schema which, with suitable additions and refinements, will account for substantial change up to the highest level of the sensible world.

Now in *GC* I. 4 we read this:

But when the thing changes as a whole, with no perceptible subject retaining its identity—for example, when *the seed as a whole is converted into blood*, or water into air, or air as a whole into water—such a process is the coming to be of a new thing and destruction of the old. (319^{b}14–18; emphasis added)

As with the two previous examples, a careful look finds Aristotle in *GC* I unobtrusively anticipating other contexts than the immediate one for the application of his results. The first sentence of *GC* I was no slip of the pen.

---

[12] Ross (1924), ad loc.

[13] εἴρηται in cross-references often connotes more than a mere mention: e.g. *Metaph.* *Z* 11. 1037^{a}21–2 has the whole of *Z* 4–5 in view.

2. Foundations

My suggestion, then, is that *GC* I really does have a lot more in view than the elements which are its immediate concern, and more than the homo-eomerous mixtures at which Joachim drew the line. This is confirmed by a pivotal passage in *Meteorologica*, I. 1:

(1) We have earlier (πρότερον) dealt with the first causes of nature [in *Physics*] and with all natural motion [in *Physics*, esp. books V–VIII]; (2) we have dealt also with the ordered movements of the stars in the heavens [in *Cael.* I–II], (3) and with the number, kinds and mutual transformations of the bodily elements, and with *becoming and perishing in general* (καὶ περὶ γενέσεως καὶ φθορᾶς τῆς κοινῆς) [in *Cael.* III–IV and *GC*]. (4) It remains to consider a subdivision of the present inquiry (λοιπὸν δ' ἐστὶ μέρος τῆς μεθόδου ταύτης ἔτι θεωρητέον) which all our predecessors have called meteorology. Its province is everything which happens naturally, but with a regularity less than that of the primary bodily element [sc. ether, the fifth element], and which takes place in the region which borders most nearly on the movements of the stars … (5) After we have dealt with all these subjects, let us then see (διελθόντες δὲ περὶ τούτων, θεωρήσωμεν) if we can give some account, on the lines we have laid down (κατὰ τὸν ὑφηγημένον τρόπον), of animals [in the zoological works, including *De Anima*] and plants [in the lost *De Plantis*], both in general and in particular; for when we have done this we may perhaps claim that the whole investigation which we set before ourselves at the outset has been completed (τούτων ῥηθέντων τέλος ἂν εἴη γεγονὸς τῆς ἐξ ἀρχῆς ἡμῖν προαιρέσεως πάσης). (338ᵃ20–ᵇ22; 339ᵃ5–9; emphasis added)[14]

This is a large-scale map of Aristotle's natural philosophy,[15] beginning with the *Physics*, going on to *De Caelo* and *De Generatione et Corrup-tione*, pausing here for the *Meteorologica*, looking forward to *De Anima* and the biological works. Aristotelian physics is depicted as a systematic whole (one προαίρεσις) in which each treatise has its part to play.[16] The role of *GC*, we learn once again, is *both* to consider the elements and their mutual transformations *and* to study becoming and perishing *in general*. This is no mere conjunction of goals. For what we found earlier was Aristotle anticipating that he would adapt *GC* I's general schemata of explanation for use in the quite different context of scientific psychology. Getting to grips with the elements will equip us to study other, more complex, things. To adapt a famous phrase from the far end of the

---

[14] Trans. Lee (1952), modified. The numeration is his too, as is the accompanying annotation, with which I entirely agree.

[15] A charmingly conclusive vindication of its authenticity is Capelle (1912). Compare *Sens.* I. 436ᵃ1–17, a small-scale map of the treatises we know as the *Parva Naturalia*; these are expressly introduced as a sequel to *De Anima*.

[16] λοιπὸν δ' ἐστὶ μέρος τῆς μεθόδου ταύτης may also imply a major grouping of treatises into a μέθοδος comprising *Ph.*, *Cael.*, *GC*, *Mete.*, and another μέθοδος concerned with living things.

Aristotelian cosmos, below the moon the elements are 'universal because first' (*Metaph. E* 1. 1026ᵃ30–1). They are not merely involved, ontologically, in all sublunary changes. The structure of their changes is the epistemological starting point from which to understand becoming and perishing *in general*.

A word to press into service here is 'foundational'. It was a word heard more than once during the Symposium at Deurne, as people tried to capture the peculiar character of *GC* I. No doubt Aristotle would tell us that 'foundational' is said in many ways. But all of them seem appropriate to *GC* I. I shall consider three.

(*a*) *Physical foundations.* One way in which *GC* as a whole is foundational is that it deals with the lowest, most basic, level of the cosmos. It is the physics of the bottom in a world that is not to be viewed and explained—certainly not fully explained—from the bottom up, as happens on the atomists' approach so severely criticized in *GC* I. 2 and 7. Moreover, this physics, in contrast to the physics of Leucippus and Democritus, is to be qualitative through and through. The atomists' key device for explaining change, the combining (σύγκρισις) and dissolution (διάκρισις) of material constituents, is dethroned to the status of a mere facilitator (I. 2. 317ᵃ20–30), and this despite the unusually high praise accorded to Leucippus and Democritus in contrast to Empedocles, who also appeals to processes of combination and dissolution. Empedocles contradicts both the observed facts and himself (I. 1; cf. II. 6). Only the atomists have a theory of sufficient power and generality to give a genuinely physical explanation of all forms of change (I. 2. 315ᵃ34–ᵇ15, 316ᵃ5–14; I. 8. 324ᵇ35–325ᵃ2). Yet their theory is completely wrong.

We need not be surprised to find Aristotle praising an approach so diametrically opposed to his own. His studies in rhetoric would tell him that the more you build up your main competitors against *their* rivals, the more wonderful it is when you win the prize. Orators preparing a speech in someone's praise may be well advised to compare him with illustrious personages: 'that will strengthen your case; it is a noble thing to surpass men who are themselves great' (*Rh.* I. 9. 1368ᵃ21–2; Trans. Rhys Roberts). I do not mean that Aristotle's praise is insincere.[17] It is still true today that a good philosopher is one who tackles the opposition in its strongest, most systematic form. The comprehensive scope of the atomists' theory is the very thing that helps us to see why it is so wrong.

As the physics of the bottom, *GC* is twin to *de Caelo*. Not only because *de Caelo* has much to say about the four sublunary elements, but also because *de Caelo* I starts from the very top of the cosmos. Certainly,

---

[17] There are other places, e.g. *GA* II. 8. 747ᵃ25–7, and IV. 1. 764ᵃ1–23, where Aristotle gives better marks to Democritus than to Empedocles.

de Caelo III–IV deal at length with the natural motions of the four elements and with the contrariety light–heavy, while *de Caelo* III. 7–8 refute Democritus' and Plato's explanations of how the elements are generated from each other. But the treatise as we now have it leaves us looking forward (III. 8. 307^{b}19–24) to Aristotle's own positive account of elemental transformation in *GC* II, where the important contrarieties are hot–cold and wet–dry. Only when this is complete can our understanding of the sublunary elements match the detailed explanation of the properties of aether in *de Caelo* I–II. Accordingly, we might think of *de Caelo* I and *GC* I as a pincer movement, one starting from the very top and moving down to the elements, the other starting from the very bottom and moving up to homoeomerous mixtures. The two work together to fix the large-scale contours of the Aristotelian cosmology, thereby establishing the habitat for the living things to which Aristotle will devote his most scrupulous attention. (Recall the order of topics in Plato's *Timaeus*, where the demiurge first constructs the heavens, then the four elements, and finally has the lesser gods see to the creation of living things.) This pincer movement may help explain why the first books of both treatises are methodologically unique.

Where knowledge of the stars is concerned 'we have very little to start from, and we are situated at a great distance from the phenomena we are trying to investigate' (*Cael.* II. 12. 292^{a}15–17, trans. Guthrie. Cf. *PA* I. 5). This means that we cannot find out about the stars by the usual Aristotelian procedures. Humanity may have had numerous sightings of them over the years, but these data are nowhere near as elaborate and varied as those that Aristotle was able to gather on animals and political constitutions, rhetorical speeches and drama. For the stars we lack even an equivalent to the everyday familiarity we have with animals and their behaviour, or with the interactions of solids and liquids, air and fire. There is no reason to think that the reputable opinions on the subject of the heavens are likely to contain, between them, most of the truth we are seeking. Hence, although it is good to cite the ancient belief that the stars are divine (*Cael.* I. 3. 270^{b}5–9; II. 1. 284^{a}2–6), dialectic will be of limited use. In this predicament, Aristotle turns to the method of hypothesis.

Take a series of hypotheses, most crucially the hypothesis of natural places and natural motions, and deduce their consequences as rigorously as you can. *De Caelo* I contains an unusually high number of occurrences of words like ἀνάγκη which express the *necessity* of valid deductive argument. But then remember that these conclusions, even if validly deduced, depend on the initial hypotheses, about whose truth it is difficult to be certain. *De Caelo* I contains an unusually high number of occurrences of words like εἰκότως and εὔλογον which express epistemic modesty: this or that is a *reasonable* thing to believe. Understandably, for if it is difficult to be certain of the hypotheses, the conclusions deduced from them cannot be certain either. Such a combination of rigorous necessity and epistemic modesty is without parallel in the corpus.

GC I is methodologically unique too, but in a different way and for different reasons. Its subject matter is not so far from human experience. Instead of the physics of the superlunary realm, we are now to examine and define some of the fundamental concepts of sublunary physics: coming to be *simpliciter*, alteration, growth, and mixture. None of these applies to the heavens (for the proofs see *Cael.* I. 3); all of them are exemplified in everyday experience; so dialectical sifting of the reputable opinions is a viable tool to get started with. And dialectic, relentless dialectic, is what we are given. Little more. This is what makes the argumentation so knotty and abstract. The puzzle is that the concepts under discussion are ones we are already supposed to be familiar with from our reading of the *Physics*,[18] which (as will be seen) is constantly referred to as 'earlier' (πρότερον). It is as if we have to retrace our steps and problematize concepts we thought we had learned.

But it is important to appreciate that Aristotle's aim is not just to problematize, and then to clarify, these concepts. They are to be *shaped* for the specifically Aristotelian theoretical use to which they will be put throughout the physical works, up to *de Anima* and beyond.

Take first a relatively trivial illustration. *GC* I. 10. 328^a2-3 acknowledges that ordinary language speaks of a 'mixture' of barley and wheat, when grains of each are thoroughly mixed, side by side. But that is of no help in understanding what happens when wine is mixed with water, let alone when all four elements are mixed with each other, as they are in every single body we meet in the sublunary world (*GC* II. 8. $334^b31-335^a23$). Aristotle's solution is to distinguish 'composition' (σύνθεσις) from 'mixture' (κρᾶσις or μίξις), reserving the latter for the case where every part, however small, exhibits the same ratio between its constituent elements as does the whole (328^a5-18).

A more significant illustration is I. 6's narrow definition of contact in terms of reciprocal or non-reciprocal influence. To understand action and passion, and a fortiori to understand mixture, which involves reciprocal action and passion, the Aristotelian physicist requires a properly physical notion of contact. This has to be narrower in scope than the general definition of contact given in *Physics* V. 2, according to which there is contact whenever two distinct magnitudes have their extremities together. That suffices for mathematics (*GC* I. 6. 323^a1-3), but the student of physics (323^a34: ἐν τοῖς φυσικοῖς) must reckon with the causal consequences of contact. One common consequence is the imparting of

---

[18] Not to mention *Cat.* 14.

motion: a travelling body pushes, or rebounds from, a body at rest.[19] Another is alteration or change of quality—think of the myriad consequences of contact, direct or indirect, with fire.[20] Contact is also the trigger for formative processes in biology (*GA* II. 1. 734[a]3–4; 4. 740[b]21–4).

In many of these cases, moreover, the two things in contact affect each other: the pushing body loses some of its momentum, the fire some of its heat. But there is also the non-reciprocal case where someone behaves hurtfully towards me: he touches me, as Aristotle puts it, without my touching him in any sense at all (323[a]32–3). The example might well make one think of the prime mover moving things as an object of love, even though the prime mover has no extremities to coincide with the extremities of something else. So Joachim prefers, no doubt rightly, to suppose that Aristotle has in view contact between the first heaven and what lies below it, which does not react on its mover.[21] Another case of contact without interaction is food: the food is affected by the feeder, but not vice versa (*de An.* II. 4. 416[a]34–[b]1). It is also worth returning to the case of perception (pain is an exercise of the power of perception towards what is bad, because it is bad: *de An.* III. 7. 431[a]10–11). Perception requires indirect contact with a perceiver through a medium (*Ph.* VII. 2. 244[b]2–245[a]11; *de An.* III. 13. 435[a]18–19), but neither the perceiver nor the medium affects the object perceived (otherwise perception would always mislead). Here again, as with nutrition, *GC* I anticipates conceptual needs that will arise in more distant, more complicated areas of natural philosophy.

But the place where the idea of reciprocal interaction comes most strikingly into prominence is Aristotle's biology. To explain inherited family resemblances he appeals to the simple cases he discussed in *GC* I, optimistically supposing that they will illuminate the interaction between male and female movements as they form an embryo. This is the most interesting, most difficult case of coming to be *simpliciter*.

The key idea is that of a movement's slackening (λύεσθαι) into a nearly connected one; for example, a movement of the semen from the biological father slackens into that of his grandfather or some more remote male ancestor. The actual sex of the offspring depends on whether the male movements prevail over the female or vice versa, but in the course

---

[19] Another case to mention is contact imparting (unnatural) stability, as when the columns of a temple uphold the pediment.

[20] Indirect contact is acknowledged at *GC* I. 9. 327[a]3–6. For the multiple effects of heat see *PA* II. 2. 648[b]11–649[b]8.

[21] Note ad 322[b]32–323[a]34. Philoponus (*in GC* 138. 26–139.2) feels free to list a variety of unreciprocated movers: a picture, one's beloved, any object of desire, an insult, plus the heavenly movers of the sublunary world.

of their struggle one or more of the two sets of movements may slacken. This helps to explain the production of male offspring who resemble their mother or their grandfather more than their father, and of females who resemble their father or grandmother. It is a complicated process—about that, Aristotle is surely right.[22] But if we ask why the movements are liable to slacken, he replies by referring us back to *GC* I. 6–7:

> The agent is itself acted upon by that on which it acts; thus that which cuts is blunted by that which is cut by it, that which heats is cooled by that which is heated by it, and in general (ὅλως) the moving cause (except in the case of the first cause of all) does itself receive some motion in return; e.g. what pushes is itself in a way pushed again and what presses on something is pressed in return. Sometimes it is altogether more acted upon than acting, so that what is heating or cooling something else is itself cooled or heated, sometimes having produced no effect, sometimes less than it has itself received. This question has been treated in our discussion of action and reaction [*GC* I. 6–7], where it is laid down in what classes of things action and reaction exist. (*GA* IV. 3. 768ᵇ16–25; trans. Platt, with modifications)

The slackening is a special case of *GC* I's reciprocal action and passion. A reader may be forgiven for finding Aristotle's examples unhelpful, to say the least, when it comes to understanding the interaction between the movements of complexly concocted biological stuffs such as male semen and the corresponding female catamenia. How many refinements and adaptations are required to reach the level of this *very* special case?[23] But the stronger our worries, the more they underwrite the importance of *GC* I. Clearly, children do sometimes resemble a parent of the opposite sex or one of their grandparents. But how to explain this on a model according to which the male parent provides the form, the female the matter? *GC* I has to contain the key to the solution of a problem which Aristotle's empirical honesty will force him to confront.

There can be no doubt, I take it, that the *GC*-type examples are seriously meant to help. Aristotle is deeply committed to the idea that the sublunary cosmos is a unity. At all levels the same or analogous causes are at work, as he insists in *Metaphysics Λ* 1–5. We can expect the lower and the higher to proceed in much the same way, however much the details vary. *GC* I is truly foundational.[24]

---

[22] For a strenuous attempt to sort out the complications, see Cooper (1988).

[23] See Cooper (1988: 31–3) (from whom I take the phrase 'special case'). He is more sanguine than I am that the difficulties he acknowledges can be resolved.

[24] Readers familiar with the first book of the Hippocratic treatise *De Victu* may like to explore the points of similarity and difference. *De Victu* I is bafflingly abstract because it seeks a level of description that will bring out the kinship of microcosm (human nature, human activities) and macrocosm. The same kinds of process are to be found at all levels. The author's predecessors (Heraclitus, Empedocles, Anaxagoras, and others) are a constant presence—but as inspiring allies, not as opponents to think against. For the work is

(*b*) *Conceptual foundations.* In remarking earlier that *GC* I examines and defines some of the fundamental concepts of sublunary physics, I strayed into a second sense in which the first book of our treatise is foundational. To explain its significance, I need to take up a point already mentioned, that *GC* is written for an audience who already know the *Physics*. It is as if we are to retrace our steps and problematize concepts we thought we had learned.

Among the numerous references from *GC* to the *Physics*, there are six clear cases where *GC* refers to the *Physics* as *prior*:

(i) *GC* I. 3. 318ᵃ3–4: 'We dealt with the other [sc. efficient] cause earlier (εἴρηται πρότερον) in our discussion of motion'. This reminds us of *Physics* VIII. 5–10, esp. 258ᵇ10–11.

(ii) *GC* I. 6.323ᵃ3–4: 'If, therefore, as was previously defined (ὥσπερ διωρίσθη πρότερον), for things to be in contact they must have their extremities together'. This, already discussed, refers to the definition of contact at *Physics* V. 2. 226ᵇ23.

(iii) *GC* II. 9. 336ᵃ13: 'We have previously explained our own view of causes in general (ἡμῖν δὲ καθόλου τε πρότερον εἴρηται περὶ τῶν αἰτίων)'. This sends us to Aristotle's extended discussion of the four causes in *Physics* II. 3–9.

(iv) *GC* II 10. 336ᵃ18–20: 'At the same time it is evident that we were right to say earlier (τὰ πρότερον καλῶς εἴρηται) that the primary kind of change is motion, not coming to be'. This refers to *Physics* VIII. 7. 260ᵃ26–261ᵃ26.

(v) *GC* II. 10. 337ᵃ18: 'If there is to be movement, there must be a mover, as has been explained earlier elsewhere (ὥσπερ εἴρηται πρότερον ἐν ἑτέροις), and if the movement is to go on always, the mover must go on always'. Aristotle's enumeration of the requirements for ceaseless change in the sublunary world is grounded on the arguments of *Physics* VIII. 4–6.

(vi) *GC* II. 10. 337ᵃ24–5: 'Time, then, is a way of numbering some continuous movement, and therefore cyclical movement, as was determined in our discussions at the beginning (καθάπερ ἐν τοῖς ἐν ἀρχῇ λόγοις διωρίσθη)'. This refers to the proof in *Physics* VIII. 9 that only cyclical movement is continuous; for time's relation to continuous movement see *Physics* IV. 14. 223ᵃ29–ᵇ1.[25]

rhetorical rather than dialectical. Nonetheless, there is a clear sense in which the book is meant to be foundational with respect to the detailed medical matter of *Vict.* II–IV. *De Victu* is a work that Aristotle may well have read, since *PA* I. 1. 640ᵇ11–15 is reminiscent of the Hippocratic's account of stomach and nostrils in I. 9.

[25] There is textual uncertainty about (vii) *GC* I. 5. 320ᵇ28: 'That a separate void is impossible has been explained earlier elsewhere (εἴρηται ἐν ἑτέροις πρότερον)', i.e. in

Conversely, the *Physics* contains three references which can be taken, with more or less plausibility, to look forward to *GC* as 'later' ($\H{\upsilon}\sigma\tau\epsilon\rho o\nu$): I. 9. 192^{b}1–2; II. 1. 193^{b}20–1; IV. 5. 213^{a}4–5.[26] The question is: What does Aristotle mean in such contexts by 'earlier' and 'later'?[27]

Consider the word 'earlier' ($\pi\rho\acute{o}\tau\epsilon\rho o\nu$) in the first sentence of *Meteorologica* I. 1, quoted at the start of Section 2 above, and the various temporal phrases that follow. If they have a chronological meaning, they ask us to believe that Aristotle has by now finished the *Physics*, *de Caelo*, and *de Generatione et Corruptione*, but has not yet written a word on biology. A most unlikely story.[28] Much better to take the temporal phrases as indicators of the order in which the treatises should be read: the order of argument and exposition. The *Physics* introduces the basic principles of Aristotelian physics, which are then applied in departmental studies of increasingly complex phenomena, climaxing in what *de Anima* I. 1. 402^{a}1–7 calls the most important and valuable part of physics, the study of soul. Only then will we be equipped to tackle biology.

It is undeniable that Aristotle *sometimes* uses temporal phrases like 'earlier' and 'later' to indicate the order of exposition. A case in point is the continuation of example (i) above:

One signification of 'cause' is that from which we say movement originates, and another is the matter. It is the latter with which we have to deal here. For we dealt with the other cause *earlier* ($\epsilon\H{\iota}\rho\eta\tau\alpha\iota\ \pi\rho\acute{o}\tau\epsilon\rho o\nu$) in our discussion of motion [*Physics* VIII. 5–10, esp. 258^{b}10 ff.], when we said there is something that remains immovable through all time and something else which is always in motion. Treatment of the first of these, the immovable original source, is the task of the other and *prior* philosophy ($\tau\hat{\eta}s\ \acute{\epsilon}\tau\acute{\epsilon}\rho\alpha s\ \kappa\alpha\grave{\iota}\ \pi\rho\sigma\tau\acute{\epsilon}\rho\alpha s \dots \varphi\iota\lambda\sigma\sigma\varphi\acute{\iota}\alpha s$), while regarding that which moves all other things by its own continuous motion, we shall have to explain *later* ($\H{\upsilon}\sigma\tau\epsilon\rho o\nu$) [*GC* II. 10] which of the particular causes does that. *At present* ($\nu\hat{\upsilon}\nu$) let us speak of the cause which is placed in the class of matter, owing to which passing-away and coming-to-be never fail to occur in nature. For perhaps, if we succeed in clearing up this question, it will *simultaneously* ($\H{\alpha}\mu\alpha$) become clear what we ought to say about the thing that perplexed us *just now* ($\nu\hat{\upsilon}\nu$) [*GC* I. 3. 317^{b}18–33], namely, the problem of unqualified coming-to-be and passing-away. (*GC* I. 3. 318^{a}1–12)

Ph. IV. 6–9. A number of other references to the *Physics* use a past tense without adding the qualification 'earlier': *GC* I, 2. 316^{b}17–18 refers thus to *Ph.* VI. 1. 231^{a}21 ff.; *GC* I. 3. 317^{b}13–14 to *Ph.* I. 6–9; *GC* II. 10. 336^{a}15 and 11. 338^{a}18 to *Ph.* VIII. 7–9.

[26] *Cael.* also refers several times to the *Physics* as prior (Bonitz (1870) 98^{a}43–^{b}8), and is itself called prior at *GC* I. 8. 325^{b}34. *Meteorologica* confirms the ordering it sets out in I, 1 by referring to both *Cael.* and *GC* as prior: I. 2. 339^{b}16 and 36–7, I. 3. 340^{b}17–19, III. 1. 371^{b}1.

[27] What follows may be read as a particular case study for a thesis about Aristotelian cross-referencing which I argue for at length in chap. 5 of Burnyeat (2001).

[28] So says also Pellegrin (2000: 25): 'Position bien naïve'. His treatment of the *Meteorologica* passage is in complete accord with mine.

Of the temporal words and phrases I have italicized, the last four plainly refer to the sequence of argument within the treatise *De Generatione et Corruptione*. They tell us nothing about the chronological order in which Aristotle composed the different portions of that work. It is equally clear that the phrase 'the other and prior (προτέρας) philosophy' has nothing to do with chronology. 'Prior' means 'earlier in the order of understanding', because the reference is to first philosophy as prior to physics. My suggestion is that when the same word πρότερος occurs (in adverbial form) in the back-reference to *Physics* VIII it is best taken to refer to priority in the order of learning, which for Aristotle is the converse of the order of completed understanding. The last four temporal adverbs sign-post (part of) the sequence of argument within the treatise. The initial πρότερον does the same on a larger scale, announcing that Aristotle is presupposing the results of arguments developed elsewhere for the exist-ence of the prime mover and the first heaven. Even if he did compose *Physics* VIII before he began *De Generatione et Corruptione*, that bio-graphical fact is not the message here. The message is logical, not chronological. In the sequence of argument and exposition *Physics* VIII comes earlier.

This way of reading Aristotelian cross-references allows for the possi-bility that, given two treatises *A* and *B*, each may refer to the other as prior. On one topic *A*, on another *B* comes first in the order of argument and exposition. For example, *de Caelo*. II. 2. 284^{b}13–14 refers in the perfect tense to *de Incessu Animalium* 4–5. On the non-chronological interpretation I favour, this means that, while in general the biological treatises presuppose the cosmic setting provided by the *Physics, de Caelo, GC*, and *Meteorologica*, on the particular issue of right and left, above and below, front and back, *de Caelo* presupposes *de Incessu Animalium*. As *de Caelo* explains, these distinctions are proper (οἰκεῖα) to the nature of animals, so it is a good idea to get a clear understanding of how they apply to the animals we are familiar with before venturing to ascribe a right and a left or a top and a bottom to the heaven itself.

I believe that Aristotle was a systematic philosopher in the sense that he held strong views about the appropriate order of learning and study. Just as *de Sensu* 3, *de Anima* II. 5, and *Metaphysics H* 1 presuppose that you have mastered *GC* I, and just as *de Caelo* II. 2 presupposes acquaint-ance with *de Incessu Animalium* 4–5, so *GC* as a whole presupposes familiarity with the *Physics*. Never mind in what order the several trea-tises were composed. Perhaps they were all composed concurrently, gradually, over a considerable period of time, with constant adjustments to fit each to the others and to the evolving overall plan. There is a sense, indeed, in which that has to be true. None of the treatises we have was published, so they could always be added to or revised. There is abundant evidence that they often were added to and revised. In a certain sense, then, all of them are contemporaneous with each other. Of none of them can we say that it went out into the world before that other, for the simple reason that, unlike Plato's dialogues and Aristotle's 'exoteric' works, none of them was sent out into the world by the author.

But that does not mean it would make sense to *read* them in any arbitrary order. Imagine starting the first-year Aristotle course with *GC* I. The students would be utterly baffled. Familiarity with the *Physics* is not a sufficient condition for understanding *GC* I, but it surely is a necessary condition. If we did not know the theory of categories, and did not know the categorial analysis of change in *Physics* III. 1–3 or V. 2–3, and much else besides, we would be at a loss to know what was at stake as we laboured through the abstract, dialectical argumentation of *GC* I. Aristotle's cross-referencing the *Physics* as prior merely confirms an obvious truth: *GC* I is for people who are already fairly familiar both with the Aristotelian cosmology, from the elementary bodies to the prime mover, and with the fundamental concepts that serve to explain it: coming into being *simpliciter*, alteration, growth, mixture, natural and enforced locomotion.

This is pedagogically sound. You need a strong grasp of a discipline before it makes sense to tackle questions about its conceptual foundations. A course on the foundations of mathematics would mean little or nothing to students who were not already well trained in mathematics itself. Mathematics is an abstract discipline, but meta-mathematics is more abstract still. Gödel's famous incompleteness proof, to the effect that any system of Peano arithmetic will contain a theorem which is true but unprovable in its system, moves at a level stratospherically high above the familiar whole-number arithmetic he is discussing. Or take the more accessible example of Frege's *Die Grundlagen der Arithmetik* (1884). He offers a long mordant critique of his predecessors' conception of what numbers are, from Euclid to modern times, with remarkably little acknowledgement of the fact that many of these people (e.g. Descartes and Newton) were themselves outstanding mathematicians. For his foundational purposes, that is not to the point. Then he propounds an account of number in terms of the extension of concepts which many readers find difficult to relate to the numbers they learned to deal with at school. That too is not to the point. Coming closer to Aristotle's concerns, J. H. Woodger is happy to confess that in his avowedly foundational *Biological Principles* (1929) the proportion of 'biology' to 'philosophy' is very small.[29] Likewise, it would be irrelevant to complain

---

[29] J. H. Woodger, *Biological Principles: A Critical Study*, reissued with a new introd. (London/New York, 1967), 6.

that Aristotle's foundational treatise makes familiar concepts seem harder to understand than they were before. In his view, as in Woodger's, dialectical debate with one's predecessors, with an emphasis on explicit definition, is the route to real insight. Those concepts are crucial to biology.

Yet there is one noteworthy feature of *GC* I which seems designed to make it more friendly to readers than it would otherwise be. This is the unusual number of striking concrete images that Aristotle introduces to get his point across. Some of his images are opaque to a modern reader, but only because we lack the relevant background information, not for philosophical reasons. Let me collect them up. In I. 2, the sawdust; in I. 5, the beaten metal, water-measuring, and the αὐλοι (however the word should be accented and whatever it refers to); the hurtful person of I. 7; the lunatic and the Eleatic in I. 8; I. 9's veins of metal; the eyes of Lynceus in I. 10; perhaps also, in the same chapter, the metals which stutter at one another (ψελλίζεται πρὸς ἄλληλα), reluctant to make a proper alloy. My favourite is the beaten metal of I. 5, which I find a really neat way to make the point that growth involves change of place in a different way from locomotion. I know of no study of Aristotelian imagery. I propose it as a topic worth investigating.

(*c*) *Teleological foundations*. It is Aristotelian doctrine that, in general, the earlier stages of development are for the sake of the later (*PA* II. 1. 646^{a}35–^{b}10). Try applying this to the series of works which develop his natural philosophy, in the order indicated by *Meteorologica* I. 1. The implication would be that *de Caelo, GC,* and *Meteorologica* are for the sake of the biological works that come later in the order of exposition. Nowadays, astrophysics, chemistry, or meteorology may be studied for their own sake, because their subject matter is interesting and worthwhile in its own right, regardless of how it relates to other disciplines. That is not, it seems, how Aristotle would teach them. The order he insists on is directed towards a definite goal, the understanding of life and living things. That, according to *Meteorologica* I. 1, is the τέλος of the entire προαίρεσις.

The rationale for this order might be simply pedagogical: start with easier, less complex things and proceed to the life sciences, where mixtures abound and the four elements still have a key role to play. But it is more likely to reflect a cosmic scale of values which grades living things as *better* than non-living (*GA* II. 1. 731^{b}28–30) and knowledge of better things as a finer, more valuable kind of knowledge (*de An.* I. 1. 402^{a}1–4). As we work through the treatises on natural philosophy we approach the best kind of knowledge the sublunary world has to offer.

It is tempting to take this thought a stage further and wonder whether Aristotle might not believe that his chosen order of study is an appropriate response to an orderly universe, in which the elements and mixtures at the lower levels exist for the sake of plants and animals. The eternity of the species cannot be maintained without a constant supply of materials to constitute the homoeomerous and anhomoeomerous parts of living bodies. That constant supply is guaranteed by the eternal cycle of elemental transformation, which ensures the continued presence in our neighbourhood of a quantity of each of the four elements; they do not all separate into their natural places, which would put a stop to life as we know it. In the sublunary world two types of cycle are said to imitate the divine, eternally circling heavens. One is the eternal cycle of elemental transformation (GC II. 10. $336^{b}25–337^{a}15$, $Metaph.$ Θ 8. $1050^{b}28–30$), the other the eternally continuing life cycles of the biological species (de $An.$ II. 4. $415^{a}26–^{b}7$, GA II. 1. $731^{b}24–732^{a}11$), and the former is necessary for the latter. Since it is axiomatic for Aristotle that 'being is better than not being' (GC II. 10. $336^{b}28–9$, GA II. 1. $731^{b}30$), it is tempting to infer that the cycle of elemental transformation, as the necessary prerequisite for a good overall cosmic state of affairs, is for the sake of that most excellent of results, the eternity of the species.

Sober readers may find the temptation resistable. I have no clear text to make them succumb. But remember: Aristotle does believe that everything in the cosmos is ordered towards the good of the whole ($Metaph.$ Λ 10. $1075^{a}11–25$).

3. Conclusion

I have described three ways in which GC I is foundational: a physical way, a conceptual one, and a third having to do with teleological ordering. It seems appropriate that as Aristotle prepares to build up his cosmos from the bottom he should at the same time turn back to analyse and, as it were, rebuild some of the basic concepts of his physical theory. Those two constructions, the physical and the conceptual, run parallel, because both the four elements themselves and concepts such as unqualified coming to be and passing away, alteration, growth, and mixture will be needed, with appropriate adaptations and refinements, over the whole range of natural philosophy. Especially in biology. That is what it is all for.

So I end on the note with which every introduction should end: Read on. Read on to De $Anima$ and beyond.[30]

[30] I should like to thank the members of the Symposium at Deurne for their vigorous criticisms, and Michael Frede, Jaap Mansfeld, and David Wiggins for invaluable help.

I

On Generation and Corruption I. 1: A False Start?*

JACQUES BRUNSCHWIG

The first chapter of an Aristotelian treatise is usually easier to read and to understand than the following ones. At first sight, *GC* I. 1 looks like a standard Aristotelian introduction: according to a well-entrenched method of exposition, Aristotle first briefly lists the theoretical problems which he plans to deal with (314^{a}1–6); then he introduces the discussion of these problems by way of a critical account of the views of his predecessors about them; the whole of the rest of the chapter is devoted to this discussion (314^{a}6–315^{a}25).

However, this apparent simplicity is largely deceptive. It seems to me that when one reads the chapter a bit more carefully it turns out that it contains many perplexing features, and raises a lot of fairly difficult problems. Yet there are a few passages which seem to be rather plain sailing; hence, I shall not try to offer a running commentary on the whole chapter. Instead, I shall concentrate on what I see as the main and most interesting difficulties, such as are revealed either by the disagreements between modern scholars or, less often, by their silence. I want to discuss first some problems which, though having a textual basis in I. 1, bear on more general problems concerning *GC* as a whole (Sects. 1–4), and then discuss some particularly problematic passages (Sects. 5–12); at the end, I shall try to offer some general conclusions (Sect. 13).

* This paper is a revised version, almost completely rewritten and largely corrected, of the draft presented to the *Symposium Aristotelicum* on *GC* 1 in August 1999 at Deurne, in Holland. I have benefited from the many observations and objections of my fellow symposiasts, either on the spot or later *per litteram*. I would like especially to thank John Cooper, Andrea Falcon, Geoffrey Lloyd, Jaap Mansfeld, Marwan Rashed, and Christian Wildberg. They are in no way responsible for what remains questionable in the paper.

1. The traditional title of *On Generation and Corruption*

The very first line of the chapter, Περὶ δὲ γενέσεως καὶ φθορᾶς κτλ. (*Peri de geneseôs kai phthoras*, 314ᵃ1), raises two problems, a general one and a specific one. First, what conclusion, if any, are we to draw from the fact that the traditional title of the treatise is simply borrowed from this line?[1] Secondly, Aristotelian treatises, as a rule, begin without any connective particle;[2] what are we to make of the unusual δέ? These two features should of course remind us, first of all, that the neat division of our *Corpus Aristotelicum* into separate and well-delimited treatises does not necessarily come from Aristotle's own hand.

To begin with the problem of the title, the most interesting parallel, I think, is provided in the *Sophistical Refutations*. Briefly speaking,[3] the fact that the traditional title of that book comes directly from its first sentence (Περὶ δὲ τῶν σοφιστικῶν ἐλέγχων), after removal of the δέ, should be compared with two other facts: (1) in *Topics* I. 1.100ᵇ23–101ᵃ4 Aristotle mentions and briefly analyses the *eristikos sullogismos*,[4] on a par with the *apodeixis* and the *dialektikos sullogismos*; the latter is clearly described as the proper subject of the treatise (100ᵃ22–4), and Aristotle does not say anything which might indicate that he plans to include in it a specific study of the *eristikos sullogismos*; (2) on the other hand, when he summarizes the whole of his *pragmateia*, at the end of *Sophistical Refutations* (34. 183ᵃ37–ᵇ16), he clearly makes the whole of *Topics* plus *Sophistical Refutations* into a strongly unitary work.[5] These data seem to be consistent with the following story: Aristotle first conceived *Topics*. I–VIII as a self-contained study about the dialectical syllogism; some time later he decided to append to it his analysis of sophistical refutations. Thus, to a certain extent, the tradition was right to consider *Sophistical Refutations* as an autonomous work, deserving a title of its own (and the obvious way of getting a title for it was to copy this title from its first words); but in another way the tradition was wrong, and it would have been more respectful of Aristotle's latest thoughts at least to count *Sophistical Refutations* as the ninth book of *Topics*.

---

[1] Apart from some minor works, the traditional title of which is more or less freely taken from the initial sentence (*MA*, *Mem.*, *Insomn.*, *Div. Somn.*), this feature of *GC* is shared only by *SE*, and in a much less significant way by *Rh*.

[2] See *de An.*, *APo.*, *APr.*, *Cael.*, *Cat.*, *EN*, *HA*, *Int.*, *Metaph.*, *PA*, *Ph.*, *Po.*, *Pol.*, *Rh.* Exceptions: *EE*, *Top.* (μέν), *Mete.* (μὲν οὖν), *GA* (δέ), *GC* (δέ).

[3] For more arguments and bibliographical references see Dorion (1995), 24–5.

[4] The συλλογισμὸς ἐριστικός is the same thing as the σόφισμα (*SE* 11.162ᵃ16–17).

[5] Among other arguments for the same interpretation (cf. Dorion (1995) 24), let us notice that *SE* begins with a δέ, like all the books of *Top.*, except I. But the main argument is that Aristotle himself refers to passages of *SE* by way of the formula ἐν τοῖς Τοπικοῖς (cf. Bonitz (1870) 102ᵃ48–9).

Can we imagine some similar story about *GC*? Is the way it is commonly entitled an indication that it was perhaps first conceived by
Aristotle as a supplement, not planned initially but justifiably added to
some already written treatise, and eventually integrated into it, and not
transmitted, initially, as an originally independent work?

In contrast with *Sophistical Refutations*, it is hardly thinkable that
Aristotle might have planned his study of the physical world, from the
outset, without knowing that he would have to deal with the all-
important notions of generation and corruption, already put right to
the fore by his *phusikoi* predecessors. But of course this does not mean
that he intended to write a comprehensive and in some sense independent
course of lectures devoted to the subject as a whole. The passages of
Physics and *de Caelo* sometimes taken as 'promising' to offer a *Peri
geneseôs kai phthoras*[6] are not specific enough, I think, to support this
reading; they merely announce that such or such question will be dealt
with later on, and in some cases at least it is clear that the fulfilment of
this promise might be found in later parts of *Physics* and *de Caelo* as well
as in particular passages of *GC*.

Similarly, and once again unlike *SE*, Aristotle's own backwards references to *GC*,[7] with only one exception to which I shall come later (the
preamble of *Meteorologica*), refer neither to *GC* as such, nor to some
bigger whole, itself included in the entire set of physical treatises; they
refer either to particular chapters or groups of chapters in *GC* (on action
and passion, the elements, mixture)[8] or quite generally to the *peri phuseôs*
works, or even more generally to 'somewhere else'.

Thus far, therefore, we have found no constraining reason to think
that either before or after writing what we read as *GC* Aristotle conceived
it as a self-contained and independent *pragmateia*. It was left to the later
tradition, so it seems, to isolate it and to give it a specific title, quite easily
taken from what we read as its first sentence. This provisional conclusion
is obviously supported by the fact that among the ancient lists of
Aristotle's works the latest one, that of Ptolemy, is the only one which
mentions *GC* as such, and with this title.[9]

---

[6] Cf. Bonitz (1870) 102^{b}47–9.

[7] Bonitz (1870), 102^{b}39–47.

[8] Gohlke (1958: 12) notices that several subunits of *GC*, devoted to specific topics,
contain surveys of earlier views: cf. I. 7. 323^{b}2–17 (on action and passion); I. 8. 324^{b}26–
326^{b}28 (on action and passion again); II. 1.328^{b}33–329^{b}5 (on the elements); II. 3. 330^{b}7–21
(on the elements again). He claims that they could have initially been independant mini-
treatises. Cf. the discussion of this sort of view in Migliori (1976: 19–26), who nevertheless
writes (25): 'noi intendiamo solo affermare che l'opera può, e deve, essere affrontata come
un tutt'unico, logicamente organizzato', but also 'questo non vuol dire...negare una
genesi storica dei singoli brani probabilmente complessa'.

[9] For details see Moraux (1951).

2. The beginning of *On Generation and Corruption* and the end of *de Caelo*

We shall perhaps go a step further if we now take on the second of the problems raised by the first sentence of *GC*; namely, the presence in it of a somewhat unusual δέ. Admittedly, 'inceptive δέ' is not at all an unheard of phenomenon.[10] But in the present case it is generally agreed that the unusual δέ at the beginning of *GC* answers to the solitary μέν which we find in the last sentence of *de Caelo* (IV. 6.313^{b}22: περὶ μὲν οὖν βαρέος καὶ κούφου κτλ.: 'about the heavy and the light and the properties connected with them, we have now finished our examination').

But what are we to conclude from this apparently strong connection between the end of *de Caelo* and the beginning of *GC*? Here many options are open.[11] Some people have thought that *de Caelo* and *GC* were originally one and the same work, or, more specifically, that *GC* was originally a part of a whole containing also *de Caelo* III–IV; that is, two books which do not bear any more on the heavens, like I–II, but on sublunary generation and the elements of sublunary bodies, and thus are closer to *GC* than to *de Caelo* I–II. A weaker and more modest conclusion would be that *de Caelo* and *GC* were written one after the other, more or less at one stretch; a still weaker and still more modest one would be that they were intended to be heard and read one after the other.

This last conclusion, which means that there is both a real distinction and a strong link between *de Caelo* and *GC*, seems to be at least the minimal one supported by the famous proem of *Meteorologica*, where Aristotle summarizes the whole of his works, past and to come, on natural philosophy, from the *Physics* to the zoological and botanical treatises (338^{a}20–339^{a}10).[12] Let us reread the part of this summary which directly concerns us.

---

[10] Cf. W. J. Verdenius 'Notes on the Presocratics', *Mnemosyne*, 3/13 (1947), 274–5, 'Notes on Hippocrates *Airs Waters Places*', *Mnemosyne* 4/8 (1955), 14–18, and 'Inceptive ΔΕ again', *Mnemosyne*, 27/2 (1974), 173–4; P. W. Van der Horst 'Some Late Instances of Inceptive ΔΕ', *Mnemosyne*, 32/3–4 (1979), 377–8. I thank Jaap Mansfeld for referring me to these studies.

[11] Cf. Migliori (1976), 19–26.

[12] The authenticity of this passage, sometimes suspected a long time ago, was successfully and definitely established by Capelle (1912), and is now, it seems, quite generally accepted (cf. e.g. Lee (1952), p. ix; Louis (1982), p. xix n. 6; Pepe (1982), 9 n. 1, 13, 37). But it is equally generally agreed that Aristotle is not describing here the actual chronology of his physical treatises; he is rather giving a largely retrospective overview of the ordered mapping of the topics he has dealt with and intends to deal with; he is probably indicating also the order in which he would like his treatises to be read. This overview certainly influenced the order in which the physical treatises were put in the so-called Andronicos' 'edition' (if we can still use this familiar description of what Andronicos did, after the doubts raised by Barnes (1997)), as well as in Ptolemy's' catalogue of Aristotle's works (cf. n. 9 above), and still of course in the medieval manuscripts and all our modern editions.

We have already discussed (περὶ μὲν οὖν...εἴρηται πρότερον) the first causes of nature [*Ph.* pt. I] and (καί), all natural motions [*Ph.* pt. II[13]]; also (ἔτι δέ) the stars ordered in the motion of heavens [*Cael.* I–II] and (καί) the corporeal elements— enumerating and specifying them and showing how they change into one another [*Cael.* III–IV]—and (καί) becoming and perishing in general (καὶ περὶ γενέσεως καὶ φθορᾶς τῆς κοινῆς [*GC*]).

It is not completely clear, however, what this text is linking to what. Some observations are here in order.

(1) A widespread view has it that *Meteorologica* establishes an especially narrow link, not between the whole of *de Caelo* and *GC*, but between *de Caelo* III–IV and *GC*;[14] this view might be related to the interplay of μέν and δέ between the end of the former and the beginning of the latter.

However, *Meteorologica* does not really support this idea, appearances notwithstanding. If we pay attention to the articulated structure of the passage, we can notice that Aristotle seems deliberately to use two different ways of ordering the elements of his list of topics. There is first a large-scale distinction, marked by the correspondence περὶ μὲν οὖν...ἔτι δέ; the effect of this articulation is to isolate the whole of *Physics* from all the rest, that is to say from the whole of *de Caelo* plus *GC;* this distinction seems strongly to separate the abstract and general topics studied in *Physics* from the already a little more concrete topics studied in the whole of *de Caelo* plus *GC*, which successively bear on heavenly bodies and motions, sublunary elements and changes, and generation and corruption in general; that is to say, on the whole set of physical bodies and processes, whether supralunar or sublunar. Then, within each of the wholes contrasted by περὶ μὲν οὖν...ἔτι δέ we find several subunits, separated by the weaker conjunction καί, which is repeatedly used. Three subunits are thus introduced; they are put exactly on the same level, in an ordered but non-hierarchic sequence, respectively corresponding to (i) *de Caelo* I–II, (ii) *de Caelo* III–IV, and (iii) *GC*. Nothing in the *Meteorologica* passage indicates the existence of any *specific* link between (ii) and (iii). The only conclusion so far supported by this passage is that *GC* was conceived as the (logically) last part of a larger unit, containing two other parts. Within this large unit *GC* is of

---

[13] Aristotle here seems to give some support to those commentators, ancient and modern, who think that there are two parts in *Ph.*, the first on principles, the second on movement. I deliberately use vague phrases ('Part I', 'Part II'), in order to avoid committing myself here to any solution to the age-old question of where to separate them (I gave a summary account of the debate in Brunschwig (1991); see now the much fuller discussion in Barnes (1997)).

[14] As implied e.g. by the figures introduced in his translation by Lee (1952), ad loc. Similarly Tricot (1955), nn. ad loc.

course what follows *de Caelo* III–IV;[15] but this does not mean that *de Caelo* III–IV has to be set apart from *de Caelo* I–II, and thereby brought closer to *GC*.

Moreover, the affinities between *GC* and *de Caelo* III–IV, as described in the *Meteorologica* preamble (and as filled in, but only to a certain extent, by the texts themselves), should not be exaggerated. The *Meteorologica* preamble clearly contrasts the subject of *de Caelo* III–IV, namely the processes through which the corporeal elements change into one another (περὶ τῶν στοιχείων τῶν σωματικῶν … καὶ τῆς εἰς ἄλληλα μεταβολῆς),[16] and the official subject of *GC*, namely 'common' generation and corruption (καὶ περὶ γενέσεως καὶ φθορᾶς τῆς κοινῆς—that is, generation and corruption in general).[17] So far, thus, there is no constraining reason to think that *de Caelo* III–IV and *GC* once constituted a single treatise.

(2) If we read the *Meteorologica* passage as contrasting generation and corruption in general (iii) with elemental generation and corruption (ii), we must notice that the official subject of *GC*, as labelled in *Meteorologica*, is far from corresponding exactly to *GC* as we have it. The focus on generation and corruption in general, if anywhere, is limited to *GC* I. 1–5 (where nevertheless elemental changes are taken as examples more often than not); the beginning of I. 6 neatly marks a shift towards the problems concerning 'the so-called elements'; and nearly the whole of *GC* II (1–8) is devoted to elemental questions.

In this respect, the preamble of II. 1 also has some remarkably strange features. It first summarizes I, and then officially announces a study of 'the so-called elements of bodies'. But the summary of book I is spelled out in an order which corresponds neither to the actual order of topics in book I as we have it, nor to the exactly reverse order: it puts first the subjects of I. 10 (mixture), I. 6 (contact), I. 7–9 (action and passion), then

---

[15] Let us notice, however, that it is not at all obvious that the study of generation and corruption 'in general' should *follow* the study of elemental generation and corruption. The reverse order could also have some justification.

[16] Echoed in *Cael.* III. 1. 298^b7–11, where the problems concerning generation and corruption are raised, at least primarily, with respect to the elements. I thank Andrea Falcon for this remark, already made in another way by Migliori (1976: 24 and n. 32) ('gli ultimi due libri del *Cael.* (…) trattano degli elementi corporei, e delle trasformazioni che, sulla base della tralazione secondo alto e basso, si determinano. A questo punto si può passare [with *GC*] a vedere analiticamente queste trasformazioni in generale e soprattutto la trasformazione più importante, la generazione e la corruzione'). Migliori himself refers to Germain (1954).

[17] Echoed in *GC* I. 1. 314^a2 (ὁμοίως κατὰ πάντων). I take it that κοινή is used for contrasting generation and corruption in general with elemental generation and corruption; when the contrast is between generation *simpliciter* and the various kinds of γένεσίς τις, the usual idiom is ἁπλῶς.

of I. 2–3 (generation and corruption *simpliciter*[18]), and finally of I. 4 (alteration); and it omits the subject of I. 5 (growth). Roughly speaking, all the topics studied *after* the shift towards the elements (at the beginning of I. 6) are listed first, whereas all the topics studied *before* this turning point are listed later. This perhaps is a sign that at some time Aristotle wavered about the order in which he would put some of his earlier mini-studies.[19]

More generally speaking, there is a problem about the exact status of the elemental theory in *GC*, concerning which I can content myself with referring the reader to the illuminating considerations introduced by Carlo Natali in his contribution to this volume (Ch. 7).[20]

3. 314[a]1–6: the agenda of *On Generation and Corruption* and the focusing on the 'G/A problem'

All this being said, it is impossible to deny that with 314[a]1–6 we have a fresh start, whether the beginning of a new *pragmateia* or of a new part in a bigger *pragmateia*.[21] The tone is clearly programmatic:

On the other hand (δέ), our task is to pick out the causes and definitions of generation and corruption common to all those things which come to be and perish in the course of nature; and secondly (ἔτι δέ) to investigate growth and

---

[18] There is a textual problem in 328[b]28–9. I prefer the variant readings which do *not* introduce the contrast between generation *simpliciter* and γένεσίς τις at this point (like Joachim (1922), Forster (1955), Mugler (1966), and Williams (1982)). *Contra* Tricot (1951) and Migliori (1976).

[19] See n. 8 above. Migliori (1976) does not seem to have commented upon the ordering of the summary of I in II. 1 either in his introduction or in his commentary. He just tries to justify the omission of growth, saying that 'questo non è tra i processi necessari per la comprensione degli elementi come causa materiale della generazione' (p. 219). This is not a very good argument, since I, 5, on growth, *precedes* the beginning of I. 6, i.e. the official shift towards the study of elements.

[20] Cf. his way of contrasting what he dubs 'Philoponus' interpretation' ('*GC* discute les aspects communs à toutes les choses qui naissent et se détruisent, y compris les quatre éléments') and 'Zabarella's interpretation' ('*GC* discute seulement la génération des corps naturels, c'est-à-dire des homéomères et des mixtes, les quatre éléments n'étant étudiés que comme des causes matérielles de la génération et de la corruption de ces corps-là').

[21] Marwan Rashed kindly drew my attention to a very interesting fact, which is not mentioned in the critical editions of *Cael.* and *GC*: at the end of (what is now) *Cael.*, the scribe of E (Parisinus gr. 1853, fo. 106 v°) has copied (what are now) the first words of *GC* (with δέ), without marking any break. He then crossed these lines out, wrote the title περὶ γενέσεως καὶ φθορᾶς in an official style, and copied again the lines he had crossed out (this time without δέ, but the particle was added by a later hand). This seems to show that his model had no break in the text, but probably a marginal note indicating that a new treatise was beginning at this point.

alteration (περὶ αὐξήσεως καὶ ἀλλοιώσεως), asking what each of them is, and whether we are to suppose that the nature of alteration and generation is the same or different, as they are certainly distinguished in names... (*GC* I. I. 314ᵃ1–6, trans. Williams (1982), with occasional slight modifications here and in what follows)

What is immediately striking in this agenda is that, in the space of six lines, Aristotle is very quickly focusing on a particular problem; namely, the problem of whether alteration and generation are identical or different processes (a problem which hereafter I shall call the 'G/A problem'). This problem will dominate the critical review of earlier theories (and hence, the major part of I. 1, at least till 315ᵃ3), as is already revealed by the very next sentence (314ᵃ6–8): 'Of the old philosophers some say that what is called coming to be *simpliciter* (ἁπλῆν γένεσιν) is alteration, some that alteration and coming to be are different.'

This sequence seems to show that the central theoretical importance which Aristotle attributes to the G/A problem is the product of his reflections on his predecessors' views and of his way of classifying them. But if so, a question arises. As is well known, Aristotle defines *alloiôsis* as a special case of non-substantial change (of γένεσίς τις, as opposed to γένεσις ἁπλή); namely, *qualitative* change, as distinct from quantitative change (growth and diminution) and local change (motion in space). By doing so, did he feel he was innovating to any extent? It is not easy to answer this question. On the one hand, the suffix -οιος, characteristically present in ἀλλοῖος, ἀλλοίωσις, ἀλλοιοῦσθαι, as well as in οἷος, ποιός, seems to indicate by itself that *alloiôsis* is a change of ποιότης, 'quality'; but, on the other hand, ποιότης itself is a πολλαχῶς λεγόμενον ('term with several meanings') in his opinion, and that implies that *alloiôsis* too is such a term.[22] In any case, we might think that Aristotle

---

[22] Philoponus (*in GC* 8. 31–9.3), commenting upon 314ᵃ4, interestingly quotes *Od.* 16. 181, where Telemachos says to his father, rejuvenated by Athena: ἀλλοῖός μοι, ξεῖνε, φάνης νέον ἠὲ πάροιθεν (the following line says that his clothes are ἄλλα and his complexion οὐκέθ' ὁμοῖος). Philoponus then adds: 'please note that he did not say ἄλλος, but ἀλλοῖος; the γένεσις makes something ἄλλο, e.g. fire out of water, whereas the ἀλλοίωσις makes something ἀλλοῖον, e.g., say, dark out of bright'. However, on the fact that Aristotle's notion of ἀλλοίωσις as change of ποιότης also differentiates according to the distinction between various senses of ποιότης itself, a broad one including the essential διαφορά, and a narrow one limited to inessential πάθη, cf. *Ph.* V. 2. 226ᵃ26–9: 'motion in respect of quality let us call ἀλλοίωσις, a general designation [of change of any kind?] that has been attached [in a more restricted sense?] to it (τοῦτο γὰρ ἐπέζευκται κοινὸν ὄνομα); by quality I do not here mean a property of substance (in that sense, that which constitutes a διαφορά is a ποιότης), but τὸ παθητικόν in virtue of which a thing is said to undergo something or be incapable of undergoing'. Cf. also the various meanings of ποιόν listed in *Metaph.* Δ 14, especially 1020ᵃ33–ᵇ1, ᵇ8–12. *Top.* VI. 6. 145ᵃ3–12 is an interesting piece of evidence in this respect: it seems to show that the distinction between πάθος (which can be lost without damage for the subject) and διαφορά (which cannot) was common stuff, at least in the Academy circle.

should be wary of attributing his specific concept of alteration to the earlier physicists, even if he finds words like ἀλλοίωσις or ἀλλοιοῦσθαι in their writings, although that by no means implies that he has *actually been wary* of doing so. Such words as these, in a pre-Aristotelian context, could simply refer to any kind of change affecting any pre-existent being, as opposed to the (apparent) coming to be of a brand new being out of nothing.

Now, is it in this broad sense or in his own technical narrow sense that Aristotle uses *alloiôsis* in chapter 1? It seems to me that it is difficult to give a clear and brief answer to this question.[23] The narrow sense is quite probably used at 314ª3–4 and ᵇ13–15, where *auxêsis* and *alloiôsis* are distinguished; and such is certainly the case at 314ᵇ27–8, where we find the standard doctrine about the kinds of change 'according to place... growth and diminution' and 'alteration' (κατὰ τόπον...κατ᾽ αὔξησιν καὶ φθίσιν,...κατ᾽ ἀλλοίωσιν). In all these passages it is clear that Aristotle is speaking on his own behalf.

On the other hand, when he speaks about his predecessors the situation is much less clear. It is perhaps worthwhile immediately to draw attention to a couple of occurrences of *alloiôsis, alloiousthai.*

(i) As we shall see, Aristotle thinks that monist philosophers are committed to identifying generation (and corruption) with *alloiôsis* (314ª8–11). The reason he gives for this commitment is that 'according to them the substratum (*hupokeimenon*, τὸ ὑποκείμενον) remains one and the same throughout; and this is just the sort of thing which we say to *alloiousthai*' (314ᵇ3–4). Here it seems that the only condition for a change to qualify 'for us'[24] as an *alloiôsis* is that the changing thing itself (the *hupokeimenon*) persists as such through the change, no matter what kind of features it might lose and acquire by virtue of the change. Local motion and quantitative growth or diminution could apparently meet the condition as well as qualitative change, and possibly still other kinds of changes;[25] *alloiôsis* here seems to refer to *any* kind of non-substantial change, including *alloiôsis* in the narrow sense, but by no means restricted to it.

---

[23] Because of this uncertainty I shall leave ἀλλοίωσις untranslated in what follows. I was put on the track of this important problem by Mugler (1966) who, unlike the other modern translators, translates ἀλλοίωσις most of the time (in I. 1) as 'changement', not as 'altération'. However, he does not explain his reasons for doing so.

[24] 'We' ordinary people, no doubt, not Aristotelian philosophers.

[25] e.g. Anaximenes generates his universe through the rarefaction/condensation of his preferred basic stuff, air. Now, Aristotle, all things considered, prefers *not* to classify μανόν and πυκνόν as qualities: they indicate rather the positions of a thing's parts (*Cat.* 8. 10ª16–22). It is even 'not clear into which category Aristotle would wish to put openness of texture, etc.' (Ackrill (1963: 107)). But this remark, I think, only widens the gap between Presocratic basic 'categories' and the Aristotelian categorial scheme, and, hence, between the broad and the narrow sense of ἀλλοίωσις. Cf. also n. 44 below.

(ii) Another remarkable passage is 314^{b}28–315^{a}3, where Aristotle explains that there is a two-way implication between unicity of underlying matter[26] and *alloiôsis*: 'for [a] if there is *alloiôsis*, both the substratum is a single element and there is one matter for all things capable of changing into one another, and [b] if the substratum is one there is *alloiôsis*'. If I am not mistaken, the implication [a] is correct whether we take *alloiôsis* in the narrow or in the broad sense: in both cases *alloiôsis* requires a persistent substratum. But not so in the case of the implication [b]: if we take *alloiôsis* in the narrow sense it is simply not true that the persistence of a unique underlying matter implies that the change is a qualitative one, since (as Aristotle himself has just said, at 314^{b}26–8) there is such a unique matter also in the cases of local motion or growth and diminution. On the other hand, the implication [b] is unproblematic if we take *alloiôsis* in the broad sense: *any* non-substantial change, as we already saw from 314^{b}3–4, requires a substratum which 'remains one and the same throughout'.[27]

This passage is all the more puzzling in that it immediately follows the most unmistakably narrow use of *alloiôsis* in the whole chapter, namely at 314^{b}28. Perhaps the transition through ἔτι δ[έ] indicates that 314^{b}28–315^{a}3 has been appended to the main text as a kind of footnote, as is often the case. As a matter of fact, it seems to be one among many signs of a certain uneasiness lingering in Aristotle's mind, throughout *GC* I. 1, as a result of his growing awareness of a sort of mismatch between his own conceptual framework and the doxographical data he tries to bend to it, that is, between what theory suggests things should be like and what history shows them actually to be. But much more on this later.

4. Two introductions to *On Generation and Corruption*?

Before coming back to the actual contents of I. 1 we have to say something about a problem which has been aptly raised and discussed by Migliori (1976: 22–3). He writes: 'se noi guardiamo attentamente il testo, ci accorgiamo che il primo e il secondo capitolo del *GC* I presentano entrambi una introduzione all'argomento, con alcune differenze'. Let us therefore compare the beginnings of both chapters:

---

[26] τοῦτο (314^{b}29) unmistakably refers to μίαν ἀεὶ τοῖς ἐναντίοις ὑποθετέον ὕλην (314^{b}26–7), as is shown by the following explanation (314^{b}29–315^{a}3).

[27] It has been tentatively suggested (by Geoffrey Lloyd) that ἔστιν (315^{a}3) should be taken in the sense of 'it is possible', in order to save the narrow sense: so, 'if the substratum is one there possibly is ἀλλοίωσις'. Right; but that would ruin ὁμοίως ἀναγκαῖον (314^{b}28–9).

[I. 1. 314^{a}1–6:] On the other hand (δέ), our task is to pick out the causes and definitions of generation and corruption common to all those things which come to be and perish in the course of nature; and secondly (ἔτι δέ) to investigate growth and alteration (περὶ αὐξήσεως καὶ ἀλλοιώσεως), asking what each of them is, and whether we are to suppose that the nature of alteration and generation is the same or different, as they are certainly distinguished in names.

[I. 2. 315^{a}26–9:] As a whole [ὅλως], our subject is both [τε δή] generation and corruption *simpliciter* [περὶ γενέσεως καὶ φθορᾶς τῆς ἁπλῆς], whether or not there is such a thing and how it exists, as well as [καί] movements of the other kinds,[28] e.g. growth and alteration.

It is hard to deny, I think, that both passages look equally like introductions to *GC*. My problem here is not, at least primarily, to decide whether one of them is more exact, more faithful to the actual contents of *GC* than the other;[29] it is rather to ask what the fact that they coexist could mean. In order to do that, we must look at the 'alcune differenze' between them, whether pointed out or not by Migliori (1976).

A first difference (not pointed out by Migliori) lies in the initial particles: δέ in I. 1, τε δή in I. 2. τε δή is difficult and controversial.[30] According to Denniston (1954: 260–1) τε can mean either 'both' (referring forwards to a later καί) or 'and' (referring backwards to what comes before); when it does mean 'both' (as is certainly the case here, see the responsive καί at 315^{a}27) 'we might either take δή as giving the connection, or assume asyndeton', for 'δή in τε δή is sometimes emphatic, sometimes connective'; however, Denniston adds, 'the two particles seem to cohere closely, and the supposition of asyndeton is, I think, to be preferred'. The need for an emphatic δή rather than a connective one, is not difficult to understand: Aristotle wants to stress the large scope of his enquiry (τε ... καί), in contrast to Plato, who dealt only with the

---

[28] Some MSS and modern editors (Bekker (1831), Forster (1955), Mugler (1966)) read 'of the other simple kinds'; for the details see Joachim (1922), app. crit. ad loc.

[29] Several symposiasts, in particular Geoffrey Lloyd and Jaap Mansfeld, have drawn my attention to the fact that we should not expect too much accuracy from ancient programmatic pronouncements. Cf. J. Mansfeld, 'Notes on the *Didascalicus*', in M. Joyal (ed.), *Studies in Plato and the Platonic Tradition* (Aldershot, 1997), 256–7: 'Alcinous' introductory chapters, and especially his divisions and subdivisions of philosophy, should not be taken as a table of contents of what is to follow. It is sufficient (...) if they provide a general idea of what is to follow in the rest of the treatise'; Mansfeld, 'Parménide et Héraclite avaient-ils une théorie de la perception?', *Phronesis*, 44 (1199), 328: 'il suffit, dans un ouvrage ancien, qu'une introduction donne au lecteur une impression assez générale de ce qui l'attend, et (...) l'auteur n'est pas du tout obligé de donner une table des matières précise'.

[30] Jaap Mansfeld has kindly sent me a whole batch of TLG searches of τε δή, from which he concludes that 'τε links up with what comes before, and δή provides emphasis'. I have doubts about the first part of this conclusion, as far as the passage in question is concerned; see below in the main text.

generation of elements, and left aside alteration and growth (315^a29–33). Thus, if the beginning of I. 2 is an alternative introduction to *GC*, it is not linked by any connective particle to the end of *de Caelo* in the same way as the beginning of I. 1 seems to be.

Migliori provides a number of more substantial arguments, to the effect that the differences between the two introductions are 'tutte a vantaggio del cap. I. 2'. Let us examine and discuss these arguments.

(i) 'La presentazione dei problemi [in I. 2] è piú sobria e schematica, e punta sulla generazione e corruzione assoluta, piú che sulla distinzione tra generazione e alterazione, come fa invece l'introduzione del cap. I. 1.' This is quite right, and could even be developed a little further. I. 2 not only introduces right away the basic notion of generation *simpliciter* ($\gamma\acute{\epsilon}\nu\epsilon\sigma\iota\varsigma$ $\acute{\alpha}\pi\lambda\hat{\eta}$)[31], but also neatly contrasts it ($\tau\epsilon$ ... $\kappa\alpha\acute{\iota}$) with the other kinds of changes ($\kappa\iota\nu\acute{\eta}\sigma\epsilon\iota\varsigma$), exemplified ($o\hat{i}o\nu$) by growth and alteration. On the other hand, I. 1 does not even mention the notion of generation *simpliciter* within the programme of the treatise properly speaking (314^a1–6), but only later on ($\tau\grave{\eta}\nu$ $\kappa\alpha\lambda o\upsilon\mu\acute{\epsilon}\nu\eta\nu$ $\acute{\alpha}\pi\lambda\hat{\eta}\nu$ $\gamma\acute{\epsilon}\nu\epsilon\sigma\iota\nu$, 314^a6–7), in the first lines of the review of earlier doctrines. It is equally true, as we already saw, that I. 1 seems to be in a hurry to concentrate on a quite special problem, namely the G/A problem. On the other hand, this problem does not play any similar role in I. 2. As Williams (1982: 63) has it, in I. 2 'the topic of the difference between generation and alteration *is left aside*, and *a new start* is made on the task of discussing the existence and the nature of generation, etc.' (emphasis added).

(ii) Migliori also claims that 'l'introduzione del cap. I. 2 cita anche il problema della mescolanza e del rapporto azione-passione, che non risultano nemmeno accennati nell'introduzione del cap. I. 1.' This is false if 'l'introduzione del cap. I. 2' means the lines 315^a26–9, as Migliori seems to suppose (he refers (p. 23 n. 28) to 315^a26–8), but true if it means 'the introduction to *GC* provided by I. 2 as a whole' (the relevant reference should then be to 315^b4–5).

(iii) Other arguments proposed by Migliori are based on further comparisons with other chapters. For instance, he points out that 'quando nel cap. I. 4 si riprende la questione della differenza tra generazione e alterazione [i.e. the G/A problem] non c'è alcun riferimento al I. 1.' True, but there is still more to it: I. 4 also discusses the G/A problem, but without any reference to the basic choice between monism and pluralism, which dominated the treatment of the same problem in I. 1.

---

[31] I don't think (*pace* John Cooper) that this abrupt way of using the notion of generation *simpliciter,* compared with the cautious introduction of that phrase in I. 1. 314^a6–7, might indicate that the readers or hearers of I, 2 are supposed to have already read or heard I. 1. As a matter of fact, some acquaintance with *Physics* would be enough to familiarize them with this notion.

(iv) Migliori also remarks that 'quando in chiusura si riassumono i risultati di questi primi capitoli, lo schema che si ripresenta è chiaramente quello dell'inizio del secondo capitolo'. This again is perfectly true. The final summary referred to by Migliori is the end of I. 4, namely 320^{a}5–7: 'this, then, is our way of deciding the questions about generation— whether or not it exists (εἴτε ἔστιν εἴτε μή) and how it takes place (καὶ πῶς ἔστι)—and about alteration'. This summary has indeed a much greater degree of similarity with the introduction of I. 2, which also distinguishes the question of the existence or not of generation *simpliciter* and the question of its mode of being (315^{a}27),[32] than with the introduction of I. 1, which makes no such distinction at all. It is pretty clear, therefore, that the end of I. 4 refers to I. 2, and not to I. 1, as *the* introduction to *GC*.

But what conclusion exactly do Migliori's arguments support? His position does not seem quite clear to me. He writes: 'è quindi possibile pensare che il primitivo inizio dell'opera fosse quello che troviamo nel cap. I. 2, e che solo in un successivo rimaneggiamento la parte finale del *De caelo* sia stata riadattata come inizio del *De generatione*, finendo col costituire l'attuale cap. I. 1.' Thus, if I understand him rightly, he seems to think that, *as a first step*, the end of *de Caelo*, together with the whole of *GC* I. 1, was the end of something, and that *GC* I. 2 the beginning of something else. Then, *as a second step*, Aristotle would have reshaped the whole in the form we still read.

I must say that it seems to me totally unlikely that *the whole* of *GC* I. 1 might have been, at any time, part of *de Caelo* IV, let alone its 'parte finale'. Perhaps we might accept that, at some early stage, the end of *de Caelo* IV included *the first lines* of *GC* I. 1, if it makes any sense to speculate about this sort of largely artificial question. But then we do not know what to do with the rest of this chapter: In what place and with which function might it have been conceived and written? I therefore prefer to postpone (see § 13 below) any attempt to answer the question why we seem to have two distinct introductions to *GC*, until we have looked more carefully at the contents of I. 1 itself.

5. 314^{a}6–13: the earlier doctrines and their theoretical implications

As we already saw, Aristotle's review of earlier doctrines in I. 1 is dominated by the G/A problem. Right at the beginning he says: 'of the

---

[32] On these fundamental types questions or enquiries see *APo.* II. 1.89^{b}23–35, *Ph.* IV. 1. 202^{a}28 ff.; cf. Mansfeld (2002), 276 n. 14, who refers to some of his earlier papers, as well as to Algra (1995). I saw Mansfeld's article before it was published.

old philosophers some say that what is called coming to be *simpliciter* is *alloiôsis*, some that *alloiôsis* and coming to be are different'.[33] But these two positions are said (without any argument, for the time being) to depend on a more primitive choice, standardly used by Aristotle in his doxographical classifications, namely, the choice between *monism* and *pluralism*.[34] Monists—that is, people who say that 'the universe is some one thing' (none of them mentioned by name, or even by any characteristic individual tenet)—are committed to thinking that generation is the *same* thing as *alloiôsis* (let us call that position the 'S answer' to the G/A problem); on the other hand, pluralists—that is, people 'who assert a plurality of matter' (here Empedocles, Anaxagoras, and Leucippus are explicitly mentioned)—are committed to thinking that generation and *alloiôsis* are *different* things (let us call that the 'D answer' to the G/A problem).

Aristotle is remarkably positive about the logical force of these two commitments. He explicitly says that it is necessary (ἀνάγκη, 314ᵃ9) for the monists to adopt the S answer. Concerning the pluralists, the strict parallelism between 314ᵃ8–11 (ὅσοι μὲν ... τούτοις μὲν ἀνάγκη ... φάναι) and 11–13 (ὅσοι δὲ ... τούτοις δὲ ⟨ἀνάγκη ... φάναι⟩) shows that he also sees the pluralists as necessarily committed to the D answer.[35] What are

---

[33] Like Philoponus previously (*in GC* 11. 9–12), Mansfeld (2002: 274) points out that the dialectical discussion opened in these terms by Aristotle is 'a bit unexpected in that ... one would expect him to start with the Eleatic tenet that there is no γένεσις at all, and no φθορά, no perishing, either'; this makes a difference for another passage where he formally discusses γένεσις, namely *Cael.* III. 1. 298ᵇ12–299ᵃ2, where the position listed first is the Eleatic absolute denial of the real existence of γένεσις and φθορά (cf. 298ᵇ10,12). It seems to me that this difference can be explained: concerning γένεσις, the *Cael.* passage explicitly raises the question πότερον ἔστιν ἤ οὐκ ἔστιν (298ᵇ12), whereas this question, raised in *GC* I. 1, where the existence of natural generation and corruption is taken for granted (cf. 314ᵃ1–2: Περὶ δὲ γενέσεως καὶ φθορᾶς τῶν φύσει γενομένων καὶ φθειρομένων); so that there is a justification for mentioning the Eleatics in *Cael.* and for not mentioning them in *GC* I. 1. More generally, Aristotle has some reasons for saying that an examination of the Eleatic 'aphysical' position (Aristotle ap. SE *M* X. 46) is out of place in a physical treatise (*Cael.* III. 1. 298ᵇ18–20; *Ph.* I. 2.184ᵇ25–185ᵃ4), and also some reasons for introducing a discussion of this position into his own physical works all the same (*Ph.* I. 2. 185ᵃ17–20, with the famous problem where to put the comma at l. 18; I venture to suggest, by the way, that *Cael.* III. 1. 298ᵇ17–24 rather favours the reading περὶ φύσεως μὲν οὔ, φυσικὰς δὲ ἀπορίας συμβαίνει λέγειν αὐτοῖς in the *Ph.* passage).

[34] The star example is of course the beginning of *Ph.* I. 2. The difference is that *Ph.* distinguishes two versions of monism, the immobilist (Eleatic) one and the mobilist (Milesian) one (184ᵇ15–18), whereas *GC*, which does not take Eleaticism into account (see n. 33 above), only refers to monistic doctrines of the Milesian type (cf. 314ᵃ9, πάντα ἐξ ἑνὸς γεννῶσι; 314ᵇ1–2, τοῖς ... ἐξ ἑνὸς πάντα κατασκευάζουσιν).

[35] Cf. also 314ᵇ1–6, where ἀναγκαῖον (ᵇ2), applied to the monistic implication, is to be understood with the infinitive διαφέρειν (ᵇ5), this time applied to the pluralistic implication. At 314ᵇ10 ἀναγκαῖον is explicitly used in reference to the pluralists' commitment to the D answer.

the arguments which allow him to be so confident in this respect? Although these arguments are presented a little later in the chapter (314^{b}1–6), I shall examine them at once, first those about monism, and then those about pluralism.

6. The case of monism

In spite of the dominant position of the monism versus pluralism contrast in I. 1, monism does not have a major place in the chapter. This is for two connected reasons: not only is the commitment of the monists to the S answer easy to understand, but also the historical monistic doctrines confirm this commitment without any exception (in these two respects, the case of pluralism is much more thorny, as we shall see). Concerning monism, we find only two brief passages in I. 1. Aristotle first states his thesis about the entailment of the S answer in any kind of monistic doctrine: 'those who say that the all is some one thing and make everything come to be from one thing are obliged to say that generation is *alloiôsis* and what, in the strict sense, comes to be, *alloiousthai*' (314^{a}8–11). The argument for why it is so comes later (314^{b}1–4, partially quoted already in my discussion of *alloiôsis* above): 'those who construct everything out of one thing necessarily identify generation and corruption with *alloiôsis*; for according to them the substratum remains one and the same throughout, and this is just the sort of thing which we say to *alloiousthai*'. Almost by definition, the persistence of the substratum throughout the alteration implies that this change is a non-substantial one, and, if one grants that *alloiôsis* here just means non-substantial change, the implication is straightforward. Although it would be easy for Aristotle to launch a *modus tollendo tollens* attack against monism on this basis, he does not offer any specific criticism against either the S answer or its monistic foundations: he probably thinks that any theory which implies or holds the S answer should be straightforwardly rejected, simply because it ignores the obvious fact that both generation and *alloiôsis* do exist, and are different things. Nor does he find any historical exception to the theoretical commitment of monists to the S answer.

We could leave monism at that point. Nevertheless, it would perhaps be objectionable not to mention the fact that 314^{b}1–4, together with many other passages, has been quoted in the great controversy which took place in recent years about the Aristotelian theory of 'prime matter'. In this passage, as Williams (1982: 216) says, 'Aristotle seems to dissociate himself from the sorts of views which are involved in the traditional doctrine of prime matter'.

Let me summarize, as briefly as possible, why it is so. In Williams's terms (1982: 211), the 'traditional doctrine of prime matter', roughly speaking, is that when a generation *simpliciter* takes place there is of course no creation *ex nihilo* but there is some underlying *prima materia* which loses a quality and acquires its contrary; for instance, when one element, say air, is generated, it is generated out of another one, say water; the underlying matter loses coldness and acquires heat. This *prima materia* persists through the change; it is not perceptible; it is nothing in actuality, whereas it is everything in potentiality; nor can it exist or subsist by itself—that is, separately from any formal characteristic. It is, so to speak, a theoretical requisite of the very notion of generation *simpliciter*.

This traditional interpretation has been challenged by some modern scholars,[36] who claim that in the case of elemental generation the only thing that plays the role of matter is not the ghost-like *prima materia* but simply the element from which the new one comes—for instance, water in the generation of air. Replies to King (1956) and Charlton (1970) have been published;[37] Williams (1982: 211–19) devotes a whole appendix to the question of whether and how *prima materia* appears in *GC*, with the conclusion that Aristotle is hopelessly confused about this 'internally incoherent' notion.

Without actually entering into this large and controversial issue, let us see whether *GC* I. 1 has anything to say about it. The monists, Aristotle says, 'make everything come to be from one thing' (314^{a}9); that this one thing may be called 'matter' is clear from the contrast with pluralists, 'who assert a plurality of matter' ($\pi\lambda\epsilon\acute{\iota}\omega$ $\tau\grave{\eta}\nu$ $\mathring{\upsilon}\lambda\eta\nu$ $\acute{\epsilon}\nu\grave{o}s$ $\tau\iota\theta\acute{\epsilon}\alpha\sigma\iota\nu$, 314^{a}11). This single matter is 'the substratum which remains one and the same throughout' (314^{b}3). If this view is mistaken, and leads itself to the mistaken identification between generation and *alloiôsis*, is it not a similar mistake to think (as in the traditional view of prime matter) that in each apparently unqualified generation there is a single matter, namely *prima materia*, which persists through the change as a permanent substratum? Is the disagreement Aristotle has with monism and the S answer compatible with his holding any theory like that of *prima materia*?

A long time before the modern discussion ancient commentators were at pains to explain in what way the material monists' conception of generation actually differs from the Aristotelian conception, which they obviously took as being what was to become the traditional theory of *prima materia*. Philoponus (*in GC* 9. 20–10. 13 Vitelli) explains at length

---

[36] See King (1956), 370–89; Charlton (1970), 129–45.
[37] See respectively Solmsen (1958) and Robinson (1974).

that the permanent substratum of generation *simpliciter* is importantly different in the two conceptions: for Aristotle this substratum is 'the formless matter' (ἀνείδεος ὕλη)—that is, nothing in actuality; whereas for the material monists it is 'an existing element already informed' (εἰδοπεποιημένον ὑπάρχον τὸ στοιχεῖον)—that is, something actual, like water or air.[38]

Is this traditional distinction supported by the account given of *alloiô-sis* in I. 4, a chapter entirely devoted to that notion and to the difference between *alloiôsis* and generation? Sarah Broadie, in ch. 4 of this volume, powerfully argues against that idea; I shall not enter into the intricacies of the chapter and of Broadie's subtle analysis. However, if I may play the *advocatus diaboli* for a little while, I would like to quote some parts of I. 4. 319[b]8–18:

> it is *alloiôsis* when the substratum remains, being something perceptible (ὑπομένοντος τοῦ ὑποκειμένου, αἰσθητοῦ ὄντος), but change occurs in the affections which belong to it (ἐν τοῖς αὐτοῦ πάθεσιν) ... For example, the body is well then ill, but remains the same body.... When, however, the whole changes without anything perceptible remaining as the same substratum (μὴ ὑπομένοντος αἰσθητοῦ τινὸς ὡς ὑποκειμένου τοῦ αὐτοῦ), but the way the seed changes entirely into blood, water into air ..., then ... it is a case of generation (and corruption of something else).

Aristotle here contrasts *alloiôsis*, in which something *perceptible* remains as the substratum, with generation, in which nothing *perceptible* remains as the substratum.[39] Given the first branch of this contrast ('something perceptible remains'), one might wonder what is the correct contrasting branch. Is it 'nothing perceptible remains—but something non-perceptible does' (Philoponus, and the traditional interpretation)? Or is it 'nothing at all remains in the function of a substratum'?[40] Perhaps the second option is not ruled out; but then, it seems to me that the reader would be entitled to ask: And what if something non-perceptible remains?[41] In that way, I. 4 could be taken, to some extent, as

---

[38] Cf. also pseudo-Thomas Aquinas ed. Spiazzi (1952), 324 n. 12: 'nos autem ponimus omnium generabilium et corruptibilium esse unum subiectum primum, quod tamen non est ens actu, sed in potentia. Et ideo ex eo quod accipit formam, per quam fit ens actu, dicitur simpliciter generatio; ex hoc autem quod, postquam est ens actu factum, suscipit aliam quamcumque formam, dicitur alteratio'.

[39] Admittedly, as Geoffrey Lloyd pointed out, the contrast between 'perceptible' and 'not perceptible' is not as neat as one could wish: air is said to be ἐπιεικῶς ἀναίσθητον (319[b]20–1).

[40] The wording of this question has to take into account the important and difficult qualification introduced by 319[b]33–320[a]1: ὅταν δὲ μηδὲν ὑπομένῃ οὗ θάτερον πάθος ἢ συμβεβηκὸς ὅλως (to be read in connection with the equally difficult passage 319[b]21–4).

[41] Such a question, already asked by Philoponus ad loc., would be logical enough, I suppose, rather than 'rhetorical' (Broadie, p. 127 below). Sarah Broadie very honestly

supporting the ascription of the traditional notion of *prima materia* to Aristotle.

This being said, it must be acknowledged that if I. 4 can help Aristotle to make compatible his rejection of monism and his (supposedly) own theory of *prima materia*, I. 1 cannot render him a similar service; for the crucial distinctions introduced in I. 4 are not to be found in I. 1. There is no mention there of any difference between perceptible and imperceptible *hupokeimena*, let alone any allusion to the difference between potentiality and actuality. From that we can draw, at least, the conclusion that in I. 1, unlike I. 4, Aristotle does not have at his disposal (or does not want, for some reason, to make use of) the tools which would permit him to preserve his favourite D answer to the G/A problem, and to dissociate himself neatly from the monists, committed as they are to the S answer. When criticizing monism, he seems to reject here some assumptions which are basic to the traditional doctrine of prime matter. Compared to I. 4, it seems to me that I. 1 is remarkably rudimentary on this point.

7. The case of pluralism

Concerning now the pluralists and their theoretical commitment to the D answer, Aristotle first makes some assertions which seem to show that, in his opinion, there is nothing more problematic in their case than in the monists' one. At 314^a11-13 he says that 'those who assert a plurality of matter, such as Empedocles, Anaxagoras and Leucippus, <necessarily think that generation and *alloiôsis* are> different things'; at 314^b4-5, that 'those . . . who allow a plurality of kinds have to distinguish *alloiôsis* from generation'; at 314^b10-11, that 'they . . . are bound to admit the existence of *alloiôsis* as something other than generation'. However, he does not seem to have a *theoretical* argument to support this commitment; at any rate, he does not offer one in I. 1.[42] Instead, he relies on a *historical* argument:[43] the justification of 314^b4-5 is that for the pluralists, 'generation and corruption occur when things come together and separate'

concedes that I. 4 'does not logically rule it out that substantial change requires its own sort of ὑποκείμενον, one that is imperceptible'; it is noticeable that her rejection of this reading is primarily based upon Aristotle's criticism of atomism in I. 2.

[42] One might even suspect that he tacitly reasons as follows: monists are committed to the S answer; pluralists are not monists; therefore, pluralists are committed to the D answer. But ascribing such a fallacy to Aristotle would be contrary to the principle of charity.

[43] It is already significant, in this respect, that Aristotle does not name any monist philosopher when he introduces monism (314^a8-11), whereas he mentions Empedocles, Anaxagoras, and Leucippus as soon as he introduces pluralism (31^a11-13).

(συνιόντων γὰρ καὶ διαλυομένων, 314^b5–6), as is clear from Empedocles' case in particular.

This argument is not completely clear and satisfactory:
(i) Williams (1982: 61) acutely observes that

it is not...*qua* Pluralist that he [the Pluralist] has necessarily to make this distinction [between cases of apparent generation and corruption and cases of alteration]...It is not obviously self-contradictory to assert that there exists more than one object but none which has a beginning or end of existence, and that what appear to be generation and corruption of impermanent objects are in fact only alterations in one or more of the eternal substances...But the Pluralists Aristotle has in mind, *had in fact* another theory about generation and corruption...This account [through aggregation and segregation of elements], which is not exactly Pluralism but *is typical of the Pluralists Aristotle knew*, does make generation and corruption something distinct from alteration (emphasis added)

This, I think, is a very good diagnosis of the trouble which permeates the whole discussion of pluralism in I. 1: Aristotle needs the history of earlier doctrines to back up his theoretical assertions, but there is, more than once, something of a mismatch between the lessons he wants to get from history and what it actually offers to him.

(ii) In order to get a clear contrast between the pluralists' account of generation (and corruption) and alteration, one would wish to know not only how they account for generation and corruption but also in what *different* way they account for alteration; now, nothing is said about this last point. A way out would be, of course, to take *alloiôsis* in the narrow sense of qualitative change, and to find a way of putting association and dissociation into a clearly different category of change. But the trouble is that association and dissociation do not fit easily into Aristotle's categorial scheme, presumably because they are processes in which several subjects are involved, whereas the predicates which the categorial scheme concerns are predicates of one subject only.[44] It is understandable that, in the later tradition, association and dissociation have been somewhat forcibly introduced into the category of quantitative change;[45] but the textual basis for this categorizing in Aristotle himself seems to be rather slim.[46]

---

[44] See the illuminating remarks of Dorothea Frede about mixture at the beginning of her contribution to the present volume (Ch. 11, p. 290, below), '*mixis* is not easily classified as a kind of change within one of the ten categories ... it is a change that involves different substances and then properties in a complex way.' On the similar case of condensation/rarefaction see n. 25 above.

[45] Cf. Aët. *Plac.* I. 24.2 Diels, on the interpretation of generation and corruption through association and dissociation in doctrines like those of Empedocles, Anaxagoras, and Democritus: οὐ γὰρ κατὰ ⟨τὸ⟩ ποιὸν ἐξ ἀλλοιώσεως, κατὰ δὲ τὸ ποσὸν ἐκ συναθροισμοῦ ταύτας γίνεσθαι, a text quoted and richly commented upon by Mansfeld (2002: 284–7).

[46] According to Mansfeld (ibid.), the conclusion offered by Aëtius (see n. 45) is 'far less bad than it may seem'. The later tradition, he says, 'has made explicit what is stated by

Jacques Brunschwig

8. 314ᵃ13–16: the skirmish against Anaxagoras

Another remarkable sign of the mismatch between theory and history, as far as pluralist doctrines are concerned, comes very early in I. 1. Scarcely has Aristotle stated that pluralism implies the D answer (314ᵃ11–13) than he calls attention to something being wrong in what one of the pluralists just mentioned, namely Anaxagoras, has said (314ᵃ13–16): whereas, as a pluralist, he was committed to distinguishing generation from *alloiôsis* very sharply, 'however, he has ignored the proper word;[47] in any case, he says (λέγει γοῦν)[48] that coming to be and perishing are the same thing as *alloiousthaî*'.

This attack is brief in the extreme; nevertheless, it raises more than one interesting problem, and perhaps I may be allowed to dwell somewhat lengthily on it.

If ever Anaxagoras actually said that generation and corruption are the same thing as *alloiousthai*, where did he say this? Most commentators think that Aristotle here has in mind the famous fragment 59B17 DK, which runs thus: 'the Greeks are wrong to recognize (οὐκ ὀρθῶς νομίζουσιν) coming to being and perishing; for nothing comes into being nor perishes, but is rather compounded (συμμίσγεταί) or dissolved (διακρίνεται) from things that are (ἀπὸ ἐόντων χρημάτων). So they would be right to call coming into being composition (συμμίσγεσθαι) and perishing

Aristotle in an indirect way only', e.g. in *GC* I. 2. 315ᵇ1–3 (the trivial explanation of growth, i.e. quantitative change, is that things grow bigger because something like it accedes (προσιόντος)) and I. 5. 322ᵃ26–7 ('in so far as what accedes (τὸ προσιόν) is potentially a certain quantity of flesh (δυνάμει ποσὴ σάρξ), it is that which makes flesh grow'). Nevertheless, it seems to me that the doxographer's reduction of association to quantitative change does not do justice to the all-important difference between προς-ιόντος (singular) and συν-ιόντων (plural, 314ᵇ5). See nn. 25 and 44 above.

[47] The Greek has τὴν οἰκείαν φωνὴν ἠγνόησεν, a sentence which has been variously understood and translated. Unlike those scholars who interpret τὴν οἰκείαν φωνήν as 'his own utterance', like Joachim (1922), and more or less similarly Tricot (1951), Forster (1955), Migliori (1976), Williams (1982), and Mansfeld (2002), I take it as meaning 'the proper appellation' (so Mugler (1966)): the trouble with Anaxagoras is that he has ignored the proper application of the word ἀλλοίωσις. This is Alexander's interpretation: according to Simp. *in Ph.* 163. 9–15, Alexander used this passage of *GC* in his comments about Aristotle *Ph.* I. 4.187ᵃ30, in order to show that the statement τὸ γίνεσθαι τοιόνδε καθέστηκεν ἀλλοιοῦσθαι, anonymously quoted there by Aristotle, should be referred to Anaxagoras; in that statement, Alexander said, Anaxagoras οὐ γὰρ οἰκείῳ ὀνόματι τῷ τῆς ἀλλοιώσεως κατὰ τῆς συγκρίσεως καὶ τῆς διακρίσεως ἐχρήσατο (Philoponus understands the passage in the same way (*in GC* 11. 15–16, 19. 1–2)). Alexander probably thought that the statement quoted in the *Ph.* passage made sense only if ἀλλοιοῦσθαι was given the broad meaning of non-substantial change in general, whereas the only οἰκεῖον meaning of the word, in his opinion, was the narrow, Aristotelian one, i.e. qualitative change. On the presence or not of τοιόνδε in the various occurrences of this statement see below in the main text.

[48] The standard confirmative force of γοῦν would be lost, I think, if λέγει were taken as meaning 'he means'.

dissolution (διακρίνεσθαι)'.[48a] But, then, commentators are at a loss to understand Aristotle's objection: this fragment reduces generation and corruption to *summixis* and *diakrisis*, not to *alloiôsis*, so that it appears to *distinguish* them from *alloiôsis*, not to identify them with it (Joachim (1922: 64)), or at least to be compatible with such a distinction (since it does not mention *alloiôsis* at all). In order to make sense of Aristotle's objection, they are obliged to add that, given Anaxagoras' conception of τὰ ἐόντα χρήματα, 'the things that are' (which include qualities like bright, dark, sweet, etc. as well as 'seeds' of homogeneous tissues like flesh and bone), *summixis* and *diakrisis* get a special meaning in his theory.[49] This solution, however, does not seem to be wholly satisfactory: it is not plausible that Aristotle might have had the text of the fragment B17 DK in mind when blaming Anaxagoras for having reduced *genesis* to *alloiôsis*, in the first place because this fragment does not say anything about *alloiôsis*.[50]

The simplest way out of this difficulty would be, of course, to suggest that Aristotle here is quoting *another* passage from Anaxagoras' book, where the reduction of generation to *alloiôsis* is explicitly stated. Zeller thought that this passage exists, that it has been textually preserved in Aristotle's *Physics*, namely at I. 4. 187ª30: 'a thing's becoming such and such consists in a process of *alloiôsis*' (τὸ γίγνεσθαι τοιόνδε καθέστηκεν ἀλλοιοῦσθαι), and that this genuinely Anaxagorean formula is also the basis of Aristotle's assertion in *GC* I. 1. 314ª13–15.[51]

In order to assess the acceptability or not of Zeller's suggestion, it is worthwhile to have a look at the fairly problematic context of this

---

[48a] Trans. Kirk/Raven/Schofield in *The Presocratic Philosophers*, 2nd edn. (Cambridge, 1983), p. 358.

[49] Cf. Joachim (1922: 64); Gershenson and Greenberg (1964: 480): 'He linked qualities to the molecules. Thus every time molecules are rearranged, change of quality must occur; so that in the theory dissociation and recombination constitute qualitative change'.

[50] Another solution, which also assumes that Aristotle's formula τὴν οἰκείαν φωνήν means 'his own words' and refers to Anaxag. fr. B17 DK, is offered by Mansfeld (2002: 288–9): since according to Anaxagoras things not only were 'all together' at the beginning (fr. B1), but still are so now (fr. B6), 'the set of corporeals in the world may be considered to be one, which indeed comes close to the (Aristotelian) *archê* of the early monists (...) Anaxagoras' association and dissociation can be interpreted as modifications of this basic πάντα ὁμοῦ, that is to say as *alloiôseis*'. Migliori (1976: 138), quoting *Ph.* I. 4. 187ª21–3, had already suggested that 'Aristotele gioca sulla possibilità di interpretare Anassagora come monista (partendo della mescolanza) e pluralista'. I am afraid it would take too much space to discuss these interpretations. Against the idea that Aristotle blames Anaxagoras for not being a pure and genuine pluralist, I would observe that this is precisely what he objects to Empedocles later on (315ª19–25), and that nothing indicates that he has here the same objection in store against Anaxagoras.

[51] I refer to the Italian revised edition, namely Zeller and Mondolfo (1969: 363 n. 19). Zeller's suggestion was approved by Ross (1936: 484). Zeller, who knew everything, does not seem to be aware that such was already Alexander's opinion (see n. 47 above).

allegedly Anaxagorean fragment in the *Physics*. From 187ᵃ26 to 31 and after Aristotle deals specifically with Anaxagoras' theory:

Anaxagoras probably made his elements unlimited in this way [i.e. by positing an unlimited number of homoeomerous elements and of opposites] because he accepted as true the general opinion of the physicists (τὴν κοινὴν δόξαν τῶν φυσικῶν) that nothing comes to be out of what is not. It is on this ground (διὰ τοῦτο) that (a) they say (λέγουσιν) that things were once 'all together' (ἦν ὁμοῦ πάντα), and (b) that a thing's becoming such and such (τοιόνδε) consists in a process of *alloiôsis*,[52] (c) while they (οἱ δέ) <have recourse to> association and dissociation.

The trouble with this passage is that Aristotle first attributes the most characteristic features of Anaxagoras' theory to his agreement with 'the general opinion of the physicists', namely the rejection of any generation *ex nihilo,* and then uses the plural λέγουσιν when he introduces statements (a)–(c) as following (διὰ τοῦτο) from this rejection. This state of affairs induced Porphyry to distribute these statements over different philosophers: (a) to Anaxagoras, (b) (quoted or summarized in the form τὸ γίγνεσθαι εἶναι τὸ ἀλλοιοῦσθαι) to Anaximenes, and (c) to Democritus and Empedocles (Simp. *in Ph.* 163. 16–18). On (a) he was clearly right: ἦν ὁμοῦ πάντα is of course a paraphrase of the notorious beginning of Anaxagoras' book (ὁμοῦ πάντα χρήματα ἦν, fr. Β1 DK). This shows very well that the plural λέγουσιν does not exclude what comes after it from being the opinion of an individual philosopher; and this conclusion is confirmed, I think, not only by the parallel standard use of the phrase οἱ περί τινα, but also, and still more clearly, by 187ᵇ1–7, where the plural φασι introduces a whole batch of distinctly Anaxagorean doctrines.

The case of (b), the 'Zellerian fragment', is more difficult. As we already saw, Alexander did not try to ascribe it to any other philosopher than Anaxagoras, and invoked *GC* I. 1. 314ᵃ13–15 in order to justify its attribution to Anaxagoras too. But there are some complications I have not yet mentioned. Though *Physics* 187ᵃ30 (τὸ γίγνεσθαι τοιόνδε καθέστηκεν ἀλλοιοῦσθαι) is uncommonly close to *GC* 314ᵃ14–15 (ὡς τὸ γίνεσθαι καὶ ἀπόλλυσθαι ταὐτὸν καθέστηκε τῷ ἀλλοιοῦσθαι), there are significant differences. The addition of καὶ ἀπόλλυσθαι in *GC* is unimportant, but this is not the case with the addition of τοιόνδε, 'such-and-such', in the *Physics* passage. We also have to acknowledge that this τοιόνδε is present in what appears as a quotation of *GC* by Alexander in his argument using *GC* in favour of the ascription of statement (b) in the *Physics* passage to

---

[52] Here, i.e. on the 'Zellerian fragment' (τὸ γίνεσθαι τοιόνδε καθέστηκεν ἀλλοιοῦσθαι), I diverge from Charlton's translation (1970), which, similarly to many others, is: 'he makes the coming to be of a thing of a certain sort alteration'. Given the parallelism with *GC* I. 1. 314ᵃ14, the subject of καθέστηκεν must be τὸ γίνεσθαι τοιόνδε, not Ἀναξαγόρας.

Anaxagoras: λέγει γοῦν [cf. *GC* 314ᵃ13–14!] ὡς τὸ γίνεσθαι καὶ ἀπόλλυσθαι τοιόνδε καθέστηκεν ἀλλοιοῦσθαι (Simp. *in Ph.* 163. 13–14).[53] How are we to account for these variants? I suggest that the original version is the one preserved in our text of *GC* (and also in Porphyry's abbreviated quotation), namely the version without 'such-and-such' (τοιόνδε), and that the addition (both in the *Physics* passage and perhaps in the text of *GC* used by Alexander) of τοιόνδε, with its connotation of quality, was a rather clumsy attempt to reduce the distance between generation and *alloiôsis*.[54] If τοιόνδε were an ancient addition and could be eliminated from the original wording of the *Physics* passage, that would only make still greater the similarity between it and the *GC* passage; and if Alexander read the *Physics* sentence without τοιόνδε it would only have made it easier for him to attribute it to Anaxagoras, in line with the *GC* passage, where the same sentence without τοιόνδε is explicitly attributed to him.

Now, if (a) and (b) turn out to be Anaxagorean, what about (c)? Against Porphyry's attribution of (c) to Democritus and Empedocles, Simplicius very reasonably objects that *sunkrisis* and *diakrisis* are fundamental Anaxagorean concepts: 'Anaxagoras', he says, 'clearly writes in the first book of his *Physika* that to come to be and to be destroyed is to be combined and to be separated'; and he immediately quotes our fragment B17 DK, which establishes the point beyond doubt. But then, why does Aristotle misleadingly write οἱ δὲ σύγκρισιν καὶ διάκρισιν? I am not sure how to answer this question. Perhaps we have to understand (c) as qualified by a tacit 'only', μόνον, as is often the case: there are people who invoke association and dissociation *only* (Empedocles?), whereas Anaxagoras invokes both association and dissociation, and *alloiôsis*. Another solution (given the rather harsh syntax of the sentence) would be to think that it is an interpolated marginal gloss first written by somebody who had more or less vaguely heard of association and dissociation but did not know to whom to attribute them in this context where Anaxagoras' position among the *phusikoi* is somewhat blurred by the interplay of singular and plural verbal forms.

With some qualifications, then, it seems possible to interpret the whole of *Physics* I. 4. 187ᵃ29–31 (including the 'Zellerian fragment') as stating a series of Anaxagorean tenets, like the whole of what follows (187ᵃ31–ᵇ7). Up to now, therefore, we have got two distinct Anaxagorean reductions:

---

[53] But Simplicius' text might have been altered, by himself or by some copyist, in order to bring it into line with (b); so I would not be positive about what text Alexander read in his copy of *GC*.

[54] The way the author of this addition was motivated seems to have been roughly the same as the one supporting a recent Italian translation of the *Ph.* passage: 'il generarsi di una data qualità è alterarsi' (Zanatta (1999)).

a reduction of *genesis* to *summixis* (B17), another one of *genesis* to *alloiôsis,* quite probably in the broad sense of the word (*GC, Ph.*). How did Anaxagoras articulate these two reductions together? Did he think that one of them was more basic than the other one? It would be interesting to get some evidence about what sort of relationship he was setting up between *summixis* and *alloiôsis.* Now, perhaps we have got such a piece of evidence, which would enable us to attribute to him the (not surprising) view that things change through mingling and being separated; that is to say, that the reality underlying apparent changes is in fact *summixis* and *diakrisis.* Admittedly, this evidence comes from a highly suspect source, the pseudo-Hippocratic *De Victu,* a hodgepodge of multifarious theories, which should be used with great caution.[55] Nevertheless, the many echoes it contains, in particular of Anaxagoras' and Empedocles' theories, might have some interest, albeit no decisive force. At I. 4 (quoted up to ἀλλοιοῦται as 59A52, 3rd text, in the Anaxagoras section of DK), the author writes, in his most Anaxagorean vein: ἀπόλλυται μέν νῦν οὐδὲν ἁπάντων χρημάτων οὐδὲ γίνεται, ὅτι μὴ καὶ πρόσθεν ἦν· συμμισγόμενα δὲ καὶ διακρινόμενα ἀλλοιοῦται· νομίζεται δὲ παρὰ τῶν ἀνθρώπων κτλ. This paraphrase of B17 has perhaps the merit of having preserved an occurrence of *alloiousthai* in the relevant Anaxagorean context, and hence a trace of Anaxagoras' interpretation of *alloiôsis* as being in fact *summixis* and *diakrisis.*

9. The trouble with Empedocles

Immediately after this brief skirmish against Anaxagoras, Aristotle offers a *diairesis* of pluralist doctrines (314^{a}16–^{b}1), which roughly reproduces what he said about pluralist doctrines on principles and beings at the beginning of *Physics* (I. 2.184^{b}18–25). Here as there, the main division is between finitist (Empedocles) and infinitist (Anaxagoras, Leucippus, and Democritus) versions of pluralism. But here in *GC* Aristotle is more robustly pedagogical than in the *Physics*: he gives some details about each doctrine, he distinguishes briefly but clearly the continuist (Anaxagorean) version of infinitist pluralism from the discontinuist (atomist) one, and he draws an impressively neat contrast between Anaxagoras and Empedocles, each of them taking as simple what the other takes as composite, and vice versa.

However, the main lesson of this *diairesis* is probably that it just has to be made. Pluralism, considered at a sufficiently abstract and theoretical

[55] On this work, the date of which is hotly disputed, see the notes in Zeller and Mondolfo (1961), 108–10 and 238–43.

level, may be a unity of sorts; but when the concrete features of pluralist doctrines are taken into account this unity breaks up: there has been much more than one historical instantiation of pluralism. Hence, it is only to be expected that the commitment of pluralist theories to the D answer will take as many different forms as there have been such theories: there is no way of treating all these versions of pluralism on a par. From now on, Aristotle will therefore focus intensely on individual forms of pluralism: Empedocles in I. 1, and Democritus in I. 2.

In I. 1, after the brief episode on monism (314^b1-4) on which I have already said something (Sects. 3 and 6 above), it is Empedocles who occupies the front of the stage, exclusively and massively. True, Aristotle seems to want to take him as a representative of pluralism in general: in 314^b6-26 he constantly shifts from singular to plural;[56] but it is clear that, even so, he always thinks in Empedoclean terms.

Before dealing with Empedocles' case, Aristotle has already made a number of steps, which are as many moves in what I would like to call a continuous drift throughout I. 1:[57] he successively comes from the general question of generation and corruption to the special G/A question; from the division of earlier views between monism and pluralism to the focusing on the contrary positions these doctrines are respectively bound to take on the G/A question; from the well-balanced contrast between monism and pluralism to an almost exclusive concentration on the more complicated case of pluralism; from a joint examination of Empedocles, Anaxagoras, and the atomists to a lengthy and specific critical account of Empedocles' doctrine. Each time, I think, these shifts are motivated by some mismatch between what was theoretically to be expected from the doctrines under consideration and what they actually offer.

This drift does not stop when Empedocles comes to the fore; that is, from 314^b4 to 315^a25 (more than half of the whole chapter: roughly, fifty lines out of eighty). Quite the contrary: Aristotle tries to show that what Empedocles said and held constantly and increasingly deviates from what he should have said and held. Before returning in more detail to some salient episodes of this progressive drift, let me give an overview of its main moves, throughout which historical facts turn out to be more

---

[56] See λέγει (7), φησίν (20), διορίζει (22), compared to αὐτῶν (9), λέγουσι (10), τούτοις (10), ἐκείνων (12), λέγουσιν οἱ πλείους ἀρχὰς ποιοῦντες μιᾶς (16). In the last part of the chapter (315^a3-25), however, the singular is dominant (the only exception is αὐτῶν, 315^a20, unless one takes, implausibly, the reference to be to the elements). Philoponus (in GC 17.14 ff.) explains at length that what is true of Empedocles is not necessarily true of other pluralists, like Anaxagoras or Democritus.

[57] Not precisely 'la relativa inconcludenza del capitolo I 1 e il suo andamento contorto', in the terms of Migliori (1976: 136–7), but something like it.

and more in conflict with the theoretical statements which they should have illustrated and supported.

(i)   First of all, Empedocles is the star example of pluralism: among pluralist philosophers he is the first mentioned, at 314^a11–12 ff. and 16 ff.

(ii) He is also the star example of pluralism as committed to the D answer to the G/A problem (314^b4–11).

(iii) But he is no less the star example of pluralism as having serious worries with *alloiôsis*, and eventually going so far as to make it 'impossible' (314^b11–26). Here the divorce between theory and history is much deeper than in Anaxagoras' case: the trouble is that various elements of Empedocles' sayings, explained at great length and exemplified by textual quotations, reveal themselves as incompatible with the recognition of *alloiôsis* as something real and different from generation, a recognition to which he was nevertheless committed by his pluralistic assumptions. He thus seems to contradict the phenomena (315^a2–3), since the reality of *alloiôsis* and its difference from generation is sufficiently attested by empirical observation (314^b13–15).

(iv) Not only does Empedocles contradict the phenomena. He also contradicts himself (315^a3–4): within his doctrine, there is an irreducible conflict between his elemental theory and his cosmology. In his elemental theory he wants to have his elements immutable and ungenerable from one another; but his cyclical cosmology (which was neither mentioned nor exploited in the earlier arguments) forces him to admit that they change into one another, not only at the beginning of a cycle, but still now (315^a4–19). Let us notice that this new salvo of objections is directed against Empedocles quite specifically,[58] and that, unlike the previous objections, it is based on his cosmology, and no longer has anything to do with the G/A question (*alloiôsis* is not even mentioned in the whole of 315^a3–25).

(v)   But the worst, and the most ironical, is still to come: ultimately it turns out that Empedocles' being a genuine pluralist is highly questionable. There are serious reasons, still drawn from his cyclical theory, to consider him a monist of sorts as well (315^a19–25). As Aristotle tersely says; 'it is unclear whether we ought[59] to make the One his principle or the Many—that is to say, fire, earth, and the others in the list'. Not a glorious exit for the great man of Acragas.

---

[58] See n. 56 above.
[59] Williams translates 'he ought', I think mistakenly.

10. 314ᵇ7–8: the quotation of Empedocles fr. B8. 1 and 3 DK

This quotation is the first point on which I would like to come back with more detail. Its context *a parte ante* is as follows (314ᵇ4–8):

Those who allow a plurality of kinds have to distinguish *alloiôsis* from generation, since (γάρ) for them generation and corruption occur when things come together (συνιόντων) and separate (διαλυομένων). Accordingly (διό) Empedocles in fact speaks in this way: 'there is no such thing as the birth (φύσις) of anything, only mixing (μίξις) and the διάλλαξις of what has been mixed (διάλλαξίς τε μιγέντων).

A first problem is to know what exactly this quotation, in Aristotle's opinion, is supposed to back up. The context, as a matter of fact, offers us two options: *either* (a) it is Empedocles' adoption of the D answer, '*alloiôsis* differs from *genesis*' (διαφέρειν τὴν ἀλλοίωσιν τῆς γενέσεως, ᵇ5), which is presented as a consequence (γάρ) of his having reduced (apparent) generation and corruption to the coming together and separation of pre-existing things, *or* (b) it is *only* the latter reduction itself.

We might well think that (b) is much more probably faithful to Empedocles' own meaning; but our problem here is only to know, if possible, what meaning Aristotle himself read in Empedocles' lines. Another, more serious argument in favour of (b) could be drawn from the difficult lines which follow the quotation (314ᵇ8–12): 'there is no doubt, then, that this statement is in accordance with their position and that they do speak in this way; but they too are bound (ἀναγκαῖον δὲ καὶ τούτοις) to admit the existence of *alloiôsis* as something other than generation, although (μέντοι) this is impossible according to what they say'. A way of reading this passage could be as follows: the quotation describes the reduction of generation and corruption to mixing and separation; this reduction is in line with 'their position' (that is to say, with pluralism, which is obviously needed to enable things to mix and to separate); *but*, on the other hand, pluralism also implies a distinction between generation and *alloiôsis*; now, Empedocles says things which make *alloiôsis* impossible, as will be shown at 314ᵇ15–26.

However, if we read the passage that way a question arises: if Empedocles' fragment, in Aristotle's opinion, illustrates only his account of generation and corruption, on what basis can Aristotle attribute to him a necessary commitment to the D answer? There is nothing left in the text which could perform that function, except an appeal to observation: 'just as, whilst the substance stays the same, we see (ὁρῶμεν) change in it in respect of size—what is called growing and getting smaller—so we also see *alloiôsis*' (314^{b}13–15).[60] But this empirical argument does not show at all why the D answer should be mandatory for the pluralists any more than for the monists. We are thus led first to try a different reading of 314^{b}8–12, which would be compatible with (a), and then to try to justify (a) itself.

Concerning 314^{b}8–12, I think it possible to read it in the following way:

> there is no doubt, then, that this statement is in accordance with their position [that is to say, not merely with pluralism, but with pluralism as committed to the D answer] and that they do speak in this way; *but* it is necessary for them *both* to say, on the one hand (μέν), that *alloiôsis* is something other than generation, although, on the other hand (μέντοι), this is impossible according to what they say.[61]

In other words, what is necessary, ἀναγκαῖον, for them is not merely the D answer, but the *contradiction* between their endorsement of the D answer and other sayings of theirs which imply that *alloiôsis* is impossible.

If that reading is correct, we must suppose that the attribution of the D answer to the pluralists has already been justified before 314^{b}8, and the only place for that justification is the quotation of Empedocles' fragment; and this amounts to what I have called option (a).

In order to find out what meaning Aristotle might have given to this fragment, we must point out at least three puzzling facts about it: (i) although Aristotle has mentioned both *genesis* and *phthora* as accounted for (respectively, to all appearances) by association and dissociation (314^{b}5–6), there is a line missing in his quotation, the very line which obviously bears on *phthora* (. . . οὐδέ τις οὐλομένου θανάτοιο τελευτή);[62] (ii) two further words are also missing in Aristotle's quotation, namely ἁπάντων θνητῶν, lines 1–2; (iii) if we insist on thinking that, according to Aristotle, these lines prove that Empedocles endorsed the D answer, we must acknowledge, however, that they say nothing explicitly about *alloiôsis*.

---

[60] One could wonder why Aristotle takes this circuitous route, from growth to alteration, as if growth were a more visible process than alteration. Don't we often see things which simultaneously undergo both processes, like tomatoes getting bigger and turning from green to red at the same time? Philoponus (*in GC* 16.20 ff.) raises this question and tries to answer it by saying that, on the basis of Protagoras' relativism, the reality of alteration could be questionable, whereas it is supposed not to be the case with growth. As good an answer as any other; but perhaps Aristotles simply means that growth and alteration are *equally* obvious realities.

[61] The interplay of particles in this passage should be carefully observed. There is a first contrast between μέν (^{b}8) and δέ (^{b}10); then, there is a second contrast between μέν (^{b}11) and μέντοι (^{b}12), nested in the second branch of the first one.

[62] The complete text of the fragment is preserved by Plu. *Adv. Col.* 1111F, and by Aët. I. 30. 1 Diels (Ps.-Plu. 885D). On this situation see Mansfeld (2002), 287–9.

On (i), we must admit that, since the same line is missing in another Aristotelian quotation of the same fragment 8 of Empedocles (*Metaph. Δ* 4.1015ᵃ1-3, where however ἐόντων replaces ἁπάντων θνητῶν), it is quite possible that Aristotle's copy was lacunose, and that he did not make any intentional cut in his quotation. So, let us try to imagine how Aristotle interpreted a text different from the one we are accustomed to. Once more, I think, we have got two options, depending on what sense he might have given to *diallaxis* (διάλλαξις) in the fragment.

(a) Let us suppose that he understands *diallaxis* as 'separation'[63] (which is generally taken as what Empedocles himself meant). Then *mixis* (μίξις) is bound to describe the physical reality underlying *genesis*, and διάλλαξίς μιγέντων the physical reality underlying *phthora*.[64] But on this hypothesis Aristotle is facing a difficulty. His text of Empedocles speaks only of *phusis*, a word which he almost certainly understands, at least in this context, as meaning *genesis*.[65] One could possibly suggest that *phusis* tacitly covers *phthora* as well as *genesis*, either because *genesis* includes *phthora*, or because *genesis* implies *phthora*.[66] But this solution, I think, is forbidden to Aristotle. Although he does not quote it here in *GC*, he does know line 4 of fragment 8, which he quotes in *Metaph. Δ* 4 (φύσις δ' ἐπὶ τοῖς ὀνομάζεται ἀνθρώποισιν),[67] which unmistakably shows, I think, that *genesis* and *phthora* cannot be the two processes covered by the plural ἐπὶ τοῖς:[68] even if a late doxographer could think

---

[63] Like the majority of modern interpreters of *GC*: see e.g. Joachim (1922) ('dissolution'), Tricot (1951) (who notes, however, that 'le sens ordinaire [of διάλλαξις] est *échange*'), Forster (1955), Williams (1982), Mansfeld (2002). I leave aside the Empedocles scholars; there are too many of them. See, however, the original interpretations put forward by van der Ben (1978), and more recently by Martin and Primavesi (1998), 55, 246.

[64] The standard interpretation since Plu. *Adv. Col.* 1112A, Simp. *in Ph.* 161. 19, *in Cael.* 306. 5, etc.

[65] However, Philoponus' interpretation of φύσις meaning οὐσία, 'being' or 'substantial being' (*in GC* 14.15-7), probably influenced by Arist. *Metaph. Δ* 4. 1014ᵇ35-1015ᵃ3, is accepted by some modern interpreters, e.g. Burnet (1930), 10-12, 363-4; van der Ben (1978), esp. 204-7. I am afraid it is not possible here to discuss the latter's rich argumentation properly.

[66] Such an extended sense of φύσις seems to be present in the doxography. Aët. 1. 30 Diels (Ps.-Plu. 885D) contains two lemmas which clearly presuppose it, first Ἐμπεδοκλῆς φύσιν μηδὲν εἶναι, μίξιν δὲ τῶν στοιχείων καὶ διάστασιν (followed by a complete quotation of Emp. B8 DK), then Ἀναξαγόρας ὁμοίως τὴν φύσιν σύγκρισιν καὶ διάκρισιν, τουτέστι γένεσιν καὶ φθοράν. On all this see Mansfeld (2002), 287-9.

[67] Text as in *Metaph*. MSS EAᵇ, and also Ps.-Arist. *MXG* 975ᵇ7, Plu. *Adv. Col.* 1111F. Other *Metaph*. MSS read φύσις δ' ἐπὶ τοῖσδ' (cf. DK app. crit.). Aëtius reads φύσις δὲ βροτοῖς.

[68] Admittedly, there is another way of understanding ἐπὶ τοῖς, namely with reference to ἁπάντων θνητῶν, ll. 1-2 (thus Burnet (1930), 206; van der Ben (1978), 203); this construal could be the origin of Aëtius' variant reading, φύσις δὲ βροτοῖς. But since ἁπάντων θνητῶν is not present either in the *GC* quotation or at *Metaph. Δ* 4.1015ᵃ1ᵃ (where his text is φύσις οὐδενός ἐστιν ἐόντων), it is ruled out as far as Aristotle is concerned. Van der Ben (1978), 214 n. 9 very neatly writes: 'it is clear indeed that if φύσις means γένεσις [the view he

that *genesis* might include or imply *phthora*, Empedocles himself would certainly not say that 'people' give the name of *phusis* both to *genesis* and *phthora*. And so, it is not likely that Aristotle would have read him that way.

(b) We are thus led to explore an alternative solution; namely, that, in Aristotle's opinion, Empedocles' *mixis* and *diallaxis* of what is mixed (διάλλαξις μιγέντων) designate two *constructive* processes, two apparent *geneseis*.[69] What might these two processes be? The ordinary meaning of *diallaxis*, as already noted (n. 63 above), is not 'separation', but rather 'exchange' or 'interchange'; the occurrence of the word in Empedocles fr. 8. 3 has sometimes been taken that way.[70] This interpretation could be motivated by an attempt to make μίξις and διάλλαξις μιγέντων almost synonymous;[71] but given the phrase μίξις τε διάλλαξίς τε μιγέντων, which seems to name two clearly different processes, I doubt that this would have been Aristotle's interpretation. Now, if, as I argued above, he quotes fr. 8 DK in order to show that Empedocles endorsed the D answer, then he might have understood *mixis* as what Empedocles sees as the physical reality underlying the apparent *genesis* of a new *substance*, and διάλλαξις μιγέντων as what Empedocles sees as the physical reality underlying the apparent *genesis* of a new *quality* in a given substance; that is, an *alloiôsis* in his sense. Admittedly, this suggestion supposes a neat distinction between substance and quality, in other words a strong injection of Aristotelianism into Empedocles; but this does not

---

rejects], τοῖς *must* refer to μίξις τε διάλλαξίς τε'. In this sentence I would be tempted to write 'iff' instead of 'if'.

[69] This interpretation might be supported by another quotation of Empedocles' μόνον μίξις τε διάλλαξίς τε μιγέντων, at *GC* II. 6. 333[b]14–15 (I owe this suggestion to Andrea Falcon). Aristotle is explaining that Empedocles is unable to account for the natural generation of beings like men or corn or bones; the whole passage 333[b]3–11 clearly shows that he means generation proper, not generation-cum-corruption. He then writes: 'what, then, is the cause of this [generation]? Because Fire, for certain, will not do, or Earth. What is more, nor will Love and Strife, for the former is the cause only of aggregation, the latter of segregation [the text here is not sure—note the interesting omission of γὰρ μόνον, τὸ δὲ διακρίσεως in E¹, even if it might be explained by homoeoteleuton]. The cause [of generation] is in fact the essence of each thing, not μόνον μίξις τε διάλλαξίς τε μιγέντων.' Even if we keep the mention of 'segregation', Love and Strife here are introduced as rejected but eligible explanatory factors of generation only. A little later (333[b]20–2) Aristotle repeats his familiar criticism, to the effect that it is not Empedocles' Strife, but Love which segregates the elements; and this implies, by way of symmetry, that Strife is also an aggregative force.

[70] 'Austausch' (DK), 'interchange' (Burnet (1930)), 'échange' (Mugler (1966)), 'redistribution' (Martin and Primavesi (1998)), and even 'conciliazione' (Migliori (1976)). See also Verdenius and Waszink (1968), 60, who note that διαλλάσσειν is used by Empedocles in the sense of 'interchange' in fragments B17. 12 and 35. 15 DK. This does not mean that all these authors agree on the doctrinal signification.

[71] Cf. Van der Ben (1978), 214 n. 10.

seem to be something that should be completely unexpected from Aristotle. Another possible objection (raised by John Cooper) would be to ask if Aristotle is likely to speak of the appearance of a new *quality* as a kind of *phusis* or *genesis*. Two passages may be quoted in order to answer the objection. First *GC* I. 3. 317[b]20–2: 'for the question might be raised whether substance, i.e. the "this" comes to be at all. Is it not rather the "such", the "so great", or the "somewhere", which comes to be?' (ἀπορήσειε γὰρ ἄν τις ἆρ' ἔστιν οὐσίας γένεσις καὶ τοῦ τοῦδε, ἀλλὰ μὴ τοῦ τοιοῦδε καὶ τοσοῦδε καὶ ποῦ). Then also 318[a]33–5: 'such-and-such comes to be something, but does not come to be without qualification; for we say that the student comes to be learned, not comes to be without qualification' (τοδὶ δὲ γίνεται μέν τι, γίνεται δ' ἁπλῶς οὔ. φαμὲν γὰρ τὸν μανθάνοντα γίνεσθαι μὲν ἐπιστήμονα, γίνεσθαι δ' ἁπλῶς οὔ). A comparison between these two passages shows that Aristotle does not hesitate to speak of *genesis* (without specifying γένεσίς τις) each time it is normal to use the verb *ginesthai* in some way or other.

A last question must be answered in order to defend the suggestion I just tried to make about Empedocles' quotation; namely, in what way Aristotelian alteration could be accounted for, in Empedocles' doctrine as read by Aristotle, through διάλλαξις μιγέντων? It seems possible to propose that the 'birth' of a new quality in a persistent substance is in fact an exchange (of place, respective positions, proportions, etc.) between the constituents of the given *mixis*, and perhaps also between these constituents and those of other *mixeis*.

Up to this point (314[b]10), therefore, we might paraphrase [b]8–10 in the following way: 'there is no doubt, then, that this statement [Emp. fr. B8 DK as quoted] is in accordance with their position [namely pluralism, which provides the materials necessary for *mixis* and διάλλαξις μιγέντων], and they do speak in this way [namely, in a way which distinguishes generation as being in fact a *mixis* and alteration as being in fact a διάλλαξις μιγέντων]'. Thus Aristotle seems to have rounded up his examination of pluralism, and to have checked the commitment of pluralism to the D answer to his satisfaction. But he does not stop here.

11. 314[b]15–26: Empedocles makes *alloiôsis* impossible

In 314[b]13–17 Aristotle undertakes to show that he was right in pointing out a contradiction within the pluralist position: on the one hand, pluralists distinguish (and are bound to distinguish) *genesis* from *alloiôsis*; on the other hand, other statements of theirs imply that *alloiôsis* is impossible. The first branch of this contradiction having been already satisfactorily checked (if I am not mistaken), he contents himself with adding the empirical argument already mentioned (314^b13–15). The second branch needs more space and argument (314^b15–26).

'It is a consequence of what is said by those who posit a plurality of principles that *alloiôsis* is impossible.' A strange assertion indeed, which deeply shakes the initial theoretical assertion that the pluralists are bound, on the contrary, to recognize the specific reality of *alloiôsis*. Once more, although he uses the plural, Aristotle's attention is more and more concentrating on Empedocles (to the detriment of other pluralists).

The main thread of Aristotle's argument is that *alloiôsis* is made impossible by an essential feature of Empedocles' theory of elements; namely, that they cannot transform themselves into one another (314^b23–5). The whole argument, which is far from clear, can be summarized, I think, in the following way.

(1) All the 'affections' (*pathê*)[72] involved in *alloiôsis*, according to common opinion,[73] 'for instance hot and cold, bright and dark, dry and wet, soft and hard, etc.', are taken by Empedocles to be 'differentiae of the elements'.[74]

(2) As a proof of (1) Aristotle offers a (once more partial) quotation from Empedocles, fr. 31 B21 DK, l. 3 and 5: 'The sun is bright to see and hot all over, but rain is dark and cold all through.' He adds that Empedocles 'similarly assigns properties to the other elements', an addition which shows that this time he has a complete text at his disposal, since the two remaining elements are mentioned or alluded to in Empedocles' lines 4 and 6: air in line 4, but in a fairly obscure way and without its name, probably the reason why Aristotle does not care to quote this line; earth in line 6, quite explicitly this time, but without any mention of its specific *pathê*—probably the reason why he does not quote it either.[75]

---

[72] Sometimes ἀλλοίωσις is defined as change κατὰ τὸ ποιόν, sometimes as change κατὰ τὸ πάθος (references in Bonitz (1870) 34ᵃ56–9). Cf. *GC* I. 4. 319^b11–12 (ἐν τοῖς αὑτοῦ πάθεσιν), 33 (ὅταν δὲ κατὰ πάθος καὶ τὸ ποιόν, ἀλλοίωσις).

[73] I suppose that φάμεν (314^b17) refers to 'we ordinary people': the examples which follow include (under the single label πάθη) hot and cold as well as bright and dark, dry and wet, soft and hard, etc.; now, Aristotle himself would draw a distinction between (i) hot and cold, which are (with dry and wet) not only 'a matter of perceptible bodies' (*GC* II. 1. 329ᵃ24–5) or 'of composite bodies' (*PA* II. 1. 646ᵃ16–17), but also the basic ἐναντιώσεις the various combinations of which essentially and always define the 'so-called elements' (*GC* II. 1. 329ᵃ26–7), and (ii) the other διαφοραί or πάθη τῶν σωμάτων, which are 'secondary' or 'derivative' (ἀκολουθοῦσιν) in respect to the former (*PA* II. 1. 646ᵃ17–20, quoted below, n. 80). On the reducibility of qualitative contrarieties to the two basic ones cf. *Mete.* I. 3. 340ᵇ16–18, and the whole of *GC* II. 2–3.

[74] That this phrase is supposed to express Empedocles' view is made certain by the fact that if we jump over the list of πάθη in 314^b18–20 we get to ὥσπερ καὶ φησὶν Ἐμπεδοκλῆς (with καί meaning 'actually', 'precisely', not 'also').

[75] However, Empedocles' Earth is mentioned as 'heavy and hard' at 315ᵃ11.

(3) Aristotle then concludes with the following inference (ὥστ(ε), 314ᵇ23): 'if, therefore, it is impossible for water to come into being from fire or earth from water,[76] it will be equally impossible for anything to come to be dark from bright or hard from soft, and the same reasoning will apply to the other properties; but precisely this is what constitutes *alloiôsis*'. In other words, the Empedoclean denial of generation from one element into another implies the denial of *alloiôsis* from any qualified composite thing into the same thing differently qualified.

For instance, Empedocles would be unable to account for human blood, a compound of determinate portions of the immutable elements, turning now brighter and now darker, because such a change would necessitate part of the fire in the blood becoming water or vice versa, and that is an impossible change; but even if it were possible, that change would entail a disruption of the original composition of the defining mixture which constitutes blood: hence, blood could not get brighter or darker without ceasing to be blood.[77]

In order to make some points clearer, let us come back for a moment to the premiss (1) of the argument. The *pathê* involved in *alloiôsis* are treated as 'differentiae of the elements' by Empedocles, in Aristotle's opinion. These different names correspond to crucial differences in ontological status. In I. 4 Aristotle makes clear that a *pathos* is a kind of accident (320ᵃ1: πάθος ἢ συμβεβηκὸς ὅλως); that is, a contingent property of its perceptible substratum, such that this substratum can lose it without ceasing to be what it is. On the other hand, the concise phrase 'differentiae of the elements' has a rich and complex meaning. It first implies '*differentiae* of the elements'; that is, *defining* features of their substratum, *essentially* belonging to it and to its definition, so that it cannot lose them without ceasing to be what it is.[78] This is quite probably how Aristotle understands ἁπάντηι and ἐν πᾶσι in Empedocles B21: properties present 'through and through', 'throughout', do belong to their subjects always and essentially.[79]

But these differentiae are also differentiae *of the elements*. Williams (1982: 62) found this hard to understand: 'A necessary premiss of this argument is that *every* affection is a differentia of some element, so that

---

[76] A notoriously Empedoclean principle, which Aristotle does not care to support with any pieces of evidence.

[77] I am indebted to Geoffrey Lloyd for this observation.

[78] It is relevant, in this context, to recall the Aristotelian texts already quoted at the end of n. 22 above.

[79] Philoponus rightly glosses 'differentiae of the elements' with εἰδοποιοὺς διαφορὰς τῶν στοιχείων εἴρηκεν (*in GC* 16. 17–18) and εἴδη εἶναι τῶν στοιχείων (*in GC* 17. 5). These phrases are authorized by passages such as *GC* II. 1. 329ᵃ24–7: ἡμεῖς δὲ φαμὲν μὲν εἶναί τινα ὕλην τῶν σωμάτων τῶν αἰσθητῶν, ἀλλὰ ταύτην οὐ χωριστὴν ἀλλ' ἀεὶ μετ' ἐναντιώσεως, ἐξ ἧς γίνεται τὰ καλούμενα στοιχεῖα. Cf. n. 73 above.

any qualitative change involves a change of one element into another. It is hard to see why Aristotle should credit Empedocles, let alone pluralists in general, with such a strange belief as this' (his emphasis). An answer could probably be drawn from the example of blood which I offered above. But, admittedly, Aristotle himself does not here say anything like that, and we might wonder where he found a justification for his premiss. I suggest that it is precisely in the lines of Empedocles which he is quoting, if they are read the way he does read them. In those lines Empedocles attaches the properties 'bright' and 'hot' to the sun, and the properties 'dark' and 'cold' to the rain. He thereby shows that he does not differentiate between qualities which are, in Aristotle's view, essential and basic properties of matter (still more basic than the 'so-called elements' themselves, cf. the texts referred to in n. 73), like hot and cold, and qualities which are, still in Aristotle's view, accidental properties involved in the processes of *alloiôsis* affecting the composite bodies, like bright and dark.[80] Moreover, Empedocles attaches these properties to his elements fire and water, transparently designated as sun and rain, showing thereby that all of them have one element or other as their primary substratum. The belief which strikes Williams as 'strange' could thus be read into Empedocles' B21 DK without too much strain.[81]

12. 315ᵃ3–25: the last salvo of criticisms against Empedocles

I have already said (sect. 9 above) what I had to say about the final part of I. 1, and stressed all the quite peculiar features of the additional series of objections which Aristotle, as if carried along by an irrepressible polemical impulse, addresses to Empedocles again. With this new salvo of criticisms, and even within that salvo itself, it seems to me that we are

---

[80] Cf. *PA* II. 1. 646ᵃ16–20: 'wet and dry, hot and cold, form the material of all composite bodies; and all other differences are secondary (ἀκολουθοῦσιν) to these, such differences, that is, as heaviness or lightness, density or rarity, roughness or smoothness, and any other such properties of bodies as there may be'.

[81] Let us note already (we will need the observation again later on) that there is a different argument, also claiming to show that Empedoclean pluralism makes alteration impossible, in *Metaph. A* 8. 989ᵃ26–30: 'and in general those who speak in this way [the pluralists, like Empedocles] must do away with alteration, for on their view cold will not come from hot nor hot from cold. For if it did there would be something that accepted those very contraries, and there would be some one entity that became fire and water, which Empedocles denies.' This argument differs from the one offered in *GC* I. 1. 314ᵇ23–6 in the sense that it infers the immutability of the basic qualities (hot and cold) from the immutability of elements, whereas the *GC* passage infers from it the immutability of *non*-basic qualities (such as bright and dark, hard and soft). One could suspect, therefore, that the *Metaph.* argument shows the impossibility of ἀλλοίωσις in the broad sense, and the *GC* argument its impossibility in the narrow sense (cf. Sect. 3 above).

assisting at the final stage of the continuous 'drift' of which we have observed the successive stages throughout I. 1.

There has been some disagreement about the exact number of Aristotle's new objections. Williams (1982: 63) counts two of them: (i) 315ᵃ4–19 (given the cyclical cosmology, it is possible that an element should turn into a different one, which *ex hypothesi* it cannot do); (ii) 315ᵃ19–25 (the single unity from which the four elements emerge and these elements themselves have equally good claims to be regarded as elementary in the system). Migliori (1976: 142) counts them as three, rightly in my opinion. 315ᵃ4–19, as a matter of fact, contains two distinct objections: (i) 315ᵃ4–15 (the four elements, supposed to be unable to change into one another, are bound to do so by the cyclical theory); (ii) 315ᵃ15–19 (they are supposed to be ungenerated, but they are bound to be generated out of the *sphairos* by the cyclical theory). Whereas (i) concentrates on the statement 'the elements have to come to be out of one another', (ii) concentrates on the statement 'they have to be generated out of the *sphairos*'. These statements are different, so the objections too must be different. The second one seems to be the converse of the first one: (i) starts from what happened to the elements *at the beginning* of the cycle and concludes that they are able, *still now*, to change into one another (οὐ τότε μόνον ἀλλὰ καὶ νῦν, 315ᵃ14); (ii) starts from what they are *now* able to do and concludes that, *at the beginning*, they must have been generated out of the one (ἔτι ... διόπερ καὶ τότε, 315ᵃ17–18).

The first new objection (314ᵃ4–15) is the most complex of the three. But since Philoponus' interpretation (*in GC* 19. 13–26) has been, as far as I can see, substantially followed by all modern commentators, and rightly in my opinion, I shall perhaps be forgiven for not adding a new version of this standard exegesis to an already lengthy enough chapter.[82]

Leaving aside the second new objection, which I have already briefly commented on, I would like to stress the dramatic impact of the third one (315ᵃ19–25): after all, it is simply unclear whether Empedocles is a pluralist or a monist. On the one hand, the One, allegedly a correct name for the *Sphairos*, could be considered as his single basic element,

---

[82] On the question whether Aristotle is right to attribute to Empedocles the tenet that, after the whole of nature except Strife has been gathered together into one, from this One everything again comes into being (315ᵃ6–8), see Burnet (1920), 235 n. 4, and Joachim (1922), 68, who point out that Aristotle has substituted for the 'all-togetherness' of Empedocles an 'all-oneness'; that is, he interprets the statement about Love bringing all *into one* (but 'remaining as they are', Emp. B17. 34, B21. 13 DK) as if it meant that Love reduces all things *to the One*, i.e. to a completely undifferenciated whole, where they lose their distinctive character (cf. 315ᵃ18–19). Let us notice, however, that later on (315ᵃ23–4) Aristotle describes 'the One' as 'coming to be through the coming together of the elements', ἐκ συνθέσεως γίνεται συνιόντων ἐκείνων, a phrase which seems to show that he suspects that there is something wrong or unclear in his earlier description of the Sphairos.

since it is the material substratum out of which earth, fire, etc. came to be by a process of change initiated by Strife; but on the other hand, the One is said to have come to be through the *sunthesis* of the four 'roots'. These latter seem to be 'more of the nature of elements' (στοιχειωδέστερα) and prior in nature, no doubt because their nature and constitution are supposed to be simpler than those of the Sphairos.[83]

13. Conclusions: from drift to shipwreck?

It is high time to come back to a general assessment of the status of *GC* I. 1 as an introduction to *GC*. I have already evoked the problem raised by the fact that two passages seem to compete for such a status, namely the beginning of I. 1 and the beginning of I. 2 (see sect. 4 above). In addition I have stressed the progressive drift which I think we can observe throughout I. 1, and which deepens, step by step, the distance between what theory leads us to expect and what history (as seen by Aristotle, of course—how could it be possible otherwise?) seems to show. At the end of I. 1 a point of extreme tension between facts and theory is reached: the ironical *desinit* about Empedocles' pseudo-pluralism retrospectively undermines the whole tenor of the chapter, and looks like a *desinit in piscem*.

This sort of situation, I take it, is one that Aristotle most disliked; he is usually very fond of finding a confirmation of his theoretical views in the instructively contrasted spectacle of his predecessors' doctrines. In the penultimate draft of this paper I ventured to suggest that, once aware of the situation into which he had let himself be carried away, Aristotle said to himself: Well, my introduction is perhaps a decent criticism of Empedocles, but as an introduction to what I am about to say it is a disaster; let us stop there, and write another one. Then he certainly did not throw I. 1 straight in the papyrus basket, since we can still read it; either he kept it because he thought that as a criticism of Empedocles it was still worthwhile, or pious hands preserved it for us later on. But he set out to write the beginning of I. 2.

Against the admittedly bold suggestion that *GC* I. 1 was a sort of 'false start', eventually recognized as such by Aristotle himself, many objections have been raised by a number of my fellow symposiasts. The most formidable is certainly the one drawn from *GC* II. 1. 329[b]1, where Aristotle says: 'these [fire, water, etc.] change into one another, and it is

---

[83] This argument is probably unfair to Empedocles, who could reply that the Sphairos and the four elements do not play the role of principle(s), if indeed they do so, *at the same moment* of the cosmic cycle; now, Aristotle himself had notoriously stressed the requisite of *simultaneity* in his analysis of genuine contradiction.

not as Empedocles and others say (for there would be no alteration).' On this passage John Cooper wrote (*per litteram*):

it is one place in the text of the treatise after I. 1 where Aristotle shows that he did not intend to scrap I. 1 and instead begin the treatise with the present I. 2. The remark there, that if we follow Empedocles and do not hold that the primary bodies or so-called elements change into one another, the consequence will be that there can be no alteration at all, seems clearly to recall, without any elaboration at all (as would be needed if when he wrote these lines Aristotle did *not* intend his readers to have previously read the argument of I. 1.314^{b}11–315^{a}3), the argument here in I. 1.

In the face of such a powerful objection, is it possible to say anything? Yes, perhaps. First, we can notice that 329^{b}1 only mentions that alteration is made impossible if one follows Empedocles' (and others') theory of immutable elements. This point, undeniably, is substantiated and argued for in I. 1; but in I. 1 it is only one arm of the tongs in which Aristotle wants to catch Empedocles, the other arm being that, as a pluralist, he had to recognize the distinctive reality of alteration, as contrasted with generation; and this peculiar strategy, I think, marks out I. 1 from other related texts. Secondly, the passage of *Metaphysics A* which I have already quoted in note 81 above (8. 989^{a}26–30) shows that the inability of pluralism to account for alteration was a familiar theme for Aristotle (hence, for his audience), and that he had more than one argument to this effect. Lastly, there is another passage in *GC* (II. 4. 331^{a}7–11) which shows that Aristotle is quite ready to see a purely theoretical link, without any appeal to historical doctrines, between the assumption of ungenerable simple bodies and the impossibility of alteration:

Since it has been settled earlier[84] that generation for the simple bodies is from one to another, and since, moreover, it is apparent even to perception that they come to be (for <otherwise> there would be no alteration,[85] for alteration is in respect of the affections of tangible objects), we must now discuss the way in which they change into one another.

In sum, the brief parenthesis of 329^{b}1 does not necessarily imply that Aristotle intended his audience to be already familiar with I. 1 *specifically*.

---

[84] Williams (1982), 161, interestingly comments: ' "Earlier" probably refers to *Cael*. III. 6. 304^{b}23 ff. The discussions of the topic earlier in the present work, at I. 1. 314^{b}15–26 and II. 1. 329^{a}35–^{b}2, are scarcely any fuller than what we have here and not worth referring back to.' *Cael*. III. 6 does indeed carefully argue that the (so-called) elements come to be from one another; but it must be acknowledged that it does not mention that alteration is thereby secured.

[85] Compare 331^{a}9 (οὐ γὰρ ἂν ἦν ἀλλοίωσις) with 329^{b}1 (οὐδὲ γὰρ ἂν ἦν ἀλλοίωσις). Almost a mechanical association.

Even when ignorant of this chapter, his students could presumably hear these few words without getting lost.

Let me add a couple of final observations.

(i) I think it worthwhile to quote a long but striking passage from I. 2 (315^a29-^b6):

Plato investigated only generation and corruption, and how they apply to objects; nor did he treat of every case of generation, but only that of the elements; there was no discussion of the case of flesh or bones or the rest of the things of this sort, nor yet of alteration and growth and the way in which they apply to objects. Altogether no one seems to have paid more than superficial attention (παρὰ τὰ ἐπιπολῆς) to any of these things, with the exception of Democritus. He seems to have given consideration to them all, and to excel from the start by <explaining> how <they come about>. For none of them laid anything down about growth, as we are saying, beyond what the man in the street (ὁ τυχών) may have to say, namely, that things grow by the accession of like to like. There was still no discussion of how this is effected, nor of mixing, nor, practically speaking, of any of the other topics such as action and passion—how one thing acts and another is affected by natural actions.

Even if an examination of atomistic doctrines normally was to be expected after their brief descriptions in I. 1 (314^a12, 18, 21–4), I cannot keep myself from finding that this passage sounds like a self-criticism by Aristotle of his own chapter I. 1. Not only does it offer a much more complete and exact overview of the problems to be treated later on[86] but it marks an enormous contrast with I. 1 in Aristotle's judgement about his predecessors. If the prehistory of the subject is such a desert and barren place as he now says, why should we have bothered to investigate and to criticize in depth the superficial, trivial, and sadly incomplete views of the *archaioi* other than the great Democritus? Why should we have made use of the standard division of these views into monism and pluralism, finitism and infinitism, continuism and discontinuism, in order to classify such jejune conceptions as these about generation and corruption? Aristotle here actually seems to draw the gloomy conclusion about his earlier attempt, and to consider that it has led him to nothing really valuable and helpful.

(ii) On the other hand, it is impossible to ignore the fact that in the following chapters Aristotle comes back to Empedocles more than once, in particular in I. 8; he obviously does not think a discussion of his views completely unhelpful.[87] However, in his contribution to the present

---

[86] Like its introduction (315^a26-9), already discussed in this respect (cf. Sect. 4 above).

[87] Geoffrey Lloyd observes (*per litteram*): 'Aristotle has to be worried about Empedocles especially—since Empedocles' theory is so close to his own. In practice, if one takes the Corpus as a whole, Empedocles gets referred to many times more than Leucippus and Democritus and Anaxagoras put together.'

volume (ch. 9, p. 244), devoted to I. 8, Edward Hussey describes the structure of this chapter in the following way:

> The two parts of the discussion of Empedocles begin and end the chapter, like the outsides of a sandwich. Inside the sandwich is a long discussion . . . of atomism as a physical theory, which goes well beyond the topics of 'action—passion'. All this has the effect of throwing the spotlight on the atomists, and of metaphorically, as well as literally, marginalizing Empedocles.

On the basis of this description, I would suggest that the structure of I. 8, as quite aptly described by Hussey, reflects the 'golden mean' position which Aristotle eventually took, after having twice altered his course, one bitterly hostile to Empedocles (I. 1), the other one a little more than usually laudatory towards Democritus (I. 2). Now, in I. 8, things are better balanced. However, perhaps as an after-effect of I. 1, Empedocles is still 'marginalized'.

   All in all, then, I would not swear that my story about *GC* I. 1 is true. But I do believe that there are some serious clues in its favour, and I offer it as such.

2

On Generation and Corruption I. 2

DAVID SEDLEY

1. Introduction

This second chapter of *GC* has been widely discussed as evidence for the nature and inferential basis of Democritean atomism, and, not infrequently, for Aristotle's own response to Democritus' argument.[1] Much less has been said about the chapter's overall strategy. At the risk of seeming to perpetuate this imbalance, I shall read the chapter from the centre outwards. I aim to establish just how Democritus' argument is presented and criticized, before moving on to Aristotle's broader goals. Unlike the majority of earlier discussions, mine will not be concerned with the question whether authentically Democritean material can be recovered from the chapter. However, my findings would, if accepted, have significant consequences for those asking that question.

The first aspect to tackle is structural. Where is the transition between Aristotle's report of Democritus and his own ensuing reply? The usual impression given by editors and translators[2] is that the break occurs at 316^{b}16, where Aristotle appears to say the time has come to answer Democritus. Unfortunately, however, that is not what happens next. Instead he remarks that the Democritean puzzle needs to be restated from the beginning, which is what he proceeds to do. It is not

---

[1] The most recent contribution is Taylor (1999), 76–9, 164–71, with select bibliography on pp. 293–4.

[2] Philoponus (*in GC* 34.5–9, *ad* 316^{b}16–18): σημειωτέον οὖν ὅτι νῦν οὐ πρόκειται αὐτῷ προηγουμένως δεῖξαι μὴ εἶναι ἄτομα μεγέθη (ἐν γὰρ τοῖς εἰρημένοις βιβλίοις αὐτὸ καθ᾽ αὑτὸ τὸ δόγμα τοῦτο ὡς ἀδύνατον ἤλεγξεν), ἀλλὰ λῦσαι τοὺς εἰσάγοντας τὰ ἄτομα μεγέθη λόγους. ἀναλαμβάνει οὖν τὸν τοῦ Δημοκρίτου λόγον ἐν συντόμῳ καὶ διαρθροῖ μᾶλλον, καὶ οὕτως τὸν ἔλεγχον ἐπιφέρει; Thomas Aquinas, *in GC* 34, 'praemissa ratione Democriti, hic procedit ad eius solutionem'; Joachim (1922), 83, *ad* 316^{b}18–19; Migliori (1976), 144; Williams (1982), 72, *ad* 316^{b}19: 'Aristotle begins to expound his own solution of the paradox. It is to rely on the distinction between actuality and potentiality. For the moment, though, it is not worked out in detail, but Democritus' arguments against infinite divisibility are further summarized'. An honourable exception is Mugler (1966), whose marginal headings imply that the reply to Democritus does not begin until 317^{a}2.

until 316^b34 that Aristotle's answer finally begins, with signposting as explicit as one could ask for: 'That, then, is the argument which is thought to make it necessary that there should be atomic magnitudes. Let us now say that, and where, it contains a concealed fallacy.'

So, what are we to make of the false start back at 316^b16? It is important to scrutinize Aristotle's words closely:[3]

ὥστ᾽ εἴπερ ἀδύνατον ἐξ ἁφῶν ἢ στιγμῶν εἶναι τὰ μεγέθη, ἀνάγκη εἶναι σώματα ἀδιαίρετα καὶ μεγέθη. οὐ μὴν ἀλλὰ καὶ ταῦτα θεμένοις οὐχ ἧττον συμβαίνει ἀδύνατα. ἔσκεπται δὲ περὶ αὐτῶν ἐν ἑτέροις. ἀλλὰ ταῦτα πειρατέον λύειν, διὸ πάλιν ἐξ ἀρχῆς τὴν ἀπορίαν λεκτέον. (316^b14–19)

So, if it is impossible for magnitudes to consist of contacts or points, there must be indivisible bodies and magnitudes. On the other hand, for those who posit these too there follow no less impossible consequences. They have been discussed elsewhere. But these are things we must try to resolve, and hence the puzzle needs to be restated from the beginning.

'But these (ταῦτα) are things which we must try to resolve' ($^b18$). What are 'these'? Since Philoponus, the universal assumption of commentators and translators has been that the reference is to Democritus' arguments, or more specifically to the puzzles which underlie them, which Aristotle would be announcing his intention to resolve. But not only does that create the problem from which I started, that Aristotle's own solution does not in fact begin here; it also leaves the anaphoric pronoun without any natural point of reference in the text. There is no suitably located mention of Democritus' puzzles, or of the arguments founded on them, for ταῦτα to pick up. If guided by the immediate context, we might expect the reference to be either to the indivisibles, already designated with the pronoun ταῦτα in the previous sentence, or to the 'impossibilities' (ἀδύνατα) which are said to result from positing those indivisibles. But one cannot make much sense of the idea of 'resolving' indivisibles, and equally the idea of resolving *impossibilities*, as distinct from difficulties, is a surprising one, for which I have found no parallel in Aristotle. Rather than any of these options, then, we must take the reference to be to the impasse which has now come about between two sets of impossibilities—those which arise from the supposition of infinite divisibility and those which arise from the thesis of atomism. It is this stalemate, with equally balanced impossibilities on both sides, that requires resolution: the argument must be taken a step further.

---

[3] In this paper I follow the text of Joachim (1922) (apart from minor matters of punctuation), except where indicated.

What I propose is the following construal.[4] Aristotle has down to this point presented Democritus' arguments in historical or quasi-historical fashion. The reasoning at $316^a14–^b16$ has in its entirety been meant to capture the way in which Democritus himself arrived at his atomist thesis (see its introduction at $316^a13–14$: 'Democritus would appear to hold his view on the basis of appropriate physical arguments. What I mean will be clear when we proceed'). At 316^b16 the historical reconstruction ends, but, I suggest, the thinking continues to be in effect that of Democritus. He is made to speak as if he acknowledged the difficulties consequent upon his argument for indivisibles—difficulties which we as readers are asked to recognize as ones formulated in Aristotle's own writings (ἔσκεπται δὲ περὶ αὐτῶν ἐν ἑτέροις, $^b17–18$). Thus it is still from Democritus', not Aristotle's, point of view that the text acknowledges the need to resolve the conflict, and proceeds accordingly.

For that, I submit, is how the argument does proceed. Democritus is fictionally permitted to reformulate his argument in terms which acknowledge, and even incorporate into his own defence, the key Aristotelian distinction between potentiality and actuality. This is a distinction which Aristotle had used elsewhere in his refutation of the arguments for atomism, but which he, one may conjecture, knew better than anyone not to have been deployed by the historical Democritus.

There is, I confess, an inaccuracy involved in this, but not one grave enough to put the interpretation in serious doubt. The 'impossibilities' to which Democritus is made to respond are not, as we have perhaps been led to expect (καὶ ταῦτα [sc. atoms] θεμένοις οὐχ ἧττον συμβαίνει ἀδύνατα), difficulties consequent upon the actual positing of atoms, such as the conflict with mathematics which Aristotle notoriously alleges at *de Caelo*. III. 4. $303^a20–4$, but rather, as we shall see, ones consequent upon the *arguments* used in favour of atomism.

The point of Aristotle's unsolicited gift is, I take it, to enable Democritus to marshal his strongest possible defence, even turning some of Aristotle's own weapons against him, before Aristotle's own refutation kicks in at 316^b34.[5] However unusual this strategy may be for Aristotle, it earns him credit for scrupulous methodology, and it coheres with the

---

[4] The bare outline of this construal (although without the proposed way of reading $316^b14–19$) is already to be found in Luria (1933), 129–35. If it has gone virtually unnoticed, the reason may be that it appeared to have been successfully refuted by Mau (1954), 25–6. However, this was primarily because Luria had failed to account for the presence of Aristotelian-seeming material at $316^b9–14$, a problem which no longer arises if my proposal for transposition (pp. 72–3, 75 below) is accepted.

[5] On this I go beyond Luria (1933), 135, who does not see the revised argument as different in content, but only in form, from the first version.

overall tenor of the chapter, in which Democritus is built up into the truly professional physicist who makes Plato look a rank amateur.

In the light of the above sketch, I propose to read the defence of atomism in two separate halves. The first half, 316^a14-^b16, which I shall call the Democritean argument, I shall read as a historical reconstruction, consciously free of Aristotelian presuppositions. The second (316^b16-34), by contrast, which I call the neo-Democritean argument, I shall present as a fiction—the argument which Democritus might, anachronistically, have used in reply to Aristotle's own criticisms of him, drawing freely on Aristotelian concepts. (My expectation that Aristotelian presuppositions should be *consciously* excluded from the first argument arises simply from the carefully signalled contrast with their presence in the second.)[6] Aristotle's ensuing reply to Democritus will succeed only if it refutes the neo-Democritean as well as the Democritean version of the argument.

2. The Democritean argument

[D1] A puzzle would arise if one were to posit that some body and magnitude is divisible everywhere, and that this is possible. For what will there be to escape the division? If it is divisible everywhere, and this is possible, it could also be in that divided state simultaneously, even if it has not undergone the division simultaneously;[7] and if this did happen there would be nothing impossible about it. Thus the same applies also at the midpoint; and generally too, if it is by nature divisible everywhere, then if it gets divided nothing impossible will have happened. For not even if it is divided into a hundred million pieces[8] is there any impossibility, although perhaps no one would so divide it. (316^a14-23)

It seems clear that for a magnitude to be divided, as distinct from divisible, into *n* parts is for some substantive separation of its parts to

---

[6] Cf. Luria (1933), 135, for a similar observation, although I suspend judgement on the question whether, as Luria believes, the first argument is a direct report of Democritus, or just Aristotle's reconstruction.

[7] 316^a17-18, κἂν ἅμα εἴη τοῦτο διῃρημένον, καὶ εἰ μὴ ἅμα διῄρηται. One might have expected εἶναι διῃρημένον and διῃρῆσθαι to be synonymous, both referring to the object's present state of division, so that the meaning would be: 'It *could* be simultaneously in a divided state everywhere, even if it *isn't* simultaneously in that divided state'. However, by Aristotle's day the perfect often, perhaps even regularly, has a past temporal designation (P. Chantraine, *Histoire du parfait grec* (Paris, 1926)); cf. e.g. *Ph.* 217^b34, γέγονε καὶ οὐκ ἔστιν; *Cat.* 5^a34-5, εἴρηταί τε καὶ οὐκ ἔστιν ἔτι τοῦτο λαβεῖν; *Po.* 1457^a17-18, τὸ δὲ βαδίζει ἢ βεβάδικεν προσσημαίνει τὸ μὲν τὸν παρόντα χρόνον τὸ δὲ τὸν παρεληλυθότα. In the light of this, it makes more sense to follow the regular translation, as I do above; the point made will be one that corresponds closely to 316^b29-31. The anomaly that διῄρηται is indicative, where the sense should strictly be 'even if it *would not have* undergone the division simultaneously', does not much harm intelligibility.

[8] I retain the MS reading at 316^a22, well defended by Verdenius and Waszink (1966), 10–11, against Joachim's (1922) διῃρημένα ⟨διαιρεθ⟩ῇ.

occur—certainly more than the merely conceptual operation of someone entertaining the thought that it contains *n* parts, boundaries, or points. Otherwise there would be little motivation for the closing words of the above excerpt, 'although perhaps no one would so divide it', or for the repeated proviso that not only is the magnitude divisible everywhere but also 'this is possible', which must in the context mean 'and this division can actually be carried out'. Thus far the process might still be a fundamentally mental one, where every division is discretely thought of. But the later speculation about some kind of sawdust being produced by the division process (316^{a}34 ff.) confirms that something more than this is envisaged.[9] The entire Democritean argument will prove to be one about the actual decomposition—and not merely the analysis—of a magnitude into its ultimate constituents.

[D2] Since, therefore, the body is like this everywhere, let it have been divided. What magnitude will be left, then?[10] There cannot be one, for then there will be something undivided, but it was said to be divisible everywhere. On the other hand, if there is going to be no body or magnitude left, but the division is going to exist, either the body will consist of points and its components be sizeless, or they will be nothing at all, with the consequence that it could come to be and be composed from nothing, and the whole thing would be a mere appearance. Similarly, even if it consists of points, there will be no quantity. For when the points were in contact and there was a single magnitude and they were together, they did not make the whole thing any bigger; for when the magnitude was divided into two or more, the whole was no smaller or bigger than before; hence even if they are all put together they will produce no magnitude. (316^{a}23–34)

This is perhaps the most lucid part of the argument. If the magnitude is potentially divisible at every point, let that potential division be realized, which, as we have seen, means 'Let the magnitude be fully decomposed by separation at every point'. The problem is then how you can reassemble it out of the resultant parts. These parts are either nothing at all, Democritus argues, or else points. If they are nothing at all then their sum, the original magnitude, is also nothing at all. If they are points they are sizeless, and therefore still cannot contribute to its magnitude.

A striking sign of Aristotle's attempt to recapture Democritus' own reasoning, and not simply to apply his own presuppositions,[11] is that the

---

[9] My remarks on this owe much to Barnes (1979), ii. 56–7.

[10] 316^{a}24, τί οὖν ἔσται λοιπόν μέγεθος; I cannot see why the editors have preferred the scarcely natural punctuation τί οὖν ἔσται λοιπόν; μέγεθος.

[11] Mau (1954), 25–6, argues for Aristotelian contamination, but see n. 4 above. Migliori (1976), 151, goes so far as to comment 'Per comprendere queste critiche, bisogna ricordare che per Aristotele il punto non è un elemento, ma il limite della linea e della divisione delle parti. Abbiamo quindi un classico caso di rilettura dei presocratici all'interno delle categorie aristoteliche.'

inability of points to compose a magnitude is not taken for granted, but is supported by a specific sub-argument: 'when the magnitude was divided into two or more, the whole was no smaller or bigger than before' (316^a31–3). Why is this relevant? Because Democritus assumes that the division process would either diminish or increase the number of points in the magnitude, yet fail to alter the magnitude itself. Accounting for the idea of increase here is relatively simple:[12] if a line is separated into two lines by the imposition of a division at point A, point A is replaced by two points, the (formerly united) extremities of the two resultant lines. But why might anyone have thought, alternatively, that division could *diminish* the number of points in the magnitude?[13] I suggest that points are for this purpose equated with contacts, which elsewhere in the argument are several times listed alongside points as if the two notions were somehow interchangeable (esp. 316^b6–8): if so, then every division realized means one less contact, and hence one less point. (The dialectical offer of a choice between two conceptions of a point should be read as a hint that Democritus' own positive theory is not built on any specified conception of a point.)

[D3] [a] But even if during the process of division something is produced like sawdust from the body, and in this way some body is removed from the magnitude, the same applies: *it* is somehow divisible. [b] If on the other hand what has been removed is not body but some separable [or 'separate'] aspect or affection, and the magnitude is a set of points or contacts to which the affection belongs, we get the absurdity of a magnitude consisting of non-magnitudes. (316^a34–$^b5$)

Here [a] envisages some of the magnitude not as vanishing into nothing but as somehow leaking out during the division process, like sawdust. The editions at this point read ἐκεῖνο γὰρ πῶς διαιρετόν; (some follow EHJL in omitting the γάρ): 'how is *it* [the sawdust] divisible?' I propose instead to read ἐκεῖνο γὰρ πως διαιρετόν, and above I have accordingly translated '*it* is somehow divisible'. Thus read, Aristotle is making the point that were we to identify a portion of sawdust which had escaped during the division, there would be some dividing still left to do, namely on the sawdust itself, before we could claim to have divided the original magnitude at every point. (On the interrogative reading he would seem to be raising a problem about how you *can* divide sawdust, but I fail to see what that problem would be or how it would help his case for atomism; it is atoms, not sawdust, that cannot be divided.)[14]

---

[12] See Furley (1967), 84–5; Migliori (1976), 151; Williams (1982), 70.

[13] This half of the argument is usually overlooked. Luria (1933), 133 n. 71, does, however, attempt an elucidation of it, while Williams (1982), 70, notes it in passing, expressing doubt whether it is meant seriously.

[14] If, alternatively, the question meant 'How *far* can it be divided?', πῶς would be a poor choice of interrogative, where what was meant was e.g. εἰς πόσον.

[b] is a trickier stretch of argument, too condensed to yield a single clear reading. We are asked to think of the leakage not this time as that of a body, such as sawdust, but as that of a property. For convenience I shall call this hypothesized property 'mass', although Democritus' own term for it might well be 'continuity', 'solidity', or perhaps best 'fullness' (ναστότης). A body's loss of its mass as a result of the envisaged decomposition into points would be a property change analogous to the loss of colour or shape. The motive for this alternative suggestion is presumably that it offers the advantage of reversibility. Whereas the *exhaustive* decomposition of a magnitude into points offered no components from which it could later be reassembled, on this revised model the recombination of the points would not itself already reconstitute the magnitude, but the bodily mass of the magnitude would be enabled to return in the way that colour and shape can return to, say, a piece of chalk which has been pulverized and then reconstituted.

Democritus' objection to this alternative model is the absurdity of a magnitude consisting entirely of non-magnitudes. His wording (^{b}3–4, καὶ ἔστι τὸ μέγεθος στιγμαὶ ἢ ἁφαὶ τοδὶ παθοῦσαι) makes it clear that these non-magnitudes are not to be taken as the points *plus* the property, but as the points alone, viewed as that to which the property belongs. Take again the analogy of a reconstituted piece of chalk. Qualitatively it may be white, cylindrical, etc., but what it is constitutively is just a collection of grains or particles, in the absence of which the whiteness and cylindrical shape would have nothing to belong to. In the case of division everywhere, the counterpart of the chalk grains is a set of mere points. If they, recombined, cannot constitute a magnitude, there will be nothing for the returned bodily mass to belong to. Thus the model envisaged in [D3] [b] proves to offer no advance on the kind of decomposition already rejected in [D2].

[D4] [a] Moreover, *where* will the points be, and will they be immobile or moving? [b] And a single contact is always between a pair of things, which implies that there is something over and above the contact and the point and the division. (316^{b}5–8)

This pair of arguments illustrates an interpretative principle which I advocated at the outset. Commentators since antiquity have looked for specifically Aristotelian tenets underlying them. Thus Philoponus, followed by Joachim and Tricot, detects in [a] the Aristotelian doctrine of natural place: if the points allegedly constituting a magnitude were separated out, how could they find natural places, being neither heavy like earth and water nor light like air and fire? In fact, once one sets off on that path, one could raise even more pertinent questions about how a free-standing point can have a place at all, given Aristotle's definition of place as the inner *surface* of the container;[15] and equally one could invoke Aristotle's argument at *Physics* VI. 10 to show why something partless could never be in motion.

But this kind of speculation is misdirected. The argument is Democritus' own, and Aristotle is not—at least not yet—offering him any help. The question asked in [a] is an intuitively powerful one even without any special Aristotelian presuppositions. Suppose we watch a body decompose into its constituent points, and I then tell you that these points are now spread all over the table, or alternatively that they are travelling slowly towards the ceiling. You do not need to be an Aristotelian to ask me (i) what are the truth-conditions of such claims, (ii) what could, even in theory, cause a free-moving point to acquire a specific location or trajectory, given its total lack of physical properties, and (iii) what it would mean for a point, all by itself, to be moving.

Similarly with [b], it is misleading to spell out, with Philoponus, Joachim, Williams, and others, what grounds Aristotle himself might have for insisting that there are always two parties to a contact. The argument is, once again, Democritus' own, and simply trades on the meaning of the word 'contact': you cannot exhaust a magnitude by division into 'contacts', if that would entail nothing's being left over for the contacts to be between.

[D5] These are the consequences if someone posits that any body, or a body of any magnitude, is divisible everywhere. [Again, if I divide and put back together a stick, or anything else, it is once more equal and one. Clearly then the same applies whatever point I may cut the stick at. Hence it has been potentially divided everywhere. What then is there over and above the division? For if there is also some affection, how is it dissolved into these and how does it come to be out of these? Or, again, how do these get separated? (316^b9–14)] So, if it is impossible for magnitudes to consist of contacts or points, there must be indivisible bodies and magnitudes. (316^b8–16)

In bracketing 316^b9–14, I am agreeing with the judgement of Prantl and Williams that these lines cannot belong here,[16] both because they interrupt the sense and because they largely repeat points already made, in their proper place, at [D3]. At the same time, however, I agree with Joachim that the lines are unmistakably by Aristotle. The correct response, therefore, is surely neither to delete them, with Prantl and Williams, nor to retain them as they stand, with Joachim, but to transpose them. I believe that the distinction between the Democritean and the

---

[15] One might also have considered invoking the claim at *Ph.* IV. 1. 208^b22–5 that mathematical entities have no place, just relative position for an observer. However, that view is contradicted at *CG* I. 6. 322^b32–323^a3.

[16] Prantl (1857), 490 n. 15, argues that these lines are an interpolation by a later hand.

neo-Democritean argument enables us to see where they must be relocated, and why. These lines do indeed repeat the substance of the earlier argument at [D3], but this time, crucially, with the benefit of an Aristotelian potentiality–actuality distinction. They therefore belong in the neo-Democritean argument. We will meet them there, renamed [ND2], in due course.

Leaving aside the intrusive lines, the remainder of [D5] simply rounds off the Democritean argument, formally stating its atomist conclusion.

3. The neo-Democritean argument

We can now move on to the restatement of the atomist argument in its neo-Democritean form. I have already, at the beginning of this chapter, dealt with Aristotle's transition to it, 316^b16–19. We can therefore move directly to its first section.

[ND1] That every perceptible body is subject to division ($\delta\iota\alpha\iota\rho\epsilon\tau\acute{o}\nu$) *and* not subject to division ($\dot{\alpha}\delta\iota\alpha\acute{\iota}\rho\epsilon\tau\sigma\nu$) at every point is no absurdity: for it will be subject to division in potentiality but not subject to division in actuality. But that it should be simultaneously subject to division everywhere in potentiality would seem to be impossible. For if it is possible, it might happen (not so that it is simultaneously in actuality both not subject to division and divided, but so that it is simultaneously divided at any point whatsoever). Thus there will be nothing left, and the body will have perished into something incorporeal, and would come to be again either out of points or out of nothing at all. And how is that possible? (316^b19–27)

I have in this context translated $\delta\iota\alpha\iota\rho\epsilon\tau\acute{o}\nu$ and $\dot{\alpha}\delta\iota\alpha\acute{\iota}\rho\epsilon\tau\sigma\nu$ as, respectively, 'subject to division' and 'not subject to division', rather than with the usual 'divisible' and 'indivisible'. This is because Aristotle's distinction between the potentially and the actually $\delta\iota\alpha\iota\rho\epsilon\tau\acute{o}\nu$ does not seem to be one either between first and second potentialities or between what is divisible merely in theory and what is capable of actually undergoing division. Rather, it looks like his way of distinguishing two senses of the -τον termination, '(in)divisible' and '(un)divided'.[17] Hence the first sentence

---

[17] Cf. *de An.* III. 6. 430^b6–11, τὸ δ' ἀδιαίρετον ἐπεὶ διχῶς, ἢ δυνάμει ἢ ἐνεργείᾳ, οὐθὲν κωλύει νοεῖν τὸ ἀδιαίρετον ὅταν νοῇ τὸ μῆκος (ἀδιαίρετον γὰρ ἐνεργείᾳ), καὶ ἐν χρόνῳ ἀδιαιρέτῳ· ὁμοίως γὰρ ὁ χρόνος διαιρετὸς καὶ ἀδιαίρετος τῷ μήκει. οὔκουν ἔστιν εἰπεῖν ἐν τῷ ἡμίσει τί ἐνόει ἑκατέρῳ· οὐ γὰρ ἔστιν, ἂν μὴ διαιρεθῇ, ἀλλ' ἢ δυνάμει. Although the interpretation is controversial, I believe that by the 'potential' sense of ἀδιαίρετον Aristotle must here mean not e.g. what is potentially indivisible even if actually divisible but what is ἀδιαίρετον in the sense of that word where the termination expresses potentiality, not actuality—i.e. indivisible rather than undivided. I here agree with, among others, J. A. Smith in Barnes (1984). For a similar case of Aristotle's potentiality–actuality language being used to disambiguate the -τον

serves mainly to focus us on the sense of the word διαιρετόν as 'having the potentiality to be divided'. The second sentence then returns us to the main Democritean argument, as we encountered it at [D1–2], but with the notion of potentiality now firmly in the frame.

By this manoeuvre the neo-Democritean is being allowed to acknowledge an Aristotelian countermove to the atomist argument, with a view to rebutting that countermove in the next sentence. The Aristotelian countermove seems to be the one found at *Physics* VIII. 8. 263^{a}4–^{b}9 (with theoretical foundations laid at *Physics* III. 6–7). Aristotle, who is aware of the close kinship between Democritus' decomposition argument and Zeno's dichotomy paradox (*Physics* I. 3. 187^{a}1–3), maintains that such Zenonian paradoxes fail because the infinite division which they postulate is infinite *only in potentiality*. Very well, the neo-Democritean argument now goes, let us concede that to call a magnitude 'simultaneously διαιρετόν everywhere' is (in line with the distinction between two senses of the -τον termination) no more than to indicate a potentiality, not an actuality. However, the neo-Democritean continues, surely to call a certain state of affairs 'potential' is to allow that it could be actual.[18] He therefore proceeds to repeat, in summary, the argument of [D2]: this supposedly realizable state of affairs would resolve the magnitude into components which were either sizeless points or altogether non-existent—leading to consequences with which we are by now all too familiar.

Aristotle need not be read, here or later, as conceding the neo-Democritean objection. In fact as early as the next chapter (318^{a}20–1) he will be reaffirming his own belief that division is infinite only in potentiality, no doubt relying on the remark at *Physics* III. 6. 206^{a}18–21 that the 'potential' being of an infinite division is of a kind which does *not* entail realizability.[19] He is, however, in the present context acknowledging that a satisfactory refutation of atomism cannot afford to rely on so debatable a premiss. We will see in the next section how his actual refutation has been so redesigned as to avoid any such reliance.

termination cf. *Ph.* VIII. 5. 258^{a}32–^{b}4. If Aristotle feels the need to disambiguate the termination in the present passage too, that is no doubt because he considers its modal sense, on which he here wishes to concentrate, to be a secondary one (*Cael.* I. 12. 282^{a}27–30).

[18] Alternatively, one could translate 316^{b}22: 'For if it were possible, it would [not just "might"] happen', in which case the principle of plenitude would be being invoked or assumed. Since versions of that principle have been ascribed both to Aristotle (esp. on the basis of *DC* I. 12) and to Democritus (Makin (1993), ch. 7), its presence in the neo-Democritean argument would be no surprise.

[19] I do not intend to get diverted into discussion of this very problematic concept, on which cf. esp. Hussey (1983), pp. xx–xxiii, and Charlton (1991).

It is at this point in the neo-Democritean argument that it seems natural to insert the displaced lines 316^b9-14:[20]

[ND2] [a] < Again, if I divide and put back together a stick, or anything else, it is once more equal and one. Clearly then the same applies whatever point I may cut the stick at. Hence it has been potentially divided everywhere. What then is there over and above the division? For if there is also some affection, how is it dissolved into these and how does it come to be out of these? [b] Or, again, how do these get separated?> Yet that it does, at any rate, get divided into magnitudes which are separ*able*, and into ones which are continually smaller and non-adjacent and separat*ed*, is clear. Now, neither could gradual division yield infinite fragmentation, nor can it be simultaneously divided at every point (that is impossible), but only within some limit. [c] Therefore it must necessarily contain unseen atomic magnitudes—especially if generation is going to be by aggregation and destruction by disintegration. (316^b9-14, + 316^b28-34; emphasis added)

The argument of [a] is too condensed for its meaning to be immediately clear,[21] but I suggest that it expands into the following sequence of ideas. Think first of physically bisecting a stick and then rejoining the two parts. Next try applying that same thought to *every* point on the stick. You have now divided the stick everywhere—not actually, of course, but potentially. That is to say, Aristotle's expression: 'Hence it has been potentially divided everywhere' (316^b11-12, πάντῃ ἄρα διῄρηται δυνάμει), does not mean merely that it could in the future be divided everywhere,[22] but that this potential division *has now been carried out*.

If the meaning of this expression has gone undetected, it is because editors have failed to notice that the construction used in it, δυνάμει (or κατὰ δύναμιν) + perfect, is unique in the entire Aristotelian corpus.[23] Aristotle must be struggling to convey something beyond the usual

---

[20] If the displaced passage belongs within the neo-Democritean argument at all, it cannot stand at the beginning of it, since its opening ἔτι indicates that it follows another argument for the same conclusion; nor can it come any later than here, because by then the atomistic conclusions are already being drawn. Moreover 316^b28-9, if, as I am proposing, it is read as the direct continuation of the passage, appropriately takes up its theme of 'separation'.

[21] Cf. Philoponus ad loc. (*in GC* 33. 7), διὰ περίνοιαν συντόμως πέφρασται.

[22] Even more implausible, but at least a welcome recognition of the expression's oddity, is Aquinas' gloss: ' "omnino divisum potestate", idest in omnia in quae poterat dividi' (*in GC* 33, quoted by Migliori (1976), 152–3).

[23] I say this on the basis of a *TLG* search of the corpus covering all 413 occurrences of δυνάμει and all 52 of κατὰ δύναμιν. Myles Burnyeat points out to me that at *de An.* II. 5. 417^a30 we may be expected to supply κατὰ δύναμιν with the aorist ἀλλοιωθείς. However, all the editors and translators I have consulted agree that Aristotle is there elliptically (or even explicitly, if one adopts Ross's supplement) describing the actuality corresponding to the potentiality described in his preceding clause. Whether or not they are right, the prevalence of such a reading confirms how strange it is to find 'potentially' attached to a past tense.

range of his potentiality talk. Now modern discussions of Democritean atomism have introduced a distinction between physical and conceptual division, debating whether it is to one or both of these that atoms are supposed to be immune. Such a distinction between two kinds of divisibility has never, to my knowledge, been identified in any ancient source.[24] But in the present passage, if I am not mistaken, we have encountered the nearest that Aristotle can get to expressing such an idea. In his terms, when you have run through a purely mental procedure of registering divisions within some magnitude, you have performed a potential division—a *virtual* division, one might say—though not an actual division.

The neo-Democritean argument helps itself to this Aristotelian (or quasi-Aristotelian) notion of a potential division, and maintains that, even if no actual division at every point were to be carried out (that is, even if one did not, as in [ND1], insist on the realizability of an exhaustive division), the mere 'potential' division carried out in thought, i.e. the conceptual analysis of the magnitude into sizeless components, is already enough to replicate exactly the problems which we have already encountered at [D2–3], and which are now briefly summarized at the end of [ND2][a].

This new twist in the argument would, if accepted, threaten to prove too much, since even within a single atom such 'potential' divisions could arguably be registered in thought, so that the only true indivisibles would be either altogether sizeless or at any rate partless. It is widely recognized that if atoms were altogether partless that would clash with the well-attested tenet that they vary in shape and size. It is, then, fortunate for Democritus that this whole extension to the atomist argument turns out to be an openly unhistorical addition on Aristotle's part. By including it only in the neo-Democritean argument, Aristotle is in effect providing testimony that, so far as he is aware, nothing corresponding to 'conceptual' indivisibility featured in Democritus' own atomist thesis.

Moving on to [b], we should assume that its opening question: 'Or, again, how do these get separated?', still refers by 'these' to the same ultimate components (whether points, or points plus properties) as were yielded by the conceptual, or 'potential', analysis outlined in [a]. But as the argument proceeds the topic is explicitly extended from these potential components to the actual components yielded by an actual division process: division yields not just separa*ble* but actually separat*ed* parts. [a] has shown us the disastrous consequences of positing divisibility everywhere. [b], which directly paves the way to the argument's atomist conclusion, reassures us that, fortunately, division everywhere is not

---

[24] For a critique of this distinction, as applied to Democritean atoms, see Makin (1989).

possible. When we are asked *how* to conceive of the sizeless components as undergoing the actual process of being separated from each other, no answer is forthcoming. Clearly a decomposition process can, for as long as we keep it up, separate the magnitude out into ever smaller parts. But that gets us no nearer to division at *every* point, which could not be achieved either by progressive or by simultaneous division.

The conclusion to the entire neo-Democritean argument follows at [c]. Since division at every point is impossible (both [a] because of its ruinous consequences, and [b] because of its conceptual and actual impossibility of realization), the necessary alternative is that division must eventually reach its limit (see the end of [b]). Wherever that limit may lie, it marks the end of division and thus the threshold of atoms, indivisible magnitudes.

We have witnessed the following progression within the neo-Democritean argument. First, in [ND1], the hypothetical opponent responded to Aristotle's use of potentiality as a weapon in the debate, by showing why it fails to disarm the main atomist argument. Second, in [ND2][a], Aristotelian potentiality was shown, on the contrary, to offer the neo-Democritean a strengthened version of his own argument, since potential divisions to infinity, unlike actual ones, could, on the hypothesis of infinite divisibility, be successfully performed, thus exposing the unacceptable consequences of that hypothesis. At [ND2][b] we are shown that not only the 'potential' but also the actual division of a magnitude must be constrained by certain limits, since *no* conceivable process could result in division at literally every point. This finally leads in [c] to the conclusion that there are atoms.

That the atoms are 'unseen', and that they underlie generation and destruction, are parts of the conclusion not warranted by the argument itself. The invisibility claim reflects a well-known independent feature of the atomist theory, and one which will become relevant in the light of Aristotle's own stipulation (ch. 4) that in substantial generation, unlike alteration, there should be no perceptible subject which endures. The further point that atoms underlie generation and destruction—to which we will return later—represents Aristotle's own primary motive for scrutinizing atomism within the context of the present work.

4. Aristotle's reply

[AR] [a] That, then, is the argument which appears to make it necessary that there be atomic magnitudes. Let us now say that, and where, it contains a concealed fallacy. [b] Since no point is adjacent to a point, there is one way in which divisibility everywhere *is* a property of magnitudes, but another way in which it is not. [c] When this divisibility is posited, it seems that there is a point anywhere and everywhere, with the result that the magnitude is necessarily divided into nothing, because the result of there being a point everywhere is that it consists either of contacts or of points. [d] The sense in which it *is* a property of the magnitude everywhere is that anywhere at all there is one point, and all the points are like each. [e] But there are not more than one in sequence (for points are not <in sequence>),[25] and hence it does not belong everywhere. For if it is divisible in the middle, will it also be divisible at an adjacent point?[26] No, because no point is adjacent to a point,[27] and it is a point that serves as a division or a join. (316^b34–317^a12)

This reply is remarkably brief (the more so once we recognize that what I have called the neo-Democritean argument is not part of it), and has caused frustration to Aristotle's admirers, since it is never quite clear whether he is saying what it is felt he ought to say.[28] Its bare bones are very simple. Aristotle does not, as might at first appear, try to impose any qualification on the admission that there are points everywhere[29] within

[25] 317^a9, πλείους δὲ μιᾶς οὐκ εἰσίν ἐφεξῆς (⟨ἐφεξῆς⟩ γὰρ οὐκ εἰσίν). That is, you cannot get a whole row of points in sequence, because points cannot be in sequence at all. I am resurrecting, after some eighteen years, an emendation which I proposed during discussions at a Southern Association for Ancient Philosophy meeting in Cambridge, which Richard Sorabji was kind enough to adopt and publicize (Sorabji (1983), 338), and which has occasionally surfaced since (Charlton (1991), 136; Bostock (1988), 265 n. 6). It is very hard to make sense of the transmitted πλείους δὲ μιᾶς οὐκ εἰσίν, ἐφεξῆς γὰρ οὐκ εἰσίν, since (a) there obviously *are* more points than one, and (b) no way (short of emendation) of filling out the meaning of the first clause so as to avoid this objection would help make it plausibly inferable from the second clause. Postulating a simple haplography seems the suitable cure.

[26] At 317^a11 I punctuate διαιρετόν; οὐ γάρ ἐστιν..., rather than, with Joachim (1922), adopt the supplement of T. W. Allen,...διαιρετόν· ⟨οὐκ ἔστι δέ,⟩ οὐ γάρ ἐστιν....

[27] 317^a11–12, οὐ γάρ ἐστιν ἐχόμενον σημεῖον σημείου ἢ στιγμὴ στιγμῆς. I have not given the last three words a separate translation, because I assume σημεῖον and στιγμή to be synonyms but cannot find an English synonym for 'point'. For competing attempts to prise the meanings of the two words apart see Joachim (1922), 86, and Mugler (1966), 81 and for the correct antidote see Netz (1999), 113, who explains that σημεῖον eventually ousted στιγμή for no more subtle a reason than that mathematicians intuitively preferred a neuter noun for points, so that an elliptical reference to a point (τό..., sc. σημεῖον) would be instantly distinguishable from one to a line (ἡ..., sc. γραμμή).

[28] The important distinction between 'potentially: everywhere divided' and 'everywhere: potentially divided' is widely seen as the correct solution to the Democritean argument and (therefore) often attributed to Aristotle. Just how far Aristotle's actual solution accommodates this insight has proved to be an unproductive way to approach the passage (cf. Williams (1982), 72–9, on the difficulties of extracting a fully coherent reading along these lines). One may hope to find Aristotle's equivalent of this distinction in one between divisibility 'everywhere' and divisibility 'at any point' or 'anywhere'. Throughout the neo-Democritean argument, however, καθ᾽ ὁτιοῦν σημεῖον is used interchangeably with πάντη, a conflation which Aristotle is still found assuming in chapter 5 (321^a3). In Aristotle's crucial moves against Democritus at 317^a2–9 one may suspect that an emergent distinction between the two terms (albeit with ὁπηοῦν replacing καθ᾽ ὁτιοῦν σημεῖον) is doing some of the work, but if so there is little sign that Aristotle sees that it is.

[29] That 'there is a point everywhere' may appear to amount to the truism that there is a point at every point. Properly, however, I suppose it means that there is a point at every *position* (θέσις) in the magnitude, where positions are determined by their geometrical coordinates.

the magnitude. What he does qualify is the claim that it can be *divided* at every one of those points: in a way it can, in a way it cannot ([b]).[30] The way in which it can is given in [d]: there is nowhere in it where there is not a point, and, since there is no difference between one point and another, if it can be divided at one it can be divided at all. The way in which it cannot be divided at every point is found at [c]: division at every point would produce the impossible consequences pointed out by Democritus. But what intervenes to save us from those consequences? The fact, with which Aristotle opens at [b] and concludes at [e], that points are not adjacent to each other,[31] so that no number of divisions could exhaust the magnitude. Between any two divisions further divisions will remain possible. Aristotle's aim in this is to show that, *even within an infinitely divisible continuum*, division at every point would be impossible, and thus to block off the atomist inference from the impossibility of division at every point to the non-existence of an infinitely divisible continuum—or, in other words, to the existence of atoms.

Why do interpreters in so far as they read Aristotle's answer along similar lines to the above tend to find it unsatisfactory? It may seem that from the non-adjacency of points it simply does not follow, as Aristotle may seem to think it does, that something could not be true of a magnitude at every point. A mathematician can generalize over all the fractions between 1 and 2, despite the fact that between any two of these there are others. And if I can, for example, paint the table-top blue at every point, why can I not divide it at every point?

Aristotle clearly is not concerned with the assignment of just any predicate to every member of such infinite sets as these, but with the assignment of divisibility in particular. The question which the neo-Democritean argument addressed at the end was how an exhaustive division might be actually carried out. It concluded that simultaneous division everywhere was impossible, and that a progressive division could never exhaust the magnitude. I suggest that Aristotle's way of responding to the atomist argument is largely conditioned by the terms in which it has been presented.

Aristotle shows no wish to defend, against the Democriteans, the idea of simultaneous division everywhere. Whether the divisions are envisaged

[30] Strictly 317^a7–8 appears to speak of a sense in which 'divisibility everywhere' is a property of the magnitude 'everywhere'. The pleonasm is harmless: Aristotle has simply slipped into thinking of unqualified 'divisibility' as the subject. There can be little doubt that divisibility, rather than e.g. 'a point', is the intended subject, since $^a7$–8, ἐστὶν ὡς ὑπάρχει πάντῃ, carefully picks up $^a3$–4, τὸ πάντῃ εἶναι διαιρετὸν ἔστι μὲν ὡς ὑπάρχει.

[31] At 317^a311–12 no two points are 'adjacent', whereas at $^a9$ (with or without my emendation, see n. 25 above) no two points are 'in sequence'. Since for Aristotle (e.g. *Ph*. VI. 1. 231^a23) two items are in sequence if there is nothing *of the same kind* between them (like neighbouring detached houses), clearly points could be in sequence only by being altogether adjacent.

as carried out with a knife, a pen, or a thought process, simultaneity makes little sense. It is only to be expected that he will for preference approach the problem in terms of progressive division. We should think of the following kind of series (taking a one-dimensional magnitude, for simplicity's sake):[32]

    (whole magnitude: 1 cm)
    set 1   1/2 cm between divisions
    set 2   1/4 cm between divisions
    set 3   1/8 cm between divisions

Aristotle's task would then be to show why we should not aspire to eventually reaching

    set ∞   no distance between divisions

There is a fairly obvious reason why we should not allow ourselves this aspiration: it is a mistake to think that there is such a set as set ∞. The temptation to think that there is such a set results from the realization that division goes on ad infinitum. But that in fact shows only that the series

    set 1, set 2, set 3 . . .

is an infinite series, and to say that it is an infinite series is to say that it has no last member; that is that there simply is no set ∞. Why then does Aristotle not simply make this point? In explaining why he does not, we can at last begin to see the difference that the neo-Democritean reformulation has made to Aristotle's own strategy for dealing with atomism.

The solution envisaged above is, I take it, in effect the one which Aristotle sketches in *Physics* VIII. 8 when he describes a magnitude as only *potentially* divisible to infinity. To say that it cannot actually be divided to infinity amounts to saying that there is no set ∞, just an endless series of sets. But in seeing this we also can recognize why Aristotle is debarred from invoking that solution here. The neo-Democritean, in [ND1], has turned Aristotle's own notion of potentiality against him: if the magnitude is potentially divisible to infinity (in the sense of being potentially divisible at every point), that should entail the possibility of such a division being realized. Unless Aristotle wishes to defend here and now the thoroughly counter-intuitive idea of a potentiality which is altogether incapable of actualization, he must answer the neo-Democritean in dialectically more acceptable terms.

---

[32] For a series of this kind see Porphyry *ap.* Simp. *in Ph.* 139. 27–32; and cf. Barnes (1979), i. 246 ff.

This, I believe, explains Aristotle's chosen strategy. Instead of arguing that we can never *reach* a set ∞ in the first place, he assumes hypothetically that there is such a set, and scrutinizes its mathematical properties, in order to arrive at an alternative account of why it cannot represent any actual or possible set of divisions.

Above I described set ∞ with the formula 'no distance between divisions'. Aristotle himself puts this by saying that the division points in set ∞ would need, impossibly, to be *adjacent* to each other. Is his intuition sound? There does after all exist a set consisting of all the *points* in the magnitude, despite the fact that no two of them are adjacent. Why should there then not equally exist a set consisting of *divisions* at all the points in the magnitude? The Aristotelian answer should be clear. It is because coexistent divisions, unlike coexistent points, have to be simultaneously actualized. A sufficient truth-condition for the ubiquity of points is that wherever you may look you are guaranteed to find one. But when it comes to the ubiquity of divisions it is hardly enough to explain it by saying that wherever you want to make a division you *can* do so. The neo-Democritean argument has forced Aristotle to allow that if there is such a thing as division everywhere it either is actual or at least could at some time become actual; and that actuality consists in the real separation of part from part (cf. [ND 2][b]). Once the parts are separated, we have to accept that each of them has no positive magnitude, or within it there would be further points at which the original magnitude had not yet been divided. But if each part has zero magnitude it follows that there is no distance separating the divisions on either side of it. Nor, on the other hand, can those divisions be altogether in one and the same place, or the original magnitude, far from being divided exhaustively, would turn out to have been divided at only one point. Hence the divisions really would have to be in a dense sequence, each of them directly adjacent to its neighbours. In short, Aristotle's conclusion is justified: a magnitude could be divided everywhere and reassembled, as envisaged in the Democritean and neo-Democritean arguments, only on the impossible hypothesis that there are adjacent points.

But if Aristotle here flags an impossible implication of allowing division everywhere, is he not simply reinforcing the case for denying division everywhere; that is, for postulating atoms? It is important to get it clear why he is not simply stating Democritus' own case for him. Democritus argued by drawing unacceptable consequences of an exhaustive division. Aristotle responds by producing mathematical reasons why, even allowing that the magnitude is divisible everywhere, one could in any case not get as far as completing an exhaustive division of it. Thus, if Aristotle is right, the question of its finite or infinite divisibility is simply irrelevant to explaining the fact on which he and Democritus agree; namely, that an exhaustive division cannot, on pain of absurdity, be carried out. To block the absurdity, there is no need to postulate atomic magnitudes: the non-adjacency of points already does the necessary work.

5. The reductive thesis

Why this elaborately contrived refutation of Democritean atomism? Aristotle makes it abundantly clear throughout the chapter that atomism is highlighted because it offers the only plausible version of the position he most urgently needs to refute; namely, the thesis that reduces generation to aggregation and destruction to disintegration—henceforth, the 'reductive thesis'. We may, for example, recall the conclusion of the neo-Democritean argument: '[ND2][c] Therefore it must necessarily contain unseen atomic magnitudes—*especially if generation is going to be by aggregation and destruction by disintegration*' (316^b33-4). Implicitly, the reductive thesis somehow relies on atomism and can therefore, if accepted, even constitute an additional ground in its favour. Why should it? To find out, we must read on and see how the chapter continues and concludes:

[C] [a] Hence there are aggregation and disintegration, but neither out of and into atoms, given the many impossibilities that follow from that, nor in such a way that division occurs everywhere (that is what would have been the case if point were adjacent to point). Rather, disintegrations are into small parts and then smaller ones, and aggregations are out of smaller parts.

[b] But absolute and complete generation <and destruction> are *not* defined by aggregation and disintegration, as some people think, adding that it is change in what is continuous that constitutes alteration. This is where all the errors lie. For absolute generation and destruction are not due to aggregation and disintegration: they are when there is a total change from x to y.

[c] Others believe that all this kind of change is alteration, but actually it is different. For in a subject some things are present definitionally, others materially. Hence when the change is in these, there will be generation and destruction, but when it is in the affections and accidental, there will be alteration.

[d] By being disintegrated and aggregated things become easily subject to destruction. For if (water) is divided into smaller droplets, it becomes air more quickly, whereas if it is aggregated it becomes air more slowly.

[e] This will become clearer in what follows. For now, however, let us take this much to be determined: that it is impossible that generation should be aggregation, such as some people say it is. (317^a12-31)

Aristotle is keen here to indicate just how destruction and disintegration *are* related. Disintegration does of course exist: it involves separation into smaller and smaller parts, but with no lower limit ([a]). Its relation to destruction is not one of equivalence, but one of *facilitation* ([d]). In the simple case of an elemental stuff like water, the more it disintegrates, the quicker it is destroyed, in this case into air: a spray of droplets evaporates quicker than a bucketful of water. But the disintegration does not itself amount to the water's destruction: any portion of water, however minute, is still water.[33]

One might want to object that the same hardly holds for non-homoeomers. A cat need be divided only once in order to stop being a cat. Nevertheless, as Aristotle insists in [b], destruction as such is a total change. The division of the cat may be a cause of its destruction, but, as [c] emphasizes, the actual destruction consists not in the cat's division but in the fact that every non-accidental constituent or aspect of it—its flesh, its bones, its blood, etc., and above all its essential form—ceases to be what it was, except perhaps homonymously.

Given that this is the kind of position which Aristotle is committed to defending, why does he perceive Democritus as presenting it with a challenge which cannot be ignored? Leaving aside here the difficult question of exactly how, where, and on what grounds Aristotle in *GC* I marginalizes those Presocratic physical theories which were in competition with atomism,[34] what should be beyond dispute is that in this book atomism is systematically singled out for its apparent explanatory power in accounting for alteration through atomic rearrangement. The point is developed early in chapter 2, alongside the atomist account of generation and destruction:

[RT] [a] But Democritus and Leucippus introduce their 'shapes' and create alteration and generation out of these—generation and destruction by their aggregation and disintegration, alteration by their arrangement and position.

[b] Because they thought that truth lies in appearance, and that appearances are contrary and infinitely many, they made the shapes infinitely many, so that through changes in its composition the same thing could appear in contrary ways to different people, and a small admixture could produce a transposition, and one transposition could produce an altogether different appearance: for a tragedy and a comedy are composed out of the same alphabet.

[c] Since nearly everybody thinks that there is a difference between generation and alteration, and that, while generation and destruction depend on aggregation and disintegration, alteration depends on changes of a thing's affections, we must dwell on this theory and study it. For it raises many reasonable problems. For if generation is aggregation, many impossible consequences follow. Yet there are further arguments, cogent and resistant to solution, showing that it cannot be otherwise. And if generation is *not* aggregation, either there is no

---

[33] Cf. I. 10. 328ᵃ10–12, 33–5, where a closely parallel point is made about mixture.
[34] See Chapters 1 above (by Brunschwig) and 9 below (by Hussey).

generation at all, or it is alteration. Or else we must try to solve this, difficult though it is. (315^b6–24)

The point made in [b] reinforces a perceived merit of atomism. The properties of macroscopic bodies being not absolute but observer-relative,[35] even quite radical changes in those properties—i.e. in the way they strike observers—may be the result of mere atomic rearrangement within the body. This contrasts favourably with the Empedocles and Anaxagoras already encountered in chapter 1, who identified qualities with specific elements (314^b15–26), and who therefore, by implication, could produce alteration only by means of adding or subtracting property stuffs. (Strictly, the atomists do not eliminate addition altogether from alteration, but its role is, according to [b], the minimal one of triggering the atomic rearrangements which actually constitute alteration[36]).

However, as [c] underlines, atomism seeks also to account for generation and destruction, and—given the glaring inadequacy of Plato's alternative—Democritean atomism offers the only rational support for the widely held assumption that generation and destruction amount to aggregation and disintegration. In doing so, however, it raises a whole cluster of issues which need to be debated, Aristotle adds: we may take these to be, more or less, the arguments for and against atomism set out in the main body of the chapter.

In all this Aristotle speaks as if atomism and the reductive thesis stand or fall together. But why? I shall return to this key question only at the very end, after considering the role of Plato in the story.

---

[35] The report that 'they thought that truth lies in appearance' (315^b9–10) is notoriously problematic (cf. Migliori (1976), 146–7) in view of the evidence for Democritus' anti-empiricism, evidence implicitly acknowledged by Aristotle at 316^a1–2 as regards the unreality of colour. For the purposes of the present context the apparent gesture towards empiricism need mean no more than that according to Democritus, in so far as there are truths about sensibles, these are observer-dependent, so that a thing's sensible properties are as various and as variable as the ways it strikes observers (cf. Mugler (1966: 78–9). However, that would not suffice to explain the parallel passage at *de An.* 404^a27–31, which in support of the same claim cites Democritus' failure to distinguish ψυχή and νοῦς.

[36] This could be a reason for hesitating to adopt, from West (1969), 150–1, the ingenious emendation of 315^b14–15, ἐκ τῶν αὐτῶν γὰρ τραγῳδία καὶ κωμῳδία γίνεται γραμμάτων to ἐκ τῶν αὐτῶν γὰρ τραγῳδία καὶ τρυγῳδία γίνεται γραμμάτων ⟨πλὴν ἑνός⟩ (τρυγῳδία being a rare word for 'comedy'). The emended text (treated with due caution by Migliori (1976), but adopted by Williams (1982), albeit without the final supplement) implies that the crucial change lies in the substitution of a single atom/letter. In fact, however, Democritus' real focus is not on the inserted atom but on the (consequent) realignment of the existing ones. The transmitted text conveys this better.

6. Democritus and Plato

The contrast between Democritus and Plato in the early part of the chapter is remarkable for its outspokenness.[37]

[DP][a] Plato inquired only about generation and destruction and how they belong to things; and as regards generation, he did not inquire about the whole of it, but about that of the elements, saying nothing about how flesh, bones and the like are generated. Again as regards alteration and growth, he did not inquire how they belong to things.

[b] Generally speaking, nobody has dwelt more than superficially on any aspect, except Democritus. He seems to have thought about all aspects, but to have excelled when it came to the question of *how* they belong to things. For as I have said, no one specified anything about growth beyond what *anyone* might say, namely that it occurs through something being added to what is like it (with no further comment on *how* this happens); nor about mixture, nor about virtually any of the other kinds, such as action and passion and the question how in natural actions one thing is their agent, the other their patient. (315^{a}29–^{b}6)

[Here follows [RT], see pp. 83–4 above.]

[c] The starting point of all this is whether existing things are generated, alter and grow, and undergo the opposites of these, because the primary magnitudes are indivisible ones, or whether there is no indivisible magnitude: that makes a huge difference. And again, if these are magnitudes, are they bodies, as Democritus and Leucippus say, or planes, as in the *Timaeus*? Well, this very idea of resolving everything into planes is unreasonable, as I have said elsewhere. Hence it is more reasonable that there should be indivisible *bodies*. But these too produce much that is unreasonable. Nevertheless, for these people it is possible to bring about alteration and generation, as I have said, transposing the same thing by turning, contact and differences of shape, as Democritus does (thus denying the existence of colour, since he says things are coloured by turning), whereas those who divide things into planes lose the power to do this: from the conjoining of planes nothing more than solids arises, since they do not even attempt to generate any affection out of them.

[d] The cause of a reduced ability to see things which are a matter of agreement is inexperience. Hence those who are more at home in physics (ὅσοι ἐνῳκήκασι μᾶλλον ἐν τοῖς φυσικοῖς, 316^{a}6) have a greater ability to posit principles of a kind which can connect up more extensively, while those who, coming from a background which lies primarily in discourse (λόγοι), have failed to study reality, find it easier to make their assertions after looking at just a few facts.

[e] One might observe also from the following considerations how great the difference is between those who investigate in the physical mode (φυσικῶς) and those who do so in the discursive mode (λογικῶς). On the existence of atomic magnitudes, the latter party say that otherwise the Triangle Itself will be many, whereas Democritus would appear to hold his view on the basis of appropriate

---

[37] Contrast I. 8. 325^{b}25–33, where it is Leucippus, not Democritus, who represents the atomists: the comparison between him and Plato involves no relative evaluation at all.

physical arguments (οἰκείοις καὶ φυσικοῖς λόγοις). What I mean will be clear when we proceed. (315^{b}24–316^{a}14)

Democritus' superior credentials as a physicist lie in

(i)   his attention to empirical fact ([d]);
(ii) his proper concern with explaining *how* natural processes occur ([b]);[38]
(iii) the comprehensiveness of his enquiries, compared with Plato's extreme selectivity ([a], [b], [d]);
(iv) his sticking to concepts apposite to physics, by contrast with Plato's inappropriate reliance on mathematical entities like his primary planes, which belong to the realm of pure discourse (λόγοι, [d], λογικῶς, [e]) rather than to physics.

There is much here which, adequately examined, would take us too far from our task. For instance, the line of attack summarized under (iv) reflects the *deuteros plous* in the *Phaedo*.[39] Plato is condemned out of his own mouth: Socrates' avowed abandonment of physics for *logoi* (*Phd.* 99e) in Aristotle's eyes represents Plato's confession of failure as a physicist, a failure which, when he came to focus on physics in the *Timaeus*, he merely compounded.

For the present we must stick to the bearing of Aristotle's critique on the issue of indivisibles. It is a revealingly contrived attack. Why, in [a], is Plato accused of paying attention to generation only as regards that of the elements, and not 'flesh, bones and the like', given that Timaeus explicitly turns to the latter at 73b–c? Far from overlooking the Platonic passage, Aristotle is referring to it (compare 315^{a}31–2, πῶς δὲ σάρκες ἢ ὀστᾶ ἢ τῶν ἄλλων τι τῶν τοιούτων, οὐδέν, with *Ti.* 73b, τὸ δὲ ὀστῶν καὶ σαρκῶν καὶ τῆς τοιαύτης φύσεως πέρι πάσης ὧδε ἔσχεν). His point is precisely that Plato here failed to explain *how* (πῶς, cf. (ii) above) the generation of these stuffs comes about: Timaeus simply nominates the store of triangles in the marrow as their source, adding nothing about how these triangles combine[40]—presumably by constituting

---

[38] 315^{a}35–^{b}1, οὗτος δ' ἔοικε μὲν περὶ ἁπάντων φροντίσαι, ἤδη δὲ ἐν τῷ πῶς διαφέρειν. Not, with the majority of interpreters (Joachim (1922), Tricot (1951), Forster (1955), Mugler (1966), and Migliori (1976)): 'He seems to have thought about all aspects, but to have excelled in *how* he did so', but, with Williams (1982): '. . . to have excelled when it came to the question of *how* they belong to things', as is amply confirmed by 315^{a}33, ^{b}3, 5.

[39] Aristotle's further remarks against Plato in *GC* II. 9 strengthen the impression that he has the *deuteros plous* in his sights. Note, however, that his characterization of Presocratic views on growth at 315^{b}1–3 ([DP][b]) draws on Socrates' critique of his own early (Presocratic, as it were) assumptions at *Phd.* 96c–d.

[40] Cf. *Cael.* III. 8. 306^{b}22–9, where Aristotle denies that *continuous* stuffs like flesh and bone could, as Plato required, be composed either out of the elementary particles or out of their constituent triangles.

specific elementary solids in the first instance—to produce flesh, etc. Aristotle does, it is true, seem to forget the short passage at *Timaeus* 60e–61c on stuffs which are explicitly compounded out of two or more elements, but it remains quite true that the great bulk of Timaeus' account of the constitution of stuffs at 58c–61c does indeed present each of them as a specific form of one of the four elements (despite the fact that particles of another element are in some cases said also to be present in them), and a surprising range of stuffs turn out to be, in reality, simply specific forms of this or that element. Hence it is no gross misrepresentation of Plato if Aristotle reads him as making absolute generation the combination not of separate elements into a compound but of discrete triangles into elementary solids.

The primary triangles (i.e. the basic half-equilateral and right-angled isosceles triangles out of which the faces of the elemental solids are composed) are taken by Aristotle to be indivisible (cf. I. 8. 325^{b}26–7, 33, 326^{a}22), following the interpretation defended in his day by Xenocrates,[41] the probable author of the desperate-sounding argument for the indivisibility thesis (cf. *LI* 968^{a}9–14) which Aristotle carefully selects for citation in [e]. Thus Aristotle's picture of Platonic generation and destruction is as occurring not in aggregation and disintegration at just any level but specifically at the very lowest level, below which further separation is actually impossible. Plato, however misconceived his actual theory may be, does to this extent conform to Aristotle's at first sight surprising assumption—the one which governs the entire content of this chapter—that the reductive thesis, which equates generation with aggregation and destruction with disintegration, stands or falls with the postulation of indivisibles. Why the triangles need be indivisible I shall consider shortly.

But how could Democritean atomism be viewed in the same light? In the case of Platonic physics, separation of, say, fire into its primary particles does not yet constitute its destruction, and only the further resolution of a pyramidal fire particle into its ultimate constituent triangles does. If so, parity of reasoning would suggest that Democritean fire, whose primary particles *cannot* be thus subdivided, is altogether indestructible: a single spherical fire atom should still be fire. Democritean destruction will, it seems, make sense only for stuffs which are compounds of two or more types of atom. Take a compound, X, requiring two type-y atoms to every one type-z atom. The disintegration of some initial quantity of X, all the way down to single y-y-z portions,

---

[41] That Xenocrates' thesis of indivisible lines applied to the Timaean triangles, and served his defence of the Timaean world's everlastingness, I argue in Sedley (2002), 67–8.

continues to yield nothing but X. Only when one of these final molecular portions is separated out into its constituent atoms is X destroyed.

We can see, then, that although Plato and Democritus both do, in their own ways, conform to Aristotle's assumption that the reductive thesis depends on indivisibles, they do so in different and even incompatible ways. For Plato the assumption is true only for simple elemental stuffs, for Democritus only for compound stuffs. Do they then have enough in common to be bracketed as they are in the present chapter?

Now if Democritus' account is thought by Aristotle to depend on the atomicity of the ultimate particles, that is presumably because on a competing continuist analysis, such as an Anaxagoras might offer, the constituents of a compound totally interpenetrate: hence no amount of fragmentation of the compound's spatial parts (as distinct from separation of its ingredients)[42] will prevent the resultant fragments from still being bits of that very same compound. Conversely, if fragmentation does end up as destruction of the original compound, that must be because the interpenetration was incomplete. To show that this incomplete interpenetration presupposes atomism, Aristotle simply has to assume—as he certainly does (*GC* I. 10. 327^{b}31–328^{a}17, cf. I. 9. 327^{a}11–14)—that in a true mixture the ingredients interpenetrate all the way down. Hence if their fusion encounters a lower limit, that is because it has reached a magnitude below which they cannot be further divided and interspersed.

If my last paragraph was on the right lines, it becomes at least a little clearer why Plato has been brought under the same heading as Democritus. For he too holds a version of the reductive thesis that the fragmentation of a stuff, taken far enough, becomes its destruction. That is already enough to show why Aristotle must assume, despite the absence of any specific indication to this effect in the *Timaeus*, that Plato's primary triangles are indivisible; otherwise there would simply be no explanation of why fragmentation and interspersal never extend below the level of these triangles.

7. Conclusion

It is, then, those who impose a lower limit on fragmentation who also hold that destruction occurs when that lower limit is reached, and who sustain the converse thesis as regards generation. And Plato and Democritus are

---

[42] It is clear from [C][a] and [d] that in I. 2 aggregation and disintegration are not identified with mixture and separation of ingredients, even though some such equivalence is introduced in I. 6. 322^{b}8.

the leading representatives of this tradition. Why then is Aristotle, as we have seen, at such pains to differentiate between the two of them? In order to eliminate a position such as the reductive thesis, he acknowledges that he must show it to be untenable *even in its strongest form*. This is achieved in two stages. First, we are shown why Democritus, as a truly professional physicist, is the legitimate spokesman for the reductive thesis, while Plato can be safely sidelined. Second, Democritus is permitted not only to expound his arguments for atomism but also to reformulate them with the help of the very latest conceptual tools, courtesy of Aristotle. In the end, despite being permitted every advantage, Democritus' position is still found unsustainable. Aristotle expects his readers to agree that the thesis of indivisibles, and along with it the reduction of generation and destruction to aggregation and disintegration, have by now been definitively disposed of.[43]

[43] My thanks, for helpful comments on an unscripted antecedent of this paper, to various members of an audience at the Padua Aristotle seminar in December 1998 (kindly organized by Enrico Berti), and to a Cambridge M.Phil. class in January 1999. The subsequent scripted paper benefited from a thorough critique at the Symposium Aristotelicum itself; I am grateful to all participants in that discussion (especially to Christian Wildberg for clarifying to me the point now developed in the last paragraph of p. 66), and to John Cooper, Alan Code, and Geoffrey Lloyd for further correspondence. I have subsequently presented to audiences at Ann Arbor, Toronto, and Princeton a paper on Democritean atomism which incorporated a large part of the present chapter: I am grateful to audiences on all three occasions for their helpful input, and especially to Sylvia Berryman, my commentator at Princeton.

3

On Generation and Corruption I. 3: Substantial Change and the Problem of Not-Being

KEIMPE ALGRA

Introduction

My contribution to this book deals with the 'chapter' in which Aristotle discusses coming to be *simpliciter* (*simpliciter* is the standard rendering of ἁπλῶς). This 'chapter' constitutes a relatively autonomous section of *GC* book I. To bring this out I provide an overview of its structure and argumentation in Section 1 below. Comments on particular points of detail will be appended here as footnotes. In the three sections that follow (2–4) the discussion will focus on three separate, though interrelated, issues. Section 2 will deal with the problem concerning the referent of 'not-being *simpliciter*' (τὸ ἁπλῶς μὴ ὄν) in *GC* I. 3. Section 3 will examine how Aristotle's account in *GC* I. 3 relates to an analysis found in *Physics* book I. It will appear that, contrary to what some commentators have suggested, these two treatments of the problem of coming to be *simpliciter* are in the relevant respects not different—let alone incompatible. Section 4, finally, will discuss Aristotle's use of the term ἁπλῶς, here in *GC* I. 3 as well as in *Physics* book I. Finally, by way of conclusion I shall append a few notes of a more general nature about Aristotle's use of common language.

Discussing the referent of 'not-being *simpliciter*' (τὸ ἁπλῶς μὴ ὄν) in Section 2 will inevitably get us involved in the thorny controversy over whether or not the notion of *prima materia* plays any role in this text. I shall argue that it does not. Some may find that this amounts to flogging the proverbial dead horse. After all, today the politically correct view appears to be that there is no such thing as prime matter in Aristotle at all, and that this is in fact how it *should* be, the notion itself being basically un-Aristotelian, or even intrinsically incoherent. However, I believe that it is unwise to take this new *communis opinio* for granted. The alleged incoherence of the notion of prime matter can hardly be established without circularity. Moreover the fact that quite a few serious philosophers and scholars have failed to regard this notion as incoherent

at all, or as odd, should certainly make us pause.[1] And if the supposition
is that Aristotle himself was of the opinion that there really can be no
such thing as prime matter, one is entitled to wonder why he never clearly
said so, especially since the idea of prime matter would readily have
suggested itself to anyone familiar with the 'receptacle' of Plato's
Timaeus—as Aristotle, after all, was. Although he does attack Plato's
account of the receptacle, he does not, to my knowledge, criticize Plato
for having illegitimately introduced some kind of prime matter.[2]

A full answer to the question whether or not the tradition of Aristotelian commentators has been right to credit Aristotle with the concept of
prima materia would involve not only exploring the *Wortlaut* of many
individual passages in Aristotle, but also examining the philosophical
presuppositions which have guided the interpretation of these passages
by others. This would of course lead us way beyond the limits set to the
present chapter, or even the present book. All the same a few introductory generalities concerning prime matter will be needed to put our
analysis of *GC* I. 3 into perspective.

Where matter figures as the *ex hou* (ἐξ οὗ, the 'that-out-of-which') of
substantial transformation, that is as its *terminus a quo*, the notion of
prime matter is not explicitly presupposed by Aristotle (our 'chapter' will
prove to be a case in point), not even at the level of the transformation of
the four elements. Here matter, in the sense of *terminus a quo*, is a
particular substance, regarded under a particular description; namely, as
hupokeimenon (ὑποκείμενον) of a particular substantial change.[3] In other
words, at what we might call the semantic level—i.e. in so far as it comes to
describing the physical processes involved—Aristotle does not need the
concept of *prima materia*. But the fact that, for descriptive purposes, a so-
called 'proximate' matter is fit to play the role of the *ex hou* of substantial
generation does not in itself preclude any commitment to prime matter as
such on Aristotle's part. After all, matter as the *hupokeimenon* of substantial change is not merely the *terminus a quo*, for Aristotle also claims that it
in some way or other *persists* in substantial change.[4] It surely is legitimate
to ask what exactly this is supposed to mean.

---

[1] The notion of prime matter figures, in various versions, in all important commentaries
on *GC*: Philoponus, Thomas Aquinas, Joachim (1922), Tricot (1955), Williams (1982). See
further, below n. 10.

[2] Aristotle's main point against Plato at *GC* II. 1. 329ᵃ24–6 appears to be that he
conceived of matter (i.e. the receptacle) as *separable* (and of course he criticizes Plato's
account of the receptacle as being unclear in various respects, 329ᵃ14). But he expresses no
qualms about the idea as such of the τιθήνη being πρώτη ὕλη (329ᵃ23).

[3] This is why Aristotle can claim that matter is a relative (*pros ti*), and that 'for different
forms there is different matter', *Ph.* II. 2. 194ᵇ8–9.

[4] It is for this reason that the product of the transformation may be called ἐκείνινον; cf.
Metaph. Z 7. 1033ᵃ5–23 and Θ 7. 1049ᵃ18–ᵇ3.

One could in principle try to make sense of this notion of persistence as well by taking it to operate merely at the level of description. On such an interpretation we may *say* that, when water turns into air water-qua-matter persists in air, in the sense that we may *say* that *what* is now air formerly was water. But neither the water as such nor any supposed indefinite substratum physically persists and survives the change. Although this solution may work at the level of categorization, or Aristotelian semantics, it is not clear whether it provides us with a workable physical theory. For doesn't this way of accounting for persist-ence confuse *explanans* and *explanandum* in a way that recalls Molière's doctors?[5]

Of course one might simply accept this as an inevitable concomitant of Aristotle's phenomenological approach in physics.[6] Alternatively, how-ever, one might fall back on the traditional notion of prime matter and consider the possibility that Aristotle did try to go beyond a more or less formal or semantic approach. After all, he may well have thought that, at least at the level of the elements, the 'continuousness' in change—the fact that we may say that 'what' was water is now air—is to be explained with reference to some persisting ultimate subject (now of one set of proper-ties, now of another).[7] There are some passages which at first (and perhaps also at second) reading appear to allow, or even suggest, such an interpretation. Thus there is *GC* II. 1, where matter is said to be 'inseparable from but underlying the contraries' (τὴν ἀχώριστον μέν ὑποκειμένην δὲ τοῖς ἐναντίοις, 329ᵃ30–31), and to be 'that which poten-tially is a perceptible body' (τὸ δυνάμει σῶμα αἰσθητόν, 329ᵃ33), and as

---

[5] The famous Molièrian parody (in the *troisième intermède* of his *Malade imaginaire*) of what an Aristotelian might regard as the formal cause runs that 'opium facit dormire [. . .] quia est in eo | virtus dormitiva | cujus est natura | sensus assoupire'. But here the *virtus dormitiva*, though inept as an explanatory factor, is at least identified as an entity in its own right, contrary to the 'persisting something' in the interpretation discussed in the text to this note.

[6] By this I mean an approach on reality through the ways in which we think and speak of physical processes, with first principles such as matter being a kind of functional terms or *Leerstellen*. Cf. Wieland (1962), 143: 'Wenn er sich nähmlich mit seinen Vorgängern auseinandersetzt [. . .] so stellt er den Lehren dieser Denker mit seiner eigenen Prinzipien-lehre überhaupt nichts entgegen, was mit diesen Lehren auf derselben begrifflichen Ebene stünde. Denn wenn Aristoteles allgemein von den Prinzipien redet, so gibt er überhaupt keine sachhaltige Bestimmung, und er sagt nicht *was* das Prinzip, bzw. die Prinzipien eigentlich sind'.

[7] It is not intuitively obvious, to say the least, that in the course of the process of elemental transformation from, say, water to air, water itself, qua matter, persists in the same sense in which bronze persists in a brazen statue. This problem appears to be overlooked when one simply treats Aristotelian matter as a 'functional term for whatever it is that endures through a change in the capacity of substratum' (Code (1976), 365).

such a kind of *archê* different from the elements as such (329^a35).[8] There are also other contexts—especially those in which the focus is not so much on substantial change (with matter in the role of the *ex hou*) but on the ontological analysis of static substances—where matter does appear to play the role of fundamental subject of properties and where an interpretation in terms of prime matter easily suggests itself (cf. *Metaph.* Z 3. 1029^a17–18; *Ph.* IV. 2. 209^b10 and 211^b30–$212\ ^a2$).[9]

Against this background we need not be too surprised to find that commentators have disagreed on whether or not the notion of prime matter as a fundamental substrate was at the back of Aristotle's mind when he discussed, for example, the process of elemental transformation in *GC*.[10] To my mind the only responsible way to deal with individual passages discussing these subjects is to assume neither that Aristotle *must* have been thinking of prime matter, nor that he *cannot* have been thinking of it, but to examine what he actually says and to proceed on the basis of the signposting of his own text. This is what I shall try to do in the present chapter. Accordingly my conclusions about matter in *GC* I. 3 are just that: they merely answer the question of the role of matter in the account of *GC* I. 3. As such they leave the *general* controversy about prime matter largely as it is.

1. The structure of the argument

GC I. 3 discusses a series of questions which are more or less clearly separated in the text. To facilitate the discussion, I have numbered these questions Q1–Q6:

Q1 $(317^a32$–4): Is there such a thing as coming to be *simpliciter?*

Q2 $(317^b18$–19): How can coming to be *simpliciter* be described (in particular: How are we to describe its *terminus a quo*)?

Q3 $(317^b34$–5): How can we explain that coming to be and perishing always go on and never fail?

---

[8] Also Aristotle's claim at *Ph.* I. 7. 191^a7–11 that the 'underlying' can be 'grasped by analogy' has often been taken as pointing to prime matter, but see the rightly sceptical comments of Charlton (1970), 78–9.

[9] For interpretations (Neoplatonic and other) of the famous passage in *Metaph.* Z in terms of prime matter see Sorabji (1988), 3–43. For a different interpretation see Schofield (1972), and the sceptical comments of Frede and Patzig (1988), ii. 46. The two passages from *Ph.* IV figure in a dialectical context in which Aristotle may primarily have had Plato's receptacle in mind, but there is no indication that he criticizes Plato for introducing prime matter *as such*; the critique aims rather at Plato's identification of matter *and place*.

[10] For a survey of passages from *GC* which have been believed to express commitment to prime matter see the appendix, 'Prime Matter in *de generatione et corruptione*', in Williams (1982), 211–19.

Q4 (318^{a}27–9): If the coming to be of one thing is the perishing of another, why do we speak of some substantial changes as coming to be *simpliciter* whereas in other cases we say that a thing comes to be this/something (similarly with passing away)?

Q5 (319^{a}2–3): Why in general (i.e. apart from the cycle of substantial generation) do we apply 'coming to be *simpliciter*' to some things and 'coming to be this' to others?

Q6 (319^{a}29–^{b}4—actually a series of questions): How should we further characterize the not-being *simpliciter* from which coming to be *simpliciter* originates?

On the basis of Aristotle's own signposting we may now have a closer look at how the chapter is structured by these questions and by the problems generated in turn by the answers that are given.

317^{a}32

Using a brief introductory formula Aristotle begins by linking the investigation he is about to embark on to the distinctions that have been made in what precedes (διωρισμένων δὲ τούτων, 317^{a}32).[11] He is presumably referring back to the end of ch. 2, where we have been told—after an elaborate discussion of the atomists' explanation of coming to be (and passing away) and the physical principles involved—that coming to be cannot be identified with aggregation (σύγκρισις) but instead takes place 'when something changes from this to that as a whole' (ὅταν μεταβάλλει ἐκ τοῦδε εἰς τόδε ὅλον, 317^{a}21). Since some other philosophers have regarded precisely this formula as the formula of alteration or qualitative change (*alloiôsis*), we have also been told briefly (a more eleborate discussion will follow in ch. 4) how *genesis* and *alloiôsis* differ.

317^{a}32– 317^{b}18

The first question (Q1) to ask now is whether there is anything that comes to be *simpliciter* (πότερον ἔστι τι γινόμενον ἁπλῶς, 317^{a}33), a question which is identical to the question whether coming to be exists *simpliciter* (ἁπλῶς ἔσται γένεσις, 317^{b}2), which is in its turn apparently equivalent to the question whether there is such a thing as unqualified coming to be, or coming to be *simpliciter* (ἁπλῆ sc. γένεσις, 317^{b}5). The problem is that such a *genesis* must be 'from not-being *simpliciter*' (ἐξ ἁπλῶς μὴ ὄντος, 317^{b}5). The term *simpliciter* (ἁπλῶς) in this formula

---

[11] According to Joachim (1922), ad loc. Aristotle has the 'meaning of the terms γένεσις and φθορά' in mind, or their 'nominal definitions'. This is perhaps a shade too specific, for no full definitions have been given thus far.

may according to Aristotle be interpreted in two ways: it may single out the highest genus in each category (in the present case, where we are dealing with the category substance, the not-being *simpliciter* would accordingly be 'non-substance');[12] or it may be used to indicate that the word(s) it qualifies are used in the most general sense (τὸ καθόλου καὶ τὸ πάντα περιέχον), in which case the not-being *simpliciter* would be absolute not-being. On both readings—also on the former, for not-being in the sense of non-substance cannot be anything else— we end up with a conclusion which is prima facie absurd; namely, that coming to be *simpliciter* is coming to be from absolute non-being. This aporia has been treated elsewhere in more detail (διηπόρηται καὶ διώρισται, 317ᵇ14)—below I shall defend the view that the reference is to *Physics*. I. 8—but the solution must be 'briefly restated here as well' (συντόμως δὲ καὶ νῦν λεκτέον): the not-being at issue is 'that which is potentially but is not actually' (δυνάμει ὂν ἐντελεχείᾳ δὲ μὴ ὄν). As that which pre-exists it is 'said in both ways' (317ᵇ17–18, λεγόμενον ἀμφοτέρως).[13]

---

[12] It is a bit odd that after having spoken of the highest genus in *each* category, Aristotle abruptly adds that in that case *substance* would come out of non-substance, but I follow Philoponus, Aquinas, Joachim, and Williams in assuming that he simply takes it for granted that in the present context the substantial category is the primarily relevant one. Note that Thomas Aquinas' position on this issue is slightly misrepresented in Williams (1982), 82. According to Williams, Aquinas' phrase 'uno modo ut significat id quod est primum inter omnia praedicamenta entis' represents an *alternative reading* of the Greek τὸ πρῶτον κατ' ἑκάστην κατηγορίαν, a reading which, he claims, may be linguistically impossible (reading 'all' for 'each') but makes better philosophical sense. However, we are not dealing with an alternative *reading* or *translation* of Aristotle's Greek, but with a *reconstruction* or *interpretation* which *assumes* that the argument is about the category of substance. This is clear from the way Thomas continues: 'uno modo ut significat id quod est primum inter omnia praedicamenta entis, *prout scilicet simpliciter ens dicitur de substantia*; alio modo secundum quod simpliciter ens dicitur ipsum ens universale, quod omnia praedicamenta comprehendit' (*In GC* lb.1, lo.6, n5). In other words, in Aquinas' reconstruction we get basically the same argument as in the interpretations of Philoponus, Joachim, and Williams. Note, incidentally, that Thomas of course used a Latin translation, probably a version of the *translatio vetus* (now available in the 1986 edition of Joanna Judycka, in vol. ix. 1 of the *Aristoteles Latinus*), which has recently been attributed to Burgundio of Pisa by Vuillemin-Diem and Rashed (1997). The *translatio vetus* in fact renders the Greek phrase at issue quite adequately as 'primum . . . secundum unumquodque predicamentum entis'.

[13] The same model is presupposed at *Cael*. III. 2. 301ᵇ31–302ᵃ9, where Aristotle rejects coming to be *simpliciter* (in the sense of absolute coming to be or coming to be *ex nihilo*) on the basis of the impossibility of the existence of a separate void. The details of the argument need not concern us here. What is relevant in connection with *GC* I. 3 is the fact that ordinary substantial generation is presented as starting from 'what is potentially a particular kind of body' (δυνάμει ὂν σῶμα) which is 'in actuality some other kind of body beforehand' (ἄλλο σῶμα ἐνεργείᾳ πρότερον, 302ᵃ6–7).

317ᵇ18–33

But even if these things have been sorted out (καὶ τούτων διωρισμένων), a second question (Q2) must be answered which involves a 'most remarkable aporia' (θαυμαστὴ ἀπορία): *How* can there be coming to be *simpliciter*? In other words, after the question of 'whether' (πότερον) has been answered, we are still faced with the question of 'how' (πῶς).[14] Should we say that there is coming to be of substance, but not of quality, quantity, and 'where'? If we assume, that these properties are themselves also only potentially present in what is potentially a substance, we must conclude, absurdly, that there is something which exists in its own right without being qualified in any way (χωριστὸν το μὴ οὕτως ὄν).[15] If, on the other hand, they exist in full actuality in what is potentially a substance, we must conclude—equally absurdly—that properties (πάθη) exist apart from (actual) substances.

317ᵇ33–318ᵃ3

These questions (subquestions of Q2, which thus turns out to be a question about the nature of the *terminus a quo* of coming to be *simpliciter*) are to be addressed in connection with the question why coming to be never ceases (περί τε τούτων ... πραγματευτέον καὶ τίς αἰτία τοῦ γένεσιν ἀεὶ εἶναι, i.e. Q3). The latter question will here have to be addressed from the point of view of the material cause only (18ᵃ9).[16] Identifying this material cause may at the same time contribute to the solution of

---

[14] In his comments on 317ᵃ32 Joachim (1922), 88, suggests that the second main question is the question 'what is the cause of there always being generation', which is broached later on, at 317ᵇ34–5. But although the question of the cause of the ceaseless cycle of generation and perishing is important, it is itself only introduced to help in clearing up the 'how' question. Moreover the end of the section dealing with the first question (the question 'whether'), and the beginning of the section dealing with the second, are clearly signposted at 317ᵇ18, where we are told that 'now that these things have been settled' (τούτων διωρισμένων) the question of the 'how' presents itself next. The structure of the argument is thus determined by the sequence of these two familiar question types, in accordance with the programmatic statement at the beginning of ch. 2 (315ᵃ26: περὶ γενέσεως καὶ φθορᾶς τῆς ἁπλῆς λεκτέον, πότερον ἔστιν ἢ οὐκ ἔστι καὶ πῶς ἐστίν, καὶ περὶ τῶν ἄλλων ἁπλῶν κινήσεων κτλ.). See also the way Aristotle winds up the whole discussion of *genesis* and *alloiôsis* (i.e. of the first four chapters) at the end of ch. 4 (320ᵃ6: περὶ μὲν οὖν γενέσεως, εἴτε ἔστιν εἴτε μή, καὶ πῶς ἔστι, καὶ περὶ ἀλλοιώσεως διωρίσθω τοῦτον τὸν τρόπον.

[15] For this interpretation of the words το μὴ οὕτως ὄν see Joachim (1922), ad loc. Philoponus *in GC* 48. 25 takes το μὴ οὕτως ὄν as equivalent to τὸ μὴ ὂν οὕτως ('what is not in this way'), and as referring back to what has just been described as τὸ μηδὲν ὂν κατ᾽ ἐνέργειαν. The two interpretations appear to be equivalent *ad sententiam*.

[16] For a closer study of the efficient cause in this connection Aristotle refers us to (1) to 'the treatise on movement' (τοῖς περὶ κινήσεως λόγοις), i.e. presumably *Ph.* VIII. 6.

Q2 (ἅμα γὰρ ἄν ἴσως τοῦτο γένοιτο δῆλον, καὶ περὶ τοῦ νῦν ἀπορηθέντος, πῶς ποτε δεῖ λέγειν καὶ περὶ τῆς ἁπλῆς φθορᾶς καὶ γενέσεως).

318ᵃ13–27

But however helpful an answer to Q3 may be in the context of our attempts to answer Q2, question Q3 itself presents enough problems in its own right (ἔχει δ' ἀπορίαν ἱκανὴν καὶ τί τὸ αἴτιον τοῦ συνείρειν τὴν γένεσιν, 318ᵃ13)[17] given that passing away is passing away into not-being, and that the sum total of the available material must be finite. Shouldn't, in that case, the cosmos have been annihilated long ago? The answer at any rate is not that the *ex hou* is infinite—whether actually or potentially (i.e. in so far as it can be cut down to ever smaller pieces).[18] The correct answer is only very briefly stated: the fact that the passing away of one thing constitutes the coming to be of another provides us with a sufficient explanation (ἱκανὴν αἰτίαν).[19]

318ᵃ27–ᵇ33

A further question (Q4) arises: What are the conditions which govern our use of 'coming to be' (or 'passing away') *simpliciter*, as opposed to 'coming to be something' (and 'passing away as something').[20] This

---

258ᵇ10 ff., where in general both the unmoved and the moved are discussed; (2) to first philosophy, where the study of the first unmoved mover properly belongs; and (3) to his treatment ὕστερον, i.e. in *GC* II. 10, in so far as not only the πρῶτον κινούμενον, i.e. the first moved mover, but also the subsequent, and for sublunar phenomena more directly relevant, movement of the sun 'in the inclined circle' (κατὰ τὸν λόξον κύκλον) is concerned.

[17] Note that the formula τί τὸ αἴτιον τοῦ συνείρειν τὴν γένεσιν ('what is the cause of the continued succession of generation') simply rephrases Q3 (τίς αἰτία τοῦ γένεσιν ἀεὶ εἶναι) in different words. Hence, the particle καί in the phrase ἔχει δ' ἀπορίαν ἱκανὴν καὶ τί τὸ αἴτιον τοῦ συνείρειν τὴν γένεσιν does not mark off a *new* question, as is suggested by the translation of Mugler (1966): 'une question assez difficile est *aussi* celle de savoir quelle est la cause de l'enchaînement de la génération' (my emphasis). In fact Q3 has already been presented as a question that can be used to solve Q2, and we are now told that also (καί) Q3 involves enough problems in its own right. This is better brought out in Forster's translation ('what is the cause of the continuous process of coming to be is a perplexing enough problem'), or in the revised Oxford translation (Barnes (1984): 'our new question too . . . is sufficiently perplexing').

[18] The former possibility (actual infinity) is theoretically excluded anyway (318ᵃ20: 'nothing is actually infinite'), the latter simply doesn't square with what we see (318ᵃ21–3: 'so the only possible inexhaustible generation would be due to something smaller always coming into existence—but in fact this is not what we see').

[19] For a similarly brief statement of the principle (in the context of Aristotle's discussion of infinity) see *Ph.* III. 8. 208ᵃ8–11.

[20] Williams (1982), 89, notes that we are here dealing with 'a new use of *haplôs*'. This, I think, is not the case (see my remarks on *haplôs* in the context of *GC* I. 3 in Sect. 3 below. We are rather dealing with a more careful look at the criteria which govern our *use* of the expressions ἁπλῶς γίνεσθαι and ἁπλῶς φθείρεσθαι.

question is all the more pressing since the passing away of one thing is the coming to be of another (εἴπερ τοαὐτό ἐστι γένεσις μὲν τουδὶ φθορὰ δὲ τουδί).[21] We are not dealing with individual cases, but with the general pattern (τὸ δὴ ταῦτα ἢ ἕτερα ὑποτίθεσθαι διαφέρει οὐδέν· τὸν γὰρ τρόπον ζητοῦμεν, ἀλλ' οὐ τὸ ὑποκείμενον). It appears that ordinary usage applies 'coming to be *simpliciter*' (as opposed to 'coming to be something)' in two ways (τρόποι); or, perhaps we should say: its use is governed by two rules.[22] Both turn on one of the two termini being either more or less of a *tode ti*:

(1) Whenever of two termini the *terminus ad quem* represents being whereas the *terminus a quo* represents not-being, the process of coming to be may be described as 'coming to be *simpliciter*'.

(2) Whenever the distinguishing marks of the matter involved in the process signify being, we are dealing with a substance (i.e. being); when they signify privation we are dealing with not-being.[23] At this point most people go astray, in focusing on the wrong distinguishing mark. They assume that the issue hinges on perceptibility or imperceptibility: they speak of coming to be *simpliciter* when there is a change from the imperceptible to perceptible material. But *doxa* and *alêtheia* do not

---

[21] Why this addition? Presumably because, although we now know that the same process may be described at the same time as a process of coming to be and as a process of passing away, it cannot be described as both coming to be *simpliciter* and passing away *simpliciter*. And in practice it *is* not, for there will always be a 'preferred perspective'; cf. 318^b33–4: 'coming to be *simpliciter* is the passing away of something, and passing away *simpliciter* is the coming to be of something' (τὴν μὲν ἁπλῆν γένεσιν φθορὰν οὖσάν τινος, τὴν δὲ φθορὰν τὴν ἁπλῆν γένεσιν οὖσάν τινος).

[22] The difference between the two τρόποι may not be entirely clear at first sight. It will be helpful, however, to recall that we are dealing with rules governing ordinary language: what we are offered are not two entirely different explanations on a technical philosophical level, but rather two reasons (which may ultimately turn out to be related) which in ordinary (hence comparatively unreflective) usage determine our willingness to speak of 'coming to be' *simpliciter*. I take it then that the first τρόπος is concerned with cases where the two *termini* are immediately recognized as being and not-being respectively (318^b11: οἷς οὖν διώρισται, εἴτε πυρὶ καὶ γῇ εἴτε ἄλλοις τισί, τούτων ἔσται τὸ μὲν ὂν τὸ δὲ μὴ ὄν), whereas the second τρόπος focuses on cases where one of the *termini* is only *indirectly* recognized— i.e. by focusing on the distinguishing marks of the matter—as being 'to a greater degree being' (μᾶλλον οὐσία, 318^b15). Note that the two τρόποι and the mistaken view of 'the many' (οἱ πολλοί) are recapitulated at 318^b35–6: '[our speaking of coming to be *simpliciter*] is due to a difference of matter, either in respect of its being substance or not (διὰ ... τὴν ὕλην διαφέρειν ἢ τῷ οὐσίαν εἶναι ἢ τῷ μή, first τρόπος), or in respect of its being more substance or less substance (ἢ τῷ τὴν μέν μᾶλλον τὴν δὲ μή, second τρόπος), or in respect of matter being more perceptible in the one case, and less perceptible in the other (ἢ τῷ τὴν μὲν μᾶλλον αἰσθητὴν εἶναι τὴν ὕλην κτλ., mistaken view of "the many")'.

[23] Apparently the idea is that only things belonging to the former class are said to be coming-to-be (and passing-away) *simpliciter*. Aristotle's (untechnical) use of the term 'matter' (ὕλη) should not lead us to infer that he is here focusing on the *terminus a quo*; for talk about the ὕλη (in the sense of 'material') of the *terminus ad quem* in this same context see 318^b20, εἰς αἰσθητὴν μεταβάλλῃ ὕλην.

coincide in this case: an element like air, which ordinary people take to be less real than earth, because it is less perceptible, is actually more real (because more of a *tode ti* or *eidos*, 318ᵇ32–3).

318ᵇ33–319ᵃ17

Having discovered the reason why coming to be *simpliciter* of one thing is said to be the qualified passing away of another thing and why the passing away *simpliciter* of one thing is said to be the qualified coming to be of another thing (τοῦ μὲν οὖν εἶναι ... εἴρηται τὸ αἴτιον)—i.e. having answered Q4—we now move on to a different question (Q5); namely, why some things are said to come to be *simpliciter* whereas others are *only* said to come to be 'this' (τοῦ δὲ τὰ μὲν ἁπλῶς γίνεσθαι λέγεσθαι, τὰ δέ τι μόνον). This is not the same question as Q4, which was concerned with why, given the cycle of coming to be and passing away, we do not distribute the terms γίνεσθαι ἁπλῶς and φθείρεσθαι ἁπλῶς equally among the changing objects (i.e. substances), but use them in some cases only. Q5, however, addresses a different problem (τὸ δ'ὕστερον εἰρήμενον οὐ τοῦτο διαπορεῖ); namely, in which cases we exclusively use 'coming to be *something*'. Why, for example, is a plant growing from a seed said to be coming to be *simpliciter* whereas some one who is learning is said to be coming to be *something* (in this case: learned). The answer to this question is that the difference is in fact a difference of the categories involved (ταῦτα δὲ διώρισται ταῖς κατηγορίαις). Things which are not substances are not said to come to be *simpliciter*. But in all cases coming to be is connected with the positive column (ἐν τῇ ἑτέρᾳ συστοιχίᾳ).[24]

319ᵃ17–29

We have now established (εἴρηται) why some things are said to come to be *simpliciter*, whereas others are not—both in general (Q5) and within the category of substance (Q4)—and we have determined the material cause of the continuous process of generation (Q3): the coming to be of one thing is the passing away of another. On this model the problem—raised earlier in connection with (Q3)—of how things can still come to be, despite the fact that they keep on perishing into not-being (διὰ τί γίνεται

---

[24] This is another way of saying that coming to be always starts out from a relevant *sterêsis*. For Aristotle's use of *sustoicheia* as a two-column list of opposites governed, in a sense, by a single criterion see e.g. *Ph.* I. 5. 189ᵃ2, which discusses the earlier physicists and the sense in which the opposite principles they put forward might be said to be the *same*: 'they take [their principles] from the same table of columns' (ἐκ τῆς αὐτῆς συστοιχίας). For this use of the concept of *sustoicheia* see also *Ph.* III. 2. 201ᵇ25; *Metaph.* Γ 2. 1004ᵇ27; Λ 7. 1072ᵃ31.

ἀεὶ ἀπολλυμένων 19ᵃ22–3), turns out to be no problem after all: if a thing's perishing involves the coming to be of not-being, a thing's coming to be involves, conversely, the perishing of not-being—however we define not-being; that is, whether or not we take there to be a persisting substrate, and hence whether or not we speak of *absolute* not-being (εἴτ᾽ ὄντος τινὸς τοῦ ὑποκειμένου εἴτε μή). There will be an equilibrium either way, so that coming to be will never fail (εἰκότως οὖν οὐχ ὑπολείπει).

319ᵃ29–ᵇ5

Yet a question, or rather a set of related questions, may still be raised (Q6) as to the nature of this not-being *simpliciter*. Are we to call earth not-being and fire being? Or is earth being as well, so that not-being turns out to be matter of earth and fire alike? Should we conclude that their matter is different, or would it rather be impossible for things to come to be from opposite termini, or from termini with opposite qualities? Or is their matter in a sense different, in a sense the same? The same, that is, in so far as 'whatever it is that underlies is the same' (ὃ μὲν γάρ ποτε ὂν ὑπόκειται, τὸ αὐτό), different in so far as their being or essence differs from case to case (τὸ δ᾽ εἶναι οὐ τὸ αὐτό)?[25]

The chapter as a whole, and especially the first half, thus reveals itself as fairly closely structured. We are not dealing with a disjointed set of problems, but with a series of linked, sometimes nested questions. Philoponus brings this out well, when he summarizes the first part of the chapter as follows:

Wishing to make us alert to possible objections and to prevent our accepting unexamined whatever may happen to be said, he first of all attempts to get rid of coming to be by means of various persuasive arguments, attempting to prove

---

[25] Part of the difficulty of this passage stems from Aristotle's use of the convoluted formula ὃ μέν ποτε ὄν. We get some guidance for possible interpretations from the discussion of time in *Ph.* IV, which shows that the logical subject of this phrase (i.e. 'whatever being it...', or 'whatever it is that...'), when contrasted with 'the essence' (τὸ δ᾽ εἶναι), may either be any *definite* particular (*x*) which remains numerically the same, but which gets ever different definitions, or a *variable* (*x*), which stands for *any* (*x*) which falls under a particular definition, but which may be numerically different from case to case. An example of the former use is to be found at *Ph.* IV. 11. 219ᵇ17–21, where the φερόμενον ᾧ τὴν κίνησιν γνωρίζομεν is described as follows: τοῦτο δὲ ὅ μέν ποτε ὄν τὸ αὐτό (ἢ στιγμὴ γὰρ ἢ λίθος ἤ τι ἄλλο τοιοῦτόν ἐστι), τῷ λόγῳ δὲ ἄλλο, ὥσπερ οἱ σοφισταὶ λαμβάνουσιν ἕτερον τὸ Κορίσκον ἐν Λυκείῳ εἶναι καὶ τὸ Κορίσκον ἐν ἀγορᾷ. An example of the latter use is 219ᵇ26–8: ὃ μέν ποτε ὄν νῦν ἐστι, τὸ αὐτό (τὸ πρότερον γὰρ καὶ ὕστερόν ἐστι τὸ ἐν κινήσει), τὸ δ᾽ εἶναι ἕτερον (ᾗ δ᾽ ἀριθμητὸν γὰρ τὸ πρότερον καὶ ὕστερον, τὸ νῦν ἔστιν). If we take the contrast in our passage in *GC* I. 3. 319ᵇ2 in the former sense (as has usually been done by commentators), the phrase ὃ μὲν γάρ ποτε ὂν ὑπόκειται seems to refer to prime matter. If we take it in the latter sense it refers to matter as a *Funktionalbegriff*, i.e. to *any* (*x*) which as proximate

that there is no such thing [a reference to the aporiasi which have to be solved in order to answer Q1]. Then, in finding a way out of this difficulty, as a result of the solution itself he encounters another difficulty [i.e. the 'how' question, Q2], only to add a third difficulty [the question concerning the everlasting cycle of coming to be, Q3]; and having enquired how it comes about that coming to be never ceases [Q3], from his solution of this third difficulty [Q3] he extracts a solution of the second [Q2] ... (*in Ph.* 43. 23–8)

When the first part of the chapter (317^a32–318^a25) has thus dealt with an analysis of what coming to be *simpliciter* amounts to, and in particular with how its *terminus a quo* can be characterized, the second part (318^a25–319^a17) continues by broaching the question of which criteria govern our willingness to speak of coming to be *simpliciter* (as distinguished from coming to be something). The final part (319^a17–$^b5$) then summarizes the argument of the first two parts, and adds what appears to be the most difficult passage of the whole chapter: the final aporia (319^a29 ff.), the upshot of which is, roughly, as follows. Thus far, the analysis of how the concept of coming to be *simpliciter* is used in common parlance has revealed that not every substance qualifies as a *terminus a quo* for coming to be *simpliciter*, because not every substance qualifies as not-being in the relevant sense. Aristotle now appears to ask whether from a pair of opposites (for example earth, being heavy, on the one hand, and fire, being light, on the other) only one (earth) should—presumably 'intrinsically'—be labelled 'not-being' and the other 'being'. Or is earth to be labelled 'being' as well, having not-being as matter in the same way as fire has its matter? This leads to the more general question of whether the elements can be treated on a par and whether and in what sense their matter is the same or different. The elements might be thought to have different matter (in so far as they come to be from *each other*, i.e. from opposites), or their matter might be thought to be in a sense the same, and in a sense different. In the present context this aporia remains unsolved.[26]

After this survey of the contents and structure of *GC* I. 3, a few additional observations on the way in which this chapter relates to

---

matter may serve as a *hupokeimenon* (and only as such be subsumed under a common definition). See further Sect. 2 below.

[26] On two different senses in which their matter may be considered 'in a sense the same, in a sense different', see the previous note. I there pointed out that the second of these senses does not involve any commitment to the notion of prime matter. Elsewhere, however, in *GC* II. 1. 329^a30–2, Aristotle exclusively focuses on the sense in which the matter of the various elements may be said to be the *same*: 'we take as a principle that is really first the matter which, though inseparable, underlies the contraries (ὑποκειμένην δὲ τοῖς ἐναντίοις), for neither is the hot matter for the cold, nor the latter for the hot, but the substratum is matter for them both (τὸ ὑποκείμενον ἀμφοῖν)'. It should be admitted that this mode of presentation does invite, although it does not necessarily imply, an interpretation in terms of prime matter as a common substratum for the elements.

what precedes may be in order. At the end of chapter 2 Aristotle has claimed that coming to be *simpliciter* is not simple aggregation (σύγκρισις) (317ᵃ20–1), but that it occurs 'when something changes from this to that as a whole'. It might seem odd that after this provisional characterization of the kind of change we are looking for chapter 3 appears to start afresh with the question 'whether there is anything that comes to be *simpliciter*' (317ᵃ33), which, as noted above, appears to be equivalent to the question whether there is coming to be *simpliciter*.[27] Apparently the provisional characterization of coming to be as the transformation of something into something else *as a whole* should not itself be taken to have settled the question whether there really *is* such coming to be. On the contrary, as soon as we go on to investigate the characteristics of this kind of genesis, at the beginning of chapter 3, we are faced with a formidable aporia which might in principle lead us to doubt the very existence of this kind of change.

This is a perfectly decent procedure from the point of view of Aristotelian dialectic. We may compare, for example, what happens at the begining of the discussion of place in the first chapter of *Physics* book IV.[28] There we are told, after some first and provisional characterizations of place, that the aporiai involved in answering the question 'What is it?' (*ti estin*) on the basis of these first characterizations are such that we may even doubt *whether* place exists (*ei estin*). One of these aporiai is Zeno's paradox of place: If everything that exists is in a place and place exists, then place must be in a place, etc. This aporia is eventually solved by showing that place in the Aristotelian sense, i.e. place qua surrounding surface, is indeed *in* something else, though not in the specifically local sense of 'being in'. In a comparable way *GC* I. 3 solves the prima facie aporia concerning the existence of coming to be *simpliciter* by showing that there is a harmless sense in which coming to be *simpliciter* is from not-being (namely, from not-being which is potential being).

In his commentary Joachim claims that the 'proof' that there is such a thing as coming to be in the proper sense begins with chapter 3.[29] Now of course Aristotle does not himself use the language of proof in this dialectical investigation and the investigation as such appears to leave some loose ends (think of the final aporia). Yet Joachim is surely right to the extent that it is only in chapter 3 that Aristotle begins to establish what genesis, or coming to be *simpliciter*, is. He does so by resolving the

[27] On the equivalence see my comments on 317ᵃ32–317ᵇ18, at p. 95–6 above.

[28] For an analysis of the discussion of *topos* in *Ph*. IV in terms of Aristotle's dialectical method (taking account of the role of initial *phainomena* and of *aporiai* in the context of that method) see Algra (1995), 153–82.

[29] Joachim (1922), 63.

relevant aporiai, as indeed the agenda of his dialectical method requires. In the context of a dialectical procedure this is as much of a proof as one can obtain.

2. The referent of not-being *simpliciter*—some observations

From this analysis of the structure of *GC* I. 3 we may already infer that the problem of determining the kind of not-being involved in coming to be *simpliciter* dominates most of the chapter. Q1 (Is there such a thing as coming to be *simpliciter*?) arises because coming to be *simpliciter* would seem to imply a pre-existent not-being *simpliciter*, and generation from such not-being would be absurd. The answer to Q1, which briefly recapitulates points made elsewhere (on which see below, Sect. 3), turns on the claim that the not-being at issue is not absolute not-being, but rather in a sense not-being and in another sense (potential) being—a familiar way of solving an Aristotelian aporia. Q2 then arises because we may well ask how this 'something' which is potential being should be further characterized. Two possible characterizations—namely (1) that the not-being we are looking for is mere potentiality (i.e. potentially substance and potentially accidents), or (2) that the not-being at issue is a potential substance displaying *actual* accidental properties—are rejected, and Q3 is introduced to help find an answer. However, the answer which is given still confronts us with various problems. This is why at the end of the chapter the complex Q6 again raises the problem of the nature of the not-being *simpliciter* which is involved—and so to speak recapitulates what is left of Q2 after the preceding discussion.

It is clear that Aristotle thinks he can dodge the problems connected with the introduction of the notion of not-being by redefining, or rather specifying, the not-being involved as a kind of not-being that is at the same time being, in the sense of potential being, or being potentially something. Yet it is not all that easy to go beyond this and to further characterize this Aristotelian not-being, especially since the chapter ends with an aporia. As we noted in the previous section, commentators have been divided as to what ultimately constitutes the referent of the not-being (i.e. the (x) which is not) which serves as the *terminus a quo* for coming to be *simpliciter*: Is it what we call 'proximate matter' or is it 'prime matter'? It is worthwhile to pause and consider in some more detail what these two alternatives actually amount to.

If the referent of the not-being Aristotle is thinking of is proximate matter, we are dealing with a *thing*, an actual substance which can be said to be 'not-being' in the sense of not actually (but merely potentially) being a particular other thing. It is a substance 'endowed' with the privation relevant to the description of the particular instance of coming to be that is at stake. Its being is twofold: it is potentially what it can come to be, but it also has its own actual existence. The potentiality involved must be the potentiality to become (x), where (x) is the *terminus ad quem* of a *particular* transformation. If, on the other hand, the not-being at issue is taken to be *prima materia*, the referent is *not* a substance, but the diffuse nothingness of pure potentiality. It has no actual existence of its own, its only mode of existence is that of *potential* being. The potentiality involved is a *general* potentiality, the potentiality of becoming *anything*.[30]

As noted in my introductory section, these two conceptions of *matter* are not necessarily incompatible, and may in principle have coexisted in Aristotle's work. After all, the view that coming to be takes place from a proximate matter which displays the relevant privation does not in itself preclude the possibiliy that at the most elementary level such a substance consists of prime matter and a particular form (or qualities). Conversely, even if we assume that Aristotle believed that the not-being which serves as a *terminus a quo* is the kind of 'hypostasized' privation which we call 'prime matter', we may qualify this claim by stressing that this prime matter cannot exist in its own right and is always in fact endowed with a particular substantial form, so that in practice it always *figures* as proximate matter. In fact those commentators who credit Aristotle with the conception of prime matter and who think the not-being he is looking for in *GC* I. 3 actually *is* this prime matter tend to add that this prime matter only figures as a *terminus a quo* in so far as it *is* already informed.[31] Even so the fact remains that the referent of not-being *simpliciter* is different in both cases, and for the interpretation of *GC* I. 3 it is important to find out which of the two perspectives Aristotle adopts in this particular context when he speaks of 'that which is not'.[32]

---

[30] As Philoponus puts it at *in Ph.* 173. 3: δυνάμει γὰρ ἐστιν ἡ ὕλη πάντα τὰ φυσικὰ εἴδη, ἐνεργείᾳ δὲ οὐδέν.

[31] Cf. Joachim (1922), 97: 'Since the substratum never exists as bare matter, but is always formed, there always is a positive actual substance'; Tricot (1933), 29 n. 3: 'Aussi bien que la perpétuité de la génération, son existence même est expliqué par la πρώτη ὕλη prise au sens de substance concrète informée, mais transformable en un autre état positif'; Solmsen (1960), 331: 'What kind of existence should one assign to such potential being which in some way must certainly be not-being? What is really needed ... is prime matter which never exists by itself and another element whose destruction makes possible the "absolute" *genesis*'. Migliori (1976), 31, speaks of 'la materia prima, come essere reale, ma potenziale, reale nella sintesi con le opposizioni che la determinano, ma assolutamente incapace di esistere separatamente'. Cf. also Williams (1982), 218: 'It is earth which is capable of ceasing to be earth and becoming fire; but that which is capable of being and not-being [i.e. prime matter] is in an important sense different from earth, though inseparable from it'.

[32] My use of the term 'reference' may call for some further comments in so far as Joachim's interpretation is concerned. It sometimes appears as if Joachim takes a different

In some cases our choice for either prime matter or proximate matter as the supposed referent of not-being *simpliciter* appears to be underdetermined by the text. A clear example is 317^{b}14–18, where Aristotle first introduces the distinction between the actual and the potential, and where he claims that

> we must say that in a way a thing comes to be from not-being *simpliciter*, whereas in another way it always comes to be from something that exists. For there must pre-exist that which *potentially* is, but *actually* is not. And this is spoken of both as being and as not-being.

Here, to quote Joachim, 'the description of the presupposed basis of γένεσις . . . would apply either to the proximate ὕλη of τὸ γιγνόμενον . . . *or* to πρώτη ὕλη, the ὑποκείμενον conceived in abstraction from all the forms which it acquires in its transformations'.[33] In such cases commentators may read the text as suits their general view—that is, their conviction that the notion of prime matter is indispensible, so that it *must* be present or, on the contrary, incoherent, so that it *cannot* be present. Philoponus, for

approach, preferring to discuss the problem of the nature of the *terminus a quo* not in terms of *reference*, but in terms of *description*. Thus Joachim (1922), 93, speaks of the substratum as something which we can 'in thought *abstract* from all its forms and *conceive as* matter undetermined'. On closer view, however, what Joachim here implies appears to be merely that when we use the *concept* of prime matter we conceive it as something in its own right, whereas it does not exist as such (i.e. on its own and devoid of all form) in reality—just as one might conceive of space *as such* even if one doesn't believe there is such a thing as empty space. I do not think that his perhaps slightly unfortunate talk of prime matter as a 'logical abstraction' should be taken to imply that, on his view, the concept of prime matter has no referent, or that the referent is merely an informed substance *under a certain description*. For he also speaks of prime matter as a 'permanent substratum [which] drops one form and takes on another' (1922: 97) and as something '*to which* Aristotle's description [at 317^{b}14–18] might apply', rather than as something which itself merely exists at the level of description. See also the formulation in his introduction, Joachim (1922), p. xxvii: 'πρώτη ὕλη is shown to be presupposed as the ground for γένεσις and φθορά, and of their never-failing alternation in the Lower Cosmos'. Note also that talking about prime matter at the level of description rather than reference would not provide a way out of the dilemma sketched in the text to this footnote. For also if 'proximate matter' and 'prime matter' are two descriptions under which one and the same substance might be viewed, we are still left with the question which of these two descriptions Aristotle had in mind when talking of not-being in *GC* I. 3. I am grateful to David Charles for having drawn my attention to these matters, in particular to the problems involved by Joachim's use of the term 'logical abstraction'.

[33] For similar remarks see Tricot (1933), 25 n. 3: 'le résumé de la *Physique* qui précède ne précise pas, en effet, comment on doit concevoir le siège de la génération: est-ce déjà un σύνολον, un composé de form et de matière . . . ou bien n'est-ce qu'une πρώτη ὕλη?' Migliori (1976), 160 n. 13, thinks the identification with proximate matter is 'meno probabile, sia per l'insistenza dello Stagirita sulla qualifica "potenziale", sia perché la materia formata può essere sostrato proprio in quanto c'è una materia prima'. The latter reason appears to beg the question, the former can carry no weight, since also proximate matter is, qua matter, a 'potenziale'.

example, both in his comments on the same passage (*in GC* 47. 36–48. 17) and in his initial comments on the chapter as a whole (*in GC* 44. 20–5) appears to assume all along that we are dealing with prime mattter— presumably because he cannot think of any other reading that makes sense. However, on closer view, and on an unprejudiced reading, Aristotle's text does appear to contain some indications that in the context of *GC* I. 3—at least before the final aporia—prime matter is *not* what is envisaged as the referent of the 'not-being *simpliciter*' from which coming to be *simpliciter* takes its start. It is to these pointers that we shall now turn.

We get a first indication from the phrasing of the aporia which Aristotle connects to an affirmative answer to QI. It runs as follows:

For if there is to be coming to be *simpliciter*, this coming to be *simpliciter* would take place from not-being (ἁπλῶς ἄν τι γίνοιτο ἐκ μὴ ὄντος), so that it would be true to say that not-being belongs to some things (ὑπάρχει τισὶ τὸ μὴ ὄν): coming to be something is from not-being something, e.g. from not being white or not being beautiful, whereas coming to be *simpliciter* is from not-being *simpliciter*. (317ᵇ1–5)

As Williams points out in his commentary, the proposition ἐκ is ambiguous: it may mean (a) 'out of' or (b) 'from'.[34] In the present context 'from' appears to be the more natural translation. In the exemplified case of 'coming to be *something*' we are of course dealing with a subject *S* becoming *y from* not being *y* (ἐκ μὴ λευκοῦ etc.); that is, becoming something it formerly was not. Now Aristotle appears to apply the same 'model' to the cases of coming to be *simpliciter*, witness his claim that the supposition that there is such a thing as simple coming to be would involve 'that not-being *belongs to* some things' (ὅτι ὑπάρχει τισὶ τὸ μὴ ὄν).[35] The latter formula seems to indicate that the not-being at issue here applies to, that is can be predicated of, a subject *S* (or, to put it differently, that a certain *S* can be *called* μὴ ὄν). Apparently we are supposed to think of a situation where an *S* does not exist (and can be called not-being) at time t1 whereas it does exist (and can be called being) at t2, so that it can be said to come to be *from* a former state of not-being.[36] The supposed continuity (implied by the talk of 'from a former state of . . .') results in the absurdity that at t1 we are already dealing with

---

[34] Cf. Williams (1982), 80–1. For Aristotle's distinction between these two senses of ἐκ cf. *Metaph.* Δ 24. 1023ᵃ26–9 and ᵇ5–7.

[35] Note, however, that the MSS are not unanimous: τισι is left out in two MSS (HJ). But ὑπάρχει τισι is to be preferred as obviously the *lectio difficilior*, which moreover occurs in the majority of the MSS, in Philoponus, and in the *versio Latina*.

[36] Williams (1982), 81, rightly points out that the puzzle would lose its sting if we should think of an S coming to be *out of* not-being, and that in that case the talk of ὑπάρχει τισι τὸ μὴ ὄν would be hard or even impossible to accommodate.

the same subject *S*, so that there *is* an *S* which nevertheless is a not-being.[37] This way of presenting the crux of the aporia is significant, because it suggests that in Aristotle's view we are dealing with some *things* (τισι)—i.e. substances, i.e. proximate matter—which may each be *called* 'not-being' (μὴ ὄν). After all, he *could* have simply said 'in that case not-being exists'.[38]

We find a second indication in the way Aristotle answers Q2 at 317ᵇ18–318ᵃ13. As we saw, Q2 (the 'how' question) is in fact a question concerning the *nature* of the not-being (i.e. of that which we call 'not-being') which serves as the *terminus a quo* of coming to be *simpliciter*. Thus far (in the answer to Q1) the *terminus a quo* has been merely characterized from the point of view of its potential mode of being. Now the focus shifts to its actual mode of being. This is said to involve a most remarkable aporia (θαυμαστὴ ἀπορία). Two possibilities are rejected. First, we are not dealing with something which is not actually qualified in *any* way, that is something that is mere potentiality, for such a thing cannot exist in its own right (χωριστόν). Neither, secondly, are we dealing with a *potential* substance which displays *actual* properties (πάθη), for properties, being ontologically dependent on substances, cannot in this way exist in their own right either. This aporia will somehow have to be solved in what follows by showing that there is a third way, and that indeed the not-being we are looking for can be successfully characterized in a way that manages to avoid the kind of absurd consequences here described.

As we noted, Aristotle suggests that this question should be studied in connection with Q3, in that the answer to Q3 (the cycle of coming to be and passing away) may help us to find an answer to Q2. Now the answer we obtain through the answer to Q3 is one in rough outlines only: the

---

[37] Cf. Williams (1982), 81: 'If we say that something came to be *simpliciter* from not-being, we imply that at one time it was and at another, previous, time it was not. To say this is to attribute to one and the same thing existence at time t2, and non-existence at an earlier time t1'. The reference to 'one and the same thing' appears to be crucial, for otherwise the analysis might be taken to locate the alleged absurdity in the mere fact that a certain *S* which exists at t2 can be said to have been non-existent at t1. However it is not absurd to predicate *previous* non-existence of an existent. The central point rather seems to be that at t1 the subject was already, in a sense, *S*. The element of continuity is also stressed by Thomas Aquinas ad loc.: 'illud enim ex quo aliquid generatur potest dici esse illud; sicut si ex ligno generatur arca potest dici quod lignum est arca. si ergo ex non ente simpliciter generatur ens, verum erit dicere quod non ens existit, idest est ens'.

[38] This *is* in fact what he says if we follow the reading of two of the MSS, but see on this n. 35 above. Note that Aristotle's solution to the problem (317ᵇ17) appears to retain the 'model' applied in the aporia, while defusing the aporia itself by specifying the kind of 'not-being' that is involved. What 'pre-exists' or 'precedes' (προϋπάρχει) is something 'said in both ways' (λεγόμενον ἀμφοτέρως); in other words: a *thing* which may be called 'being', but also 'not-being'.

question whether it is because the corruption of one thing is the generation of another, and vice versa, that the change is necessarily unceasing (318^a24–5) may apparently be answered affirmatively (this is said to provide us with a 'sufficient explanation', 318^a27).

This may indeed count as a brief, though straightforward enough, answer to Q2 as well, *if* we assume that the not-being we are here trying to characterize is a *thing*, a substance which can be *said* to be in some sense not-being, but in another sense being. We now hear that its actual mode of being is that of being a substance which is part of the chain of becoming. It is hard to see this reference to the cycle of becoming as a straightforward attempt to characterize the not-being we are looking for, if that not-being should be supposed to be prime matter. True, we might come up with the familiar response that prime matter is always in fact informed. But, precisely because in the aporia itself the idea of a self-subsistent pure potentiality has already been rejected, we would expect Aristotle to have made explicit at this point why the prime matter he supposedly has in mind is not vulnerable to the same objection (namely, because it does not exist in its own right and is always in fact informed). If he had prime matter in mind all along, the mere reference to the cycle of change would be an extremely vague and implicit way to make his point.

A third indication is to be found at 319^a20–2, where Aristotle summarizes the results arrived at thus far by claiming (among other things) that 'the coming to be of one thing in the case of substance is always the corruption of another, and the corruption of one thing is the coming to be of another' καὶ ἔστιν ἡ θατέρου γένεσις ἀεὶ ἐπὶ τῶν οὐσιῶν ἄλλου φθορὰ καὶ ἡ ἄλλου φθορὰ ἄλλου γένεσις). He adds that, given this state of affairs, the paradox of genesis continuing while things perish into not-being ceases to exist. The amount of coming to be from not-being will always match the amount of perishing into not-being (on any interpretation of not-being, i.e. whether not-being is taken to be a *hupokeimenon* or not). So it is understandable after all that coming to be never fails. He then rephrases the mechanism at issue as follows: 'for coming to be is the corruption of what is not, and corruption the coming to be of what is not' (ἡ γὰρ γένεσις φθορὰ τοῦ μὴ ὄντος, ἡ δὲ φθορὰ γένεσις τοῦ μὴ ὄντος, 319^a28–9). If we map this formula on to 319^a20–2 (i.e. the phrase we just quoted), it appears that 'not-being' (or 'what is not') here figures as a substitute for 'another [thing]' (ἄλλου) in the former passage, and hence refers to a substance, so that we are dealing with not-being in the sense of proximate matter. It is hard to see, to say the least, how Aristotle could speak of the 'corruption of what is not' (φθορὰ τοῦ μὴ ὄντος) if the not-being at issue were supposed to be prime matter.

Finally, we may turn to the way the aporia at the end of the chapter (319^a29 ff.) is introduced:

But is this not-being *simpliciter* one of a pair of contraries—for example is earth, the heavy element, what is not and fire, the light element, what is?

This question would scarcely make any sense if it had been supposed all along that not-being *simpliciter* is prime matter. It does make sense, however, on the supposition that not-being *simpliciter* is a substance (proximate matter) as part of the cycle of generation. After all, it has been suggested in what precedes (318^{b}33–319^{a}16), on the basis of an analysis of how we *speak*, that not *all* substances qualify for the position of *terminus a quo* of coming to be *simpliciter*.

It appears, to conclude, that the interpretation of *GC* I. 3 can do without general philosophical observations on the feasibility or absurdity of the notion of prime matter. The *Wortlaut* of the text provides enough indications that at least in this particular context prime matter was not what Aristotle had in mind when speaking of 'not-being *simpliciter*'.

3. *On Generation and Corruption I. 3* and *Physics I*

As we saw, Aristotle gives his solution to the problem of coming to be from not-being at 317^{b}13–18 (Q1), and he does so only very briefly (συντόμως), because he claims the problems at issue have been studied—and the necessary distinctions have been made—in more detail elsewhere (περὶ μὲν οὖν τούτων ἐν ἄλλοις τε διηπόρηται καὶ διώρισται τοῖς λόγοις). Various commentators have taken this as a reference to *Physics*. I. 6–9, although usually without specifying which elements of that text are relevant to the present discussion.[39] Williams, however, formulates some reservations, as follows:

The summary which Aristotle proceeds to give makes the distinction between actuality and potentiality do the whole work of resolving the difficulty about what it is that a thing comes to be from *simpliciter*. The notions of actuality and potentiality, however, play an exiguous role in these chapters of the *Physics*. Briefly, at the end of chapter 8 Aristotle alludes to the distinction between *actual* and *possible* as an alternative way of dealing with precisely the difficulty he is considering here.[40]

He notes in addition that the solution of the *Physics* is 'at least verbally inconsistent' with the solution put foward in *GC* I. 3:

here we have 'in one way it is from what is not that a thing comes to be *simpliciter*, though in another way it is always from what is'; there, 'we ourselves

---

[39] Cf. Philoponus. *in GC* 48. 1 (who in general terms refers to book I of the *Physics*); Joachim (1922), 91 (*Ph.* I. 6–9); Tricot (1951), 25 n. 2 (*Ph.* I. 6–9); Migliori (1976), 160 n. 10 (*Ph.* I. 6–9, in particular I. 8).

[40] Williams (1982), 84.

maintain that nothing comes to be *simpliciter* from what is not, but in a way it does come to be from what is not, sc. *per accidens*' ... (191^{b}13–15) Here 'that from which a thing comes to be *simpliciter* is held to be potentially existent, though actually non-existent'. There it is coming to be *simpliciter* which is itself rejected in favour of coming to be *per accidens*.

I believe the differences sketched by Williams do not affect the core of the matter, and that it is reasonable to take the reference to be to *Physics* I, more particularly to *Physics* I. 8. In what follows I shall try to show, first, that there is more in *Physics* I that is relevant to the interpretation of *GC* I. 3 than merely the distinction between actuality and potentiality; secondly (as against Williams), that the approaches of *Physics* I and *GC* I are not inconsistent or incompatible; and, thirdly, that it makes sense for Aristotle in the context of *GC* I. 3 to refer to the argument of *Physics* I only as briefly as he does (συντόμως).

As for the first point, we may note to begin with that at *GC* I. 3. 317^{b}13–15 the words 'these things' in the phrase 'about these things we have set out the aporiai and made the necessary distinctions elsewhere' cannot refer to just the solution in terms of potentiality and actuality, a distinction which is only first mentioned in the next sentence. It must refer to what precedes, that is to the *problem* that has just been set out (317^{b}1–13)—the problem of (coming to be from) not-being—which indeed is also the problem that dominates the discussion of *Physics* I. 8, from 191^{a}23 where Aristotle claims that he will now show (λεγῶμεν μετὰ ταῦτα) how the analysis provided thus far will be able to solve 'the aporia of the early thinkers' concerning not-being. In what follows (ἡμεῖς δὲ λέγομεν κτλ, 191^{a}35 ff.) this problem is discussed more or less *in extenso* and solved by making the necessary conceptual distinctions (or rather, distinctions of categorization)—which happens to be just what Aristotle's brief reference at *GC* I. 3.317^{b}14 claims: it couples the discussion of problems and the making of the necessary distinctions (διηπόρηται καὶ διώρισται τοῖς λόγοις). So from a formal point of view—i.e. when we focus on the problem at issue and the way it is approached—*Ph.* I. 8 would seem to be a good candidate for the text Aristotle was referring to at *GC* I. 3. 317^{b}13, and I do not think that any other Aristotelian text answers the description equally well.[41]

Yet, and this brings us to our second point, one might still be inclined to follow Williams in so far as he argues that the contents of *Physics* I. 8 are in part 'at least verbally inconsistent' with what we find in *GC* I. 3. Let us therefore have a closer look at the contents of *Physics* I. 8, in

---

[41] Other Aristotelian texts which more briefly discuss, or at least refer to, the problem are listed below at n. 43.

particular at the distinctions introduced there to dodge the aporia of coming to be out of not-being. The relevant analysis is to be found in 191^a34-^b19, a rather difficult passage, which I shall here summarize only in so far as it is relevant to the present discussion.

In the account of *Physics* I. 8 the different ways in which a particular thing may be 'labelled' appear to play a crucial role. Thus Aristotle begins his discussion by arguing that the phrase 'a physician's acting' can be used in two ways ($\delta\iota\chi\hat{\omega}_S$ $\lambda\acute{\epsilon}\gamma\epsilon\tau\alpha\iota$); namely, to describe what a physician does qua *physician* (example: 'a doctor doctors qua doctor', 191^b5) or what he does, not qua physician, but qua being something else (example: 'a doctor builds a house not qua doctor, but qua house-builder', ibid.). The point appears to be that a thing (in the case of the example, a person who is a physician, but is also building a house) can be described in many ways. Different descriptions may single out different aspects of the same entity. Ordinary language does not always pick out what is strictly speaking the right descriptive perspective: when we say 'the doctor is building a house' ($o\mathring{\iota}\kappa o\delta o\mu\epsilon\hat{\iota}$ $\acute{o}$ $\mathring{\iota}\alpha\tau\rho\acute{o}_S$), we might be taken (but do not mean) to imply that the person we are describing is a doctor *and nothing else* (in which case we might be taken to imply that it is in virtue of his medical skills that a physician builds). However, what we mean to say is that there is a person (substance), who happens to be in the first place a physician (and who may therefore be truly called 'a physician'), but who also exhibits other characteristics such as being a house-builder (in virtue of which he is now building). Now just as we correctly speak ($\mu\acute{\alpha}\lambda\iota\sigma\tau\alpha$ $\lambda\acute{\epsilon}\gamma o\mu\epsilon\nu$ $\kappa\upsilon\rho\acute{\iota}\omega_S$) of 'a physician doing (x)' whenever he is doing (x) precisely qua physician, so the phrase 'coming to be from not being', when correctly applied, means: 'coming to be from not being *in so far as* it is not being' ($\delta\hat{\eta}\lambda o\nu$ $\acute{o}\tau\iota$ $\kappa\alpha\grave{\iota}$ $\tau\grave{o}$ $\acute{\epsilon}\kappa$ $\mu\grave{\eta}$ $\acute{o}\nu\tau o_S$ $\gamma\acute{\iota}\gamma\nu\epsilon\sigma\theta\alpha\iota$ $\tau o\hat{\upsilon}\tau o$ $\sigma\eta\mu\alpha\acute{\iota}\nu\epsilon\iota$ $\tau\grave{o}$ $\hat{\eta}$ $\mu\grave{\eta}$ $\acute{o}\nu$, 191^b10). In other words, we need not suppose that we are dealing with something which is *mere* not-being (absolute not-being). Rather, in using the locution $\acute{\epsilon}\kappa$ $\mu\grave{\eta}$ $\acute{o}\nu\tau o_S$ we are speaking about something which may well display other characteristics as well (and which hence may also be described in other ways).

It was through their failure to make these distinctions that the earlier thinkers went astray and 'denied that nothing ever comes to be, or is <except being>, but did away with coming to be' (191^b10-12). In other words, they failed to see that what is 'being' can at the same time have other characteristics (and be called by other names) as well—and, we may supplement in thought, that similarly what is called not-being may have other characteristics as well and hence need not be absolute not-being. Aristotle now claims (191^b13 ff.) that 'we too' say that nothing can come to be in the absolute sense from not-being, but that a thing may come to be from not-being *in a way*, namely accidentally (πῶς μέντοι γίγνεσθαι ἐκ μὴ ὄντος, οἷον κατὰ συμβεβηκός), presumably from a substance which happens not-to-be-*S*, where *S* is the *terminus ad quem*.[42]

We are next given an alternative 'way of looking at these things' (*tropos*); namely, that the same things can be spoken of in terms of potentiality and actuality (εἷς μὲν δὴ τρόπος οὗτος, ἄλλος δ'ὅτι ἐνδέχεται ταὐτὰ λέγειν κατὰ τὴν δύναμιν καὶ τὴν ἐνέργειαν, 191[b]28). But, or so Aristotle claims, this is something which has been analysed with greater precision elsewhere (ἐν ἄλλοις διώρισται δι' ἀκριβείας μᾶλλον).[43] It is clear anyway that both approaches (τρόποι) serve to solve the problem of not-being by redescribing the not-being at issue.

We may now return to Williams's point: the (real or 'at least verbal') inconsistency of the main argument of *Physics* I. 8 (i.e. the first *tropos*—the analysis of not-being as not-being *per accidens*) with certain elements in the discussion *GC* I. 3. On closer view the inconsistency might appear to concern two points:

(1) the way the not-being of the *terminus a quo* is being redescribed according to the first approach of *Physics* I. 8 on the one hand (accidental not-being), and according to the second approach of *Physics* I. 8 and in *GC* I. 3 on the other (potential being); note, by the way, that if we are prepared to speak of an 'inconsistency' here, the inconsistency can be found *within Physics* I. 8—i.e. between the first and second approaches—as well);[44]

(2) the way in which the qualifier *simpliciter* (ἁπλῶς) is used in *Physics* I. 8 on the one hand (there is no coming to be from not-being *simpliciter*, 191[b]13–14) and in *GC* I. 3 on the other (in a sense there *is* coming-to-be from not-being *simpliciter*, 317[b]15–16).[45]

I shall deal with (2) separately in the next section, and now first concentrate on (1).

---

[42] *Pace* Williams (see the end of the second quotation printed above (pp. 110–11)), the qualification *per accidens* (κατὰ συμβεβηκός) here must apply to the words ἐκ μὴ ὄντος, not to γίγνεσθαι. We are not dealing with coming to be *per accidens* (after all we are dealing with coming to be from the relevant *sterēsis*), but with coming to be *from not-being per accidens*.

[43] One might think of one or more of the following: *Metaph*. Δ 7; Z 7–8; Θ, or even the very brief summary in Λ 2.

[44] As for the *being* of the *terminus a quo*, the descriptions are different but certainly not incompatible. The second τρόπος characterizes this being as *potential* being, the first τρόπος (implicitly: it only gives examples) as *actual* being.

[45] In both cases the adverb ἁπλῶς primarily appears to qualify the formula γίγνεσθαι ἐκ μὴ ὄντος (cf. *Ph*. I. 8.191[b]13–14, *GC* I. 3. 317[b]2). *GC* I. 3, however, appears to assume that this formula equals ἁπλῶς εἶναι γένεσις (317[b]2), which in its turn implies the existence of ἁπλῆ γένεσις, which is γένεσις ἐξ ἁπλῶς μὴ ὄντος.

It appears that Williams's assessment should at least be qualified. For whether or not we are inclined to see a substantial difference (or even an inconsistency) between the two ways of redescribing the not-being of the *terminus a quo* will depend on our identification of the referent of not-being *simpliciter* in *GC* I. 3. *If* we take this referent to be prime matter, as Williams does, it is clear that we are indeed dealing with two different redescriptions: in that case *GC* I. 3 (but presumably also the second approach of *Ph.* I. 8!) redescribes not-being as the not-being but potential being of the *terminus a quo* regarded qua prime matter, whereas the first approach of *Physics* I. 8 redescribes not-being as the accidental not-being of the *terminus a quo* regarded qua substance (i.e. as the relevant *sterêsis*). Thus interpreted the texts we are dealing with offer two different and independent ways of solving the problem of not-being.[46] In that case we may go along with Williams in concluding that the largest part of the discussion of *Physics* I. 8 loses its relevance for *GC* I. 3, so that a reference in the former text in the context of the latter would be rather pointless.

If, on the other hand, we interpret the referent of the actual not-being (but potential being) of *GC* I. 3 in the way outlined in the previous sections of this chapter—i.e. as proximate matter—the two approaches of *Ph.* I. 8 and the account of *GC* I. 3 are not only compatible but represent (two different aspects of) a single account of not-being. They both characterize the *terminus a quo* of the coming to be of a substance *S* in terms of the *terminus ad quem*; that is, as not-being-*S*. The account of *GC* I. 3 and the second approach of *Physics* I. 8 then both stress that from the perspective of a description of this *terminus ad quem* this not-being is *potential being*. The first approach of *Physics* I. 8 makes what we may regard as an *additional* point; namely, that from the perspective of a description of the *terminus a quo* as a whole this not-being (i.e. not-being-*S*) is *accidental* not-being. This is not at all to say that this additional point is irrelevant: indeed it may be said to provide precisely the kind of conceptual clarification that Aristotle may have had in mind when he stated at the beginning of *GC* I. 3 that 'the necessary distinctions concerning these matters have been made elsewhere' (περὶ μὲν οὖν τούτων ἐν ἄλλοις (...) διώρισται τοῖς λόγοις, 317ᵇ14). All the same there is no reason for Aristotle to restate it or even summarize the *whole* account of *Physics* I. 8 here at the beginning of *GC* I. 3. For his present purpose—which is the restricted one of trying to answer Q1 by establishing that the not-being we are talking about in the case of coming to be *simpliciter* is not

---

[46] Cf. Solmsen (1960), 334 n. 53: 'In the *Physics* the μὴ ὄν is found in the στέρησις, i.e. the contrary, not in the substratum (I. 8. 191ᵇ13 ff.). But the μὴ ὄν which Aristotle there recognizes is a relative one, not as in our treatise an absolute μὴ ὄν.' See also ibid. 331 n. 48.

absolute not-being—a brief reference to the *second* approach of *Physics* I. 8 alone will suffice. Aristotle explicitly claims that he will here mention only briefly (συντόμως) what had elsewhere been discussed in a more elaborate form (ἐπὶ πλεῖον). This means that he can pick out only one relevant aspect of an otherwise continuous and coherent account.

But there is more to it. Even though the *term* 'accidental being' does not occur in *GC*,[47] the corresponding concept may be said to be present in the background all along. For the very idea that there are various ways of describing the *terminus a quo* (which each single out different aspects of its being or not-being), which is at the basis of the analysis of not-being *per accidens* in *Ph.* I. 8, plays a central role in the course of *GC* I. 3 as well. In fact the whole treatment of Q2 may be regarded as an attempt to determine how the *terminus a quo* can be described *apart* from being potentially the *terminus ad quem* (i.e. apart from the aspect of *sterêsis*). And the answer to this question, the reference to the cycle of generation, shows that the not-being out of which a substance *S* comes to be is another substance (being) which is not (yet) *S*, and which accordingly could in principle be labelled not-being (i.e. not-being *S*) *per accidens*.

In Section 2 I provided some arguments against the identification of not-being *simpliciter* in *GC* I. 3 as prime matter. We may now add a further one to the list. It does not matter much whether or not we are prepared to take the actual reference at *GC* I. 3. 317 ᵇ13–14 to be a reference to the first book of the *Physics*. For in each case we shall have to acknowledge that *GC* I. 3 as well as *Physics* I. 8 deal with the same problem: the problem of not-being in the context of an account of substantial generation or coming to be. So we may expect these two chapters to match and to represent a single and coherent underlying theory. This indeed is what they do, but only *if* we take the referent of not-being *simpliciter* in *GC* I. 3 to be proximate matter, not prime matter. Although they each highlight different aspects of the theory, the two discussions dovetail into each other in that *Physics* I. 8 is primarily concerned with solving the problem of the *not-being* of the *terminus a quo* (i.e. in what sense the *terminus a quo* may be said not to be), whereas *GC* I. 3 only briefly broaches this question and then goes on to investigate the *being* of the *terminus a quo* (in what sense can the *terminus a quo* be said to be; that is, be described in positive terms (Q2)).

---

[47] The idea that 'that which is, is twofold', and that change occurs 'from that which is potentially to that which is actually' (ἐκ τοῦ δυνάμει ὄντος εἰς τὸ ἐνεργείᾳ ὄν), *does* occur explicitly in *Metaph.* Λ 2. 1069ᵇ15–16, but there the whole issue is broached only succinctly. Too succinctly, in fact, to warrant the idea that this is the text Aristotle had in mind at *GC* I. 3. 317ᵇ13–15 when claiming that 'we have gone through the problems (διηπόρηται) and made the necessary distinctions (διώρισται τοῖς λόγοις) concerning these matters elsewhere'.

4. The use of ἁπλῶς (simpliciter) in On Generation and Corruption I. 3 and Physics I. 8

This having been said, we still have to deal with the second prima facie difference between the accounts of *Physics* I. 8 and *GC* I. 3 which was outlined above: the way in which the qualifier ἁπλῶς (*simpliciter*) is used in *Physics* I. 8 on the one hand (no coming to be from not-being ἁπλῶς, 191ᵇ13–14) and in *GC* I. 3 on the other (in a sense there is coming to be from not-being ἁπλῶς, 317ᵇ15).[48] Let us first have a closer look at the context in *Physics* I and at the precise nature of the claims made there.

It is true that *Physics* I. 8. 191ᵇ13 claims that

> We as well hold that nothing can be said *simpliciter* (ἁπλῶς) to come to be from what is not. Yet we do maintain that a thing may come to be from what is not in a qualified sense, namely accidentally. For it comes to be from the privation—which is in itself not-being—which is not there (ἐκ γὰρ τῆς στερήσεως, ὅ ἐστι καθ' αὐτὸ μὴ ὄν, οὐκ ἐνυπάρχοντος γίγνεταί τι).

As we saw, this remark occurs in a context where Aristotle concentrates on the various ontological aspects of objects, on the way we may pick out these various aspects in naming the objects, and on the way we *should* pick out the *right* aspects in *correctly* naming these objects in a particular context; that is, in describing how they act, or are, or come to be, etc. We may recall that he claims that 'coming to be from not-being', when correctly applied, means: 'coming to be from not-being *in so far as it is not being*' (δῆλον ὅτι καὶ τὸ ἐκ μὴ ὄντος γίγνεσθαι τοῦτο σημαίνει τὸ ᾗ μὴ ὄν, 191ᵇ10). This 'in so far as it is not-being' is further specified by the words ἐκ...τῆς στερήσεως...οὐκ ἐνυπάρχοντος, an odd phrase which I have translated as 'from the *sterêsis* which is not there'.[49] There is no coming to be from not-being *simpliciter*—that is, from something which

---

[48] On the use of ἁπλῶς in this formula see also n. 45 above.

[49] Like all the commentators I have seen I suppose that οὐκ ἐνυπαρχόντος goes with στερήσεως (the fact that it is not a feminine form being explained by attraction to the interposed neuter ὅ ἐστι καθ' ἑαυτὸ μὴ ὄν). I concede that on my reading the phrasing (the implicit double negation: a *sterêsis* which is not there) is slightly awkward, but I think this is nevertheless the best way of making sense of the words οὐκ ἐνυπάρχοντος in the given context. In his comments on the whole of 191ᵃ36–ᵇ27 Ross observes that 'what is...comes to be *per accidens* from what is not, i.e. from a privation, which is *per se* not-being; but it does not come to be *per se* from this privation, but inasmuch as the privation belongs to a matter'. I believe this 'inasmuch as the privation belongs to a matter' is precisely what is meant by the somewhat clumsy addition of οὐκ ἐνυπάρχοντος. Ross himself, however, does not make this link. In his comments on 191ᵇ16 he glosses the words οὐκ ἐνυπάρχοντος as 'not surviving in the product' (similarly the revised Oxford Translation: 'this not surviving as a constituent of the result'). I think this is less likely to be correct, given the fact that the genitive is governed by the proposition ἀπό (ἀπὸ στερήσεως...οὐκ ἐνυπάρχοντος).

is not-being, and nothing else. There is only coming to be from a substance ('a matter', in Ross's words),[50] which apart from its own particular mode of being exhibits also a relevant, but accidental, mode of not-being.[51] To put it differently, the *terminus a quo* is a not-being-*something* (μὴ ὄν τι) in the relevant respect. We may compare the analysis provided at *Physics* I. 7. 190^{b}12 ff. where we are told that *everything* that comes to be (τὸ γινόμενον ἅπαν, i.e. whether in the substantial sense of coming to be or in any qualified way) has a *terminus a quo* (ὅ τοῦτο γίνεται) which is complex, or twofold: 'and this in two senses—either the subject or the opposite' (καὶ τοῦτο διττόν· ἢ γὰρ τὸ ὑποκείμενον ἢ τὸ ἀντικείμενον).[52] This is why, on this particular analysis, it may be concluded that 'nothing comes to be *simpliciter* from not-being' (γίγνεσθαι μὲν οὐδὲν ἁπλῶς ἐκ μὴ ὄντος), which we may regard as equivalent to the claim that coming to be does not start out from a not-being *simpliciter*—no more, in fact, than from a being *simpliciter*—even if the term 'not-being *simpliciter* (ἁπλῶς μὴ ὄν), which we do encounter in *GC* I. 3, is not used in *Physics* I. 8.[53]

We may now return to where we started from and ask whether and how these passages in *Physics* I. 8 can be squared with the claim of *GC* I. 3 that in a sense there *is* such a thing as coming to be *simpliciter*, which starts from not-being *simpliciter*. I think the answer is that we are dealing with what we may call different levels of analysis. It is true that in Aristotle's method in general, but also in the account of *Physics* I. 7–8 and *GC* I. 3 in particular, the way we *talk* is an important starting point. But it is also true that this level of analysis is often *not more than* a starting point. Aristotle may well use it to move on to the more general level of conceptual analysis, where he focuses on conceptual distinctions which need *not* correspond with any particular distinctions made in ordinary language. As an example we may take the beginning of *Physics*

[50] The claim, also made in *Ph.* I. 8, that the coming to be from this substance, regarded qua 'this thing here' (τόδε τι), is to be regarded as non-accidental—cf. *Ph.* I. 7. 190^{b}26: 'for it is more of a "this-thing" (τόδε γὰρ τι μᾶλλον) and what comes to be does not come from it accidentally'—merely implies that we are dealing with *real* substantial generation, or that we are singling out the right descriptive perspective; it has no bearing on the question of the real or accidental not-being of the *terminus a quo*.

[51] There is no tension between this claim and the claim at 192^{a}5 that the *sterêsis* is 'in itself not-being' (καθ' αὑτὸ μὴ ὄν): the *sterêsis* is accidental *to the hupokeimenon* (the *terminus a quo*).

[52] We may indeed also compare the arguments against Parmenides at *Ph.* I. 3. 187^{a}7–10: 'there is no reason why [not-being], even if it cannot be without qualification, should not be something or other' (οὐθὲν γὰρ κωλύει μὴ ἁπλῶς εἶναι ἀλλὰ μὴ ὄν τι εἶναι τὸ μὴ ὄν); and 'who understands "being itself" otherwise than as being some particular thing?' (τίς γὰρ μανθάνει αὐτὸ τὸ ὂν εἰ μὴ τὸ ὅπερ ὄν τι εἶναι;).

[53] On the equivalence see the argument of *GC* I. 3. 316^{b}32–317^{b}18 summarized above at p. 95, and cf. n. 46.

I. 7. 189ᵇ32–4 where the two perspectives are linked in the course of one sentence:

When we *say* (φαμέν) that one thing comes to be out of another, or that something comes to be out of something different, we *may be talking* (λέγοντες) either *about* what is simple or about what is composite.

Clearly, the starting point is the way we speak ('we say'), but this is immediately linked to the referent ('we may be talking about . . .') and the way this is structured (simple or composite). In what follows it becomes clear that a one-to-one correspondence between distinctions made in ordinary language and the structure of reality (and the conceptual distinctions we should be making in describing this reality) does not exist, although the two levels are not entirely unrelated, and although ordinary language actually provides important approaches towards the structure of reality. In what follows—i.e in the rest of I. 7—the two levels of analysis coexist.[54] However, by the time Aristotle has come to *Physics* I. 8 the focus has shifted predominantly to the level of conceptual analysis (how we do or should *think* of things). The *terminus a quo* and the *terminus ad quem* are now consistently treated as composite, i.e. as compounds of subject-plus-*sterêsis* and of subject-plus-form respectively.

Now the formula ἁπλῶς (x) may serve in both contexts: it may be used, as often in Aristotle, to designate what we are prepared to *call* (x) without further qualification, but it may also be used to designate what we can *regard* as, or *think of* as (x) without further qualification.[55] In *GC* I. 3 we are dealing with the former case: the starting point of the analysis is ἁπλῶς γένεσις ('coming to be *tout court*'), which is contrasted with γένεσις ἔκ τινος καὶ τί ('coming to be something from something'). Here the qualifier ἁπλῶς is added to isolate those cases of coming to be in which we (i.e. people in general) are prepared to *say* that '(x) comes to be (period)'.[56] This analysis involves that in a similar way the *terminus ad quem* of coming to be *simpliciter* is always an ὄν ἁπλῶς (a 'being *simpliciter*'), that is something of which we are prepared to *say*, eventually, that 'it exists (period)', that is a substance (although it will also become clear

---

[54] Cf. 190ᵃ29–31: καὶ γὰρ ἐξ ἀμούσου ἀνθρώπου καὶ ὁ ἄμουσος ἀνθρώπος γίγνεσθαι λέγεται μουσικός (linguistic analysis) and 190ᵇ20–3: συγκεῖται γὰρ ὁ μουσικὸς ἀνθρώπος ἐξ ἀνθρώπου καὶ μουσικοῦ τρόπον τινά. διαλύσεις γὰρ εἰς τοὺς λόγους τοὺς ἐκείνων (conceptual analysis).

[55] For a good analysis of this use of ἁπλῶς in general, and in *GC* I. 3 in particular, see esp. Bemelmans (1995), 169–74.

[56] 'Coming to be (period)', as a translation of γίγνεσθαι ἁπλῶς, has been introduced by Williams (1982), p. x. That the discussion of γίγνεσθαι ἁπλῶς in *GC* I. 3 is in an important sense an analysis of that which we are prepared to *describe* by the phrase '(x) comes to be' without any further qualification becomes especially clear at 318ᵃ28 ff.: διὰ τί δέ ποτε τὰ μὲν ἁπλῶς γίνεσθαι λέγεται καὶ φθείρεσθαι τὰδ' οὐχ ἁπλῶς, πάλιν σκεπτέον. ψφ. αλσο, 318ᵃ32: λέγομεν γὰρ ὅτι φθείρεται νῦν κτλ.

that not every substance conversely allows the locution of its coming to be *simpliciter*). And at the beginning of *GC* I. 3 we are told that *if* there is coming to be *simpliciter* it must take its beginning in not-being *simpliciter* (ἡ δὲ ἁπλῆ ἐξ ἁπλῶς μὴ ὄντος, 317ᵇ5). This claim may be translated thus: If there is something we are prepared to *describe* as 'coming to be (period)', it must come to be from something we are willing to *describe* as 'not-being (period)'. For example: 'If a tree comes to be (period), it was formerly non-existent (period)'.

As we noted, however, in the passages from *Physics* I. 8 quoted above, the level of analysis has shifted from ordinary usage to what we should call conceptual analysis. Here the word ἁπλῶς is added in order to isolate the kind of coming to be which we may *think of* as coming to be *simpliciter*; that is, which we may think of as starting out from something we are prepared to think of as 'not-being *and nothing else*'.[57] Given the analysis of *Physics* I. 8, there is *no* such kind of coming to be *simpliciter*, for, as we saw, the *terminus a quo* is invariably composite.

As I have argued in the previous section, at the level of conceptual analysis there is no real tension between the accounts of *Physics* I and *GC* I. 3. This can be illustrated from the way in which Aristotle solves the aporia which arises in connection with Q2. This aporia precisely turns on the supposition that what is not-being *simpliciter* in the sense relevant in the context of *GC* I. 3 (i.e. what we are in fact prepared to *call* 'not being', i.e. what *need* not be called anything else but 'not-being') is to be taken, absurdly, as not-being *simpliciter* in the sense that it *cannot* be called by any other name than just 'not-being'.[58] As we are now in a position to see, this supposition was mistaken. What *need* not be called by any other name than 'not-being' is not something which *cannot* be called by any other name than 'not-being', just as what *need* not be called by any other name than 'being' is not something which *cannot* be called by any other name than 'being'. The latter claim can indeed be illustrated from the first book of the *Physics* as well. There Aristotle can both maintain,

---

[57] It is γένεσις ἁπλῶς in this sense which is also excluded at *Cael.* III. 2.301ᵇ30–302ᵃ9, on which see above, n. 93.

[58] In the context of his comments on 317ᵇ15 Joachim (1922), 93, attempts to solve this apparent difficulty by suggesting that there is a difference between τὸ ἁπλῶς μὴ ὄν and τὸ μὴ ὄν ἁπλῶς, the former expression meaning 'that which is, without qualification, devoid of being', whereas the latter means 'that which is devoid of being unless you qualify the term "being"'. See also Tricot (1933), 24 n. 2, who glosses τὸ μὴ ὄν ἁπλῶς as 'ce qui n'est pas absolument' i.e. 'ce qui est en un certain sens'. However, it is difficult to get this out of the Greek word order (one would expect τὸ μὴ ἁπλῶς ὄν in that case, rather than τὸ μὴ ὄν ἁπλῶς). Furthermore, Joachim's distinction has the authority of Philoponus against it, who appears to treat the expressions τὸ ἁπλῶς μὴ ὄν (*in GC* 46. 12 and *passim*) and τὸ μὴ ὄν ἁπλῶς (*in GC* 47. 31–2) as equivalent. Finally, the claim that the *terminus a quo* is not an ὄν ἁπλῶς would make little sense, philosophically, in this context, where after all the problem concerning the *terminus a quo* is primarily that of not-being, not of being.

against Parmenides, that every being ($\check{o}v$) is a 'being-something' ($\check{o}v$ $\tau\iota$), and claim in a different context that substance is being *simpliciter* ($\dot{a}\pi\lambda\hat{\omega}s$ $\check{o}v$, 190^{b}1) and that only substances can be said to come to be *simpliciter* (190^{a}33).[59]

We might think these 'varying' applications of the qualifier *simpliciter* confusing, but when we take into account that '$\dot{a}\pi\lambda\hat{\omega}s$ (x)' basically means '(x) without further qualification', we may see that there is no real inconsistency involved. The point is merely that the rider 'without further qualification' may take on a different force, according as it is used in different contexts. Since these differences of contexts (or, as I have put it earlier, these different levels of analysis) occur within the context of *Physics* I no less than between *Physics* I and *GC* I. 3, and since the overall ontological framework appears to be the same in both cases, we may conclude that also in this respect the accounts of coming to be in *Physics* I. and *GC* I. 3 can be regarded as constituting a coherent whole.

5. Concluding remarks: the status of ordinary language

My concluding observations take up some of the things that have been said—in the previous section as well as at the end of Section 1—about the role of ordinary language vis-à-vis what we might call conceptual analysis. As I have tried to show, the practices of ordinary language, in particular our ways of naming things, play an important role in Aristotle's account. Yet, as we have seen, this is not all there is to Aristotle's method. First of all, as our analysis of *Physics* I. 8 may be taken to have shown, ordinary language does not always single out the right perspective in speaking about things, and it may thus give rise to mistaken ontological beliefs—the example of the earliest thinkers discussed in *Physics* I. 8 being a case in point. That ordinary language (and the way it names things) may sometimes simply fail to mirror certain features of reality is further shown at *Physics* I. 5. 188^{b}9–12 where we are told that although genesis always is 'from contraries' ($\dot{\epsilon}\xi$ $\dot{\epsilon}\nu\alpha\nu\tau\acute{\iota}\omega\nu$, e.g. $\mu o\nu\sigma\iota\kappa\grave{o}s$ from $\check{a}\mu o\nu\sigma os$) this tends to escape our notice in the case of composite things, such as a house, 'because the opposite conditions have no names' ($\delta\iota\grave{a}$ $\tau\grave{o}$ $\mu\grave{\eta}$ $\tau\grave{a}s$ $\dot{a}\nu\tau\iota\kappa\epsilon\iota\mu\acute{\epsilon}\nu\alpha s$ $\delta\iota\alpha\theta\acute{\epsilon}\sigma\epsilon\iota s$ $\dot{\omega}\nu o\mu\acute{a}\sigma\theta\alpha\iota$).

Accordingly, the fact that a certain distinction is made in ordinary language is not itself sufficient to establish that there is a corresponding ontological distinction. That we use different names ($\delta\iota\acute{\omega}\rho\iota\sigma\tau\alpha\iota$ $\tauo\hat{\iota}s$ $\dot{o}\nu\acute{o}\mu\alpha\sigma\iota\nu$) for coming to be (*genesis*) and alteration (*alloiôsis*) is introduced at the beginning of *GC* I as a relevant fact (314^{a}5–6), yet it is one

---

[59] On Aristotle's points against Parmenides see n. 52 above.

which is apparently in itself unable to clinch the issue. Indeed it is introduced in the context of a question which precisely asks whether we should follow this convention of ordinary language, or whether we should rather take *genesis* and *alloiôsis* to be the same thing. In other words, the subsequent dialectical discussion of the first four chapters of *GC* I is still indispensable.

I find myself unable, therefore, to go along with Graham's claim (in his discussion of *Ph*. I. 7) that 'Aristotle seems to take for granted that language ... directly mirrors reality'.[60] Nor do I think one should follow Wieland who, true to his phenomenological interpretation, attempts to destroy the whole idea of there being separate realms of language and reality in Aristotle, and who consequently concludes that 'indem er sprachliche Formen untersucht, analysiert er also zugleich die Strukturen der Wirklichkeit'.[61] Of course the ways in which we speak and think about reality provide an important starting point for Aristotle's dialectical investigations in the area of physics as well as elsewhere. However, it is *not more* than a starting point. Aristotelian physics does not remain at the level of semantics. Language may (and often does) provide indications of the structure of reality, but it often also can be a source of error.[62]

[60] Graham (1987), 480 n. 11.

[61] Wieland (1962), 145.

[62] I would like to thank Frans de Haas, Jaap Mansfeld, and the participants in the Symposium Aristotelicum, in particular John Cooper and David Charles, for their comments on earlier versions of this paper. My analysis of *GC* I. 3 is much indebted to Bemelmans (1995), an excellent Leiden dissertation which unfortunately has not (yet) been translated into English.

4

On Generation and Corruption I. 4: Distinguishing Alteration—Substantial Change, Elemental Change, and First Matter in *GC*[1]

SARAH BROADIE

There are two parts to this chapter. The first is mainly a commentary on *GC* I. 4. 319^b6–320^a7.[2] In the course of it I raise the issue of first matter, and draw a comparison between this chapter and *Physics* I. 7.[3] The second part is an attempt to come to better terms with the idea of first matter in the context of *GC*.

1. Commentary on I. 4

319^b6–8

Aristotle has argued that genesis unqualified does occur, and is a process *sui generis*, not reducible to alteration. The discussion has assumed, of course, that genesis is radically different from alteration, but the difference has yet to be explained.[4] This is the task of the present chapter.

319^b8–10

This says that the *hupokeimenon*[5] is one thing, and the *pathos* predicable of it something else, and of each of them ($\dot{\epsilon}\kappa\alpha\tau\dot{\epsilon}\rho\sigma\nu$) there is change. The

---

[1] Despite the imperfections that undoubtedly remain, not only the discussion at Deurne but written comments kindly sent me by Jacques Brunschwig, John Cooper, Mary Louise Gill, Paul Kalligas, and Geoffrey Lloyd have helped to improve this paper.

[2] I rely on H. H. Joachim's revised text (apart from his transposition at 319^b28–31).

[3] For other discussions of the issue of prime matter see the contributions of Algra and Charles to this volume (Chs. 3, 5).

[4] Actually, the explanation in I. 4 is anticipated at I. 2. 317^a20–7.

[5] i.e. subject or substratum. But for the most part I avoid using those words so as to try not to beg questions. The clearest meaning (relevant to this discussion) of *hupokeimenon* is:

next point will be that genesis is change of the one, and alteration is change of the other. Now, in one sense of 'of', both alteration and genesis are changes *of* a *hupokeimenon*: that is to say, each is predicated of a subject; for example, *Callias* in 'Callias becomes well' and *fire* or *The lump of bronze* in 'Fire becomes earth' or 'The lump of bronze becomes a statue'. But this cannot be the sense of 'of' at work here, because in this sense there cannot be change of a *pathos*. So the passage means that in alteration one *pathos* is exchanged for another *pathos*, which suggests that in genesis one *hupokeimenon* is exchanged for another *hupokeimenon*: that is, in genesis one subject of (here unspecified) qualities, quantities, relations, etc. (and also of changes and potential changes) comes to be, and another subject of qualities, etc. passes away (*phthora*).[6] The suggestion has already been defended in I. 3, and it is confirmed below by the coupling of *genesis* and *phthora* at 319^{b}17–18, 22, and 320^{a}3.

319^{b}10–18

(a) The point that in alteration the *hupokeimenon* remains or persists (ὑπομένει) while the *pathê* change[7] will soon be balanced by the thought that in *genesis* and *phthora* a *pathos* may remain while the *hupokeimena* change (21–3). (*GC* II and *Cael.* III show that in *genesis* and *phthora* of the simple bodies a *pathos*[8] not only may but must remain throughout. As for *genesis* and *phthora* of organisms and artefacts, it seems clear that there must always be attributes in common between what goes into any given metamorphosis and what comes out of it.)

(b) Here Aristotle emphasizes that the *hupokeimenon* that remains the same in alteration is perceptible, whereas in *genesis–phthora* nothing perceptible remains throughout as the self-same *hupokeimenon*. It is natural to understand him as taking the same point further, by giving a reason for it, when he says at 14–17 that in *genesis–phthora* the first thing is wholly transformed into the second. C. J. F. Williams,[9] however, has suggested that ὅλον at 14 should be understood in a logical sense contrasted with κατὰ μέρος at I. 3. 317^{b}35. In that case, Aristotle is not so much saying that the first thing is transformed through and through

---

'subject as of predication' (this in a metaphysical, not merely grammatical, sense). I believe that by the end of this paper it will have been shown, by implication, that 'subject' in this sense is always an appropriate rendering of *hupokeimenon* in the parts of *GC* under consideration. The predication in question includes predication of change or coming to be, as well as the categories of being.

[6] For an extended defence of this, the natural, reading of 319^{b}8–10 see Gill (1989), 53–7.

[7] Cf. *GC* I. 1. 314^{b}13–15; 314^{b}26–315^{a}3.

[8] More precisely, it is a διαφορά.

[9] Williams (1982), 98–9.

so that it completely disappears, as that it undergoes unqualified *genesis* or *phthora* as distinct from coming or ceasing to be F for a non-substantial predicate 'F'. But this interpretation cannot be right, for Aristotle here is engaged in explaining the difference between unqualified *genesis–phthora* and alteration considered as paradigmatic of the non-substantial changes.[10] On Williams's reading we just have a reiteration of the terminology, as opposed to an account of the distinction it labels. Since Williams himself suspects that his interpretation is 'too far-fetched' (the grounds he gives for it are subtle but not strong), one may wonder why he invests therein. Presumably it is because he accepts the traditional view according to which Aristotle postulates first matter as the *hupokeimenon* that persists through substantial change.[11] On this view, the transformed thing does not completely pass away, because one metaphysical component of it remains: the *hupokeimenon*.[12]

(c) On that traditional view, the present passage is likely to be taken as suggesting that in substantial change a necessarily non-perceptible, because non-empirical, *hupokeimenon* remains throughout. Thus the contrast between this type of change and alteration depends in part on the contrast between a non-empirical and an empirical *hupokeimenon*. On the traditional view, Aristotle presents us with three *hupokeimena* in substantial change: the imperceptible one that remains throughout, and those that respectively perish and come to be. In relation to what, then, are these latter two, the perceptible ones, *hupokeimena*? To non-substantial attributes and non-substantial changes actual or potential, of course. For each when it exists is subject of the corresponding predicates. It is very tempting to stop at this point in the conviction that (equally of course) neither of the perceptible *hupokeimena* can be thought of as a *hupokeimenon* of *substantial* change. For: (i) that which comes into being in a given substantial change logically cannot be subject *of that change*. (ii) That which passes away in the same substantial change

---

[10] Although at 319[b]31–320[a]2 alteration is listed with growth/diminution and locomotion, and all three are contrasted with substantial change.

[11] This, as John Cooper pointed out to me, is ambiguous between 'persists through a given substantial change' and 'persists through all the substantial changes there ever are'. I mean to refer to a view that (a) is tailored for the case of elemental transformation and (b) mainly considers transformation of a portion of say fire into one of earth, of that into one of water, etc., in roughly the same or a contiguous location (however tricky it would be to spell that out exactly). The view, then, is that first matter is the *hupokeimenon* that persists throughout such a cycle of transformations (and throughout subsequent and previous cycles in the same place). Nothing is to be gained for the purpose of this chapter by deciding whether traditional first matter is numerically (!) the same subject of a cycle occurring in the Netherlands and a simultaneous one in Australia.

[12] Williams *passim*, 211–19. Cf. Tricot 38, who understands ὅλον at 319[b]14 as σύνολον, i.e. the matter-form compound, 'et non la chose entière, car toujours la πρώτη ὕλη persiste à titre d'ὑποκείμενον'.

(i.e. changes into the new thing) can hardly be thought of as a *hupokei-menon* to that change. The reason is that although we quite naturally predicate the change of the perishing thing as subject, saying 'The pool of water turned into air', nevertheless, according to the traditional view (on a straightforward understanding of it) first matter is already functioning as a *hupokeimenon* of the change in question. And (iii) by parity of reasoning the new perceptible subject cannot be thought of as a *hupokei-menon* to any future substantial change in which it too will pass away. The crucial assumption of this account is that if it is correct to say that first matter is a *hupokeimenon* of substantial change, then it is incorrect to say that the perishing perceptible substance is its *hupokeimenon*, and vice versa. The account, then, leaves us with two choices: (i) It is true that Aristotle, like ordinary people, sometimes speaks as if (e.g.) the water that turns into air is the subject of that change, since he informally predicates '...changes into (μεταβάλλει εἰς) air' of water, and so on,[13] but these words hide what he considers to be the true logical form, whereby first matter is the true subject, a subject that *comes to be*, rather than *itself changes into*, air from having been water. Alternatively, (ii) Aristotle by his own lights is speaking correctly when he says 'Water changes into air', so that in one sense *water* certainly is the *hupokeimenon* of *changes into air*; but in a different and perhaps more recondite sense first matter, too, is a *hupokeimenon* of that change from water to air. The *hupokeimenon* in this new sense is not the subject of which '...comes to be air', etc. are predicated; it is, however, the *sub-stratum* of that change. The first of these alternatives carries the unwel-come implication that Aristotle is happy to predicate '...comes to be air' etc. of a complete blank, something without any nature. The second commits us to two senses of *hupokeimenon*, one of which, 'subject of predication', is straightforwardly intelligible, while the other, 'sub-stratum', is rather mysterious in so far as it is supposed to mean some-thing different from 'subject'. One tries to make sense of it by getting what one can from the image of an *under*-thing, but this does not shed much light.

---

[13] e.g. *GC* II. 5. 332ᵇ5–19. It is noteworthy that he hardly if at all uses the form 'Air *becomes* water'. And at *Ph.* I. 7. 190ᵃ25–6 he says that we (= common sense or his theory?) do not say that the bronze *becomes a statue*, but that the statue *comes to be from bronze* (here this exemplifies substantial change). (Cf. however the universal statement at 190ᵇ10–13, which in light of the examples (14–17) certainly implies that it is correct to say that the bronze becomes a statue.) If 'we do not say' at 190ᵃ25–6 is normative, the reason may be that 'X becomes Y' automatically implies that, given no impediment, it will be the case that X *is* Y. If so, then when X is matter and Y the substance it turns into we are saying either that (it will be the case that) one substantial thing is another, which is absurd, or that e.g. the bronze is statue-y, which reduces substantial coming to be to alteration.

(d) Returning to the text, let us see whether the present passage is evidence that Aristotle postulates a persisting first matter in connection with substantial change. One could argue: Why else would he emphasize the absence from substantial change of a perceptible persisting *hupokei-menon*, if not to get us to infer the presence of a non-perceptible one?[14] One could also counter this rhetorical question with another: If at this point Aristotle wants us to understand that substantial change requires a non-empirical persisting *hupokeimenon*, why does he not say so explicitly—at this point? Perhaps the answer to the first question (treated now as not merely rhetorical) is that Aristotle wants to contrast his own position with the type of theory (exemplified by atomism, discussed in I. 2)[15] that reduces all macroscopic change to non-substantial change (locomotion and turning) in imperceptible subjects. Thus he emphasizes that, for him, non-substantial change involves a perceptible *hupokeime-non*, so that where this is lacking the change is genuinely substantial. This does not logically rule it out that substantial change requires its own sort of *hupokeimenon*, one that is imperceptible; but his rejection of atomism is all the more telling if it includes the claim that, so far as subjects of change are concerned, what you perceive is just what you get.

319^{b}18–21

Presumably he thinks that the clearest cases of *genesis–phthora* are those where one term is (relatively speaking) imperceptible,[16] perhaps because where this is not so there is more purchase for supposing that the initial *hupokeimenon* remains throughout the change. (In that case—since we are now speaking only of perceptible *hupokeimena*—the change would be alteration.) It is as if one is more tempted to identify (across time) two perceptible things, or parts of them, than a perceptible with an imperceptible thing. At first sight this passage conflicts with his rejection at *GC* I. 3. 318^{b}18–33 of the vulgar equation of unqualified coming to be and passing away with coming to be from, and passing away into, something imperceptible. But there is no disagreement, for different distinctions are at issue in the two passages. Here the contrast is between substantial coming to be and passing away, and change (especially alteration) in respect of a non-substantial category. At I. 3. 318^{b}18–33 the contrast was between the coming to be/passing away of a positive thing (there called 'unqualified coming to be, etc.') and that of a privation in the same category. The crowd are wrong to think (e.g.) that earth, a robustly

---

[14] So reasons Philoponus, *in GC* 66. 12–17.
[15] See David Sedley's contribution to this volume.
[16] Air is imperceptible in the way in which fire, in earlier theories, was held to be 'the most *incorporeal* of the elements' (*de An.* I. 2. 405^{a}6–7).

thing-y thing, comes robustly to be from nothing-y air, whereas it is only in a tenuous sense that the air correspondingly perishes into earth, since air is not enough of a being for its ceasing to be to count as true perishing. The crowd are wrong, because true thingy-ness is a matter of form and positive being, and earth is a privation compared to air in Aristotle's scheme.

Let us take stock. We have considered two interpretations of the main point of I. 4. According to the first, the difference between alteration and substantial change is that the former is exchange of *pathê* in a persistent *hupokeimenon*, the latter is exchange of perceptible *hupokeimena*. According to the second, both types presuppose a persisting *hupokeimenon*, but in alteration this is an empirical substance, whereas in substantial change it is non-empirical matter. According to the first, the statement that alteration, but not substantial change, involves a perceptible persistent *hupokeimenon* is meant mainly to rule out imperceptible *hupokeimena* whose non-substantial changes, here typified by alteration, would otherwise offer a tempting reduction base for the coming to be and perishing of organisms and the like. According to the second interpretation, the statement is meant to rule in a non-empirical persistent *hupokeimenon* for substantial change.

(On either interpretation, the contrast drawn in *GC* I. 4 seems to focus on the special case of simple-body transformation, even though Aristotle claims to be distinguishing alteration from substantial change in general, and gives a biological example of the latter at 319^b16.[17] For it is only in the case of simple-body transformation that one is bound to deny the persistence of an empirical subject. 'Simple' entails no empirically distinguishable constituent. No doubt biological coming to be and perishing can be made to fit the same formula, but in their case there is no such compelling reason why it should be preferred.)

To return to the two interpretations. Adherents of the second one should be bothered by the fact that Aristotle does not take this opportunity to state outright that he postulates a persistent *hupokeimenon* for substantial change. One should also wonder why he postulates it. The usual explanation, I believe, is that he wants the structure of substantial change to fit the triadic structure set forth in *Physics* I. 7.[18] However, as long as we do not look beyond *GC* I. 4 we are not justified in resorting to

---

[17] 'The semen is entirely transformed into blood' [sc. of the offspring]. G. E. R. Lloyd reminds me that Aristotle here cites a common belief; it conflicts with his own embryology.

[18] Whether the fit is successful depends on whether the concept of *hupokeimenon* in *Ph.* I. 7 is the same as, or can be reasonably extended to cover, a non-empirical *hupokeimenon* that cannot be subject of predication.

this or any other explanation, because within this discussion of the difference between substantial change and alteration the evidence for the supposed *explanandum* (sc. that he postulates first matter as persistent *hupokeimenon* of substantial change) is almost non-existent.[19] This is in addition to the fact that the postulate has philosophically unpleasing consequences.[20]

But, in order to keep the focus on *GC* I. 4 itself, let me for the moment bracket the second interpretation along with arguments for or against it.[21] For, whatever the rest of the chapter may yield, and the rest of the treatise, no good reason has emerged so far from I. 4 itself for believing that in reading I. 4 we are reading about (*inter alia*) a matter that persists through substantial change. Provisionally, therefore, I shall proceed as if the first, the metaphysically conservative, interpretation is correct for *GC* I. 4. On this basis, consider the account here in comparison with the foundational discussion of coming to be in *Physics* I. 6–7.[22]

GC I. 4 presents a different and more developed picture.[23] Aristotle may be drawing our attention to this by illustrating alteration here with an example all but identical[24] to the one which in *Physics* I. 7 he used as a general model:[25] the uncultured man becoming cultured. In terms of that model, the *hupokeimenon*[26] was expressly said to remain,[27] and there was no suggestion that this aspect of the model was not intended to apply to change in the category of substance. On the contrary, the model was introduced to explain '*all* coming to be' (189[b]30–2). Furthermore, bronze shaped into a statue was an example of things that remain (190[a]24–5),

---

[19] It may be thought that the closing lines of I. 3. 319[b]2–4 constitute evidence for the postulate. But different translations are possible; does ἑτέρα ἑκατέρου ἡ ὕλη at I. 3. 319[a]33 ask whether the matter of fire and earth is a third thing besides them, or does it ask whether each has a different matter from the other? If the first, ἡ αὐτή at [b]2 means 'the same as fire (or as earth)'; if the second, it means 'the same for fire as for earth', a formula satisfied by first matter in the traditional doctrine. But even on this reading the passage hardly constitutes evidence that, in the immediately ensuing discussion distinguishing substantial change from alteration, Aristotle relies on that doctrine to explain the difference. For in that case he would not have indicated as he does at [b]4–5 (περὶ μὲν οὖν τούτων ἐπὶ τοσοῦτον εἰρήσθω) that one discussion is over for the time being and another about to begin.

[20] Even some of those who attribute the postulate to Aristotle see it as an embarrassment; e.g. Williams (1982), 218–19.

[21] The bracketing will be lifted before the end of these comments on I. 4.

[22] Cf. Keimpe Algra, above, pp. 110 ff.

[23] On the comparative underdevelopment of the *Physics* I approach cf. R. M. Dancy, 'On Some of Aristotle's Second Thoughts on Substance: Matter', *Philosophical Review*, 87 (1978), 385 n. 35, and M. J. Loux, *Primary Ousia: An Essay on Aristotle's* Metaphysics Z *and* H (Ithaca, NY: 1991), 125–7.

[24] In *GC* I. 4, it is the cultured man becoming uncultured. Williams (1982), 100 suggests that this is meant to match the air (positive)-to-water (privative) example at 319[b]23.

[25] See Code (1976), 358–9.

[26] Cf. 190[a]15 and 34.   [27] See 190[a]9–13 and 17–21.

and statue-making was classed as substantial change (190^b6).[28] On the other hand, the examples at 190^b4-5 of biological genesis (plants and animals from seed as *hupokeimenon*; cf. blood from semen at *GC* I. 4. 319^b16) rather suggested that in that sort of case the *hupokeimenon* passes away. In general: although in *Physics* I. 7 Aristotle was definite that the coming to be of substance is the coming to be of something in a different category from the others,[29] he did not dwell on what difference this implies for the logical structures of the corresponding types of change. For example, at 190^a21-3 he said that 'Y comes to be from X' is said where X is contrary to Y, not where X is that which remains. ('Cultured comes to be from uncultured', not 'Cultured comes to be from man'.) He then qualified this by remarking that in some cases (ἐνίοτε) the locution is used even where X does remain, 'for we say that the statue comes to be from bronze' (24–5). In the context, the latter is clearly an instance of substantial coming to be, but it is interesting that Aristotle did not point this out, let alone pause to state: 'This qualification is something that distinguishes substantial coming to be from the other kinds'.[30] Of course, his purpose in *Physics* I. 7 was to establish the coherence of *coming to be* in general, which no doubt made him attend more to likenesses than to differences between substantial change and the model case of uncultured man becoming cultured. Still, it is difficult to believe that if at that point he did hold a definite view about a distinct structure of substantial coming to be he would not have expressed it.

319^b21-4

Here we have a further refinement on the *Physics* I. 7 account, where the uncultured–cultured model was used simply to show up the relationships between that which remains and the contraries. It was just taken for granted that the something that remains remains as one and the same *hupokeimenon*. But on that assumption even a *pathos* shared by the termini of substantial change automatically functions as *hupokeimenon*

---

[28] The fact that at places in the *Metaphysics* Aristotle excludes artefacts from counting as substances cannot tell against this evidence, *pace* Charlton (1970), 76. See also *Ph.* I. 7. 190^b11: '*Everything* that comes to be is composite (συνθετόν)'; and *Ph.* I. 9. 192^a31-2 and II. 3. 194^b23-4 on matter as τὸ ἐνυπάρχον. Cf. *Metaph.* V. 2. 1013^a24-5; VII. 7. 1032^b32-1033^a1.

[29] See 190^a31-$^b1$ ff.

[30] Similarly at 190^a25: 'We do not say that the bronze becomes a statue' (whereas 'The man becomes cultured' is correct) might have been, but is not, generalized into a doctrinal mark of substantial coming to be. The only such mark given here is that substances alone are said to come to be without qualification (190^a31-3), but this is not an analysis showing a special way (i.e. unique to the substantial case) in which *hupokeimenon* and/or that which remains are or are not involved.

of the new phenomenon, and of the one that has passed away. This has the absurd result that such a change would be alteration after all.

Although I have no doubt that the above paraphrase gives the meaning of 319ᵇ21–4, there are several difficulties.[31]

(a) At line 21 πάθος ἐναντιώσεως presumably means '*pathos* that is one of a pair of contraries'. But one of the examples is the transparency of water and air (22–3). Is this one of a pair of contraries? And why, for that matter, should the common *pathos* be one of a pair of contraries? The point seems not to depend on this.[32]

(b) The main thought is: That into which the thing changes must not be (i.e. must not be seen as) a *pathos* of the common *pathos*. On this construal, τούτου at line 23, which refers to the common πάθος at line 21, is governed by πάθος at line 24, not by θάτερον. Thus πάθος at line 24 is the predicate; the subject is θάτερον, εἰς ὃ μεταβάλλει. But why this emphasis on the *terminus ad quem* alone? It is equally true that the contrary that passes away must not be viewed as a *pathos* of the common *pathos* if the case is one of substantial change. And, since the contrary that passes away has not even been mentioned, what is θάτερον other than?[33] (As a matter of fact, the passage looks as if it might conflate two thoughts: (1) the one just stated, which is surely what Aristotle intends here; and (2) the point that if the common property is one of a pair of contraries, change cannot be to (or for that matter from) the other contrary of the pair. (2) requires that θάτερον govern τούτου. Cf. *GC* II. 5. 332ᵇ1–5, and the polemical argument at 332ᵃ12–17.)

(c) For ψυχρά at line 23 Averroes's text apparently had the equivalent of 'wet', which is chemically preferable, since air is hot-wet and water cold-wet on Aristotle's theory. Joachim, following Philoponus, says that Aristotle is 'only quoting a common view [sc. that air is cold] in illustration'.[34] The error, whatever it is and whoever's, does not affect our philosophical understanding.

(d) Following Joachim, 1922 (p. 108), Mugler, 1966 (p. 17) and Williams, 1982 (p. 14), I understand οὐ δεῖ at l. 23 as 'must not', not 'need not (i.e. not-must)'; so Forster (1955), 203. (Cf. *APr.* I. 28. 44ᵃ2.) However, εἰ δὲ μή at line 24 hypothesizes that the *terminus ad quem* is (in

---

[31] I am grateful to Jacques Brunschwig for not letting me get away with a more relaxed treatment of this passage, although I fear I have not been able to rise to all his questions about it.

[32] ἐναντιώσεως may suggest that the common *pathos* is a σύμβολον as *per* the theory of *GC* II. 4–5, but 'transparent' has nothing to do with that theoretical context.

[33] However, cf. 320ᵃ1 for θάτερον as simply meaning, in effect, 'the new thing'.

[34] Joachim (1922), 109. If he is right, 319ᵇ16 (semen turns into blood) may afford a parallel; see p. 128, note 17.

fact) a *pathos* of wet or whatever, not merely that it is possible for it to be one.

(e) A philosophical question arises about the scope of the notion of 'common *pathos*' in the argument.[35] No one could suppose it to apply to every *pathos* common to some water and the air it turns into: for example, to *being in my kitchen*. In other words, the point hardly merits discussion at all if it takes seriously the possibility that *being in my kitchen* might be the *hupokeimenon* to which cold and hot successively belong. Presumably the passage is restricted to common *pathê* that are (1) what would nowadays be called intrinsic properties, and (2) constant features of both termini of the change.

At any rate, read as we have decided provisionally to read it, the discussion in *GC* I. 4 shows the *Physics* I. 7 analysis to be inadequate. For we now see that staying with that analysis poses a dilemma: either substantial coming to be, and simple-body transformation in particular, is alteration after all (because of the common *pathos* functioning as persistent *hupokeimenon*), or there is no *pathos* common between the termini. In the latter case, substantial change is scientifically unintelligible: which would be another arrow for the quiver of those who want to deny its reality. Moreover, if in the cycle of elemental transformations (e.g.) wet as common factor is allowed to function as *hupokeimenon* of the change from water to air, can wet also function, as it must, as a *pathos* in relation to the change from earth (cold-dry) to water (cold-wet)?[36]

$319^{b}25–31$

(What follows draws on the interpretation of Philoponus, but with a crucial difference: Philoponus assumes the traditional doctrine of first matter, whereas this account excludes it.)

(a) *Preliminary remarks.* The previous passage showed that if we analyse, say, the transformation of air to water as acquisition, by a common feature such as wet, of hot in exchange for cold, then we are analysing it as alteration. But this needs to be qualified, because it holds true only if we treat cold and hot as *pathê* of wet *per se*.[37] This is another way of saying: only if we take wet as the true *hupokeimenon* of the other two. But

---

[35] Thanks to Mary Louise Gill for the discussion which brought this into focus.

[36] We cannot be sure that Aristotle could not accommodate such metaphysical role-switches if he had to. Cf. the way in which the (in some sense) same bronze shows up first as subject, then, when the statue is made, in the predicate (*Metaph.* VII. 7. $1033^{a}5–23$; IX. 7. $1049^{a}18–24$; *Ph.* VII. 3. $245^{b}9–16$).

[37] Cf. *GC* I. 5. $321^{b}3–4$ and I. 4. $319^{b}11–12$.

what if instead we think of cold and hot as *pathê* of wet *per accidens*? That is to say: What if we think that 'wet is cold' and 'wet is hot' are true (one after the other) because first we have wet and cold both holding of a subject that is neither of them, and then we have wet and hot holding of one that is neither of *them*?[38] If traditional first matter is kept out of the picture, the only available subjects are water for the first pair and air for the second. These (or, more precisely, these portions of the respective simple bodies[39]) have to be numerically distinct, because one is essentially cold, the other hot. Thus we have exchange of one subject for another, hence true substantial change. By this shift of logical Gestalt from seeing cold, then hot, as successively holding *of* wet (*per se*) to seeing them as successively concurrent *with* it, we automatically find ourselves with distinct successive subjects. Equivalently, we now find ourselves hearing the 'it' with which cold and hot are successively associated as denoting a universal with successive instances, instead of, as under the previous Gestalt, a single particular. The shift depends on the doctrine that if there is a property there must be a subject. For once we deny that wet is *per se* subject to cold or hot (or either of them to it) we place them all on one metaphysical level. And now two choices are open: either we treat them all as accidents of whatever subject they are of, or we treat them as all essential.[40] In the first case we are led to traditional first matter and a change with the same logical structure as alteration; in the second we understand the change from cold to hot as the coming to be of a portion of *that which is* hot and wet out of something which, when it existed, would have been rightly termed 'a portion of *that which is* cold and wet'.[41]

---

[38] See *APo.* I. 22. 83^{a}1–14; *Metaph.* V. 7. 1017^{a}7–22. Joachim (109–10) invokes this distinction between *pathos per se* and *per accidens*, but fails to apply it in interpreting the passage. Williams (100–1) invokes it to more effect, but does not see that, just as the *per se* side of the contrast lines up with alteration in one subject, the *per accidens* side of it, in the present context, lines up with coming to be and passing away of different subjects. This may be because he is committed to the view that Aristotle distinguishes substantial coming to be by postulating first matter as its persisting subject (pp. 211–19).

[39] For one might doubt whether water, as distinct from a definite particular portion of it, can be said to have a numerical identity, unless what one means is the entirety of water in the universe at a given time. I owe this point to Paul Kalligas.

[40] So on this disjunct, given Aristotle's examples, transparency turns out to be essential to water and air. (However, it belongs to them not because they are water and air, but because they are bodies, and it plays no part in the chemistry of elemental transformation; cf. *de An.* II. 7. 418^{b}4–13.)

[41] The reason for this elaboration is that if we try to describe a particular case we use tenses (in the Aristotelian context). But '(A portion of) that which is hot, etc. comes to be out of) that which *is* cold, etc.' suggests that they exist simultaneously; while '(A portion of) that which is Hot comes to be out of (a portion of) that which *was* cold' suggests that the subject of cold survives its loss of cold. Presumably this difficulty has made it easier to believe in persisting first matter.

(b) Now, at 319^{b}25–31 Aristotle runs the argument backwards to reinforce the point that it makes all the difference whether a *pathos* is *per se* or *per accidens*. As before, we start with a pair of logical compounds, of which one ceases, the other comes, to be. In the discussion just preceding, the compounds were cold-wet, hot-wet, and so forth; now they are cultured-man and uncultured-man. We now know, what was left completely unclear in the *Physics* I. 7 discussion, that these compounds can be interpreted in two ways. If we treat culture and lack of it not as *pathê* of man *per se*, but as each coinciding with man in the same subject, so that we have first something that is man and cultured and then something that is man and lacking culture, then, since man is a substance and we treat those contraries as if they were on the same metaphysical level as man, they figure as substantial too. Thus passing away of a contrary would entail passing away of the substance of which the contrary is a substantial property. But since that substance is also a man, a man passes away and (by a parallel argument) a man comes to be. And the one that passes away must be numerically different from the one that comes to be, or the identical substance would exist and not exist at the same time. Since this is absurd, we adopt the other interpretation, according to which the contraries are *pathê per se*, so that the change is mere alteration. Of course, we can still describe it as the coming to be of the compound uncultured-man and the passing away of the compound cultured-man, but this description, while unhelpful, is innocuous as long as it is not given the first interpretation.[42]

(c) Paraphrastic translation of 319^{b}25–31:

For example, the cultured man ceases to be, an uncultured man comes to be, but the man remains as the same thing. Now if culture and lack of culture were not *pathê per se* of this [sc. thing], there would have been a coming to be of the one and a ceasing to be of the other [i.e. of the man that was cultured, and of the man that was uncultured, respectively]. (That is why these [culture and lack of it] are *pathê* [*per se*] of man, whereas the coming to be and ceasing to be are [only] of cultured-man and uncultured-man.) But as things are, this [culture, lack of it] is a *pathos* [*per se*] of that which remains. That is why changes of this sort are alteration.

I take τοῦ μὲν . . . τοῦ δέ at lines 27–8 to refer not to ἡ μουσικὴ καὶ ἡ ἀμουσία at line 27, as Joachim (p. 109), but to ὁ μουσικὸς ἄνθρωπος and ἄνθρωπος . . . ἄμουσος at line 25 (cf. 29–30). πάθη at line 29 refers to the

---

[42] Williams 102 complains that these compounds are 'incoherent', because while in general 'a cultured man Φs' entails 'a man Φs', 'a cultured man comes into existence (= comes to be)' does not entail 'a man comes into existence (comes to be)'. He does not see that the entailment would hold if cultured stood to man as wet to cold in air, which is Aristotle's point. Yet apart from that, Williams is very clear about the parallelism; see esp. 100–1.

contrary states, not to the *genesis* and *phthora* of 27–8 and 30, nor to 'the fact that a man becomes unmusical and ceases to be musical' (Verdenius and Waszink, 13–18). Similarly for πάθος at line 30. There is perhaps a slight awkwardness in the flow of thought at lines 29–30, but not enough to justify Joachim's transposition (suggested by Philoponus ad loc., though as a way to read the passage rather than an emendation).[43] The inference introduced by διό at line 28 does not follow from the preceding conditional, nor from its apodosis, but from the obvious absurdity of the apodosis.[44]

319^b31–320^a2

(a) Here Aristotle says that it is *genesis–phthora* when *nothing* remains for the contraries to qualify as *pathê* or accidents. Thus he corrects any impression that might have arisen from earlier wording in the chapter, that hot, wet, etc. are only accidental *pathê* of the simple bodies.

(b) Does this passage contradict the traditional doctrine of first matter as the persistent *hupokeimenon* of substantial change? Not if *pathê* are now understood as accidents (cf. τὸ πάθος καὶ τὸ ποιόν at 319^b33) and cold, etc. are thought of not as accidents of traditional first matter, but as standing to it in some other, presumably more intimate, though not straightforwardly essential, relation.[45]

(c) The fact that Aristotle lines up the other types of change with the categories quantity, place, and quality, but not *genesis–phthora* with *ousia*, suggests that the 'nothing remains' condition (earlier, 'nothing perceptible remains') is meant in part as a criterion for distinguishing actual processes as instances of *genesis* or *phthora* unqualified. Simply to say that these processes are in respect of *ousia* or the *ti esti* leaves room for the criticism that they do not exist in the world of nature, but are artefacts of the Aristotelian categorial scheme.

320^a2–5

(a) Williams says of this sentence: '[It] clearly indicates that first matter [sc. in the traditional sense, in which it persists] is the substratum of

---

[43] Joachim ibid.

[44] According to Verdenius and Waszink ad loc., the counterfactual ἦν ἄν at $^b28$ should be supplied as verb of the sentence διὸ ἀνθρώπου μέν ... καὶ φθορά, even though they admit that the μέν clause cannot be counterfactual. This is harsh, and unnecessary for a good sense.

[45] Cf. Williams, 103. Jacques Brunschwig has suggested in correspondence that cold, etc. meet this condition by being essential properties of what first matter is potentially, i.e. the simple bodies.

generation and corruption, as other sorts of matter are of other sorts of change. It is said to be receptive of contraries. How can it receive a new contrary after having lost the old one without remaining there throughout the change?'[46] But there is no need for this interpretation. The singular reference at lines 2–3 ('*the hupokeimenon* that admits of *genesis* and *phthora*') no more implies that just one subject is in question than the singular reference at line 4 ('*the hupokeimenon* of the other changes') implies that all alterations, locomotions, and changes in size occur in the same individual. I take Aristotle here to be talking about the *kind* of *hupokeimenon* involved in *genesis–phthora*; and given his earlier insistence that in *genesis–phthora* one *hupokeimenon* replaces another, I assume that water, air, etc. are what he has in mind. The water that is *hupokeimenon* of a particular coming to be of some air cannot also be *hupokeimenon* of the passing away of that air; only the air itself can be that, but they are of the same kind. Nor, of course, can a particular body of water be *hupokeimenon* of the process of its own coming to be as well as of its own passing away, for nothing can be *hupokeimenon* of its own coming to be. There is, however, a way in which even a particular mass of water is subject of coming to be as well as of passing away. For once the water has come to be, it is a logical subject of '. . . *has* come to be and *will* pass away'. In this way, numerically the same subject admits (δεκτικά, 320ᵃ 4) *genesis* and *phthora* without being persistent first matter. (b) I have the impression that some who see evidence for persisting first matter in this passage do so because they understand 'matter μάλιστα κυρίως' as meaning 'matter that most of all deserves to be called "mere matter"; that is, matter that is most indeterminate (hence non-empirical)'. But the point is only that the primary use of 'matter' relates to *substantial* change, because of the primacy of substance.[47] Just so, in *Metaphysics* VII. 5 definition and essence are primarily of substance.

2. First matter in *De generatione et corruptione*

A. Preliminary

In what follows I shall not survey all the passages relevant to the question whether Aristotle posits first matter, not even all those in *GC*. Other scholars between them have already done this several times over.[48] Instead, I shall first (Sect. B) state reasons why Aristotle lacks

---

[46] Williams, 103.

[47] *Pace* Gill, for whom the reference is to the simple bodies, which are said to be matter μάλιστα κυρίως because they are the ultimate sublunary materials; cf. Gill (1989), 67 and 82.

[48] The most recent and comprehensive survey is in Charlton (1970).

philosophical motivation to posit first matter in the sense of a *hupokei-menon* persisting through substantial change. Then (Sect. C) I shall proceed hypothetically and a priori (i.e. not yet looking at passages), as follows: *If* Aristotle does posit a principle which it would be reasonable for him to call 'first matter' (and therefore for us to call 'first matter in Aristotle'), then its function is…, or the reason he would posit it is…, or we should expect to find it coming in at such-and-such a point in his discussion rather than at such-and-such. I shall then come to rest on one weighty passage in *GC* (II. 1. 329ª24–ᵇ1) which in light of the hypothetical part of the discussion shows that Aristotle would have been happy to give positive employment to the phrase 'first matter' in the sense developed a priori.[49] Finally (Sect. D), I shall discuss in two stages a difficulty which seems not to have been noticed.

B. First matter as persistent through substantial change

Here are three reasons why Aristotle lacks motive for positing the above in *GC*:

(1) He is commonly thought to need it in order to bring substantial change into line with the uncultured–cultured man model in *Physics* I. 7, since there the *hupokeimenon* persists. But if (as I think is likely) *Physics* I. 7 takes it for granted there that uncultured–cultured are *pathê* of *man per se*, this is only a model for alteration according to the distinctions made in *GC* I. 4. Alternatively, if the message of *Physics* I. 7 is simply that the upshot of every change is 'something old and something new', then *GC* II. 4–5 will satisfy this, at least in the fundamental and for this treatise central case of elemental transformation, by insisting on at least one quality in common between what has perished and what comes to be.

(2) He is commonly thought to need it, at least in the case of simple-body transformation, and therefore in *GC*, as a principle that 'gives being' to the otherwise ungrounded qualities whose pairings differentiate the

---

[49] In fact, he uses the expression in *GC* only once, at II. 1. 329ª23–4, in reference to the 'nurse of becoming' in *Timaeus*.

Up to this point my account is similar to Charlton's, so far as *GC* is concerned (see esp. Charlton (1970), 132–6). I have learnt a great deal from Charlton's work on prime matter in Aristotle. There is a difference in approach, in that Charlton keeps fixed the meaning of 'first (prime) matter' (i.e. what persists through substantial change) and argues that Aristotle posits no such thing, whereas I argue that in one sense Aristotle does not posit it, in another he does. Charlton also gives less attention to the difference between matter as stuff and as potentiality. And since his purpose is to show that neither *Physics* I nor *De generatione et corruptione* provides evidence for a doctrine of first matter in the fixed sense, he does not dwell on the difference between the two accounts so far as substantial change is concerned.

simple bodies. But, as has been said over and over, what has no nature itself cannot (in Aristotle) conceivably 'give being' to anything. If Aristotle does recognize first matter, it is not in the sense of stuffing[50] for an otherwise unrealized, and therefore existentially incomplete, form, but in the sense of potentiality for change. More on this presently.

(3) Finally, Aristotle cannot, as sometimes seems to be suggested, posit persistent first matter as *hupokeimenon* because he has no other way of distinguishing the type of change in question from alteration. For he does have another way, stated in *GC* I. 4: substantial change is exchange of one *hupokeimenon* for another. Anyone who thinks that these so-called (by Aristotle) *hupokeimena* are qualities needing a 'real' *hupokeimenon* should return to (2) above.

C. What 'first matter' means for Aristotle if it means anything

(1) If Aristotle recognizes a principle he would call 'first matter' in connection with the simple bodies, it is a principle of *change* only, not of *being*. For matter is a principle of being ('substance as matter') only when it functions as a constituent. But the simple bodies lack empirical constituents. Nor, as we saw, could their being depend on a constituent altogether without empirical character. Therefore the first matter of (e.g.) fire would be what functions as *hupokeimenon* for the coming to be of fire, but not of fire itself or its differentiating *pathê*. It is of course true that first matter would certainly be the principle of *a* being; namely, the being *of a change of this type*. But the form of such an entity, which we assign by assigning the *terminus ad quem* of the change, requires for its realization not stuffing but potentiality.

(2) If our hypothetical first matter is potentiality for *substantial* change, exemplified here by the elemental transformations studied in *GC*, we should not expect the concept of it to appear where Aristotle's task is to distinguish substantial change from changes in respect of other categories. This is because every type of change presupposes a corresponding potentiality. If what we know about first matter is that it is potentiality for substantial change (or, more narrowly, for change of elementary substances), reference to first matter will not help anyone to say, or see, what the difference is between the kind of change in which it is involved and the other kinds. The reference will tell us no more than that the difference is simply the difference between substance (here, paradigmatically, elemental substance) and the other categories. Evidently Aristotle does not think this sufficiently illuminating, for in I. 4 he tries to say what

---

[50] It is in this sense that the empirical matter of something is in a way substance, as he often says.

this difference is, using the contrast between change of *hupokeimenon* and change of *pathê* (or quantities, places).

But whereas the idea of first matter as potentiality adds nothing to our understanding of the nature of *substantial* (or elemental) change versus changes of other types, it is a vital idea if we are to make sense of the thought that *the elements do change in respect of their substance*. First matter is why Aristotle's elements, the simple bodies, in their particular portions are not eternal. So we should expect first matter, if it appears explicitly at all, to appear in the context of the theory that explains the intertransformation of the four simple bodies; in other words, the theory of *GC* II in which the bodies are treated as pairs of contraries drawn from two basic contrarieties.

(3) Since an obvious reason for calling anything '*first* matter' is that it is matter in relation to the primary bodies which are the elements of everything else, we should expect first matter, if it figures at all, to be characterized by some such formula as 'not separable but always with contrariety' (*GC* II. 1. 329^{a}25–6). We should take this to mark a contrast with an empirical material (it, too, a potentiality for various types of change) that can make a difference to the world not only by moving between (e.g.) *shapeless lump* and *statue* (thereby also activating some third quality or set of qualities *common* to both terms, such as fusibility), but also (e.g.) by falling or by being perceived. For first matter, by contrast, there can be no life outside the substantial trans- formations it makes possible. There is nothing about it to be activated apart from the qualities that, three at a time (two from one set of basic contraries and the common one from the other), structure elemental coming to be and passing away. And it is only in so far as these are activated together *as* the trio structuring such change that first matter makes any difference. For instance, if the cold of water cools my hand, this is an activity of the cold or of water qua cold, not of first matter or of water qua first matter.

(4) We need to understand more clearly how first matter, if it appears in *GC*, relates to the simple bodies. Portions of two such bodies are involved in any single transformation. We have equated first matter, if it appears, with the potentiality of one to be transformed into the other: for example, the potentiality of water to change into air. It would be equally reasonable to say that first matter is, for example, water itself considered as potentially changing into air, or water considered as potentially changing into either of the bodies into which it can change; namely, air and earth. Furthermore, since *GC*'s explanation of the general nature of substantial change says nothing about a persisting *hupokeimenon*, we should infer that either first matter does not figure there as *hupokeimenon* at all (since if it did, this could only be in relation to substantial or, at any

rate, elemental change),[51] or first matter is to be identified with (e.g.) the water which does not persist since it passes away into air. That is to say, on the second alternative, first matter is (e.g.) the water qua potentially air.

Now, at least one passage[52] pulls us out of hypothetical mode:

[1] Our own theory is that whereas there is a sort of matter of the perceptible bodies, this is not separable but is always with contrariety. From this[53] the so-called elements come to be. [2] We have reached rather thorough[54] determinations about them [sc. the elements[55]] elsewhere; however, since according to the present approach too [sc. as well as that of the *Timaeus*, which he has just been discussing] the first bodies are from matter, we must [sc. now] include them too [sc. the first bodies] in our determinations. [3] We must treat as *principle* (ἀρχή), and as *first*, the matter that on the one hand is inseparable [sc. from the contraries] but on the other hand is *hupokeimenon* to the contraries.[56] [4] For the hot [i.e. the contrary] is not matter for the cold [i.e. the contrary] nor the latter for the hot, but the *hupokeimenon* is matter for both. [5] So, first, what is potentially perceptible body is a principle; and, second, the contrarieties (I mean such as hotness and coldness) [are a principle]; and immediately, third, fire and water and such [are (sc. collectively) a principle] . . . (II. 1. 329ᵃ24–ᵇ1).

The purpose of this passage is to accommodate (a) the *endoxon* that the primary bodies (whatever they are) that constitute compounds have the rank of *principles* and *elements* (329ᵃ5–8) to (b) the doctrine of elemental coming to be, which implies the more fundamental principles of elemental contrariety and matter.[57] Although certain philosophers

---

[51] In a discussion like the present one, that something is matter and potentiality for X cannot automatically be taken to imply that it is *hupokeimenon* of X.

[52] Another may seem to, namely *GC* II. 5. 332ᵃ26–ᵇ5, with its reference at ᵃ35–ᵇ1 to matter that is imperceptible and inseparable. But here Aristotle is not stating his own theory but following out the implications of the counterfactual assumption that elemental transformation involves just one pair of contraries and two elements. Cf. Gill (1989), 248–50.

[53] No doubt ἧς at 329ᵃ26 refers grammatically to ἐναντιώσεως in the same line, but the meaning also links it to ὕλην at 24, since it is in virtue of contrariety that one element is matter for the next.

[54] Or 'more thorough', with most translators. But than what? The *GC* discussion of the simple bodies, or of their matter and contrarieties (see next note), has not yet started. When it comes, it is as thorough as any.

[55] Thus Williams (1982), 155, so that 'elsewhere' means *de Caelo*, especially *Cael.* III. Philoponus, followed by Joachim (1922), 198 and Charlton (1970), 202, takes 'them' to refer to matter and contrariety, and 'elsewhere' to *Physics* I.

[56] The matter *hupokeitai* the contraries *only* in so far as they are implicated in substantial change.

[57] The passage can be translated differently at several points, and different interpretations of the aim and the flow of thought are possible. The only translation difference affecting the present discussion concerns ἧς at 329ᵃ26, on which see n. 53. For a detailed examination concluding in a somewhat different understanding see Gill (1989), 243–7.

thought that the basic perceptible bodies are eternal, in fact (according to Aristotle) there *is* a sort of matter of them, which is the *hupokeimenon* for (e.g.) the switch between hot and cold otherwise known as 'fire's changing into earth' (or vice versa). This matter is 'principle and first' (i.e. first among principles). Second come the contrarieties. But the simple bodies count as principles too—a third kind—since all other bodies consist of them.[58] (This statement, at both ends, excludes the fifth simple body, since (a) it refers only to simple bodies that come to be and pass away, and (b) the fifth body not only is eternal but is not an element of anything else.)

Now, since in this very deliberate passage Aristotle casts the matter that is first among principles as *hupokeimenon*, we must accept the second of the alternatives stated above: we must identify this matter with fire and earth, etc., the perishing *hupokeimena*.[59] But there is a difficulty. Section 5 of the passage lists *three* principles, or three lots of principles. If the matter said to be the first one is, for instance, fire or water, how can fire or water be different from this first principle? But if they are the same as it, then how can fire and water and suchlike constitute a *third* principle, as stated in sentence 5?[60]

The answer,[61] I think, is that the simple bodies play two roles in this scheme and figure as distinct principles accordingly. As matter for and

---

[58] Obviously the cycle of simple-body transformations has explanatory power for a huge range of phenomena. But it is also worth dwelling on the metaphysical implications of 'perishable–generable *elements*'—a seeming contradiction in terms. (a) The simple bodies are not just basic ingredients of compounds, for some of those composed things are animals and plants, paradigmatic Aristotelian substances. A basic ingredient of a *substance* is, in a very strong sense, a principle and element. (b) If *primary bodies* come to be and pass away, and yet are primary by being elements of just about everything else, no one should hesitate to grant full substantial status to *animals and plants* simply on the ground that they do not last for ever. (c) The elemental bodies do the donkey-work of the sublunary world. They constitute environments and materials for living beings. From an Aristotelian point of view it might well seem inappropriate that the essentially infrastructural be individually everlasting. Conversely, it would seem equally inappropriate that anything individually everlasting should constantly be bent and stand ready to be bent to the use of forms of mortal species. (This last point gives an argument against ascribing to Aristotle the doctrine of a persisting, ingenerable, and indestructible first matter. It is rather like one of Berkeley's reasons for rejecting 'material substance': he thought that only the divine and spiritual should rank as eternal.)

[59] The identification means, I suppose, that it is just in so far as fire potentially changes into earth that 'changes into earth' is predicable of fire as subject. This not trivial. At the beginning of an investigation that is one of a series (*Caelo*, DC, and *Mete*.) dealing with every aspect of simple-body physics and chemistry, it is worth making the point that such predications do not hold of fire qua light-weight or qua possible constituent of blood etc. Fire is potentially perceptible body as *per* Section 5, because it can change into (another) perceptible body. However, see main text.

[60] Solmsen (1958), 248–9, raises this question against King (1956).

[61] Seen by Charlton (1970), 201.

subject of change into (e.g.) air, water is an example of the first principle. Its potential for such change is not something about it that is perceptible, nor something that renders it perceptible. For this potentiality is nothing but a combination of qualities severally capable of recombining with others, and we cannot perceive the qualities on this level, since it is on this level that they *constitute* the primary bodies, and only bodies[62] are perceptible.[63] Fire, water, earth, and air are essentially perceptible, and also essentially capable of changing into each other. But it is not qua perceptible that they lend themselves to mutual transformation. Since it is a matter of experience that fire, water, earth, and air are perceptible, whereas their transformations are the posit of a controversial theory, it is natural for Aristotle to refer to them by their ordinary names when he is considering them as *constituted from* (aspects of) one another. Only as having been constituted (i.e. as being rather than coming to be) are they ready to function in turn as constituents of physical compounds, earning their own title of 'principles'.[64]

To summarize this interpretation: The phrase 'Aristotelian first matter' (meaning 'the matter of simple-body transformation') picks out fire or water or earth or air, or all or several of them, presenting each as what changes into another simple body, or as that out of which another one comes to be. It follows that at any given time there are numerically as many different first matters as there are portions of air, water, earth, and fire, however one chooses to distinguish portions. It also follows that none of these is a *hupokeimenon* that persists through the relevant change.[65]

---

[62] And vacua, if there are any.

[63] Cf. Gill (1989), 247 (although her overall interpretation is different from the one defended here).

[64] It is confusing when translators and commentators gratuitously refer to the simple bodies as 'the *elements*' when describing their mutual transformations. Thus Joachim and Williams *passim* in connection with *GC* II. 4–5.

[65] How exactly does 329[a]31–2 (Section [4] in the last quoted passage) fit the present interpretation? I think that 30–1 (Section [3]) says: 'What is here being called first matter is, yes (μέν), inseparable from the contraries, but (δέ) inseparable as their *hupokeimenon* (i.e. not because it *is the same as* one or another contrary'. Section [4] then justifies this distinction between the inseparability of the *hupokeimenon* from contraries and the inseparability of a contrary from itself, by reminding us that in a change from hot to cold (as when air becomes water) and in a change from cold to hot (e.g. the same in reverse) it is not the contrary *a quo* that functions as matter for the coming to be of the *ad quem*, but, in each of the two cases (and so in general), it is the *hupokeimenon* that functions as matter. 'The *hupokeimenon*' is being used generally or functionally, and in one of the two cases it picks out some air, in the other some water. Thus there is no need to take the passage to be saying (what of course supports the traditional prime-matter interpretation) that that which is *hupokeimenon* of a change to hot on one occasion is *hupokeimenon* of a change to cold on another.

D. Aristotelian difficulties

(1) 'Each changes into each'?

There is a problem.[66] Aristotle not only says that each sublunary simple body can change into either of the two others for which it has a tally (σύμβολον) (i.e. a matching quality), and that each of these resultants can change, via different pairs of tallies, back into the first and on into the fourth, which itself can change by a similar mechanism back into the second and third. He also states very deliberately: 'It is clear that all are of a nature to change into each other', meaning by this not 'They are of a nature such that each changes into one or some of the others', but 'They are of a nature such that every one changes into every one'.[67] By way of proof, he states the theory just summarized, according to which earth can change into fire or water, water can change into earth or air, air can change into water or fire, and fire can change into air or earth. But how does the conclusion follow? We are used to thinking of an Aristotelian change as defined by a pair of termini;[68] thus, while it is true to say that nature has made it possible to get from each to each of the four, it is false, one would think, that fire can change into water or vice versa. Because of the distribution of tallies, fire can only change into something that is not fire that can change into water. Neither of these two changes is *both* from fire *and* into water. Similarly with earth and air. Nor is there any Aristotelian principle according to which two changes, laid end to end so to speak, necessarily constitute one change with one pair of termini. Again, the simple-body transformations can be viewed as being from positive thing to positive thing.[69] To the extent that this is so, such transformations count as *kinêseis*[70] according to distinctions made in *Physics* V. 1. And *Physics* V also says (ch. 4) that a *kinêsis* is one (unitary) only if (in the terms which we have been using in this chapter) it has one *hupokeimenon*. But (according to the argument of this chapter so far) there is for Aristotle no one *hupokeimenon* of *the* change from fire to water or back.[71]

---

[66] As we shall see, it is as much a problem on the 'persistent' interpretation of first matter.

[67] *GC* II. 4. 331^{a}10–14; cf. 331^{a}20–2 and 332^{a}1–2.

[68] *Ph.* V. 1. 225^{a}1.

[69] Even though in *GC* I. 3 he tries to view them as from privation to positive or vice versa.

[70] Cf. Gill (1989), 54 n. 19.

[71] This is consistent with the *GC* I. 4 doctrine that substantial change is change of *hupokeimena*, for only the one changed *from* (the one that perishes) is *hupokeimenon* of the change itself. *Ph.* V. 4 (227^{b}20–228^{a}3) explains the requirement 'One *kinêsis* has one subject' by pointing to two ways in which the requirement fails to be met. Neither is the failure of an individual to persist through change. The problem here in the main text has to do with the fact (as it seems) that fire-to-air and air-to-water involve two *hupokeimena*

It may be said that we are making too much of the statement that each changes into each: this does not mean that there is a change that is one change from fire to water, but only means to include all four bodies in a cycle of distinct changes. The point is levelled against the *Timaeus*, where earth is an element that for geometrical reasons cannot transmute. However, Aristotle could have said just this if this alone had been the point. In fact he says more; namely that, the difference between a one-step and a two-step transition ($\mu\epsilon\tau\acute{a}\beta\alpha\sigma\iota\varsigma$) is that the second is slower because more 'difficult' ($\chi\alpha\lambda\epsilon\pi\acute{\omega}\tau\epsilon\rho\sigma\nu$)[72]—although the tally connections between successive stages make this cyclic method as a whole 'extremely easy'![73] And here is his explanation for the greater difficulty:

> The transition is quick for the bodies that have tallies for one another and slow for those that do not, because it is easier for one thing to change than for many to. (*GC* II. 4. 331^{a}23–6; cf. 331^{b}6)

The comparison in respect of *ease* and *difficulty* turns us away from thinking merely that in a transition from fire and to water more things change one by one than in a transition from fire to air. For this greater multiplicity, being successive, is itself enough to explain why fire-to-water *takes more time* than (e.g.) fire-to-air and air-to-water individually ($\chi\rho\sigma\nu\iota\acute{\omega}\tau\epsilon\rho\alpha$).[74] So why does he insert 'more difficult'[75] between the *explanans* ('more things change') and the *explanandum* ('slower, takes more time')[76]? Presumably, to draw us into seeing fire-to-water as essentially accomplishing the same result as air-to-water accomplishes. In other words, we are not to regard the first stage of the complex transition

---

(*termini a quibus*), one for each of two changes. Persistence of either or both is not the issue. Hence, although 'Each changes into each' may feed the impression that Aristotle postulates first matter as the persistent *hupokeimenon* of substantial change, first matter in this sense does not solve the problem, if it is one, of the unity of the transition from fire to water. For even if this were a pair of alterations in one persisting subject one could still wonder how it counts as a single change.

[72] See *GC* II. 4. 331^{a}22–5; 331^{b}6.

[73] See *GC* II. 4. 331^{b}2–3.

[74] Cf. *GC* II. 4. 331^{b}11–14.

[75] The question arises not merely because this middle term (which can also be translated 'more harsh') is unnecessary for the explanation, but because it threatens to rock the boat of Aristotle's metaphysical optimism. A natural cycle forever repeated must not involve struggle against the grain (cf. *Cael.* II. 1). Even in the sublunary realm, nature at large is not 'step-motherly' (synonymous with 'harsh', e.g. Hesiod, *Works and Days* 825). Hence (as in steering when sailing) the non-cancelling correction at 331^{b}2–3, where it is suggested that two-step transition is easy—it is just not the easi*est* kind. (*Pace* Joachim—see his Oxford translation (1922)—$\sigma\tilde{\upsilon}\tau\sigma\varsigma$ $\acute{o}$ $\tau\rho\acute{o}\pi\sigma\varsigma$ refers to one-step transitions, not to the cycle as a whole.) This zigzag, indicating that 'more difficult' carries a dialectical cost, tells us also that Aristotle needs it in his argument.

[76] These are not synonymous. 'Slower' already suggests a single change, 'takes more time' does not. But I have a better argument if the first here means no more than the second, because then 'more difficult' adds something not already present.

as a project on its own, but as belonging to the same project as the second stage. But looking at air-to-water along with the next change on, namely water-to-earth, we can see that since these are all of the same kind there is no reason not to treat air-to-water as the first stage in the single two-stage project of air-to-earth. And by similar reasoning we reach the conclusion that each simple transition is a stage in a single four-stage cyclical project in which x ultimately changes into x, the variable being arbitrarily cashed as any of the four bodies.

The difficulty raised in this section, then, does not exist, according to the present reply, because Aristotle's cycle is not made up of a series of distinct changes which happen to bring it back to the starting position. The tally metaphor brings this home. A and B are not tallies if they simply match each other, for tallies are counterparts *made to be such* and distributed to different parties *so that* they can recognize each other.[77] Since each simple body consists of two tallies and nothing else, each body essentially refers directly to two of the three others and indirectly to the third. In this way one might support not only the claim that every one changes into every one, but the further claim that it is of the nature of each to do so.

It seems, then, that we should think of the series of changes as a single process[78] each of whose stages shares in the whole. Arguably, the only real unitary change in all this is an entire turn, since any shorter section would be incomplete on its own. Thus a two- or three-stage transition has as much right to count as *a* change as a simple transition. And since we can pick any of the four bodies as that from which we view the cycle as 'starting', a portion of any one of them can be viewed as *the* perishing *hupokeimenon* of the immediately subsequent cycle, and of any immediately subsequent part of it, and of as many immediately subsequent repetitions as we care to think about if we consider all this as a single recurrent process. At the same time, any individual portions can be viewed, in relation to immediately preceding cycles, parts of cycles, repetitions, as *the* coming-to-be thing in which the cycle or part or series culminates. However we divide up the process, we can always view it as from one thing to one thing, and from one perishing *hupokeimenon* to another. In this way, the theory fits the account of *genesis–phthora* in *GC* I. 4.

In the next section, however, this solution comes under attack.

---

[77] Does it make sense to apply teleological language or imagery to an eternal arrangement (for the make-up of the elements is a law of nature)? I do not know, but Aristotle does it openly at *GC* II. 10. 336^b27–34.

[78] Though not as a rule a temporally continuous one, or there would be no stable environment and no stable nature for the elements to contribute to mixtures and compounds.

(2) 'A common matter' ?

Here are some texts that challenge the view that Aristotelian first matter (the matter of elemental transformation) is nothing but portions of the elements themselves considered *sub specie mutabilitatis*.[79] For it is fairly natural to read these passages as postulating a single persistent first matter in the traditional sense.

> On the question of the elements from which bodies are compounded: those who hold (1) that there is something common [to the elements], or (2) that they change into each other, cannot take one of these positions without the other one's following too. (*GC* II. 7. 334^a 15–18)[80]

Since Aristotle holds (2), presumably he sees himself as committed to (1). Next:

> We hold that fire and air and water and earth come to be from one another, and that each of these is potentially there in each, just as with other things that have one and the same *hupokeimenon* that is ultimate in the analysis of them (*Meteor.* I. 3. 339^a 36–^{b}2).

And (in a context where he is discussing the four natural motions of the sublunary simple bodies):

> So the kinds of matter [i.e. matter for locomotion] too must be as many as these [the four bodies], namely four, but four in such a way that there is one matter that is common to them all, especially if they come to be from one another. (*Cael.* III. 5. 312^{a}30–3)

Now how can there be a matter common to the four simple bodies if Aristotelian first matter is one or another of those bodies considered as capable of changing into another? The difficulty is similar to the one raised in the last section, but now we are going to press harder, in a way that will undermine the solution to the former unless the present one is solved independently. The problem is that there is a different description of each of the simple bodies as first matter. Fire is first matter for *the air and earth* into which it can change, air for *fire and water*, and so on. But, since all that can be said about matter on this level is what it is matter *for*, there are four first matters without a common description. The same if we substitute 'potentiality' for 'matter' here, since a potentiality is defined by what it is potentiality for.

It might seem easy to get round this by emphasizing, as above, the simple bodies' natural community in contributing to the one cycle of elemental coming to be and passing away. One can elaborate this

---

[79] Cf. Dancy, 'Aristotle's Second Thoughts on Substance: Matter', 406.
[80] Cf. 334^{a}23–5, also *Metaph.* X. 3. 1054^{b}27–9.

further by pointing out that each of these matters or potentialities refers directly or indirectly to each of the simple bodies, so that a common set of terms spells them all out, although in a different order in each case. One could go further still and devise a single description that not only fits them all but is essentially shared. For, staying with the tally analogy, one could point out that form is the important thing, not content. For a tally situation we need (a) two parties meeting for a common purpose; thus they are in some way opposites: one has what the other lacks, or they complement each other; and (b) two matching tallies assigned one to each side. It makes no difference what the opposites are and what the tallies are made of. If, as we saw, each of the four simple bodies essentially consists of a pair of tallies each set to enable *genesis–phthora* by means of the other's contrary together with its own counterpart, then it is also essentially true of each that it belongs with three others of which the same is essentially true. This essentially shared essential fact about each is an identical-thing-in-common that requires, of course, essential differences enabling each body to play its part in the pattern. But, from the perspective of pure transmutation theory, the empirically obvious differences are accidental and superficial; that is, it is accidental and superficial that the tallies–contraries are hot–cold and wet–dry, rather than one or another analogously recombinant pair of pairs.

Now, does this result validate the theory, which we are supposing for the moment to be Aristotle's, that the one common matter of the elements is fire, water, earth, and air—any or each considered in turn in their capacities as *hupokeimena* for elemental transformation? Strictly, I think not. To say that (a) A is matter or potentiality for B is to say that (b) A can change into B, for any A and B. Now if (c) B is defined as something that can change into C, it follows that (d) A can change into something that can change into C. In this way, reference to all the simple bodies is established when we spell out the *genesis*-potentials of each. But (d) does not entail that A can *change into C*, and hence, by (1) above, it has not been established that (e.g.) fire can change into each of the other elements. And if the *only* reason for holding that each can change into each of the others is that tallies and contraries enable transition (simple or complex) from each to each, then one is not justified in holding that each can change into each of the others. For the fact (even if it is essential to each and essentially shared) that transition is possible from each to each means only that each can change into one (to keep it simple) that can change into a third. And this is insufficient for the proposition that *the first can change into the third*, hence also for the proposition that *the first is matter for each of the others*. And so on for each in turn.

Crucial to the above objection is the fact that, for Aristotle, '...can change into...' is not transitive.[81] This can be deduced from what he says about matter and the potential in *Metaphysics* IX. 7:

> earth is not yet potentially a statue, for when it changes (μεταβαλοῦσα) it will be bronze. And it seems that when we call a thing not 'so and so' but 'of-so and so' (for example, we do not say that the chest is wood, but that it is of-wood, nor that the wood is earth, but that it is of-earth), a thing is always potentially what is next (without qualification). For example, the chest is not of-earth, nor is it earth, but it is of-wood. For this [wood] is potentially a chest, and it is the matter of a chest: wood without qualification is the matter of a chest without qualification, and this wood here of this chest here. (*Metaph.* IX. 7. 1049ᵃ17–24)

Let us also look again at *de Caelo*. III. 5. 312ᵃ30–ᵇ1:

> So the kinds of matter [i.e. matter for locomotion] too must be as many as these [the four bodies], namely four, but four in such a way that there is one matter that is common to them all, especially if they come to be from one another. (*Cael.* III. 5. 312ᵃ30–3)

Here the sublunary simple bodies are said each to be a distinct kind of matter, because their natural motions are different. Now, for Aristotle, in respect of natural motions and natural places, these bodies form a system. And it is a system that reflects the order of elemental transformation!

> The bodies which lie next to one another are alike [in the language of *GC*, they 'tally'], e.g. water to air and air to fire...In each case, the higher body stands to the one underneath it as form to matter. (*Cael.* IV. 3. 310ᵇ11–15)[82]

It follows that, by itself, the systematicity patterning the elemental cycle cannot justify treating the whole as a single change, or describing each element as changing into each, or as matter for all the others. For otherwise the interrelations of the natural places would commit Aristotle to saying that the 'topical' matter of the simple bodies is essentially one and common, whereas in fact he stresses that the topical matters are four.

---

[81] My discussion assumes that '...can change into...' is generally non-transitive (except when there is one agent for all the changes in question: see below in the text). However, at the Symposium Alan Code suggested that non-transitivity may be peculiar to sequences like that of *Metaph.* IX. 7. 1049ᵃ17–24, where the matter of each object remains in it: the wooden chest cannot also be an earthen chest. For full discussion of change as defined by its termini see S. Waterlow, *Nature, Change, and Agency in Aristotle's* Physics (Oxford, 1982), ch. 3.

[82] There are striking similarities between *Cael.* IV. 3. 310ᵇ16–26 and *Metaph.* IX. 7. 1049ᵃ1 ff. Obviously this is to be explained by the subject matter of each. But the similarities make it harder to believe that Aristotle says (and says undefensively) in *GC* II. 4 that each of the elements changes into each simply because it escapes his notice that elsewhere he holds that '...changes into...' is not transitive. The fact that the order of the natural places of the elements follows the order of their transformations could even suggest that '...changes into...', like '...lies next to...' (assuming a linear series) is *in*transitive!

The solution to this puzzle lies, I suggest, in understanding the non-transitivity principle of *Metaphysics* IX. 7 not as a spelling out of the concept '...changes into...' on its own, but as a spelling out that assumes a usual, but not inevitable, context. It is the context in which the agent of change from A to B differs from the agent of change from B to C. For wood is not only matter *of* a projected chest; it is matter *for* the cabinetmaker. The reason why there is no single change from earth to chest based on one change from earth to wood and another from wood to chest is that no single agency has the power, the skill, or the active nature to turn earth into a (wooden) chest.[83] If '...changes into...' were generally transitive, there could be no artifice if, as I surmise, single agency is necessary as well as sufficient for transitivity.[84] For then no one could make anything from materials which themselves had come to be unless, by the same power or skill, he had already made those materials. Consequently, where artifice is under discussion or is a prominent example, it is reasonable to take it for granted that '...changes into...' is non-transitive or even intransitive. (Such cases arise even where the chain of changes considered does not start from an unprocessed natural material, and even where all are ultimately for the same end; cf. the bridlemaker/horseman/general of *EN* I. 1. The leather for the well-made bridle does not come to be a military feat. From this we see again that 'the simple transitions belong to the same project' is insufficient to validate the claim implicit in *GC* II. 4 that it is *by* changing into air, which changes into water, that fire *changes into water*).

So we come to the sun's revolution in the ecliptic. This is the ultimate efficient cause of the endless dissolution and rebirth of elements (*GC* II. 10). Because the circling sun is *one agent*, unchanging in the manner of its agency, its effect is indeed a single process in which any ordered set of consecutive transitions counts as a single transition.[85]

But for every single transition there is a single matter and perishing *hupokeimenon*. So if, for example, we choose to view a given cycle as 'beginning from' fire, we treat the fire as matter and *hupokeimenon* not only for the proximate earth (or air), but also for the remoter water air (or earth), and fire. In this way 'one matter is common to them all'

[83] It is because wood itself lacks the skill (φύσις) to grow into a chest that it fails the general test laid down in *Metaph.* IX. 7 for X's being Y potentially, namely that X will become Y if nothing interferes. Unless the wood comes into the presence of a cabinetmaker who wants to make a chest, there is no chest-focused project to be interfered with. Once that condition is met, the wood passes the test.

[84] It depends on the rule for 'single agency'. The surmise in fact is that we shall find it reasonable to use equivalence of transitivity with singleness of agency as a constraint on what counts as the latter.

[85] This is consistent with the fact that the sun has its effect via different elemental 'means'.

(*Cael.* III. 5. 312^{a}30–3). And since we could have taken any of the four as starting point, each functions as matter and *hupokeimenon* that is one and common to all.[86]

So the passages quoted at the beginning of this section do not compel us to ascribe to Aristotle the traditional doctrine of first matter as a persisting *hupokeimenon* which functions in elemental transformation in exactly the same way as Socrates functions in his change from sick to healthy, the only difference being that first matter is necessarily imperceptible. The key to interpreting those passages without falling back on traditional first matter lies in the presumption that the elemental transformations constitute between them a single change. However, as we have seen, that presumption, and therefore the interpretation it supports, faces an Aristotelian challenge concerning the identity of changes. But we have also seen how the challenge is met from Aristotelian resources to do with singleness of agency. It is important to be clear that this solution to the problem of change-identity in the elemental cycle is not an alternative to another solution, provided by the traditional doctrine of first matter as persisting *hupokeimenon*. For no such other solution exists. The persistence doctrine may have seemed to guarantee the unity of the cycle and the cycle's sections, but in reality it does no such thing. This is because even if from-B-to-C occurs in the same *hupokeimenon* as from-A-to-B, it does not follow that there is one change, from-A-to-C. So there are still the problems of justifying 'each changes into each' and 'common matter'. The doctrine's uselessness to this end is another reason for not attributing it to Aristotle.

---

[86] In this formulation, 'one' is almost synonymous with 'common', and does not mean 'unique', since each of the *four* is matter to all. Alternatively, now that it is established that any series of elemental transformations counts as a single change (because of the single agency of the sun) we could say that the common matter is the essentially shared attribute of contributing to that single change (cf. p. 147). Viewed in this way, the matter is one but instantiated in four kinds. By contrast, Aristotle does not want to say that the tendencies of the four sublunary simple bodies to their natural regions is a power (to produce that complex natural arrangement) that they all share but manifest each in its own way. Perhaps this is because he wants to preserve an analogy between the locomotion of (portions of) those simple bodies and the locomotion of an animal conceived of as a more or less self-sufficient being or substance. Or it may be because (especially in *Cael.*) he wants to maintain a certain parity or analogy between the four sublunary simples *and the fifth body*. Because the latter is divine and eternal, its movement cannot easily be thought of as immediately governed by a single plan which also immediately governs the natural movements of the sublunary simples. Moreover, its movement (he sometimes thinks) manifests life, theirs do not. Consequently, although if he only had the sublunary simples to attend to he might consider them as instantiating a single common matter for motion and rest (or, rather, matter for a certain overall arrangement—earth at the centre, fire at the periphery, etc.— realized by the four kinds of locomotion and rest), he does not look at them in this way, since doing so would leave the fifth body too much a theoretical outsider. After all, its claim for existential recognition rests entirely on its theoretical credentials.

5

Simple Genesis and Prime Matter

DAVID CHARLES

1. Introduction: *De generatione et corruptione* I. 3

At the end of I. 3. 319^{a}29–^{b}5 Aristotle asks a series of questions. I shall begin with a translation, which is, at some points, controversial.[1]

Someone may ask: is that *which is not* (without qualification) one of the contraries: e.g. earth or the heavy, while the other contrary (e.g. fire or the light) is *what is*? Or is it rather that earth is also a case of *being*, while the matter of earth and fire are both alike *what is not*? Further, is the matter of each of these two different, for otherwise they would not come to be out of one another or out of contraries (for the contraries belong to fire, earth, water, and air)? Or is the matter of each of these in some way the same, and in another way different: for the thing, whatever it is, that underlies is the same, although it is not the same in being. That is enough on these topics.[2] (emphasis added)

---

[1] Cf. Keimpe Algra, in Ch. 3 of this volume, pp. 101–4.

[2] While I follow the text proposed by H. H. Joachim (1922), my translation differs from his in one crucial respect (ibid. 105). He takes the phrase 'ὅ μὲν γάρ ποτε ὂν ὑπόκειται' to mean 'the underlying, whatever its nature may be' and construes this as the grammatical subject of a sentence which says that the underlying, whatever it is, is the same, but different in being. On his reading, the gap marked by 'whatever it is' will have to be filled by a specification of the nature of the underlier itself (saying what its essence is). Thus, for Joachim, we have already in place an entity (the underlier), separate from the matter of earth and of fire, with its own distinctive essence. By contrast, I take this phrase to mean 'that thing, whatever it is, that underlies', and construe the first part of the sentence as saying only that that thing, whatever it is, that underlies is the same. Here, the gap marked by 'whatever it is' would be filled by a further specification of what the thing is that underlies: e.g.: a list of relevant underliers, or an abstract specification of what the matters of earth and fire have in common when they underlie. It need not be filled by pointing to the essence of a distinct thing, the underlier. The relevant contrast is clear in Aristotle's use of the same phrase in his discussion of blood in *PA* 649^{b}23–5. For 'blood, whatever its nature may be' differs in meaning from 'whatever it is that is blood'. The former refers to blood (and leaves a gap for an account of its nature), while the latter refers to something distinct from blood (such as hot liquid) which is (or constitutes) blood. In *PA* 649^{b}23–5 the latter use is intended, since Aristotle wishes to leave indefinite the precise nature of the thing, or things, which constitute blood. He is not concerned in this passage with

This difficult and condensed passage raises two questions:

(A) What is *what is not* without qualification?

(B) Is the matter of earth and fire the same or different?

In this essay I shall focus on the second question. Three answers are suggested in the text:

1. The matter of earth and of fire is the same. This answer is immediately called into question on the ground that if it were correct genesis could not occur.

2. The matter of earth and of fire is different. This answer is rejected elsewhere on the ground that if it were correct (without qualification) change would be impossible.[3]

3. The matter of earth and of fire is in some way the same and in some way different. This third answer is not rejected, but neither is it completely clear. It seems to involve three ideas: (a) there is one thing, whatever it is, which underlies; (b) the matter of earth and the matter of fire are the same in virtue of their both being that thing; and (c) that thing is nonetheless different in being.

Aristotle immediately interrupts his discussion with a brisk 'That is enough on these topics', and does not develop this answer further in *GC* I. 3. As a consequence, his third, and apparently preferred, alternative remains telegrammatic, not to say elusive, at this point. This chapter is an attempt to spell out his final proposal in more detail. My suggestion is that, properly understood, it points to a view of prime matter and simple genesis which has been overlooked in recent interpretations of Aristotle's account of these difficult topics.

2. 'Matter is the same in so far as it is that thing, whatever it is, that underlies, but it is different in being': an analogy introduced

The Greek expression, which Aristotle employs here, is distinctive: ὃ μὲν γάρ ποτε ὄν ὑπόκειται, τὸ αὐτό. What does it mean? In what way is that thing, whatever it is, that underlies the same throughout? What is the intended contrast with difference in being? Aristotle uses the same

---

the nature of blood itself. (I am indebted to John Cooper for discussion of these issues and for calling to my attention R. Brague's pioneering essay on Aristotle's use of this phrase in his *Du temps chez Platon et Aristote* (Paris, 1982), 97–144.)

[3] The first two options are discussed in the account of ποιεῖν and πάσχειν in *GC* I. 7. For the second option see 323ᵇ24–5.

expression in the *Physics* with the same contrast in his discussion of *now*.[4] In the first of these passages Aristotle writes:

The now is in some way the same, in some way different. In so far as it is in different things, it is different (this is what it is to be the now), but that thing, whatever it is, that is the now, is the same. (*Ph.* IV. 11. 219^{b}12–13)

In what way is the now different? Presumably, it is different when considered as located at different stages in a process (219^{b}13–14). Aristotle subsequently notes that the now is different when it is considered as at different numbered times (219^{b}27–8). In this way, the now at 1.01 p.m. and the now at 1.02 p.m. will be different.

In what way is the now the same? Aristotle says: it is the same because that thing, whatever it is, that is the now is the same. But what is this thing? Aristotle gives two (compatible) answers. It is

(a) the divider of time into before and after (219^{b}11–12);
(b) the divider of the before and after in change (219^{b}26–7).

If time is, in some basic way, dependent on change, (b) will be the more fundamental answer: it will be because it separates before and after in change that the now divides time into before and after. But, whether (a) or (b) is the more basic, the now will be what it is in virtue of being that thing which divides time (or change) into before and after. For the divider of time into before and after is that thing which is the now.[5]

On this account, the now, in being that thing which divides before and after, is the same, although at different moments different nows (different points of time) do, in fact, divide before and after.[6] On the one hand, the present moment, in virtue of being that thing which divides before and after, is always the same. On the other, different points of time will

---

[4] *Ph.* IV. 11. 219^{b}10–15, 25–8, 31–3; see *Ph.* IV. 14. 223^{a}27–9. I am indebted to Edward Hussey for calling these passages, and their importance, to my attention. Aristotle also uses this terminology in his discussion of the point (219^{b}17 ff.), contrasting (by implication) the point we are now at, wherever that may be, with a named specific place.

[5] I understand the phrase 'the divider of time into before and after' to refer to times which fall in what McTaggart, in 'The Unreality of Time', *Mind*, 18 (1908), 457–84, described as the A-series. So understood, which events are before and which after will change as time goes by. The phrase is not used to specify one eternally ordered chain of events, in which (e.g.) event *a* is always earlier than event *b*. (McTaggart called the latter the B-series.)

[6] These passages are difficult and their interpretation controversial. In what follows, I shall merely sketch (and do not attempt to argue for) one way of understanding them. My interpretation follows (in broad outline) that proposed by Edward Hussey (1983), 155. For, Hussey suggests that 'the before and after' in change in the abstract could be identified with the permanent present'. What is needed, as Hussey notes, is a way of talking about the now (and the something which makes it the now) which will be true for any arbitrary time. The point is a general one, not confined to any one specified sequence of before and after.

constitute the present moment at different moments (1.01 ... 1.02, etc.). In this way, Aristotle can distinguish the now, understood as that thing which divides before and after, from the now, understood as different numbered (or dated) points of time present at different times (219^{b}28). The former remains the same, the latter differs from moment to moment.

The divider of before and after is the thing in virtue of being which all the nows are the same. What is the thing in question? There is no need for it to be more than (what I shall call) a 'logical (or abstract) entity': that entity in virtue of being which all the nows are the same. What I intend by the phrase 'a logical (or abstract) entity' may be brought out by considering the sentence:

(S) It is in virtue of being the President that Mr Bush is in command.

In one analysis, one could take the phrase 'the President' in (S) to refer to an entity, namely, the President. It is in virtue of his being (for a time) the President that Mr Bush is in command. At another time Mr Clinton would have been in command in virtue of his being the President. At different times the President is constituted by different material (and perceptible) substances. However, the President is not a material (or perceptible) object present alongside (or over and above) the material (and perceptible) Mr Bush and Mr Clinton and the rest. Rather, the phrase 'the President' signifies what I shall call a logical (or abstract) object.[7] If the phrase 'the divider of the before and after' functions in a similar way, it will not have as its referent a further specific or dated point in time, present alongside (or over and above) particular dated points of time of the same type, 1.01, 1.02, etc. Rather, the same object, that which divides before and after, will be present throughout, even

---

[7] Logical or abstract objects are non-material individuals. The phrase 'logical or abstract object' is merely a label for the account of such objects to be given in this essay. In the particular example used, the relevant logical (or abstract) object might be 'an arbitrary object'. Arbitrary objects are associated with an appropriate range of material objects, and will have the properties common to all individual objects which can fall in that range. In the present example, the individual objects will be those (Bush, Clinton, and the rest) who play a given political role, and the arbitrary object will be referred to by the phrase 'the President'. In another case, the individual objects will be particular men (Socrates, Callias, and the rest), and the arbitrary object could perhaps be referred to as (e.g.) 'man' in such sentences as 'man is rational,' 'man is a biped'. (For further work on the idea of arbitrary objects see Kit Fine, *Reasoning With Arbitrary Objects* (Oxford, 1985).) However, not all 'logical or abstract objects' need be arbitrary objects. Football clubs or governments (e.g. Bush's administration) also are non-material individuals.—*Caveat*: The example of the President is used to offer some initial grip on the relevant idea of a logical (or abstract) object. I am not proposing that Aristotle adopted such an account in this case. (There is clearly an important issue, here left unresolved, as to whether Aristotle used the idea of logical (or abstract) objects in discussing individual men, taken universally: see e.g. *Metaph.* VII. 10. 1035^{b}27–31.)

though it is (or is constituted by) different dated times at different moments. So understood, the phrase 'that which divides the before and after' will specify a logical (or abstract) object.[8]

This model suggests one way to understand the *GC* passage with which we began:

Just as there is some one thing (that which divides before and after) in virtue of being which all nows are the same, so there will be some one thing in virtue of being which all cases of underlying matter are the same. Equally, just as all nows are different, when understood as being at different points in a continuum, so all the cases of matter may be different, when considered as distinct particular matters (e.g. present at different stages in a process).

The analogy can be developed further with reference to basic, elemental, change:

(1) Matter, understood as the one thing in virtue of being which all specific instances of matter underlie, will be the same (in all cases of basic elemental change), even though the specific instances of matter involved may differ. Thus, sometimes the matter of earth, sometimes the matter of fire will be the matter in question. But, in each of these cases, that thing in virtue of being which the different matters underlie will be the same. So just as that thing (the divider of before and after) in virtue of being which all nows are the same is the same throughout, so too there will be one thing in virtue of being which all matters, involved in basic elemental change, are the same. (I shall call this thing, following well-established tradition, 'prime matter'.)

---

[8] A closely parallel view could be presented without the use of the notion of a 'logical object.' Thus, one might take 'the President' to signify Mr Bush, described in a certain way, or 'prime matter' to signify (e.g.) the matter of fire, described in a certain abstract way (e.g. as what is capable of elemental change). However, while this alternative conceptualization is attractive to modern eyes, I retain talk of 'logical (or abstract) object' for two reasons:

(a) The Greek phrase (ὃ μὲν γάρ ποτε ὂν ὑπόκειται, τὸ αὐτό) is most naturally taken to invoke an entity signified by ὅ: that, whatever it is, that underlies, which is the same. The phrase seems to commit Aristotle to more than to a reference merely to the determinable concept of (e.g.) the underlier. For the latter notion see W. E. Johnson, *Logic* (Cambridge, 1921), pt. I, pp. 173–85.
(b) Aristotle, in talking of the now (as elsewhere in talking of points) appears to accept that it is an entity, although one whose nature and existence can be explained (in some measure) on the basis of the existence of other simpler entities. He does not insist on talking of the now as a mere description of dated moments. On this see (e.g.) Hussey (1983), 182–4.

In the light of (a) and (b), the more conservative route is to interpret Aristotle as speaking of logical (or abstract) objects rather than of objects under logical (or abstract) descriptions. If the latter conceptualization can be shown to apply (non-anachronistically) to the present context, it may seem (to some) to offer a preferable way of articulating some of the central exegetical claims of this essay. These issues are complex and deserve a separate study. See also nn. 13 and 17 below.

(2) At one time it will fall to 1.01 p.m. to be now, at another to 1.02 p.m. Similarly, in the case of matter, it will sometimes fall to the matter of fire to be that which underlies, sometimes to the matter of earth. Just as it sometimes falls to 1.01 p.m. to be the divider of before and after, so it will sometimes fall to the matter of fire to be that which underlies. But there will also be one thing which is the same throughout: that thing in virtue of being which all these different instances of matter (specific points of time) underlie (are the now).

(3) If that which divides before and after can be a logical or abstract object, so too can that thing in being which the matter of earth and fire underlies. In the case of times, the relevant object will be the divider of before and after. This object will exist provided that there is one (and only one) thing which persists and satisfies the description 'the divider of before and after'. There is no further dated, individual, point of time involved over and above 1.01, 1.02, etc. By analogy, nothing more will be required for that object in virtue of being which specific matters underlie to exist than for there to be one (and only one) thing which persists and satisfies some favoured description (e.g. 'the underlier'). There is no greater pressure to generate a further material (or perceptual) entity which underlies in this way than there is to generate a further material entity apart from Mr Bush who is in command. All that is required is that there be some object in virtue of being which Mr Bush (or Mr Clinton) is in command. So understood, prime matter, now, and the President will all be logical (or abstract) objects.[9]

3. Is this the right way to understand the analogy? Three issues

The suggestion made in the last section is incomplete in several respects. There are three gaps which need to be addressed.

Issue 1: So far, no positive account of what the object is, in virtue of being which particular cases of elemental matter underlie, has been offered. In the case of the now the object in question is that which divides before and after. But in the case of matter no such specification has been provided. This is why at the end of the last section it was described as 'the underlier'. But this suggestion will only yield the comparatively trivial claim:

---

[9] There is a residual, but important, disanalogy between these cases. While the now (and the President) is a logical or abstract individual, prime matter is (probably) best conceived as an abstract or logical kind or type. For while there can only be one now (President) at a time, there can be several discrete but cotemporaneous instances of prime matter. I shall continue (for simplicity of exposition) to describe all three as logical (or abstract) objects.

It is in virtue of being the underlier that some particular matter underlies.

If the analogy with now is to be sustained, we need to detect in *GC* a more informative way of characterizing the relevant logical object in the case of matter. For, Aristotle does not merely say that the relevant object (in the case of the now) is the object which is the now. Rather, he seeks to characterize it more informatively using the phrase 'that which divides before and after'.

Issue 2: No reason has been given to understand the crucial phrase ὃ μὲν γάρ ποτε ὂν ὑπόκειται, τὸ αὐτό on the basis of an analogy with Aristotle's use of this phrase in the discussion of time in the *Physics*. The phrase itself is used elsewhere to suggest a different type of object, specifiable in material terms. Thus, in discussing blood in *PA* 649^{b}23 ff., Aristotle writes τὸ δ' ὑποκείμενον καὶ ὃ ποτε ὂν αἷμά ἐστιν, οὐ θερμόν. Here, the underlying, i.e. that thing, whatever it is, which is (or constitutes) blood, certainly is a material and not a purely logical object; namely, a certain liquid. Aristotle is saying that blood, in so far as it is the liquid that constitutes blood, is not always hot, even though blood, considered as blood, is always hot. Here, the reference is to a real liquid which underlies and is distinct from blood. 'ὃ ποτε ὂν αἷμά ἐστιν' seems to refer to the stuff that makes up blood. If so, one cannot assume that the phrase 'ὃ ποτε ὂν' always specifies a logical entity. Indeed, it might refer in *GC* I. 3 to the kind of underlying material substratum, as in traditional theories of prime matter.

Issue 3: My contention, thus far, is conditional in form. It amounts to the claim that:

> If the logical object reading of the *Physics* discussion of the now is accepted, a similar interpretation of prime matter is possible.

But even if this interpretation of Aristotle's view of the now is possible, it has not been established. So, one can reasonably ask: How much support can it lend for the proposed reading of matter in *GC*? Is there anything further in *GC* which supports this interpretation?

4. What is that in virtue of being which the matter of fire underlies?
Issue 1

In *GC* I. 3 Aristotle introduces his preferred idea through the phrase 'that thing, whatever it is, that underlies' (319^{b}3–4). There is clearly a gap here which needs to be filled: what is the object in question? Since Aristotle does not attempt to make good this lacuna in *GC* I. 3, we need to look to the next chapters of *GC* I for any filling which he provides.

Aristotle makes some progress on this task in I. 4 when he characterizes matter as 'the underlying thing which takes on generation and destruction' (320^a2-3). If so, matter (in general) will always be the same in virtue of being the object which receives genesis and destruction. Compare this with the suggestion that the now is always the same in virtue of being the divider of before and after. The two logical objects, that which divides before and after and that which receives genesis and destruction, seem to be equally well specified. Prime matter, on this account, will be that which receives genesis and destruction in elemental change.

Aristotle makes further progress in characterizing the relevant object in I. 5, when he introduces the idea of *dunamis* (e.g. 320^a13), an idea to which he returns in I. 9 (326^b31 ff.). In the light of this suggestion, the relevant object may be that thing which has the capacity to become F. In a similar vein, in II. 1 (329^a33 ff.) he describes matter as that which is capable of being a perceptual body (of the relevant type). Aristotle further notes that what is capable of being a perceptual body will always exist with a contrary (329^a25-6). So, he can now characterize prime matter in a more complex way as that which is capable of being a perceptual body of a given (elemental) type. Such matter (the abstract object) does not itself have any contrary as part of its nature, although it cannot exist without having some contrary or other (e.g. when it exists together with heat, it is the matter of fire; 329^a30-1).

On this account, Aristotle continues to make progress throughout *GC* I with the task, begun in I. 3, of specifying the logical (or abstract) object in virtue of being which all the relevant cases of matter underlie. They are all one in virtue of being that which is (e.g.) capable of genesis and destruction. So understood, the matter of fire and the matter of earth will be, in this respect, the same, although in many other respects they will be different (e.g. undergoing different changes). The analogy with time can now be made more determinate: the matter of earth and the matter of fire will be different in the same way as particular dated times (1.01, 1.02) are different. But the relevant cases of matter will be the same in virtue of their being that object (namely, prime matter) which is capable of receiving elemental genesis and destruction, as the nows will be the same in virtue of their being that object which divides before and after.

5. Logical or material object? Issues 2 and 3

In this section my aim is to make more determinate the idea that prime matter is a logical (or abstract) object, which maintains (as closely as possible) the analogy between prime matter and the now introduced in previous sections. I shall argue that we can understand, on the basis of this analogy, several of Aristotle's claims about prime matter.[10]

If Aristotle sustains the analogy between prime matter and the now, he can make room for the following possibility:

> [A] When change from earth to fire is followed by change from fire to earth, the matter for the first change is the matter of earth and that for the second the matter of fire.

For, there need be no one specific type of matter of the type which is the matter of both changes. In the first the matter of earth and in the second the matter of fire may be the underlier. But there is no one specific type of matter (materially specified) which they both are. In a similar way, this proposal allows for a further possibility:

> [B] In the case of the genesis of air from the destruction of water, the matter of the destruction of water is the matter of water and the matter for the genesis of air the matter of air.

In [B], as in [A], there need be no one specific type of matter which is the matter of the whole change. For, the matter of water may be the underlying matter for the destruction of water, and the matter of air the underlying matter for the genesis of air (assuming that, in this basic elemental change, the matter of water is not present in air etc.). There need be no one materially specified type of matter which underlies throughout in either [A] or [B]. Rather, that object in virtue of being which both pairs of distinct matters (in [A] and [B]) underlie will be the possessor of the capacity for elemental genesis and destruction. But, as just suggested, what it is to be that matter will be different from change to change.

If Aristotle maintains the analogy between prime matter and the now in this way, he can allow for the possibility of a simple genesis which is

---

[10] There may be other proposals, apart from the one to be developed here, which will (1) satisfy the constraints mentioned in this section, (2) account for there being one object in virtue of being which particular cases of matter underlie, and (3) preserve some form of analogy between now and prime matter. Some interpreters may seek to achieve these goals while treating prime matter as a persisting continuant more ontologically robust than logical (or abstract) objects such as the now. The distinctive feature of the present interpretation (which marks it out from others which also meet (1), (2), and (3)) is that it aims to meet these conditions while (a) maintaining as close an analogy as possible between prime matter and the now and (b) taking prime matter to exist only in the same way as the now. It offers, in this respect, what might be described as a 'minimalist' account of the type of entity prime matter is. If there are reasons to attribute to Aristotle an ontologically more robust account of prime matter, the analogy with the now will be correspondingly less precise. While I am presently sceptical as to whether the latter moves are required, several major issues are left unresolved at this point.

not any form of quality change. For, in the cases of elemental transformation just mentioned, there need be no one material (or perceptible)
object which underlies these changes. But this possibility is precisely
what Aristotle needs if he is to make room for the possibility of elemental
change that is not itself a form of quality change, while holding on to the
idea that there is one thing which is the underlier in any such change.[11]

There are several further reasons which favour the line of interpretation currently under investigation.

1. It makes good sense of Aristotle's remark in *GC* I. 4. 319^b14–15 that
there will be nothing *perceptible* which remains as the same underlier
throughout cases of simple genesis. For, the matter of water will pass
away, and the matter of air will come into being. The first will underlie
the destruction of water, the second the genesis of air. However, that
which underlies, understood as a logical (or abstract) object, will remain
the same throughout, first being the matter of water and then the matter
of air. Prime matter, so understood, can persist throughout all the
relevant changes even though no perceptible substance (such as earth
or water) persists in elemental generation.[12] For logical objects are
imperceptible, because they are not material substances. If prime matter
is a logical object of this type, there is no need to introduce an imperceptible material substance (as in traditional theories of prime matter) to be
present throughout the relevant changes. All that happens is that it falls
first to the matter of water and then to the matter of air to be that which
underlies in virtue of their being that which is capable of undergoing
elemental change of the relevant type. It is in virtue of their underlying in
this way that each is (at various times) one and the same object.

2. This interpretation makes good sense of the phrase: 'the whole
changes, nothing perceptible remaining as the same underlier'. For this
phrase allows that something perceptible may persist, even though nothing perceptible remains as the *same underlier*. Thus, for example, if
certain perceptual properties persist, they will not be perceptible as *the
same underlier*. For they are not underliers at all. Aristotle is at pains

---

[11] It is important to note that this proposal merely allows for the possibility of one
element turning into another. It does not by itself explain how such transformations occur.
To complete the latter task, Aristotle may need other aspects of his physical theory, such
as his theory of reciprocal action and passion of contraries (II. 7. 334^a20–4) and the
circular pattern of the genesis of basic elements (II. 4. 331^b2 ff.). But these suggestions are
at a less abstract level of discussion than that pursued in *GC* I. 3–4.

[12] David Bostock (1995), 223, sees the problem in these terms. He writes as follows on
GC I. 4: 'So Aristotle is apparently affirming that some matter persists through a generation [in 320^a2–5], at the same time as he apparently describes a generation as a change in
which nothing persists [in 319^b8–18 and 319^b32–320^a2]!' This difficulty can be avoided if
the (prime) matter that persists is a logical object and there is no persisting perceptible
substance to which perceptible properties such as hot or cold belong.

to distinguish what underlies and the properties which belong to it (319^b8–10). Features such as heat and cold are most naturally taken as properties not underliers. (There is certainly no preparation in this context for taking these to be the underliers). Further, were heat and cold to be underliers in this transaction, why are they not perceptible as such? If cold were to be an underlier, why could it not be seen as such? (Again, no answer is provided in the present context.)

The crucial phrase 'nothing perceptible remaining as the underlying' allows that there may be different perceptible underliers for the destruction of water (namely, the matter of water) and for the creation of air (namely, the matter of air). What it rules out is there being one perceptible underlier which is present throughout. According to the interpretation just suggested, this is because there is no one material underlier which is present throughout. For if there were, it would be perceptible (as what underlies the destruction of earth is perceptible). Rather, we have one and the same logical underlier: that object in virtue of being which different (perceptible) matters are capable of undergoing genesis and destruction. So understood, all these different types of matter share the same general feature: being capable of undergoing genesis and destruction. They are capable of this in different ways, depending on their different specific and perceptible features. But there is no one *material* underlier in the case of elemental transformation (see 319^b32–320^a2). Rather, there are two perceptible underliers for different parts of the transition.

If this is correct, there is no need to postulate an imperceptible material underlier to account for elemental change. All that is required is that there be one logical object, the underlier, in virtue of being which different types of perceptible matter are (from time to time) capable of undergoing genesis and destruction of this type. At some time the matter of water will constitute the underlier (when water is destroyed), at another the matter of air will do so (when air is created). In this way one can separate the matter of water from water and the matter of air from air. For it is the matter of water which is the primary subject for the relevant process of destruction. There is no need, on this interpretation, to insist that the relevant matter is first water and then air, or to override the distinction drawn between (e.g.) fire and its matter in 319^a32 ff.[13]

---

[13] It is significant that Aristotle illustrates his discussion with the case of earth and fire, described as heavy and light, and not with his favoured pairings of the hot and the cold (319^a30–1). This may be because his discussion is intended (at this stage) to be independent of the details of his favoured physical theory. He may be concerned only with the 'logical' point about the way in which that which underlies is the same, not with any particular physical account of such changes.

By the end of I. 4 matter (as specified by the prime use of the term 'matter') is to be identified with that which underlies genesis and receives destruction. In the case of fire, what fulfils this role will be the matter of fire, in the case of earth the matter of earth. By contrast, what undergoes changes (such as spatial change, quantity/quality change) will be substances (such as fire or earth). This is why the latter are matter *in a way*, distinguishable from the primary case in which matter itself (and not matter construed as a substance) is involved.

3. If one focuses on the idea of the one object in virtue of being which specific matters underlie, it is natural to take this as the logical object matter has to be if it is to underlie: something capable of playing a given role. This provides a regress-stopping answer to the question: in virtue of being what does matter underlie? For the answer is: in virtue of being that which is capable of playing the relevant role of underlying. By contrast, this question would not have been answered if one had merely specified a distinctive type of imperceptible matter. For the same question could still be asked: in virtue of being what does this imperceptible matter underlie? For the question, which arises for perceptible matter, can also be raised for imperceptible matter. Indeed, there seems (on this interpretation) to be an infinite regress (which might be labelled the 'third-matter argument'). The introduction of logical objects addresses this issue, while the introduction of imperceptible matter cannot. For the relevant logical object is simply that object in virtue of being which the specific matters of fire and water etc. underlie. One cannot sensibly ask of it: in virtue of being what does it underlie? For it underlies simply in virtue of being the object it is.

6. Prime matter and elemental change

In *GC* I. 4 Aristotle is talking about the matter required in all cases of simple genesis, including the genesis of animals (319^b16–17). His discussion is not confined to elemental change. However, it can be easily extended to such cases. If matter is (strictly speaking) that thing, the receiver of genesis and destruction, in being which all cases of matter underlie, prime matter will be that thing, the receiver of genesis and destruction in the case of the primary elements, in being which cases of prime matter underlie the relevant transformations. This too will remain the same (in the way in which it is always now), even though what it is to be prime matter will differ from time to time (and from change to change). In one case it will be the matter of fire and in another the matter of earth. Prime matter, so understood, will be a distinctive logical (or abstract) object.[14] (It falls to more things to be matter than to be prime matter.)

In the case of elemental change, there need (according to the view currently before us) be no single material substratum which persists throughout the elemental change from earth to fire via air. At the beginning of the change the substratum may be the matter of earth, at the end the matter of fire. If so, features and causal potentialities will be transferred from earth to fire without there being one persisting material substratum.

Many will wonder whether this view can be Aristotle's. Can features or causal potentialities 'jump' from one Aristotelian substance (or basic element) to another in this way? Can he really dispense with the idea of a basic material substratum continuing throughout the whole change (as in the *Physics* picture)? Is he not prevented from doing so by his own metaphysics of change?

It should be noted, at the outset, that when somewhat similar issues arise in the cases of the other logical objects mentioned above (the now and the President), they do not seem to lead to insuperable problems. One might ask, in the spirit of the last paragraph, how can the powers of the President 'jump' from Mr Clinton to Mr Bush, when the latter succeeds the former? Or again, one might ask how can the power to divide past and future 'jump' from 1.01 to 1.02 as time goes by?[15] But, in the first case, we certainly talk (apparently sensibly) of one continuing object (i.e. the President) retaining its powers while the material objects who from time to time 'are' (or constitute) the President change. Further, Aristotle himself seems content to talk in this way of the now and the dated times that 'are' (from time to time) the now. So, it seems as if there is no general problem with the idea of a 'logical' object's retaining its powers even though the material objects involved change. If so, there can be no incoherence in thinking of prime matter as surviving and retaining its powers even though the specific matters that constitute it change.

---

[14] To speak of prime matter as a 'logical' or 'abstract' object is fully consistent with thinking of material substances (such as fire, air, or their matter) as the basic elements in reality. Perhaps only the latter may play a role in physical explanation. Indeed, the introduction of logical (or abstract) objects allows for phrases such as 'that...which underlies' to refer to an object, without taking its referent to be part of the basic building blocks of the physical world. (It is consistent with all that has been said here that all 'logical' objects are reducible to material substances or material kinds.) For a similar point about the ontological status of arbitrary objects see K. Fine, *Reasoning with Arbitrary Objects* (Oxford 1985), 7.

[15] Or in another example mentioned above: How can the powers of Manchester United (e.g. to play in the Premiership, etc.) 'jump' from one set of players, managers, etc. to another?

It may be that if a logical object loses all its powers at one instant we have to conclude that it has ceased to exist. So, for example, if the powers of the President changed completely overnight we might be led to say that the President had ceased to exist and been replaced (e.g.) by the Chairman of the Central Committee. But if his powers change gradually (with some being retained at each step) we can (without apparent difficulty) say that the President (or prime matter) survives. Thus, the President may survive such changes in power over time as occurred between the time in office of George Washington and George W. Bush, provided they occur in a gradual (or step-by-step) way. Since in the case of Aristotelian elemental change some of the powers of the previous element are retained in this way, there seems to be no difficulty in thinking that in this case too prime matter can survive through the various step-by-step changes it endures.

However, it will be said, the three cases just discussed differ in an important respect. In the case of the President, while Mr George W. Bush comes after Mr Clinton, the latter is not transformed into the former. Similarly with 1.01 and 1.02. But the matter of fire is transformed, in elemental change, into the matter of air. The question of how this can happen without one persisting material substratum is not resolved simply by introducing logical objects. Surely, more than this is needed to account for change involving transformation?

The basis for a reply to this objection is to be found in Aristotle's developing argument in *GC* I. In his account of mixture in *GC* I. 10, elements (it appears) can be transformed into (e.g.) alloys without one persisting material substratum ($328^{b}12$ ff.). In this case, while the original elements are present potentially in the alloy (in that they can be extracted from the mixture when it is unscrambled), they are not actually present throughout as a continuing material substratum ($327^{b}22-8$). Thus, when a mixture is created out of pre-existing elements its creation cannot require the presence of one material substratum throughout the process. At some point the matter of the elements ceases to exist and a distinct matter (that of the mixture) comes into being. Indeed, this is what has to happen if the mixture is to be a genuine mixture and not merely a rearrangement of continuing pieces of matter (as, for example, in the alternative atomist account).

In such cases, some of the causal potentialities of the pre-existing elements may be preserved, but now as potentialities of the mixture. Thus, for example, the resulting mixture may be capable of heating if it is derived (in part) from the hot. In this way, one substance can be transformed into another (and the relevant causal potentiality be preserved) without a persisting material substratum.

If this account of the creation and destruction of mixtures is (in outline) correct, Aristotle can allow in *GC* I for something similar to occur (within the *GC* framework) in the case of basic elemental transformation, such as when earth is transformed into water. For here too there can be a transformation from one substance to another (and the retention of the relevant causal potentiality) without an actually persisting material substratum. Since I cannot, within the scope of this chapter, argue for the interpretation of mixture just sketched, the current proposal must remain incomplete.[16] However, there is some exegetical reason, internal to *GC* I, for thinking that it is along the right lines: it reveals an interesting thematic unity between some of the apparently disparate discussions in this book, one which displays the coherence and radicalism of Aristotle's thought on these topics. For, on this account, one reason to discuss mixture in *GC* is to provide space for a type of change which does not require a specific persisting (*Physics*-style) material substratum. This is certainly needed if he is to avoid being driven by his own, *Physics*-style, arguments into denying the possibility of basic elemental change by his assumption that there is no real persisting underlying matter in this case (or in the case of mixture). So understood, his discussions of both topics constitute a systematic attempt to modify his *Physics*-style view that a material substratum must persist throughout any case of change. This project requires for its successful completion both his discussion of mixture and his account in I. 5 and I. 9 (mentioned in Sect. 4) of the relevant *dunameis* involved in change. If it can be carried through, nothing more is required in the case of basic elemental change than a persisting logical object (which bears its properties in the way the President or the now does). And this is precisely what prime matter (on the present proposal) supplies.

There is one qualification which should be noted: Aristotle cannot, using the notion of prime matter under discussion, determine (on this basis alone) which elements are primary at a given time. The phrase 'prime matter' offers a way of labelling that thing which is (at a given time) involved in elemental genesis and destruction. We can only find out which matter is prime matter (at a given time) by finding out which elements (at that time) are involved in elemental genesis and destruction, just as one can only find out which time is currently now by finding out whether it is now 1.01 or 1.02. As Aristotle remarks, it is the latter idea of time (as dated points of time) which is most familiar or knowable to us.[17]

---

[16] For detailed discussions of mixture consistent with the sketch offered here see Fine (1996), Code (1996), and Dorothea Frede in chapter 11 of this volume, pp. 294–6.

[17] We find particular dated times more knowable than the ever-present now: see *Ph.* IV. 11. 219^{b}26–30.

7. The role of prime matter

Why, on the present view, did Aristotle introduce prime matter at all? It provided him with a way of understanding how the matters of earth, air, fire, and water could all be one thing, as it falls to each of them to be that object which underlies the genesis and destruction of the primary elements. If understood as a logical object, prime matter can be thought of as the ultimate determinable, a kind of which the matter of fire and earth etc. constitute (from time to time) determinate subkinds, made such by the relevant determinants (e.g. the hot and the cold).[18] Without a logical object of this type Aristotle would have merely had a list of the varying matters of primary elements and would have failed to specify any matter common to them all. But, if so, he would have found it difficult, if not impossible, to make sense of transformations between the different primary elements.[19] Introduction of a logical object (that in being which specific elemental matter underlies) allowed him to make room for such transformations without recourse to one basic enduring material kind (as required in the monist accounts he rejects). Thus, he found a mid-course between the Scylla of monism and the Charybdis of pluralism, the very route he needed given his rejection of these two alternatives in *GC* I. 1 and elsewhere. For he could agree with the monists that there is one thing which all cases of elemental matter are (in certain situations) without following them in reifying this as a material (or quasi-material) substance (or substratum).

The possibility of the mid-course I have charted has remained hidden in many contributions to the long-standing exegetical debate about the nature of prime matter. Defenders of the traditional view have standardly committed themselves to two claims:

[A] Prime matter is a being, the one thing which underlies certain changing properties and conditions.[20]
[B] Prime matter is an imperishable substratum.[21]

[18] Prime matter, so understood, is a determinable kind not a determinable concept. As such, it cannot exist without one of the determinants (an opposite) which make determinate kinds (e.g. the four basic elements). See *GC* II. 1. 329^{a}24–35. Since determinables cannot exist without determinants, prime matter must be inseparable.
[19] See his critical discussion of Empedocles' view in *GC* II. 6. By analogy, in the case of time, what makes all of 1.01 ... 1.02 times would be that they may all be or constitute (at some time) that which divides before and after. Without this type of unity there would be no way of taking them all as times. See *Ph.* IV. 14. 223^{a}25–9.
[20] e.g. Zeller, *Aristotle and the Earlier Peripatetics* (tr. Costellae and Murhead, London 1897), 344.
[21] Ibid. 345.

The first claim is ontologically less committed than the second. [A] allows for the possibility that the phrase 'prime matter' may pick out that logical object in being which the matter of (e.g.) fire underlies basic elemental change. But [B] goes considerably further than this in identifying prime matter with the eternal, physically indeterminate, material (or quasi-material) substratum of all change. It is the latter which is often taken to play a basic role in Aristotle's physical theory. However, claim [B], as has sometimes been noted, resembles Anaximander's suggestions about the *apeiron*, which Aristotle attacks in several places.[22] Claim [A], by contrast, is far less controversial, as it commits him to no more than a claim about a logical (or abstract) object: (roughly) that thing which underlies. And this need come to no more than his comparable claim about the now (as that thing which divides time).[23]

Claim [A], or so I have argued, is all that is needed to analyse the *GC* passages we have discussed. If Aristotle is committed to no more than this, we can readily understand his criticism of those who move to endorse claims like [B]. Thus, in *Metaphysics* XII. 2, he censures his predecessors precisely because they 'materialized' (or reified) matter, the principle, as a specific type of matter (such as the unbounded, atoms, fire, the cosmic mixture). In that context, as in the one currently under discussion, he seeks to avoid a 'materialized' way of understanding matter.[24]

Recent opponents of the traditional view of prime matter have rejected both claims [A] and [B]. For them, 'prime matter' specifies only the collection of basic elements (earth, air, fire, and water) or their distinctive types of matter. (See, for example, the discussions by William Charlton and Montgomery Furth).[25] But their proposal does not capture

---

[22] *GC* II. 1. 328^{b}35; II. 5. 332^{a}20–5. See also *Metaph.* XII. 2. 1069^{b}22–3. In *GC* I. 5. 320^{b}2 ff. Aristotle attacks the distinct idea of matter (for growth) as a separate incorporeal thing devoid of magnitude. See Alan Code, in Ch. 6 of this volume, p. 177.

[23] Joachim (1922), it should be noted, sometimes writes as if he was committing himself only to [A], as when speaking of 'prime matter' as 'a logical abstraction' (p. 93), a 'logical presupposition' (p. 199), or as 'isolable by definition' (p. 137). However, while these passages might suggest that Joachim understands 'prime matter' not as an object but as a determinable concept (or even as a logical object), elsewhere he reverts to talking in more traditional terms of a permanent substratum which 'drops one form and takes on another' (p. 97). Keimpe Algra, in Ch. 3 of this volume n. 32, understands Joachim's proposal in the latter way. It may be that Joachim did not arrive at a stable view of the ontological status of prime matter.

[24] See *Metaph.* XII. 2. 1069^{b}21–4. I discuss this passage in my essay on *Metaph.* XII. 2 in *Metaphysics Lambda: Symposium Aristotelicum*, ed. M. Frede and D. Charles (Oxford, 2000), 97–103.

[25] Charlton (1970), 129–45; Montgomery Furth, *Substance, Form and Psyche: an Aristotelian Metaphysics* (Cambridge, 1988), 76–9, 221–7. It should be noted that Charlton (1970), 136, comes close to the present proposal, when he writes that something is a material factor 'under the description "perceptible body in possibility" or "cold body

Aristotle's insistence on the need for there to be one common matter shared by the basic contraries (329^{a}32), which underlies earth, air, fire, and water. (*Mete.* I. 3. 339^{a}36–^{b}2, *Cael:* III. 5. 312^{a}30–^{b}1. See *GC* II. 6. 334^{a}15–18). Nor does it do justice to his claim, cited at the beginning of this chapter, that the matter of fire and the matter of earth are one object: that, whatever it is, that underlies.[26] Indeed, Aristotle rejects the views of his pluralist predecessors precisely because, when they refused to accept that there is one thing which underlies change, they debarred themselves from making sense of the idea of common matter involved in transformations between differing basic elements.[27]

Claim [A] was attractive to Aristotle because it gave him a way to accommodate the idea of common matter without representing it as a

in possibility" '. However, because he does not distinguish sharply between these two descriptions, he overlooks the possibility that it is the first and not the second that captures what is common to all underlying matter.

[26] For discussion of further problems in Montgomery Furth's views see Theodore Scaltsas, *Substances and Universals in Aristotle's Metaphysics* (Cornell, 1994), 18–22.

[27] Sarah Broadie notes this weakness in the pluralist style of interpretation, favoured by Charlton, and addresses it by suggesting (on Aristotle's behalf) that common matter is to be found in any sequence of changes which begins with one of the four primary elements. Thus, earth (or its matter) might be the matter for fire, air, and water since it is the element which is turned into the others in a cyclical process brought about by one agent. In this way, she aims to accommodate the idea of a common material basis for elemental change without invoking any matter beyond that of earth, fire, etc. (See the final section of Ch. 4, above). I have two reservations about her ingenious proposal:

1. It does not seem to explain how there can be *one* matter common to all elemental changes, irrespective of whether they begin with earth, fire, air, or water. What is needed (if the suggestion is to be generalized) is not merely that there be one matter (i.e. fire) for any change beginning from fire, but that the same matter be involved in all elemental changes, no matter whether they start from earth, fire, or water. The only way to explain, on this model, the presence of one and the same matter common to all elemental changes would be to assume that Aristotle accepts (but does not state) that all elemental changes begin at one and the same starting point (e.g. earth).

2. The presence of one unchanging agent does not seem sufficient to ensure that there is only one type of matter involved. For, if a builder turns wood into beams, and then turns beams into a house, there seem to be (in Aristotle's general account) two distinct matters involved (at least in *Metaph.* IX. 7. 1049^{a}9–11) as there are two distinct subjects of the relevant changes (each in a state in which the change can occur without any further change to them). Here, the matter at each stage is precisely that which is required (without any further addition or change in the matter) for the relevant Form to be added. (A single process is required to effect the imposition of the Form.) Nor (*pace* Broadie's suggestion) is this account of matter confined to cases where the process involves artifice, since Aristotle immediately generalizes it to all cases of natural processes with an external cause (1049^{a}12) and then to all cases with an internal cause (1049^{a}13–16). Not all of these will involve artifice. Notwithstanding these (possible) disagreements, Sarah Broadie and I both aim to reject the (recently popular) pluralist interpretation whilst avoiding the traditional view of prime matter as a material (or quasi-material) but imperceptible

mysterious, indeterminate, eternal substratum (in the style of his monist predecessors). Indeed, it was precisely by accepting claim [A] and rejecting [B] that he could achieve his immediate goal in *GC* I of allowing for the *possibility* of simple genesis of basic elements, while avoiding the errors to which monists and pluralists had fallen victim. (Of course, he had to do far more than this to show, at some appropriately physical level of description, that such *genesis* actually occurs.)[28]

substratum. We differ in that she attempts to meet this challenge by looking to Aristotle's physical theory not to his general ontology.

[28] This paper grew out of discussions at the Deurne Symposium. There, Edward Hussey first alerted me to the possibility of comparing Aristotle's discussions of prime matter and the now. I am indebted to Adam Beresford, Justin Broackes, Myles Burnyeat, Kei Chiba, Ursula Coope, Michael Frede, Frans de Haas, Edward Hussey, Geoffrey Lloyd, Ben Morison, and Dory Scaltsas for their comments on earlier drafts of this paper.

6

On Generation and Corruption I. 5

ALAN CODE

After chapter 4 of *On Generation and Corruption* shows how to distinguish alteration from generation, chapter 5 begins its treatment of growth (αὔξησις), or increase,[1] by stating that it remains[2] for us to say (i) how it differs from both of these and also (ii) how growing things grow and diminishing things diminish. The growth of a child into an adult is not the same thing as the coming to be of a new human being, nor is it the taking on of new qualitative attributes. It is a different kind of change, and as such must be distinguished from both of these other kinds. Furthermore, as he will point out shortly, although as something increases or decreases in size it occupies a larger or smaller place, these changes need to be distinguished from locomotion (and revolving in place) as well.

The first topic is dealt with in a preliminary manner early in the chapter, and the text proceeds to deal with both topics as it builds upon and amplifies the initial results. An answer to the first question puts constraints on the answer to the second, and an answer to the second consists in specifying the causal mechanism that gives rise to the phenomena of growth. The view ultimately arrived at is that growth is caused by an active power in the thing that grows, a power to assimilate acceding matter to the form of that which grows when the two are together. The acceding matter is in some sense opposite to the growing thing, being potentially what the growing thing is actually. When the latter grows, its substance and form, unlike that of the acceding matter, persists.

The discussion begins with the question as to whether generation, alteration, and growth differ solely with respect to that with which they are concerned (περί + acc.), or differ also in manner (τρόπος). He takes it

---

[1] As the discussion proceeds it becomes clear that the subject matter of this chapter is not mere increase in size, but growth or αὔξησις conceived of as a certain kind of natural phenomenon.

[2] The opening remarks of the treatise indicate that investigating what growth is falls within the scope of its investigation (*GC* I. 1. 314ª3–4).

for granted that they must differ at least in the first respect in that generation, alteration, and growth are changes concerned with *substance*, *affection*, and *magnitude*, respectively. Generation is a change ($\mu\epsilon\tau\alpha\beta o\lambda\acute{\eta}$) from what is potentially a substance to what is actually a substance, alteration a change from what is potentially modified to what is actually modified,[3] and growth a change from what is potentially of a size to what is actually of a size. Initially Aristotle does not attempt to make clear the sense in which such changes are from potential to actual substances, and the like, but will turn to that task shortly. However, we have already learned from chapter 3 in connection with generation that the view that an actual substance comes to be from something that is merely a potential substance, and not also an actual substance of some sort, leads to aporia.[4] The correct view, and the view urged later in that chapter, is that the generation of one substance is the passing away of another—what is potentially but not yet actually fire is actually something else, perhaps earth. In that case, what is actually a substance of one kind (fire) is generated out of something that is both actually a substance of some other kind (earth) and only potentially a substance of the first kind. A bit later (at I. 5. 320^{a}27 ff.) he will raise this kind of issue specifically in connection with growth, but he first deals with the question as to whether generation, alteration, and growth differ from each other in the second way he has specified, in manner.

After an examination of the way in which growth and diminution involve change of place he concludes that the three kinds of change must differ in manner as well as differing with respect to that with which they are concerned. The main observation is that when something changes in size it also changes with respect to place in the sense that its parts occupy a bigger or a smaller place, or $\tau\acute{o}\pi o s$. Obviously something that grows can be—and typically is—also moving around from place to place. However, this motion is not as such a part of growth, and in so far as the thing is growing it is not moving.

Although what grows or diminishes will, as a growing or diminishing thing, itself change with respect to place, this is not the kind of change of place that is characteristic of locomotion. In locomotion the body moving 'changes its place as a whole'. It changes its place *entirely* in

[3] Although the text does not make it clear whether alteration is from potential to actual modifications or from potential to actual things that are modified, I take it that Aristotle's view is the latter. For instance, when something is heated, this is not a change from what is potentially heat to some actually existing heat, but rather a change from what is potentially hot to what is actually hot. For the purposes of a chapter on growth it is not important to get clear on this distinction. However, the analogous distinction in the case of growth is important, and 320^{a}27 ff. makes it clear that there the change is from what potentially has size to what actually has size, not from a potential to an actual quantity.

[4] *GC* I. 3. 317^{b}18–33.

that as it changes it continually occupies distinct places. By way of contrast, one could describe what happens in the case of that which grows by saying that the object comes to occupy a larger place of which its original place is a proper part. This is not, however, quite how Aristotle draws the contrast in this passage. To help us to understand this idea he compares growth with a special case of qualitative alteration, that of metal being beaten and flattened out. Although alteration as such does not require a change with respect to place, change of shape does.[5] As the metal changes its shape its parts move out in various directions along a plane, but the piece of metal as a whole 'remains'. The volume of the metal does not change and so this is not an increase in size, but nonetheless growth is like this in that the parts of the growing things also change with respect to place[6], while the growing thing 'remains'.[7] Unlike the case of the rotating sphere, in which the parts are subject to circular motion in an 'equal' place (i.e. the motion is within the same amount of space), the parts of the growing thing move over a constantly larger place,[8] and as such the growth is an expansion in all three spatial dimensions. The parts of the growing thing are here described as *moving*. Locomotion has earlier been described as change 'with respect to place' (κατὰ τόπον),[9] but we are now being told that there is a way of changing 'with respect to place' characteristic of growth which is not the same as locomotion. The sense in which the growing thing changes 'with respect to place' is explicated by reference to its parts changing 'with respect to place'. One can avoid a regress by taking this latter type of change to be locomotion, and so I take it that his view is that the parts of the growing thing move. However, the growing thing as a whole is not moving from one place to another, but rather 'remains'. Since this is supposed to contrast with the locomotion of its parts, it is natural to interpret this as meaning simply that it is not moving. So, although both that which moves and that which grows change with respect to place, the latter changes with respect to place only in the sense that its parts move over an ever-increasing place, although in so far as it grows it does not itself move as a whole.

That said, it is nonetheless clear that the growing thing must as a whole occupy larger and larger places as it grows, and hence it does occupy continually different places. In order to clarify how this differs from locomotion it would be necessary to bring in an account of the difference between the relationship between the successive places occupied by

[5] Since only some cases of alteration, but all cases of growth, involve this kind of change with respect to place, this marks out a respect in which growth and alteration differ.
[6] 320[a]21–2.   [7] 320[a]21.   [8] 320[a]24.
[9] For which see 319[b]31–2; see also *Ph.* III. 1. 200[b]33–4.

growing things and the successive places occupied by moving things. For
this we would need some way of defining the various places in question.
However, he does not here invoke his definition of the place (τόπος) of a
body as the innermost motionless boundary of the body containing it.[10]
Were he to do so he would have to bring in a modal notion of potentiality
to explicate the sense in which a larger place contains smaller places, and
how the later place of an object overlaps with the place it previously
occupied. He does not, however, treat any of these issues here, and
rightly so since that is not necessary in order to distinguish growth
from other changes or say how it occurs.

This observation about the sense in which growth requires change of
place will turn out to be important later when he comes to the distinction
between matter and form in his attempt to specify the cause of growth.
At this point, though, he gives no indication as to the connection of this
fact with the remainder of the chapter, but instead at 320^a27 ff. raises a
question about the relationship between growth and that with which
growth is concerned: magnitude. He earlier claimed that growth is a
change from potential beings into actual beings.[11] The beings in question
are magnitudes, and in order to explain how growth occurs we are going
to need to clarify the sense in which the actual magnitude of something
that has grown is the result of a change from a potential magnitude. Just
as in the case of substantial change it is impossible for an actual substance to come to be from a potential substance that is not also actual, so
too he will argue that the actual magnitude of a growing thing cannot
come from something that is merely a potential magnitude and not also
actually of some magnitude.

We will see later in the chapter that Aristotle distinguishes two different items that are potentially of a certain magnitude. In growth there is (i)
that which accedes to something, and (ii) that to which it accedes. Both of
these are corporeal, and both of these are possessed of some actual
magnitude. Additionally, both are in some sense potentially of some
magnitude that prior to the growth neither actually has. The food that
will become (say) flesh is potentially the magnitude by which it will
increase the flesh that grows, and the flesh that grows is potentially the
magnitude it will be once the food has been assimilated and added to it.
In the section at 320^a27-^b34, though, he has not yet drawn the distinction
between these two items. However, although it is not until 321^a29-^b10
that he raises the question as to which of the two is the growing thing,
this earlier section concludes at 320^b30-4 with the observation that
growth is the increase of an existing magnitude, and takes this to show
that the growing thing must have some magnitude, and hence that

---

[10] *Ph.* IV. 4. 212^a20-1.   [11] 320^a14-16.

growth cannot be from a matter lacking actual magnitude (having it only potentially) to something having an actual magnitude. These remarks deal with the growing thing as the item which must have matter with some actual magnitude, and for this reason it is best to take at least this section as dealing with this, and not the matter of that which accedes. Among other things, this thesis is relevant to the task of showing how growth differs from coming to be. If (contrary to fact) something with no actual magnitude were to grow into something with actual magnitude this would be a case of coming to be (indeed, of coming to be out of nothing actual).[12] In that case growth would not be, as it in fact is, a phenomenon that is distinct from generation.

The position for which he argues is that growth is not a change from something that potentially, but not actually, possesses magnitude. He thinks that this point is made evident by the examination of difficulties that takes place at 320^a29-^b25. Even if the overall conclusion is relatively clear, the argument itself is difficult to interpret.[13] His examination takes the form of a *reductio* argument. The argumentative strategy commences at 320^a29 where he introduces the claim targeted for refutation: the matter from which something that is a body and a magnitude comes to be is itself potentially but not actually a body possessed of size. At $^a31-4$ he considers two ways of understanding the thesis targeted for *reductio*: *either* (i) the matter is separate 'itself by itself', *or* (ii) the matter is contained in another body.[14] Either the matter exists separately, on its own, just by itself, or it does not. If it does not, then it must be in something else; if it exists in something other than itself, then it does not exist on its own and by itself. He intends to show that on either construal the claim cannot be true. Consequently, growth does not proceed from a matter that is possessed of magnitude merely potentially, but rather proceeds from an actual body that actually has some magnitude.

His argument continues at $^a34-^b2$ by distinguishing two alternative ways in which the matter of growth might exist separately while being actually incorporeal and lacking in magnitude. *Either* (a) this matter will not occupy a place, but rather will be like a point,[15] *or* (b) this

---

[12] See *GC* I. 5. 320^b28-34.

[13] I would like to thank Frans de Haas for useful discussion on the structure of this argument.

[14] Joachim (1922), 114, thinks that the thesis targeted for *reductio* implies that the matter has independent existence and is separate, and says that 'the matter is supposed to be κεχωρισμένη in *both* alternatives'. However, the claim that something X is described as potentially, but not actually, corporeal and of a size does not require that X has independent existence. The potential Hermes in the stone does exist independently of the stone.

[15] We can, as Philop. *in GC* 75. 30–76. 2 suggests, take the second ἤ in an adversative sense, and not follow Joachim in excising it.

matter will be either a void or an imperceptible body.[16] Concerning these
two alternatives, Aristotle says that one of them is impossible, whereas
on the other it is necessary for the matter to be in something. The
argument that the matter must be in something is that the item that
comes to be from it is somewhere, and for this reason that matter must
itself be somewhere, either per se or *per accidens*.

It is usually assumed that he is claiming that option (a) is impossible,
and that option (b) leads to the requirement that the matter is in something. On this interpretation the reason that (b) has this consequence
must be that a void or an imperceptible body must have a location
coincidentally, and hence be in something else that has a location per se.
This assumes that only an actual body could have a place in its own right,
and so a matter that is merely potentially corporeal would have to
occupy a location coincidentally by being in something that has a location in its own right. There is, however, in the context of this argument
no justification for the assumption that only actual corporeal bodies have
places in their own right. After all, option (a) was that the separate
matter has no place, but option (b) is that it *does* have a place. This
problem can be avoided by reading 320[b]1–5 chiastically,[17] and taking
Aristotle to be saying that option (b) is impossible, whereas option (a)
leads to the view that the matter is in something other than itself. This
would contradict the assumption from (i) that the matter exists separately itself by itself.

On this reading Aristotle is flatly denying the possibility of either a
void or a body that lacks perceptible features, and is not arguing that
voids or imperceptible bodies could not exist on their own on the
grounds that they are contained in actually existing bodies. On the
other hand, incorporeal entities that exist in the way points do are said
not to have places. However, since they have to be somewhere (since the
object that grows is in a place), they are contained in some other body
and as such do not exist on their own. Thus alternative (i) is ruled out on
both option (a) and option (b), and, since (a) and (b) exhaust the
possibilities for a separable incorporeal and sizeless matter, only alternative (ii) is left in the running.

If the matter of growth is incorporeal, then it is in something other
than itself. If so, either it can exist separately from what it is in or it

---

[16] Reading instead of καί at [b]2 'L's' ή. Philoponus, who was aware of both, reports the
text that he was using contained ή (*in GC* 76. 3–4). In notes distributed at the Symposium
Gisela Striker pointed out that Philoponus and Alexander grouped point and void
together, and took imperceptible body as the second alternative. There is an excellent
analysis of Philoponus on Aristotle's discussion of growth in chapter 3 of Frans de Haas,
John Philoponus' New Definition of Prime Matter (Brill, 1997).

[17] I owe this suggestion to David Sedley.

cannot. At 320^b5-12 he argues against the first disjunct, claiming that it leads to many impossibilities. Once it is granted that a separately existing incorporeal matter can be present in a body, nothing rules out the possibility of an infinite number of them in the same body. Each of these would be incorporeal and would actually lack magnitude, but each is potentially of some magnitude, and each such potentiality could be actualized. Although this result is supposed to be absurd, the precise nature of the absurdity is never specified. Perhaps he thinks that all of these potentialities could be actualized simultaneously, and hence the body that grows from it could be infinitely large (contrary to the arguments against an infinitely large sensible body in *Physics* V). However, it does not follow directly from the claim that something has an infinite number of potentialities each of which could be actualized that each could be actualized at the same time, and so perhaps the absurdity he has in mind is simply that there would be no limit to the growth of a body if it contained an infinite number of separately existing matters. As an additional consideration he points out that this in any case goes against experience. We do not, for instance, observe air emerging from water as if from a container that stays behind.[18]

Having dispensed with the view that an incorporeal matter of growth exists in something else as something separable from it, he urges at 320^b12-17 that it is better to say that the matter for growth is not separable. So far option (ii) has been examined only in connection with the assumption that the matter of growth is separable, and nothing has yet been said to rule out the possibility of an *inseparable* incorporeal and sizeless matter of growth that resides in some other body. We should now expect some treatment of an inseparable matter that is contained by a body. It is not immediately clear that this is what we get in 320^b12 ff., and, unless the βέλτιον of 320^b12 answers to the εἰ μέν of 320^b5, it looks as though Aristotle has overlooked this topic.[19]

This section argues in favour of a matter of growth that is not separate from that which grows, which cannot exist on its own, and which depends for its existence on the body it is in. He begins this section with the premiss that the matter is inseparable in that it is numerically

[18] Although this is in fact for Aristotle a case of generation, the point applies equally to what one observes in growth.

[19] Frans de Haas pointed out in discussion that by taking 320^b12-17 as examining option (ii) in connection with the thesis that the matter of growth is inseparable one can avoid accusing Aristotle of neglecting this option. This makes for a more elegant construal of the overall structure of the argument. The claim that the matter is inseparable in that it is coextensive with the body can be used to rule out other candidates for inseparable inherents such as points or lines. However, this claim represents just one way in which matter could be inseparable from the body it is in, and as such is a special case, and so Aristotle's treatment of this alternative would be incomplete.

one and the same as the body (or its matter), but different in account.[20]
I take it that he means that the matter of growth is the same as the matter
of the body that grows, although it differs from it in account. If so, then,
since the body that grows has actual size, the matter of growth would
have to be something that actually possesses size, and could not be
incorporeal and only potentially a body having magnitude. This rules
out the possibility that incorporeal points could serve as the matter of
growth, since they are not the same as the corporeal matter; for the same
reason lines too cannot be the matter of growth. The matter, he says, is
that of which such mathematical entities are a limit. As such, the matter
is what is marked off and delimited by points and lines. Whatever this is,
it is something that must possess shape and affections. In any event, it is
something with actual magnitude. If what points and lines mark off and
limit is spatial extension, then this matter of growth would be a spatial
extension. This is something that already has some size, and hence the
matter of growth would be something actually possessed of size.

However, 320^b17–25 invokes some general theses about generation
that rule out the possibility of a single kind of matter for all cases of
growth, and for this reason the matter of growth is not mere spatial
extension. He tells us that it has been established elsewhere[21] that the
efficient cause of unqualified generation is either (i) an actual being that
is the same in kind or species as the effect or (ii) an actuality,[22] and since
there is also a matter for corporeal substance that is different for different
kinds of substances (there being no matter common to all bodies) it
follows that this (i.e. the matter for a corporeal substance that is appropriate to that kind of substance) is also the same as the matter for
magnitudes and affections. Just as there is an appropriate type of agent
to serve as the efficient cause of a given kind of substance, so too there is
an appropriate kind of matter upon which the efficient cause operates.
However, it is this very same matter that is the matter for the size and the
qualities of the substance. We learned in I. 4. 319^b31–2 that the substratum that is receptive of contrary sizes (and hence receptive of sizes) is the
matter for growth, and thus if the matter of corporeal body is what is
receptive of size it would follow that the matter of corporeal body is also

[20] 320^b12–14.
[21] Perhaps *Metaph.* VII. 7–9.
[22] Examples of (i) would include corporeal bodies that produce generically or specifically identical corporeal bodies, and examples of (ii) would include the forms, dispositions,
or activities by virtue of which those corporeal bodies produce their kindred effects.
Richard Sorabji has proposed a different way of understanding the import of 320^b17–21
(in *Philoponus: On Aristotle's Coming-to-Be and Perishing 1. 1–5* (Cornell, 1999), p. vii).
He retains σκληρὸν γὰρ οὐχ ὑπὸ σκληροῦ γίνεται, and following Philoponus proposes that
Aristotle is claiming in (ii) that in some cases all that is transferred from cause to effect is
actuality.

the matter of growth. The matter of body just is the matter of growth, separate from it only in account but not in location.

Lines 320^{b}34 ff. mark a transition in the exposition. Aristotle has earlier argued that growth involves a locomotion of parts but not of the whole, and subsequently argued that the matter from which growth proceeds is possessed of an actual size (as well as potentially possessing the size it will attain). We also need an account of how growth takes place, and our explanation of growth and diminution should be consistent with the results of these previous arguments. Towards this end we are now enjoined to get a better grasp as to what growth and diminution are like, almost as though starting an enquiry from the beginning, from scratch. What immediately follows is not a treatment of theories of growth (either his opponents' or his own) but rather a listing of two (later three) of the phenomena of growth and diminution that an explanation must preserve. The new start requires that we say what growth and diminution appear to be according to the commonly held views. These views about what growth and diminution are like will put further constraints on his answer to the question as to how growth and diminution take place, different from and additional to the constraints imposed by the previous arguments.

The two phenomena initially listed are (i) that when something grows each part has grown[23] (and when something decreases each part has decreased), and (ii) it is on the condition of something acceding that something grows (and it is on the condition of something departing that something decreases). He will later add to these two conditions on the ordinary conception of growth the common-sense view that what grows remains and is preserved as it grows.[24]

The second of these conditions rules out the possibility that an object grows without any influx of new matter, growing simply as a result of an expansion in volume of the matter it already has. He states in *Physics* IV. 7. 214^{b}1–3 that things can grow as a result of a qualitative alteration even if nothing accedes. Water, for instance, expands as it turns into air.[25] However, this is not the kind of 'growth', or increase in size, with which he is here concerned. In *GC* I. 5 he explicitly argues against the claim that growth takes place in this way on the grounds that it violates the condition stated later at 321^{a}21–2, the condition that what grows remains.

---

[23] See also 321^{a}19–20.   [24] 321^{a}21–2.

[25] Although the generation of air from water is not itself alteration, the heating of water that can eventually lead to the destruction of the water is alteration for just so long as the water still exists. Later, in *Ph.* IV. 9. 217^{a}27–^{b}11, he discusses the expansion and contraction of air resulting from heating and cooling. That passage recognizes a case in which something gets bigger in size without anything acceding, and hence would fail to satisfy one of *GC* I. 5's conditions on growth.

When water turns to air it is a destruction of the water and a generation of air, but is the growth of neither. Furthermore, it cannot be the growth of some body that is common both to the water and the subsequent air because if it were then this body would violate condition (ii) that things grow on the condition of something acceding.[26]

Accordingly, his new conditions on growth focus the enquiry on a specific kind of natural process in which something that persists increases in size. With his new start he captures the common conceptions of growth that must be respected by any theory, and the concept of growth as commonly conceived is more restricted than mere increase in volume. Certain cases of increase can be explained by the causal mechanisms invoked to explain other kinds of changes, such as generation or alteration. However, he is here trying to isolate a kind of change that is distinct from both generation and alteration, and which is the result of a different kind of causal mechanism at work in nature. It would be a mistake to attempt to explain all cases of increase in volume by the same causes, or to classify them all as falling under the ordinary concept of growth.

In connection with these newly stated phenomena of growth he develops a new puzzle at 321[a]5–9. Since growth requires the accession of something to the thing that grows, then either something grows by the accession of an incorporeal item or by the accession of something corporeal. If it is incorporeal, then there will be a separable void. Following Philoponus, I take it that this is because the space into which the growing thing expands would have to be a void that prior to the expansion contained no body and existed separately from any body.[27] If one assumes that what accedes to a growing body is itself incorporeal, then what accedes does not itself have any volume or occupy any space. Consequently, the space into which the growing object expands could not have been previously occupied by that which accedes (since it had no space) or by some other body that previously occupied it but has now moved into a space previously occupied by that which accedes. Instead, or so this arm of the dilemma would have it, as the body grows it expands into what was previously empty space. However, this would make the matter of size a separable vacuum, and we have already concluded that the matter of size cannot be separable from the matter of corporeal body.[28] Thus it would seem that what accedes to the growing thing is corporeal. However, if what accedes is itself a body, then there will be

---

[26] See also 321[a]20–1.   [27] Philop. *in GC* 89.14–15.

[28] 320[b]23–5. I am at 321[a]6 accepting κενόν, rather than κοινόν, and attempting to treat [a]6–7 as containing one argument, not two. The thought would be that the empty vacuum into which the growing thing expands would possess a size, and this would make it the matter for that size, and hence for the increase in size.

two bodies in the same place. As the acceding body travels to each and every part of the growing thing it must pass through it, and so the thing that makes it grow (that which accedes) will occupy a place that is already occupied by some part of the thing that is growing. However, it is impossible for two distinct bodies to occupy the same place at the same time.

The reason for thinking that on this second alternative two bodies would have to be in the same place is given by another common-sense view; namely, that there is growth of each and every part of that which grows. Without this restriction it would be possible for growth to take place by simply attaching the acceding matter to the growing object as a new part, thereby making the whole bigger, but without increasing the size of any of the previously existing parts. Hence both phenomena (i) and (ii) are needed to generate the new puzzle. A satisfactory resolution of this puzzle will involve showing how growth of each part can take place by accession of matter without violating the principle that two bodies cannot occupy the same place, while nonetheless allowing that what accedes is itself something corporeal.

Before presenting an explanation of growth that enables him to solve this problem he presents an additional aporia concerning whether what grows is that to which something accedes, or that which accedes.[29] As was made clear in the statement of the previous puzzle, since growth takes place only if something accedes, the acceding something must possess the matter of size. As was also made clear in the earlier examination of the previous theories, the item that is growing possesses matter of size as well. It is now time to ask why it is not the case that the acceding item is what grows rather than the item to which it accedes. In his example he calls that by virtue of which a calf grows 'nourishment', and asks why it is not the case that both the calf and the nourishment grow.

Rather than solving the problem in this section, he draws two comparisons that are suggestive of a solution. First, he compares growth to the mixing of wine with water. This is not a case of growth,[30] but the example does satisfy the constraints he has given on growth, and one can pose the question as to why it is not the case that both the wine and the water have increased. One of the three primary conditions on growth is that the thing which increases is preserved and persists. He appeals to this condition in order to show why it is not the case that both the wine and that to which the wine is added are increased and made larger. When the two are mixed only one prevails in the sense that the new whole does the work of only one. If the mixture does the work of wine, then it is wine

---

[29] 321^{a}29–321^{b}10.   [30] See I. 10. 327^{b}13–14.

that has persisted, and that is why only the wine has increased in size, not the water as well. Only the *ousia* of that which is increased persists. He asks whether the case of somebody's calf growing is not also like this. If it is, then the *ousia* of the acceding food does not persist, and since that which is increased must persist, only that to which the food accedes is increased, but the food is not.

His other comparison is with alteration, and he points out something that has already been stated in different words in I. 4. He claims that when something continues to be what it is but has an intrinsic modification that it previously lacked, it has altered. In cases of alteration the subject that alters persists. He is here tacitly assuming that something X persists through a change only if the *ousia* of X persists through that change. More specifically, the assumption is that:

The subject X that has altered persists only if the *ousia* of X persists.[31]

He assumes that for a changing subject X there is such a thing as 'being what X is'. Furthermore, if the subject X that is altered is (say) flesh, then in such a case 'being what X is' is no other than 'being *flesh*'—for X to be what it is just is for X to be *flesh*. Given that for X to be just is for it to be flesh, one may infer that for X to continue to be is for it to continue to be flesh. That is, it is on the condition that it is flesh that it continues to exist and persists through change. He is here using the label '*ousia* of X' for 'what X is'.

The circumstantial participle 'being flesh' (σὰρξ οὖσα) gives the condition under which that which is altered persists and remains the same both during the alteration and after the alteration has been completed. Flesh has altered if (i) on the condition of its 'being flesh' it persists, and (ii) some property that did not belong before now belongs to it in its own right. The subject that alters is *flesh*, and it is as such, as flesh, that it persists and remains the same while altering. Just as a fluid is wine, not water, when it does the work of wine, so too it is flesh when it does the work of flesh. Indeed, according to *Meteorologica* IV. 12 something is truly called 'flesh' only if it is able to perform the characteristic activity.[32]

Just as there is a persisting substratum in the case of alteration (see I. 4) there is also a substratum for growth that remains, and for it to persist just is for its *ousia* to persist. Since the *ousia* of the food does not persist when an organism grows or is nourished by it, the food itself does not persist. Consequently, it is not the case that the food has grown. In the present passage he does not explicitly make the point that the *ousia* of the

---

[31] Perhaps he is here relying on the fact that each thing is thought to be no other than its own οὐσία (Z. 6).

[32] *Mete.* IV. 12. 390ᵃ10–14.

food does not persist. Additionally, he does not here make it clear what the *ousia* of a thing is, and in particular has not identified it with form as opposed to matter. However, as we shall see, his later exposition of the cause of growth involves treating that which grows as a hylomorphic composite in which the form remains intact while its matter is constantly replaced. Accordingly, the *ousia* of a thing is in fact its form, not its matter, and it is because the form (i.e. the *ousia*) of that which grows persists that the growing thing persists.

His causal account of growth is able to respect the principle that two bodies cannot occupy the same place by claiming that the thing that grows increases in size by the accession of nourishment that is a contrary, but which changes into the same form as the that which grows.[33] According to *de Anima*, it is thought that nourishment in its unconcocted state is something contrary to what it nourishes.[34] The food is acted upon by that which is nourished in such a way that it is assimilated to the latter's nature. The form (that is, the *ousia*) of the nourishment does not persist, but rather the nourishment is changed in such a way that the result has the same form (that is, the *ousia*) of the growing thing. After this transformation the nourishment fails to persist precisely because its form fails to persist, and hence it cannot be a body that competes with the growing thing for space. Rather it has been assimilated into the growing body, and although the process started with two bodies, only one survives and only one is present to occupy a place.

This brings us to a second point of comparison with alteration. He puts his point by saying that what effects alteration and the principle of change are in the thing that alters and the thing that grows.[35] In the case of growth he distinguishes that by which something grows (the food) from that which grows, and locates the efficient cause of growth in the latter, not in its food. Corresponding to this is a distinction between that by which something alters and that which is altered, and here he is locating the cause that effects alteration in the former. It would seem that he is claiming that the efficient cause of alteration is in what is altered.[36] Since it is not true in general that the efficient cause of what undergoes qualitative change or alteration is a principle inherent in the subject of change, he would here have to be thinking of some restricted

---

[33] 321ᵇ35–322ᵃ2.   [34] 416ᵃ21–2 with ᵇ6–7.   [35] 321ᵇ6–7.
[36] According to Philoponus (*in GC* 98. 1–5), to avoid the difficulty of locating the efficient cause in the thing that alters Alexander denied this and took τὸ ἀλλοιοῦν to be the principle of being altered. Later, in *GC* II. 9. 335ᵇ26, τὸ ἀλλοιοῦν is used for an active cause. However, if Alexander's interpretation is allowed then this passage cannot be used to support the idea that the efficient cause of growth is in the thing that grows. The parallel with alteration would require only that the thing that grows possesses a passive principle by virtue of which it can be made to grow. Aristotle's point about growth would then in effect be that the food does not have the ability to grow.

set of alterations. Lines 321^{b}6–7 could be read as locating a single principle that effects both alteration and growth in a thing that both grows and alters. On such a reading he is talking about cases in which a growing thing is the persisting subject of both an alteration and growth. More specifically, this could be exemplified by the case in which some flesh alters in a natural way as it grows. For instance, as the flesh in an infant's hand grows, the hand not only gets bigger but also changes shape. In any case, it is not necessary to read these lines as a general thesis about alteration as such. He may even be thinking of his own view that the soul is an internal principle both of alteration and of growth. For instance, in *de Anima* the soul is the efficient cause both of nutrition and growth[37], both of which are said to be caused by the same power of soul.[38] Food is digested and converted into blood, the primary nutrient, by heat, and the nutritive faculty of soul uses heating and cooling both to constitute the parts in embryological development and later to nourish them and make them grow.[39] Heating and cooling are alterations, and the power of growth is exercised through such changes. When flesh is a subject of growth its growth is regulated by alterations, and the efficient cause of both is a principle internal to the flesh. However, unlike what is said in either *de Anima* or the biological works, he does not in *GC* I. 5 identify the mover with either the soul or a part of soul. Indeed, the word 'soul' does not even occur.

The fact that the efficient cause of growth is in that which grows, but not in the food, by itself guarantees that the food does not also grow when the body does. Growth requires nutrition, and in nutrition there are two items, the food that nourishes and the organism that is nourished. If one of the two must be assimilated in form to the other, and the efficient cause is the same in form as the effect, then whichever of the two contains the efficient cause of nutrition within it changes the other into its own form. If the efficient cause is in the thing that is nourished, but not the nutriment, then this explains why the food does not persist but the thing that is fed does. And this in turn explains why the food does not grow when the thing that is fed does.

However, the idea that food is a contrary, and in growth is assimilated to the form of what grows, is needed in order to give this solution to the puzzle, and this had not been presented yet. The passage at 321^{a}29–^{b}10 develops, but does not solve, the puzzle. To give an explanation of growth he must now present an account that honours the constraints previously stated, while avoiding this and the other puzzles. To do this he thinks that the following six conditions, stated at 321^{b}12–16, must be met:

---

[37] *DA* II. 4. 416^{a}8–9.   [38] 416^{a}19.   [39] See esp. *PA* II. 3 and *GA* II. 4.

(1) What grows persists.[40]
(2) It grows on the condition of something acceding (and diminishes on the condition of something leaving it).[41]
(3) Every perceptible point of what grows gets bigger (and of what diminishes gets smaller).[42]
(4) The body is not a void.[43]
(5) Two magnitudes do not occupy the same place.[44]
(6) That by which something grows is not incorporeal.[45]

Having stated the puzzles and laid out the constraints on their solution, he at last begins at 321^b16 to address the explanation of growth. Although prior to this there has been talk about matter, it is at this point that Aristotle first explicitly brings in his distinction between matter and form, and the attendant analysis of living things as hylomorphic compounds. Before we are in a position to grasp the explanation of growth, he thinks it is necessary to make two preliminary observations. The first is that the *non-uniform* parts of living things increase by virtue of the increase of their *uniform* parts. The reason he gives for this is that the former are composed of the latter. Non-uniform parts are composites of matter and form, and uniform parts serve as the matter for non-uniform parts.[46] Non-uniform parts such as hands grow by virtue of the growth of uniform parts such as flesh. The shin, for instance, is a non-uniform part, and it is composed of such uniform parts as flesh and bone. Because of this, if the shin grows, it must be by virtue of the increase of the flesh and bone and other uniform parts that constitute it.

In general, the growth of some non-uniform composite is the result of an increase in size of the parts of which it is composed, and their increase in turn is the result of an increase in whatever they are composed of, and so on until we reach its uniform living parts. Non-uniform parts such as hands grow by virtue of the growth of uniform parts such as flesh. Things

---

[40] 321^a20-1.

[41] Stated as what appears to be the case at 321^a4-5; see also 321^a20-1.

[42] Stated as what appears to be the case at 321^a2-4, using μέρος instead of σημεῖον αἰσθητόν; see also 321^a19-20.

[43] If the body that grows were a void, then matter could travel through it, acceding to each and every part, without violating the condition that two bodies cannot occupy the same place. However, the growing body is not a void, and, given condition (5), condition (2) could not be satisfied if the acceding matter had to travel through all parts of the growing body.

[44] See 321^a8-9.

[45] Established at $320^a27-320^b34$.

[46] Since some non-uniform parts such as hands are composed of other non-uniform parts (e.g. fingers), this needs to be clarified. The uniform parts of which hands are composed will be the uniform parts of which their most basic non-uniform parts are composed, and hands grow by virtue of the growth of the uniform matter of these basic parts.

made of flesh increase in size because the flesh of which they are composed increases. How, then, does one account for the growth of these
uniform organic parts?

This brings us to his second preliminary point. Flesh and bone, as well as
all other such uniform living parts, are 'twofold', or spoken of in two ways,
in that terms such as 'flesh' apply both to the matter of flesh and to the form
of flesh. Although the point is specifically made about the uniform parts, it
does not seem to indicate a difference between such parts and the non-
uniform parts. He goes on to indicate that the claim holds for the former
just as it also holds for the other things that have a form in matter.[47] This
would, of course, also include non-uniform composites. The same term
that designates the form of some composite, whether that composite be
uniform or non-uniform, also applies to the matter.

Let us consider Aristotle's example in this passage: flesh. Both the
matter and the form are called 'flesh'. Although the matter of flesh may
be spoken of as 'flesh', this is not what it is in its own right. The matter
of flesh is what is potentially flesh. This matter was, prior to becoming
actual flesh, potentially flesh but not yet actually flesh. Prior to
becoming flesh it was actually something else. The most proximate
matter for flesh is blood, and at some still earlier stage it would have
been the food that the animal ingested. We are told elsewhere that flesh is
in fact a composite of elemental matter and form, as are all uniform
organic parts.[48] That is, earth, water, air, and fire are the uniform
substances out of which flesh, bone, and other uniform organic parts
are constituted.

However, what makes something actually flesh is not the matter but
the form. To specify the *ousia* or being of flesh, to say what it is for
something to be flesh, is not simply to list the inanimate uniform substances of which it is composed. As noted above, for a thing to persist is
for its *ousia* to persist, and for the *ousia* of flesh to be present to
something it must be able to perform the characteristic work of flesh.
Some elemental matter is not in truth *flesh*—does not really constitute
flesh—unless it is able to perform that function. Suppose (as a simplifi-
cation) that the function of flesh is solely to serve as the medium for the
sense of touch. Its role in the sensing of tangible qualities is the characteristic activity that makes something flesh, and for something truly to be
flesh it must actually be capable of fulfilling that role. When some matter
is potentially flesh, but actually just food, or actually blood, it cannot in
that condition serve as the medium of touch, and as such it is not actual
flesh. Some appropriate matter (what is potentially flesh) constitutes

[47] 321^{b}20–1.
[48] See *Mete*. IV. 12. 389^{b}26–8, and *PA* II. 1. 646^{a}20–2.

actual flesh when it actually has present to it the form of flesh, and is able to perform the characteristic natural function of flesh.

On this view uniform parts such as flesh are themselves hylomorphic composites, and grow in virtue of an increase in their matter. However, the manner in which the matter of flesh increases does not satisfy the conditions that in growth something accedes and that each part grows—i.e., conditions 2 and 3. That which grows is a composite of a material and a formal principle. As he will urge, the flesh can satisfy these conditions when spoken of in respect of (κατά) its form, but not when spoken of in respect of (κατά) its matter.[49]

The claim is illustrated at [b]24–8 by stating that we should think of the case of growth of the material principle on the model of what happens when one measures water with the same measure. This Heraclitean comparison is very likely the most widely cited passage from the present chapter. Although the comparison has been understood in a number of different ways, it is typically thought to show commitment to the view that the matter of which some growing thing is composed is constantly leaving the body and being replaced by new matter.[50] There is, through metabolic interchange with the environment, a constant flow of matter through a living organism. Let us call this the 'metabolic' reading of the passage.

Water is, of course, elemental matter. When one uses the 'same measure' to measure water on different occasions one is measuring different parcels of the same kind of material substance, though not the very same water. In order to get a metabolic reading of our text Joachim suggests that what Aristotle has in mind is the measure of flowing water, and that this is something like 'a bag of skin, open at both ends, inherently capable of expansion and contraction'. Water flows in through one end of the bag (the entrance) and departs through the other (the exit). Although the bag remains the same bag, and even though at any given time it is completely full of water, the water which it contains is constantly different. Water that previously was not in the bag has flowed in to occupy the portion of the bag nearest the entrance, thus pushing some water to the middle of the bag; and water that used to be in the middle has now taken the place of the water that used to be in the part of the bag closest to the exit, and it too will soon exit as it gets displaced by the water behind it. It is in this sense that what comes to be is on each occasion different.[51]

---

[49] 321[b]22–4.
[50] The most influential statement of this view has been that of G. E. M. Anscombe in *Three Philosophers* (Cornell, 1961), 55–6.
[51] 321[b]25.

If this is correct, it highlights the relevance of the claim made earlier, at
320^{a}10–27, that growth differs from other changes in its 'manner' to the
present account of how growth takes place. It is there that we learned
that a growing thing does not as such move, but in order for it to grow it
is necessary for its parts to move over an increasingly large place. Growth
is an increase in size, but it is not simply an increase in size. The increase
in size involved in growth requires that new matter accedes to the
growing thing, and this accession of matter is locomotion. The new
matter must move into the growing thing, and for this to happen at
least some of the matter that is already there must also move. If the place
were to remain the same size, then the object would be nourished without
growing, and as new matter comes in old matter must exit. An object that
is nourished but does not increase in size is not growing. In order for it to
grow, it must occupy a larger place, and matter that is already in it must
move within this larger place to accommodate the influx of the matter
that has acceded.

The upshot of this is that as new matter moves in, matter that is
already contained in the object gets pushed to new locations, either out
of the object altogether, or elsewhere within it. There is no increase of
each and every part of the *matter* of flesh, it just gets pushed around from
place to place. The matter of flesh does not satisfy Aristotle's conditions
on growth. When some flesh grows or diminishes, its matter does increase or decrease, but only in the sense that there is more or less of it.
The matter entering and leaving the flesh is not a persisting subject that
gets bigger or smaller, receiving various sizes. However, when the new
matter enters actual flesh it is informed in such a way that it performs the
function of flesh. In so far as some quantity of matter is so informed it is,
or constitutes, actual flesh. The persisting subject for growth and diminution is a composite of matter and form, and for it to persist it must
retain the form. Since the matter of which flesh happens to be composed
at any particular time is constantly changing, sameness of matter is not a
condition for its persistence. The actual flesh considered as an informed
composite is, however, a single persisting subject. When spoken of in
respect of its form, flesh is not the matter flowing in and out of various
places, but rather is a uniform, living part that as a whole occupies a
place within which the locomotion of the matter of flesh takes place.

At 321^{b}27–8 it is said that something is added to each and every part of
the shape and form. Material does not literally attach itself to the form of
flesh. It is rather the case that the matter that is added accedes to every
part of the flesh spoken of in respect of the form. That is to say, the
matter accedes to it in so far as it is actual, functioning flesh. It is
the composite that is spoken of and called what it is called in virtue
of the form of flesh being actually present, and this composite is the

persisting subject to which the matter of flesh accedes as a whole, and it is this that grows as a whole without moving. The conditions that each and every part of the flesh grows, and that the flesh grows by the accession of something, are satisfied by informed flesh, not the matter of flesh. What grows is indeed flesh. However, this flesh that is the subject of growth is a composite of matter and form.

As he indicates at 321^b28 ff., the point that growth is proportional applies both to uniform parts like flesh as well as to the non-uniform parts composed of such uniform parts, although it is easier to discern in the latter case. The hand, for instance, grows by an increase in its flesh (and bones, sinews, and the like). It should be obvious that non-uniform parts such as hands are not flowing in and out of the body as growth (or nutrition) takes place. These non-uniform parts persist through time while retaining their identity as hands, feet, and so on, and grow as such—as hands and feet—and not simply as larger collections of matter.

It is worth pausing to consider an objection to Joachim's position that might make one incline against the 'metabolic' interpretation. Joachim thinks that it is the use of the term *metron* that suggests the application of the water example to the case of growth. The 'measure' is (or stands in for) the form, and is something which can itself expand and contract. On his reading the form itself expands and contracts, and in this sense grows. However, it does not make sense to think of forms (as opposed to informed objects) as expanding and contracting, and the measure analogy does not support this false view. A 'measure' is that by which a quantity is known.[52] The point of measuring water is to determine how much of it there is, and it is not possible to apply this concept of a 'measure' to something that itself changes in quantity. The 'measure' to which Aristotle refers in the present passage is some kind of a spatial container that holds a certain quantity of water, and as such can provide a *unit* for counting. Suppose, for instance, that the unit of measurement is a 'bag'. The form of water does not provide a principle for counting units of water, but we can measure a quantity of water in terms of a unit such as a bag and answer the question 'How much water is there here?' by specifying how many bags of water there are. When I measure a quantity of water using this bag, different parcels of water fill it on different occasions. However, if it is allowed that the bag itself increases or decreases in size, one could not determine the quantity of water simply by knowing the number of bags of water of which it consists. Once we allow that the bag can change in size, there must be something else by reference to which its change of size could be measured—a cup, for instance. In that case, the cup, not the bag, would be the measure by

[52] *Metaph.* 1052^b20.

which quantity is known, and we would have to answer the question 'How much water is there?' in terms of cups, not bags.

In light of this problem I would suggest that we take the measuring example as illustrating no more than the sense in which the water that comes to constitute the cup (or bag) of water changes on each occasion. It is meant to illustrate the sense in which the matter changes, but need not be read as also an example of increase. In particular, we do not have to attempt to construe it as illustrating the claim that increase of each and every part is possible in respect of form.[53]

At 322[a]4 he turns next to the question as to what 'that by which something grows' must be like. He is here referring to the nutriment that is added to a growing thing.[54] He replies that if the growing thing is flesh, then it must be potentially but not (yet) actually flesh. This is of course connected with the earlier claim that the nutriment is a contrary. Since its form is in some way contrary to the form of flesh it is not actually flesh. Furthermore, according to the account in *de Anima* the food is not just any old contrary, but one that is not only capable of changing into that for which it is food (and vice versa) but also one that can provide for its growth.[55] When the food is destroyed it is transformed into flesh, but it does not become flesh in and of itself ($a\mathring{v}\tau\grave{o}$ $\kappa a\theta'$ $a\mathring{v}\tau\acute{o}$), all on its own and separate from the growing thing. This would be the generation of flesh, and not growth at all. In growth there is already some flesh in existence, and the nutriment that is in contact with the growing thing is changed into more flesh by an efficient cause in the flesh itself. He compares this to what happens when water is mixed with wine in a small enough quantity that the water is converted into wine, thus increasing the quantity of wine. Next he compares it to what happens when fire makes contact with something capable of burning. Just as contact with an existing fire causes a log to ignite because of a capacity of the fire to heat, so too contact with the growing thing converts food that is potentially flesh into actual flesh by the causal efficacy of an efficient cause residing in the flesh that already exists. We are told

[53] Verdenius and Waszink (1968), 28–9, reject the idea that the 'measure' is to be thought of as representing form, and offer a reading according to which in order to reach a desired quantity of water using a standard measure we must do so in discontinuous increments, and take the application of this example to the matter of flesh to require that its growth (as opposed to the growth of flesh as a whole) is discontinuous. Although I agree that the reference to a measure need not illustrate a point about the unity of form, I am not convinced that Aristotle views the accession of elemental matter as a discontinuous process. The fact that such matter is added at particular places and not everywhere at once does not show that the organism cannot be subject to a continuous metabolic process.

[54] See *DA* II. 4. 416[b]20–3 for the claim that that by which something is nourished is the food or nutriment.

[55] 416[a]21–4.

elsewhere[56] that this efficient cause is the soul, and that this is the form and *ousia* of the growing thing. Here, however, he leaves the nature of the efficient cause unspecified, except by reference to its effect.

The acceding matter is the same for both nutrition and growth. In both cases the growing thing converts the food into flesh, or whatever other uniform substance it is that is growing. Given that elemental matter is constantly leaving the organic body, new nutriment is required if the organs are going to continue to exist. The nutritive capacity is necessary in order to maintain the *ousia* of a thing, but deprived of food the organism is unable to preserve itself and continue to exist.[57] However, it is possible for an organism to be nourished and maintained in existence without growing. Even though the same part of the soul is responsible for both nutrition and growth we need to explain how the two are distinguished, and this is the aim of 322^a17–28. The nutrition that accedes to the flesh is both potentially flesh *and* potentially a certain quantity of flesh. In so far as it is potentially just flesh the food produces growth. However, the food also is potentially a certain quantity of flesh, and in so far as it is a particular quantity of flesh it produces growth. Hence nourishment is simply the process by which the food is converted into flesh considered only as such (as flesh), whereas growth is the process by which the food is converted into a determinate quantity (i.e. a determinate quantity of flesh). He does not specify here exactly which quantity is relevant, but it could hardly be the entire size that the thing has after it has grown. A small bit of food simply is not potentially something with the size of, say, the entire thigh. What he must intend is that the quantity of flesh that it is potentially just is that amount by which it is capable of increasing the size of that which is growing.

The chapter concludes at 322^a29–34 with a puzzling and somewhat cryptic discussion of form, its causal agency, and its persistence even when something nourished diminishes in size. There is a reference to 'this form'[58] and it is compared in some way to a pipe (αὐλός), and said to be a certain kind of power in matter. Since the efficient cause of growth is a power in the growing thing, not the food, it would seem that the form in question just is the form and *ousia* of the growing thing, not the nourishment. As such it is a power or capacity that exists in the matter or body of the growing thing.

It is unclear what the significance is of the reference to αὐλός. He uses this term elsewhere for certain parts of animals: funnels in cephalopods,[59] the blowhole in cetaceans,[60] and the *conus arteriosus*.[61] There is no

---

[56] See *DA* II. 4.   [57] 416^b16–19.   [58] Bracketing ἄνευ ὕλης.
[59] *HA* 524^a10; *PA* 678^b37–679^a7; see *GA* 720^b32 ff.
[60] *HA* 489^b3; 537^b1; 566^b3, 13; and 589^b2, 6, 19; *PA* 597^a17; 659^b14–19; 697^a15–697^b13.
[61] *Resp.* 478^b7–9.

indication that he has any of those uses in mind here. Nonetheless, he does seem to be using it to stand for some kind of non-uniform part of a growing thing, the kind of part that can be larger or smaller. In the absence of texts attesting to an Aristotelian usage of the word that fits this passage one might instead try to determine what he thinks is true about the growth and diminution of this kind of part, and then consider what kind of part would fit this description. What he seems to be saying about the form of an αὐλός (whatever that may be) is this. The form is not only responsible for the growth of a uniform part, but can also be responsible for its diminution. Matter that is potentially an αὐλός, and potentially of a large enough quantity, accedes to the uniform part, the αὐλός. In growth the power present in the growing thing causes an increase, and the αὐλός will grow and become larger. However, at some point the very power that in the past caused growth now instead produces a diminution in size. The power in the growing thing loses its ability to convert food into large αὐλοί, and instead makes them smaller. The acceding matter still is potentially of a great enough size to sustain larger αὐλοί, but the power in the matter is not strong enough to bring about that result. In such a case the power in the matter can still succeed in assimilating the acceding food to its form, but no longer has the ability to make the food so assimilated into the larger magnitude, and hence produces smaller αὐλοί. Even so, the form of that which grows remains, and hence the αὐλοί themselves are maintained in existence.

In certain respects this is like what happens when water is mixed with wine in continually greater quantities. Initially the wine is able to convert the water into wine, and thereby increase the quantity of wine. However, at a certain point the wine gets so diluted by the addition of water that it loses its capacity to increase its bulk by assimilating water. As Joachim points out, 'the parallel is not exact' since at the end of this process we no longer even have wine, and the form of wine does not persist. This difference between the two cases is indicated by the final words of this chapter, 'but the form remains'. Nonetheless, if we think of the comparison as illustrating only one aspect of the αὐλός case, that of a loss of the capacity to utilize what accedes in order to increase the bulk of that to which it accedes, it is instructive.

Perhaps our αὐλός passage is a sketch of what happens to the vascular system as it first grows and then later diminishes in size.[62] Other than the heart itself, the tubes or passageways leading from the heart are the first bodily parts with which the primary nutrient is in contact, and the first

---

[62] 483[b]26–8 of the spurious *Spir.* says that nourishment is distributed to flesh at the mouths of veins, as if these veins were pipes. The term for 'pipe' here is not αὐλός but σωλήν.

parts formed out of it. Although the term αὐλός is not used elsewhere for a vein or blood vessel, the account at the end of *GA* I. 5 does match at least some of the details of the account in *PA* III. 5 of the vascular system.[63] There he compares the entire system of veins to an irrigation system for a garden that starts from a single source, and progressively branches off so that water is carried to each part of the garden. All of the bodily parts grow and are nurtured not by water, but by blood, and so the animal's body requires a similar system of channels to bring this nourishment to all of the bodily parts. It too starts from a single source, the heart. Attached to the heart is a 'great blood vessel' and an aorta, and branching off from these a series of blood vessels and eventually small veins that serve as channels to bring the blood to all of the other bodily parts.

According to *GA* II. 4, in embryological development the heart is the first part to be formed, and this contains the principle that guides and controls the later development of the other parts. Among other things, the generative power in the heart converts blood into vascular tissue as it produces a series of channels through which the blood flows. As the embryo grows, a formative power in the growing thing extends and enlarges the vessels in a manner that one could describe as producing larger 'pipes' or 'tubes' out of the matter (blood) that is potentially vascular tissue of a sufficient quantity. However, blood is also the matter that is potentially flesh. According to the text in *PA* III. 5, animals become emaciated and waste away as the small veins that provide blood to the flesh actually themselves turn into flesh. This is compared to what happens when the smallest channels of a watercourse get filled up with mud. When this happens the largest of the vessels still remain intact, although the overall size of the channels leading from the heart becomes smaller. The animal's power of growth and nutrition no longer sustains the larger vascular system the animal had when in sound health, and some of the smallest components of that system are converted into flesh.[64] Despite the fact that these passageways become smaller, though, there are still blood vessels emanating from the heart and conveying nutriment. The form of blood vessel still remains, and is still present, but present now to a smaller quantity of matter.[65]

[63] Or the analogue to that in animals lacking blood.

[64] Although he does not say so, this kind of truncation of the vascular system results in less nutriment getting to the various bodily parts, and hence in the wasting away of the animal.

[65] I am grateful to John Cooper, Michel Crubellier, David Charles, Andrea Falcon, Michael Frede, Geoffrey Lloyd, Carlo Natali, Johannes M. van Ophuijsen, Marwan Rashed, and other participants in the Deurne Symposium for discussion and criticism of a previous draft, and especially to Frans de Haas and David Sedley for their detailed written comments.

7

On Generation and Corruption I. 6

CARLO NATALI

1. Division of the text

The medieval translators have unified in one chapter two different texts. The first covers *GC* 322^{b}1–26 and has the function of a general introduction to what follows: the rest of book I, or the entire work, according to different interpreters.[1] In this first section Aristotle claims that it is necessary to define some preliminary notions, before entering into the study of the elements. The second text, from 322^{b}26 (or 29)[2] to 323^{a}34, presents the discussion of the first preliminary notion, 'contact' (ἀφή).

So, chapter I. 6 does not have a conceptual unity, but it is the juxtaposition of two distinct discussions, a methodological premiss and a conceptual analysis.

2. The first part (322^{b}1–26): introduction (322^{b}1–6)

'Since we must first investigate the matter καί the so-called elements' (322^{b}1–2).[3] This καί has been understood as an explicative connective by most interpreters, from Philoponus to Zabarella, Joachim, and Migliori, who translate it as 'i.e.'. Only a minority (Williams, Mugler) translate it as 'and'. The choice depends on the understanding of the subject matter of the conceptual analysis Aristotle is introducing here. This, in turn, depends on the general idea the interpreters have of the intent of the entire work. There are two main interpretations of it, which we will call 'Philoponus' interpretation' and 'Zabarella's interpretation', even if it is possible that before Zabarella some other people maintained the same position.

According to Philoponus, *De generatione et corruptione* contains a general discussion of the common properties of things which are subject

---

[1] The first position is maintained by Zabarella *in GC* 845. 37; the second position is defended by Philoponus *in GC* 124. 3–25.

[2] For discussion of this issue see p. 202 below.

[3] We follow Joachim's translation in J. Barnes (1984), i., 512–54, with occasional minor modifications.

to generation and corruption, *including the elements.*[4] On his interpretation Aristotle criticizes, in the first chapters of the work, the opinions of his predecessors and discusses in general the notions of generation, corruption, augmentation, and local movement. Philoponus thinks also that in the second book Aristotle will discuss the generation and corruption of the elements; now, in the second part of the first book, he thinks that Aristotle wants to discuss some preliminary notions, necessary to understanding the generation of the elements.

Zabarella, on the contrary, thinks that *De generatione et corruptione* has as subject matter the generation and corruption of composite bodies only, that is homoeomers and things mixed. The four elements, air, water, earth, and fire are studied only *as material cause of the generation and corruption of composite bodies*, and not in themselves.[5] According to him, in the first five chapters of book I Aristotle gives the nominal definitions of generation and corruption, in book II he provides the real causes for it, and in the last chapters of book I he explains the preliminary notions necessary to the understanding of the four elements as the material cause of the generation and corruption of bodies. Zabarella adds that the deduction we find in lines 322^b1-5 would be meaningless, if the intent was to study the four elements in themselves. Aristotle says: 'We must ask whether they really are elements or not[6]... Hence we must begin by explaining certain matters about which the statements now current[7] are vague' (i.e. action/passion,[8] mixture, contact). But it is not true, Zabarella remarks, that in order to study the

---

[4] Philoponus *in GC* 2. 12–13; 6. 31–2; 205. 1–6; 124. 35–125. 1, etc.

[5] Zabarella *in GC* 751. 23–4: 'Elementa in hoc libro considerari non ut species subiecti, sed ut principia materialia subiecti' (cf. 847. 14–15). Since Zabarella's text is difficult to find in the libraries and has not been reprinted since 1602, I will quote in full the most important passages.

[6] Nobody, except Mugler, gives to the expression εἴτ ἐστὶν εἴτε μή an existential meaning, because they consider the existence of the four elements as evident. The commentators understand either 'If they are elements or not' (Philoponus) or 'If they are principles or not' (Zabarella). Joachim and Migliori follow Philoponus.

[7] At 322^b5 νῦν is interpreted by most commentators as 'until now' and taken as referring to the opinions of the Presocratics discussed in the preceding chapters, and discussed again in the following lines 323^a6-26 (Philoponus, Zabarella, Mugler, Migliori et al.). But usually in Aristotle νῦν indicates his contemporaries, and pseudo-Thomas Aquinas translates 'philosophi sui temporis'. Joachim translate it as 'now, at present', and Williams does the same. There are two possibilities for understanding Aristotle's words. Either the notions of contact, etc. are now obscure because they were discussed by the Presocratics in an obscure way and never investigated again. Or they are obscure because now the contemporaries of Aristotle (the Academics?) use them in a confused way.

[8] 'Action' usually translates πρᾶξις. However, I follow the usage of most translators of *De generatione et corruptione* in translating 'action' also for ποίησις in general, when the Greek word means the 'activity of the agent' (ἐνέργεια τοῦ ποιητικοῦ, Bonitz (1870), 609^b7) and has no reference to human activities.

four elements in themselves it is necessary to elucidate the notions of mixture or contact. Only if we want to study the elements as material cause of bodies is the clarification of the notions of contact, mixture, and so on necessary, and Aristotle's argument in 322^b1–5 is sound. The reason is that only in the case of the generation of bodies do the elements touch one another, act and suffer, and mix together.[9] Zabarella's interpretation has had wide success, and has been followed by Joachim, Verdenius, Tricot, Migliori, and Williams. However, pseudo-Thomas Aquinas follows Philoponus' interpretation.

The most important difference between the two interpretations is connected with the question of prime matter. According to Philoponus, the study of the generation and corruption of the elements must determine, first, what is the matter of the elements, which is, in turn, the matter of everything that becomes.[10] According to Zabarella, on the contrary, if we study the four elements as the material cause of the generation and corruption of bodies, it is not necessary to ask whether there is a common matter beneath them, and what this matter could be. Furthermore, the investigation of the elements is limited to the characteristics that belong to the elements as matter of bodies, and not to the characteristics they have in themselves. So, according to Zabarella the question of prime matter has no place in this book.

On the line of thinking characteristic of Zabarella's interpretation, it is natural to understand the καί in 322^b1 as *explicative*: we must investigate the matter of change, *i.e.* the four elements. I am inclined to agree with Zabarella's position, even if some passages in the next section do not square with it completely.

3. The first part (322^b1–26): demonstration (322^b6–26)

Aristotle now states that it is necessary to clarify some preliminary notions, and tells us what these notions are.

In chapters 1–5 Aristotle has distinguished generation properly understood from the mere association and dissociation of particles; he has also distinguished generation from alteration and growth. One would expect him to proceed from the results of the preceding discussion, now taken for granted, to demonstrating the necessity of the study of the notions of

[9] Zabarella *in GC* 849. 12–14: 'Consequentia est valida, dum antecedens sic intelligitur, agendum est de elementis, prout sunt materia mixti, nisi prout simul commiscentur & agunt & patiuntur mutuo.'

[10] Philop. *in GC* 124. 14–15: ἔστι σωματικὴ ὕλη κοινῶς πάντων τῶν γινομένων. According to Philoponus this is not the absolute first matter, because there is a more primary matter below that one.

contact, action and passion, and mixture. Instead, Aristotle wants to show that the clarification of these three notions is necessary also for the people who do not accept his theory, and who follow the rival theories of the Presocratics. In the first part of the demonstration (322^b6–21) he claims that the Presocratics presupposed some of the three preliminary notions. In the second part (322^b21–6), on the contrary, he analyses the three notions in themselves, in order to show that there is a chain of implications between them.

Aristotle starts from a division of the Presocratics into two groups, monists and pluralists, a distinction which was posited in the first chapter of book I, and then forgotten. So Aristotle takes a step back in the order of the demonstration.[11] Some authors such as Migliori[12] and Brunschwig (Ch. 1 of this volume) maintain that the first chapter of book I did not originally belong to *De generatione et corruptione* and was added to it later. But the fact that in chapter I. 6 the division of the Presocratics we have found in I. 1 is used again pleads in favour of considering the first chapter as a genuine part of the first book.

The analysis of the positions of the Presocratics is a little confused. Aristotle does not start from the main division, monists versus pluralists, but in a first phase he analyses a subdivision of the pluralists (322^b6–11); in a second phase he analyses, very briefly, the main division (322^b11–13), and immediately passes on to a comparison with Diogenes of Apollonia, which, according to some critics, is not very appropriate (322^b13–21).[13] In this way the pluralists are discussed twice, in their various species and in general (322^b6–12), while the monists are dealt with in just one line (322^b12–13).

Scholars have tried to amend this confusion by modifying the order of the different analyses. We can find different arrangements in Philoponus (125. 4–35), pseudo-Thomas Aquinas (512–14) and Zabarella (849. 15–851. 17). Philoponus violates the order of Aristotle's words too much, while pseudo-Thomas Aquinas and Zabarella follow the text closely. Zabarella's arrangement has been adopted by Joachim (1922, 140) and the others. We shall follow his opinion here.

In the first step it must be shown that all predecessors, both monists and pluralists, presuppose the notions of action and passion in their analyses. The monists do so directly (322^b12–13), the pluralists indirectly. In fact, the pluralists use the notion of dissociation and association, which in turn presupposes the notion of action and passion (322^b9–12).

---

[11] Cf. 322^b1: πρῶτον ... 332^b5 πρότερον. See also e.g. *EN* I. 3 and I. 5.

[12] Migliori (1976), 22–3.

[13] Cf. Williams (1982), 112–13. He says that Aristotle is arguing that those who postulate a single common matter are committed to action and passion—but Diogenes is arguing the converse of this; namely, that action and passion require a single matter.

Besides, all the pluralists presuppose the notion of mixture when using the notion of association (in different ways). They do not understand completely what mixture is, but they understand, nevertheless, that 'mixture' is a necessary notion. The monists, on the contrary, do not use the idea of mixture (322^b6–9). We can give the following scheme:

Monists: action/passion
Pluralists: dissociation/association→ action/passion→mixture

At this point it has been shown that the pluralists presuppose, in an obscure way, two of the notions Aristotle thinks need clarification, and the monists just one of them. The method changes at this point: now Aristotle will show that the notion of contact is logically implied in the other notions presupposed by the Presocratics. Hence, in a way, even the notion of contact is presupposed by them.

Before analysing this step, we must briefly discuss the comparison with Diogenes of Apollonia (322^b13–16). It is not very interesting in itself, but it can help us understand the meaning of some expressions Aristotle uses in this chapter, and on which there is disagreement among the interpreters. Let us quote the passage in full:

And in this respect Diogenes is right, when he argues that unless all things were derived from one, ὑπ' ἀλλήλων action and passion could not occur. e.g. the hot thing would be not cooled and τοῦτο be warmed πάλιν, for heat and coldness do not change into each other . . .

I have left in Greek the words on which there is disagreement. The expression ὑπ' ἀλλήλων is employed twice in the chapter in connection with the verbs ποιεῖν καὶ πάσχειν (322^b12, 14–15) and once in connection with κινητικῶν καὶ κινητῶν (323^a12). It indicates some sort of reciprocity, as is the case for the other expression we find in this chapter, ἅπτεσθαι ἀλλήλων, 'touch one another' (323^a4–5; 10–11). The most natural way of understanding the phrase ποιεῖν καὶ πάσχειν ὑπ' ἀλλήλων is that there is reciprocal action and passion between two things, A and B, where each acts on the other and is acted upon by the other. In other words, there are two reciprocal processes; for instance, if A is a warm thing and B a cold thing, B is cooling A at the same time as A is warming B.

We can find this meaning very clearly expressed in a similar passage in *Physics* III. 1. 201^a22–3:

Many things will act and be acted on by one another, since each of them will be capable at the same time of acting and being acted upon.

πολλὰ ἤδη ποιήσει καὶ πείσεται ὑπ' ἀλλήλων· ἅπαν γὰρ ἔσται ἅμα ποιητικὸν καὶ παθητικόν.

On the other hand, in antiquity and in modern times some interpreters have offered a different interpretation of the expression ὑπ' ἀλλήλων.

According to them ποιεῖν καὶ πάσχειν ὑπ' ἀλλήλων means: 'one thing acts on another, while the other is affected by the first'. This way, the relationship does not consist in two processes but in a single process, in which A acts and B is acted upon. And the reciprocity would be given by the fact that when A acts reciprocally B suffers. In antiquity this position was maintained by the most important commentator on Aristotle, Alexander of Aphrodisias; in modern times it has been partly renewed by Williams, and it found many supporters in the discussion at Deurne.[14] With a difference, however: Alexander and Williams tried to interpret in this way only line 323ᵃ12 κινητικῶν καὶ κινητῶν ὑπ' ἀλλήλων, which belongs to the next passage, and never tried to apply it to lines 322ᵇ12 and 14–15, where we find ποιεῖν καὶ πάσχειν ὑπ' ἀλλήλων. But the parallel could be easily made, since ὑπ' ἀλλήλων clearly has the same meaning in both cases.

Let us now see what Alexander's argument is. We no longer have his commentary on *De generatione et corruptione*, but Philoponus quotes his opinion. In the commentary to 323ᵃ8 Philoponus writes:

> He [Alexander] says that the expression ὑπ' ἀλλήλων in the phrase 'being capable of changing and being changed by one another' [323ᵃ12], must be understood as 'the first by the second' (θάτερον ὑπὸ θατέρου); in the same way in the *Categories* Aristotle uses the phrase 'genera ὑπ' ἄλληλα' to mean one genus being the genus of another (θάτερον θατέρου γένος), and not each genus being the genus of the other (ἑκάτερον ἑκατέρου γένος)... (Philop. *in GC* 135. 8–11)

Williams[15] repeats Philoponus' position without adding other arguments.

But, *pace* Alexander, the expression ὑπ' ἀλλήλων is not equivalent to the expression ὑπ' ἄλληλα. A quick search of the TLG shows that ὑπ' ἄλληλα (with accusative) is employed only in the *Organon*, and indicates a logical dependency between genera and species.[16] They can be ὑπ' ἄλληλα or μὴ ὑπ' ἄλληλα. If they are ὑπ' ἄλληλα, A is ὑπό B, and B is not ὑπό A.

On the other hand, ὑπ' ἀλλήλων (with genitive) indicates a reciprocal causal relationship.[17] There is a large number of examples. I quote just one phrase often repeated by Aristotle: ποιεῖ δὲ καὶ πάσχει τἀναντία ὑπ' ἀλλήλων 'the contraries reciprocally act and suffer action'.[18] In this case, if A causes an effect on B, B in turn causes another effect on A. As far as I know, there is no example in Aristotle, outside the controversial passages in *GC* I. 6, in which two entities ποιεῖ δὲ καὶ πάσχει ὑπ' ἀλλήλων, and what happens is just that A acts on B, while B is affected by A. This phrase always indicates a pair of opposite and reciprocal processes.

---

[14] I would like to thank here J. Cooper who sent me after the conference a long letter articulating his interpretation of this problem.

[15] Williams (1982), 115–16.

[16] Cf. Bonitz (1870), 795ᵃ34.

[17] Cf. Bonitz (1870), 794ᵇ39, and Gill (1989), 196.

[18] *GC* I. 7. 324ᵃ2–3; *Cael.* II. 3. 286ᵃ33, etc.

This is not strange. The reason is that, according to *Metaphysics* V. 15. 1021ᵃ14 ff., τὸ ποιητικόν and τὸ παθητικόν are relatives, and this means that 'that which is capable of heating is related to that which is capable of being heated, because it can heat it' (1021ᵃ16–17). So, it is clear that in every relationship in which something ποιεῖ some other thing πάσχει. The reciprocity implied in this kind of relationship based on a single process depends on the fact that the two terms are relatives, and not on the fact that they are ὑπ' ἀλλήλων. I mean that if we want say that when A acts reciprocally B suffers we do not have to add the phrase ὑπ' ἀλλήλων, because this meaning is already implied in the fact that τὸ ποιητικόν and τὸ παθητικόν are relatives.

The acting and being acted upon ὑπ' ἀλλήλων is, on our view, a particular case of ποιεῖν and πάσχειν, and the specification ὑπ' ἀλλήλων is added to express some further characteristic, which is not present in the normal case. If not, to add ὑπ' ἀλλήλων to ποιεῖν τε καὶ πάσχειν would be a mere pleonasm. The characteristic added by ὑπ' ἀλλήλων is precisely the fact that each term in the relationship acts and is acted upon by the other.

The example given by Aristotle in *GC* I. 6 confirms this interpretation. When he says 'e.g. the hot thing would be not cooled, and τοῦτο be warmed πάλιν, for heat and coldness do not change into each other' (322ᵇ15–16) some people translate πάλιν by 'in turn', but it is not necessary to understand πάλιν a temporal sense. We can understand the phrase as

the hot thing would be not cooled, and this [i.e. the cooler] would not be heated in return, for heat and coldness do not change into each other

and the example appears totally appropriate to the context. This has been clearly seen by Mugler and Williams, who translate πάλιν as 'réciproquement' and 'vice versa'.

Let us go back to the point where we left the analysis of the argument of this section of the chapter. The second part consists in the demonstration that action/passion on the one hand and mixing on the other presuppose the concept of contact: 'but if we must investigate action and passion, and mixing, we must also investigate contact' (ᵇ21–2). In fact, action and passion properly understood presuppose contact (ᵇ22–4), and mixing in general presupposes contact (ᵇ24–5).[19]

---

[19] The phrase οὔτε μὴ ἀψάμενά πως ἐνδέχεται μιχθῆναι πρῶτον at ll. 322ᵇ24–5 is a little difficult. Philoponus *in GC* 130. 2–5 finds here a *huperbaton,* and thinks it would be better to write ἀψάμενά πως πρῶτον ἐνδέχεται μιχθῆναι, connecting πρῶτον to ἀψάμενα. He has been followed by pseudo-Thomas Aquinas, Mugler, and Migliori. Tricot connects πρῶτον with μιχθῆναι 'commencer à se mélanger', which seems incorrect. Joachim thinks that πρῶτον is to be understood absolutely: 'enter into combination at all'. Verdenius and Waszink connect it to what follows.

The preceding schema now becomes:

Monists: action/passion →   contact
Pluralists:dissociation/association → action/passion → mixing → contact[20]

The monists presuppose only two of the three preliminary notions, but the pluralists fare better, and show the necessity of all the concepts Aristotle wants to analyse here. But the pluralists wrongly conceive mixture as association of particles, as a kind of σύγκρισις, and this mistake will be criticized in the last chapter of book I, when Aristotle says: 'this was the difficulty that emerged in the previous argument; and it is evident that the mixing constituents not only coalesce, having formerly existed in separation (ἐκ κεχωρισμένων συνιόντα)' (I. 10. 327^{b}26–8).

The third and last part of this section is the conclusion of the demonstration: 'hence we must define (διοριστέον) those three things: contact, mixing, acting' (322^{b}25–6). The three notions are not arranged in the order of the analysis; in the next chapters the series will become: contact, action/passion, mixing.

The short passage which follows (322^{b}26–9) can be considered in two ways: it can be seen as the conclusion of the first part of I. 6, or as the beginning of the second. Philoponus thinks that it is the first premiss of the analysis of the notion of contact,[21] while Zabarella sees it as the conclusion of the preceding discussion.[22] We think that Philoponus is right: Aristotle says κυρίως, 'in the proper sense'; that is, in a physical sense. This is the main object of the analysis of the following lines, the distinction between a κυρίως sense from other senses that are less important.

4. The second part (322^{b}26–323^{a}12): the definition of 'contact' properly understood

Here a new section starts. One could easily make it a new chapter, but there are also some reasons, as we will see, to connect it with what precedes.

---

[20] Philop. *in GC* 125. 6–8 and 16–17 tries to make the schema more regular by attributing to the monists also the concepts of association and mixing, even though this is not stated in the text. In his reconstruction the series is: monists: action/passion → mixing → contact; pluralists: action/passion → mixing → contact, thus leaving no difference between the two schools on this point.

[21] Philop. *in GC* 130. 12–13: νῦν δὲ πάλιν τὸ αὐτὸ ἀναλαμβάνει πρὸ τοῦ περὶ ἀφῆς λόγου. Joachim and Williams share this opinion.

[22] Zabarella *in GC* 850. 39–43: 'tandem Aristoteles, postquam declaravit vim consequentiae suae, et necessitatem agendi de his tribus, tandem considerat ordinem in his tribus servandum, nempe, quando dicit, principium autem accipiamus, & probat, exordiendum esse a tactu.' Mugler and Migliori agree.

'Contact' needs definition, because it is said in many ways: λέγεται πολλαχῶς (322ᵇ30–1). Aristotle adds (322ᵇ31–2) that there are two possibilities for names to be said in many ways; that is, ὁμωνύμως and ἀπὸ τῶν ... προτέρων. In the case of 'contact' it is clear that Aristotle thinks that the second possibility applies, and that there is a dependency between the different meanings of the word. But which meanings?

The majority of the commentators, as Philoponus, Zabarella and most moderns, think that there is a metaphorical usage of 'contact', as when we say 'I am touched by your kindness'; but, they say, this usage is not discussed in the present chapter, in which every attention is dedicated to the physical sense of 'contact'. There is the physical sense, which applies to the contact between bodies, and which will be defined exhaustively. Besides, they say that there are two more senses, less important and less precise: contact in the mathematical sense and the kind of contact that exists between the celestial bodies and the sublunary region. In those cases, according to the commentators, the definition of 'contact' is derivative from the definition of 'contact' in the physical sense. Aristotle will discuss them for completeness's sake and also because they help to clarify, by comparison, the characteristics of physical contact.

In sum, they say, there are three meanings of 'contact': an extremely general meaning, which applies to mathematical entities; a meaning which applies to the contact between our region and the celestial bodies; and a meaning which applies to the bodies of the sublunary world. They are connected by the fact that in order to have contact between sublunary bodies three conditions are needed, for the contact between celestial bodies and the sublunary world only two of those conditions are necessary, and for the contact in the mathematical sense there is need of only one condition.

Williams objects to this reconstruction that the contact between the celestial and the sublunary bodies is never mentioned in the text.[23] Furthermore, at the end of the chapter Aristotle expressly quotes the metaphorical sense of contact: φαμὲν γὰρ ἐνίοτε τὸν λυποῦντα ἅπτεσθαι ἡμῶν (323ᵃ32–3) without any caveat, like 'so to speak' or 'figuratively speaking'. It would seem that does not want to exclude the metaphorical sense, and that he is not concerned at all with celestial bodies. The ancient commentators' opinion seems to be wrong, and we must investigate how many meanings of 'contact', and which, are investigated here.

The important passage is 322ᵇ32–323ᵃ12. Here Aristotle gives a definition of 'contact' in the proper sense; that is, of the meaning that is relevant to an analysis of the generation and corruption of things. The

---

[23] Williams (1982), 115. Also Migliori (1976), 189–90, is sceptical about the references to the celestial bodies.

definition is reached via a sort of demonstration constructed as a series of conceptual implications, in a way very similar to the demonstration of $322^{b}21$–6. The similarity of procedures may be a reason why medieval translators decided to unite the sections $322^{b}1$–26 and $322^{b}26$–$323^{a}34$ in a single chapter.

The demonstration runs as follows.[24] The passage $322^{b}32$–$323^{a}12$ can be divided into three sections. In the first ($322^{b}32$–$323^{a}1$) Aristotle establishes the conditions necessary, but not sufficient, to have contact. In the second ($323^{a}1$–3) he confirms what he has said by a reference to mathematics. In the third ($323^{a}3$–12) he quotes the definition of contact given in the *Physics*: 'things are... in contact if their extremities are together' (*Ph.* VII. I. $231^{a}22$) saying 'as we have defined earlier, to be in contact is to have the extremes together' ($323^{a}3$–4). He shows that this definition has a series of implications, which restrict it, if properly understood, to only one case of contact between physical objects. Joachim is right when he says that in *De generatione et corruptione* Aristotle does not reverse the position he has taken in the *Physics*, but gives a further specification of it.[25] Let us have a look at the three sections one after the other.

(A) The proper sense of 'contact' applies to things which have a position (θέσις: $322^{b}33$; $323^{a}5$), but to have a position implies being in a place (τόπος: $322^{b}33$–$^{a}1$, V. $323^{a}6$). Things which have no position and are not in a place either cannot be in contact.

(B) This is confirmed by the fact that we attribute, in some special sense, place and contact also to the mathematical entities: 'in so far as we attribute contact to the mathematical entities, we must also attribute place to them, whether they exist in separation or in some other fashion' ($323^{a}1$–3). The mathematical sense derives from the physical because it is reached by subtracting some conditions from the physical sense. This squares well with the general conception of mathematics in Aristotle: mathematical concepts are established ἐξ ἀφαιρέσεως from the physical entities. Here we find the first two elements of a series of implications (θέσις → τόπος) which will continue in the next step of the demonstration. But these conditions are not sufficient to be in contact: many things have a position and are in a place without being in contact. The two conditions merely establish the possibility of being in contact.

---

[24] This reconstruction is different from Philoponus', followed by nearly all commentators. Also Zabarella has a different analysis, to which only Verdenius and Waszink adhere in part, but we cannot accept their interpretation.

[25] Joachim (1922), 141. But Gill (1989), 195, objects that the example used by Aristotle in *Physics*, teaching and learning, requires contact between the teacher and the students, but not a contact demanding that they have their extremes together. There is no necessity of being too literal. One could think, for instance, of the voice of the teacher, or of the man who commits outrage (see sect. VII), as an extension of his body which reaches someone else's ears (cf. *de An.* II. 8. $420^{b}5$–$421^{a}6$).

(C.1) To realize the possibility a third condition is needed, 'to have the extremes together' (τὸ ἅπτεσθαι τὸ τὰ ἔσχατα ἔχειν ἅμα: 323ᵃ3–4). In a sense, it is sufficient that two things have position, are in a place, and have the extremes together for being in contact. This is the sense of 'contact' which applies to mathematical entities; but it is a derivative sense. Zabarella denies that, and thinks that the adverb κυρίως in line 322ᵇ33 applies to the contact in the mathematical sense, and not to physical objects. In his interpretation this kind of contact is κυρίως because it gives the common minimal conditions of application of the concept (856. 8–9 and 14–16).²⁶ This is, in our opinion, a reversal of Aristotle's position, according to which the κυρίως meaning of contact is the one which gives a complete specification of the phenomenon, and not just the minimal necessary conditions for it. Gill²⁷ thinks that the mathematical sense of contact is 'a general account' of it, but, as we will see, with the expression 'to be in contact in general' (323ᵃ22) Aristotle alludes to something different. The mathematical sense of contact is not καθόλου, is ἐξ ἀφαιρέσεως and, in some way, a derived and uninteresting sense.

(C.2) Moreover, Aristotle proceeds to show that the definition of the *Physics* must be completed. Since the main differences of place (τόπος) are high and low (323ᵃ7, cf. *Cael.* II. 2), and since to be high or low implies to be light or heavy, consequently the things which are in contact are light, heavy, or both: 'all things which are in contact with each other will have weight or lightness, either both or just one of those qualities' (323ᵃ8–9). On the other hand, things which are heavy or light are capable of action and passion (323ᵃ9–10). From this Aristotle can derive the following definition:

Hence it is clear (ὥστε φανερόν) that those things are by nature in contact with one another, which, being separate magnitudes, have their extremes together and are capable of moving, or of being moved by, one another. (323ᵃ10–11)

This is the final conclusion, and 'contact' in the proper sense is defined. What remains to be done for Aristotle, as it seems, is to clarify some aspect of the definition and to distinguish the other senses of the term.

But first some comments are needed. First of all, why has the couple ποιεῖν–πάσχειν been substituted with the couple κινεῖν–κινεῖσθαι? And can one say that Aristotle's demonstration is sound?

Let us begin with the second question: in short, Aristotle argues the following series of implications:

ἅμα ἔχειν τὰ ἔσχατα → θέσις → τόπος → τὸ ἄνω καὶ τὸ κάτω → βάρος καὶ κουφότης → ποιεῖν καὶ πάσχειν.

---

²⁶ He also suggests that this type of contact could be said κυρίως in comparison with the metaphorical usage.

²⁷ Gill (1989), 195.

One can doubt that all those implications have the same validity. The first steps are sound, since there is no doubt that things which have the extremes together have a position (ἅμα ἔχειν τὰ ἔσχατα → θέσις). There is no doubt either that things having position are in place (θέσις → τόπος). But here a specification is needed. In fact, the implication θέσις → τόπος has two different senses for mathematical and physical objects. The former are in place *in abstracto* and in a relative sense, as when we say that an object is at the right side of another,[28] the latter are in a physical place, to which the distinction of high and low applies. This means that the following step (τόπος → τὸ ἄνω καὶ τὸ κάτω) is valid only for physical objects, and not for mathematical objects: mathematical place admits no distinction between high and low.[29] This clearly shows that from the start the demonstration is limited to the realm of physical objects and that the mathematical sense of contact is incomplete.

The following step (τὸ ἄνω καὶ τὸ κάτω → βάρος καὶ κουφότης) is self-evident in Aristotle's system; but the last one (βάρος καὶ κουφότης → ποιεῖν καὶ πάσχειν) is more doubtful. Philoponus affirms that a logical proof is not sufficient to demonstrate that things which are heavy and light are necessarily capable of acting and being acted upon reciprocally (οὐκ ἐκ συλλογισμοῦ). He says that this passage is grounded on the evidence of the senses (ἐνάργεια) and is less convincing for that reason.[30] Bäumker[31] even maintains that this passage contradicts a later text, which says that heavy and light are neither active nor passive (II. 2. 329^{b}20–4). Zabarella attempts to find an answer: 'Sunt gravia & laevia, & quod talia etiam sunt passiva & activa, quia ut dixi gravitas et laevitas sunt secundae qualitates, quae insequuntur quatuor primas alternativas, quae sunt vere activae & passivae' (855. 36–8). Joachim[32] rejects Zabarella's pos-

---

[28] Cf. *Physics* IV. 1. 208^{b}22–5. Zabarella *in GC* 854. 12 and Joachim (1922), 143 insist that mathematical objects have a position (θέσις) only as determination of physical objects; but this restriction seems too strong: we can say that a triangle is on the left hand side of a circle without thinking of the physical objects from which they are derived.

[29] Cf. Zabarella *in GC* 855. 4–7. He thinks that this passage is like a sophism: 'notate artificium Aristotelis qui, cum declaravit primam acceptionem tactus per positionem & locum hic significat secundam acceptionem tactus per locum & positionem, sed strictius accepta quam prius'.

[30] Cf. Philop. *in GC* 135. 13–15. From time to time Philoponus adds to his explanations of Aristotle's position some criticism. In doing that, he follows the opinion of his master Ammonius, who, in his commentary on the *Categories*, lists among the tasks of a good commentator noting the faults in Aristotle's arguments and correcting them. Cf. Amm. *in Cat.* 8. 17–18: δεῖ ἕκαστον κρίνοντα βασανίζειν ἐπίπροσθεν Ἀριστοτέλους θέμενον, εἰ τύχοι, τὴν ἀλήθειαν. Such criticisms are not indicative of an evolution to the anti-Aristotelian position to which Philoponus arrived much later in his life. Cf. K. Verrycken, 'The Development of Philoponus' Thought and Its Chronology', in R. R. K. Sorabji (ed.), *Aristotle Transformed: The Ancient Commentators and Their Influence* (London, 1990), 243.

[31] Quoted by Joachim (1922), 146.

[32] Joachim (1922), 146.

ition and says: it is true that physical bodies are essentially active or passive *and also* that they are essentially heavy and light, but their action and passion are not the effects of their heaviness and lightness. The criticism of Philoponus remains substantially unanswered.

Anyway, the general conclusion is in a way acceptable, because it is true that things which are separate magnitudes, have their extremes in common, and are capable of acting and being acted upon reciprocally— are in contact. It is also true that this definition of contact (323^a10–12) is the most important from the point of view of *De generatione et corruptione* the important sense of 'contact' is that which implies a reciprocal action and passion.[33] But, one could say, this is a very peculiar kind of contact, and the conditions stipulated by Aristotle (being separate magnitudes, having extremes together, reciprocal influence) cannot be the conditions without which one cannot speak of 'contact' in general.

To answer this objection we must understand in which way Aristotle calls this meaning of 'contact' κυρίως. Here the adverb doesn't mean 'consacré par l'usage'[34] but indicates 'ipsam propriam ac primariam alicuius vocabuli notionem'.[35] The meaning of 'contact' described here is the most important in the context of a study of generation, corruption, and the elements. And this is κυρίως because it realizes the nature of the process in the best way,[36] and because the other meanings derive from it ('being derived from other and prior ones', 322^b31).

5. New definitions of contact (323^a12–25)

The section which follows is the most obscure of the chapter. In general we can say that with lines 323^a10–12 the search for a definition of 'contact' in the proper sense is concluded. From line 323^a12 onward Aristotle adds some clarifications and modifications which have been read as an attempt to make clearer the proper sense of the term by distinguishing other, less precise, meanings from it. The commentators have tried to construct an argument from what is said in these lines, adding some premisses and qualifying some claims, but we cannot say that they have succeeded completely.

Let us begin with a summary of the passage. Aristotle says:

[33] Cf. *GC* I. 7. 324^a7–9, $^b1$–3; I. 10. 328^a19–21.
[34] cf. A. Wartelle, *Lexique de la 'Rhétorique' d'Aristote* (Paris, 1982), 228.
[35] Bonitz (1870), 416^a56–7.
[36] Cf. *Ph*. VII. 3. 246^a13–16: 'when anything acquires its proper excellence, we call it perfect, since it is then really in its natural state; for instance, a circle is perfect when it becomes completely circular and when it is best'.

1. There is a difference between movers (i.e. there are moved movers and unmoved movers) which applies also to the agents, and this is confirmed by the fact that people say ($\varphi \alpha \sigma \iota$) indifferently that a mover acts or an agent moves (323ᵃ12–16).[37] This amounts to saying that there *are* un-affected agents. It is a correction to what has been said at lines 322ᵇ22–4: 'action and passion properly understood are not possible between things which cannot be in contact with each other', and to the definition of the preceding lines: 'that those things are by nature in contact with one another, which ... are capable of moving, or being moved by, one an-other' (323ᵃ10–11).

2. But, he adds, on the other hand what people say is not completely true: not every mover can act, and moving is wider than acting; this is confirmed by a consideration of the element correlative to the agent; that is, the patient. Since a patient is something which changes its qualities, the movement involved in acting is a qualitative change; but qualitative change is only one of the kinds of movement, so every action is a movement, but not vice versa (323ᵃ16–20).[38] Since all $\pi o \iota \acute{\eta} \sigma \epsilon \iota \varsigma$ are $\kappa \iota \nu \acute{\eta} \sigma \epsilon \iota \varsigma$, the main point of the preceding section, that there are unaffected agents, still holds.[39]

3. At least what follows is clear: there is a sense in which movers[40] are in contact with the things moved, and a sense in which they are not (323ᵃ20–2).

---

[37] Not only 'people'. Aristotle used the words in the same way both in the preceding lines 323ᵃ9–12, when he substituted $\pi \alpha \theta \eta \tau \iota \kappa \grave{\alpha} \ \kappa \alpha \grave{\alpha} \ \pi o \iota \eta \tau \iota \kappa \grave{\alpha}$ with $\kappa \iota \nu \eta \tau \iota \kappa \grave{o} \nu \ \kappa \alpha \grave{\iota} \ \kappa \iota \nu \eta \tau \acute{o} \nu$, and in *Ph*. III. 3. 202ᵃ21 ff.

[38] This narrow sense of the term $\pi o \iota \epsilon \hat{\iota} \nu$ is not usual in Aristotle, but it is the most appropriate in the context of *De generatione et corruptione*.

[39] The problem posited in points (1) and (2) reappears, in a slightly different formula-tion, in chapter 7, 324ᵃ24–ᵇ13, which has been very well explained by C. Wildberg in ch. 8 of this volume (pp. 233–8). There Aristotle says that an argument which applies to the pair mover/moved applies also to the pair agent/patient. In fact, between movers there is a chain, and we can distinguish a first mover, which initiates movement, from the last one, which moves the object; the same applies to agents (324ᵃ24–30). The first mover can be (or must be) unmoved, the last one is necessarily moved; the same applies to agents (324ᵃ30–4). The differences between the passage of chapter 6 and the passage of chapter 7 are not profound: in chapter 6 we are told that 'moving' is a genus of which 'acting' is a species, and there are no allusions to a chain of movers, but Aristotle simply says that there are two kind of movers, moved and unmoved. In chapter 7 Aristotle starts from the idea of a chain, and arrives at the conclusion ($\delta \iota \acute{o}$, 324ᵇ9) that the first element of the chain is an unmoved mover. In chapter 6 we have an argument for the thesis that what applies to movement also applies to action and passion: action and passion are a species of move-ment. In chapter 7 we have an argument for the thesis that there are two kind of movers, moved and unmoved: the chain of movers. The two passages seem connected and illumin-ate one another.

[40] Here, 323ᵃ21, Joachim reads $\kappa \iota \nu \eta \tau \iota \kappa \acute{\alpha}$ (motiva $\varGamma$); Mugler reads $\kappa \iota \nu o \hat{\upsilon} \nu \tau \alpha$ (E^2, L, and Philoponus) which is better attested. The meaning does not change.

4. But the definition of 'contact' is twofold: καθόλου there is contact between mover and moved, πρὸς ἄλληλα there is contact between agent and patient (323ᵃ22–5). This seems to mean that this first kind of contact is different from the contact between an agent and his patient, and that there is another sense in which the mover is in contact with the object moved.

Many commentators have tried to connect the first three points of Chapter 6 by interpreting 'moved', in lines 323ᵃ13–14, as 'moved by the object moved', and to extract from it a single argument. This is pseudo-Thomas Aquinas' interpretation, followed by Zabarella, Joachim, Tricot, and others.[41] Since in the preceding lines Aristotle has spoken about contact between things that are reciprocally mover and moved, the assumption is quite natural. The argument runs like this:

(a) there are movers which are moved by the object moved, and movers which are not;

(b) ποιεῖν is a species of κινεῖν: in the case of acting the patient reacts upon the agent;

(c) in conclusion, it is clear[42] that some movers are in contact with the object moved and some are not.

In other words, they consider the distinction between κινεῖν and ποιεῖν as subordinated to the distinction between unmoved and moved movers. In the case of ποιεῖν the mover is always moved in return by the patient, whereas in the case of κινεῖν it is not necessary that the mover be moved in return by the object. As an example of a mover that is unmoved by the object moved, Philoponus (136. 32), pseudo-Thomas Aquinas (514ᵃ), Zabarella (856. 36), and the others indicate heaven: it moves the sublunary world but is not moved by it. To this case, according to the commentators, a new sense of 'contact' applies.

But Williams rightly remarks that Aristotle says nothing about movers moved by the thing which they move: he says only that there are movers which cause motion without being moved—full stop. He goes back to lines 323ᵃ10–12 and suggests that they can be interpreted as: there is contact in the full sense when a thing is capable of moving another, and

---

[41] Pseudo-Thomas Aquinas 514ᵃ: 'quoddam est movens motum, quoddam autem movens immobile (et hoc dupliciter: aliquid enim simpliciter nullo modo movetur, aliquod autem movens non movetur a moto, licet moveatur ab aliquo)'. Cf. Zabarella in GC 856. 28–41, Joachim (1922), 146–7 and Tricot (1951), 60. Philoponus in GC 136. 6–34, on the contrary, understands 'unmoved' in the sense of Ph. VIII: ἐπειδὴ δέδεικται ἐν τῇ Φυσικῇ ὅτι οὐ πᾶν τὸ κινοῦν κινούμενον κινεῖ, τοῦτο νῦν λαβὼν ἐξ αὐτοῦ δείκνυσιν ὅτι μηδὲ πάντα τὰ ἁπτόμενα ἁπτομένων ἅπτεται (136. 9–11). But in his reconstruction of the argument it is not clear how to derive from the fact that not every mover is moved the conclusion that not everything that acts is acted upon *by the thing which is affected*.

[42] Zabarella in GC 857. 14–15: 'illud igitur manifestum est'.

the other of being moved by it. We have already discussed this point. Now the definition is specified, according to Williams, in the sense that there is a difference between movers: some are moved, some are not. He thinks that Aristotle alludes to the unmoved movers which move the celestial spheres, and not to the celestial spheres themselves. In the end, however, Williams accepts the traditional interpretation: he says that the distinction between agents and movers does not cut across the distinction between moved and unmoved movers, but it applies only to the first branch of the latter distinction; all agents are moved movers, because all agents are also affected.[43]

The difference between pseudo-Thomas Aquinas' and Williams's interpretation is that in the former the agents are affected by the things they affect, in the latter they are affected by something different. And both interpreters say that there are no unaffected agents.

But this cannot be true, and there is nothing that prevents agents from being unaffected. In lines $323^{a}12$–16 Aristotle has claimed that there *are* unaffected agents. One could reply that this was only preliminary position, which is corrected in lines $323^{a}16$–22. But later, in chapter I. 7, Aristotle uses the chain argument to demonstrate that not every agent is affected: 'in motion there is nothing to prevent the first mover from being unmoved' ($324^{a}30$–1). The traditional interpretation, according to which in chapter 6 Aristotle wants to say that there are no unaffected agents, contrasts with this passage.

In chapter 7, however, it is said that the last agent, which is in contact with the patient, is always affected by it. Only for the last agent does the principle that there are no unaffected agents apply. And, in fact, only the last agent is in contact with the patient. But the problem is, affected by what? By the agent which precedes it in the chain of movers (Williams), or by the patient (pseudo-Thomas Aquinas)?

There is an asymmetry between a chain of movers and a chain of agents. In a chain of motions the first mover moves the last item, the moved non-mover, *and also* every element in the chain. A man pushes a door with a stick: he moves the stick and, by moving the stick, he moves the door. But in a chain of actions, in the restricted sense of ποίησις as qualitative change, this does not always apply: the first agent changes the last element, but not necessarily the intermediates. A doctor heals a patient by giving him wine: he heals the patient but does not heal the wine. The qualitative change of the last agent is not originated by the first agent, but by the counter-influence of the patient. As Aristotle says in chapter 7: 'the food, in acting, is itself in some way acted upon; for, in

---

[43] Williams (1982), 116–17.

acting, it is simultaneously heated or cooled or otherwise affected' (324^{b}1–3).

We think that this is the point of the distinction we find in 323^{a}16–20: when there is a ποίησις there are qualitative alterations—which do not form a chain the same way as local movements do.

Aristotle says that in a ποίησις there is a contact between the (last) agent and the patient, a contact which implies a reciprocal qualitative change. But since not all κινήσεις are ποιήσεις, other senses of 'contact' apply, and, in those other cases, the (last) mover is not in contact κυρίως with the object moved. This leads to a reformulation of the definition of lines 323^{a}10–12, to accommodate the distinctions made in the preceding lines.

But what the reformulation consists in is not certain. From a textual point of view there are no problems, and everybody agrees that Aristotle wrote the following lines:

^{a}22   ἀλλ' ὁ διορισμὸς τοῦ ἅπτεσθαι καθόλου μὲν ὁ
^{a}23   τῶν θέσιν ἐχόντων καὶ τοῦ μὲν κινητικοῦ τοῦ δὲ κινητοῦ, πρὸς
^{a}24   ἄλληλα δὲ κινητικοῦ καὶ κινητοῦ ἐν οἷς ὑπάρχει τὸ ποιεῖν
^{a}25   καὶ τὸ πάσχειν. (323^{a}22–5)

The passage begins with an ἀλλά, which answers the φανερόν of line 323^{a}21: it is clear that x (some movers are in contact with the object moved and some are not), but y (contact is said in two different ways). Joachim places a comma after δέ in 323^{a}24; Mugler places a comma after κινητοῦ in the same line, and Verdenius and Waszink agree with Mugler. Joachim understands πρὸς ἄλληλα δέ as ὁ διορισμὸς τοῦ πρὸς ἄλληλα ἅπτεσθαι, Mugler and Verdenius connect πρὸς ἄλληλα δέ to κινητικοῦ καὶ κινητοῦ. The main difference concerns the question of what is reciprocal: the contact and its definition, or the relationship between mover and moved?

Many commentators think that here we have two definitions, and that Aristotle distinguishes 'contact' in the proper sense from a more general meaning. This is Zabarella's interpretation, followed by Joachim, Verdenius, Williams, and others.[44] In Zabarella's interpretation we have two definitions, distinguished by μέν ... δέ in lines 22 and 24. The first definition is said to be καθόλου, the second is proper to a particular case, when the things in contact are πρὸς ἄλληλα. The καθόλου case requires two conditions, having the extremes together and being mover and moved; the πρὸς ἄλληλα case requires a stricter condition; namely, that the movement involved is a ποίησις, or alteration.

---

[44] Zabarella in GC 857. 20–1; Joachim (1922), 147; Verdenius and Waszink (1968), 33; Migliori (1976), 190; Williams (1982), 117; Gill (1989), 196.

But Tricot and Mugler think that here we have only one definition, a new definition of 'contact' in the proper sense.[45] In Tricot's interpretation we have two conditions at the beginning, and then a restriction of the second condition. The definition of contact in general applies to things which present the condition of having the extremes together and of being movers and moved; but to be mover and moved reciprocally it is necessary to be agent and patient.[46]

Philoponus is uncertain, and says that either here we have two (or three) definitions or there is only one definition but formulated twice: at the beginning it is expressed ἀπροσδιορίστως, and at the end ἀκριβέστερον.[47]

So, everybody admits that the definition of lines 323ᵃ10–12 is reformulated, and that from it something more general (another formulation or another definition) is distinguished.[48] The root of the difference between the two main interpretations lies in the understanding of διορισμός... καθόλου in line 22: Is it a general definition, to be contrasted with a more precise one, or it is a precise definition, expressed generally at first, and with more precision later on? Moreover, what does πρὸς ἄλληλα mean?

On the first question Zabarella's interpretation seems more plausible. We have two definitions of contact, one 'general' and the other 'reciprocal'. The text can be translated as follows:

But the definition of contact in general applies to things which have position and are capable the one of imparting motion, the other of being moved; while reciprocal [contact] applies to a mover and a thing moved between which there is action and passion... (323ᵃ22–5).

Now the second question. In lines 323ᵃ20–2 it is said that it is clear that there is a sense of 'mover' in which the movers are in contact with the thing moved, and others in which they are not. But, Aristotle adds, the

---

[45] Tricot (1971), 61; Mugler (1966), 27. Pseudo-Thomas Aquinas *in GC* 514ᵇ thinks that here we have the only definition of contact in the proper sense: 'concludit investigatam definitionem tactus'.

[46] In a footnote of his translation Tricot (1971), 61 attributes this interpretation to Mgr Diès.

[47] Cf. Philoponus *in GC* 137. 20–2 and 138. 12–16. The doubt is possible because in his interpretation there is an increase of conditions in the passage: at first we have a general condition, which can be seen either as the first definition, or as a preliminary sketch of the complete definition; then further conditions are added.

[48] What corresponds to the definition of ll. 323ᵃ10–12 cannot be what is said in ll. 323ᵃ22–3: the definition in lines 10–12 is κυρίως (cf. 322ᵇ23), the definition in lines 22–3 is καθόλου. Between the two terms there is a difference: both can correspond to πρῶτον (cf. Bonitz (1870), 356ᵇ26 and 416ᵇ1) but on different readings. Cf. also Philoponus *in GC* 137. 21–2, who interprets the καθόλου definition as κοινότερον and the other definition as ἰδικώτερον καὶ κυριώτερον.

definition of 'contact', in general, requires only that things in contact have the extremes together and are related as mover and moved. This clarifies a necessary condition for 'a sense in which' (323ᵃ21) movers and moved are in contact: the mover is in contact with the moved when they have the extremes together, and not in the other cases. There is no need to think of the first unmoved mover, as Williams does: in the next chapter Aristotle will explain that there can be chains of movers in which only the last item of the chain is in contact with the object moved. This looks like a new sense of contact: in the case of motion only two conditions are needed, having a relationship as mover and moved, and having the extremes together.

However, Aristotle adds, if we have a πρὸς ἄλληλα case, κινεῖν must be understood in the restricted sense of ποιεῖν. This restricted case clarifies ἔστι δ' ὡς οὐ: 'there is another sense in which they do not' (323ᵃ22): in the πρὸς ἄλληλα sense there is contact between a mover and a thing moved only if they are an agent and a thing affected. Because only in alteration is there reciprocal contact.

What distinguishes the πρὸς ἄλληλα case from the καθόλου case? Gill believes that here πρὸς ἄλληλα means just 'in relation one to the other' and not 'reciprocally'.[49] Even if this translation is possible, it does not fit the context. For we know that:

(a) the πρὸς ἄλληλα case is not the most general case;
(b) it applies only to a subset of movements; namely, alterations.

It is natural to think that here Aristotle alludes to a stricter notion, and not to a looser one. The most natural way of understanding the πρὸς ἄλληλα case is to see in it the case described at 323ᵃ10–12, the case of reciprocal movement, which is limited here to cases of alteration.

To sum up. Points 1–4 are all concerned with a comparison between κίνησις and ποίησις which corrects the implicit identification we have found in lines 323ᵃ10–12, when Aristotle used κινεῖν and ποιεῖν indifferently. But they do not constitute a coherent argument, and seem to be a couple of disconnected remarks. In points 1 and 2 the main thesis is the existence of an unaffected agent. Its existence is affirmed by Aristotle, together with the idea that κινεῖν is a genus of which ποιεῖν is a species. In points 3 and 4 it is said, without further proof, that it is evident that the kind of contact that applies to τὸ ποιοῦν and τὸ πάσχον is different from the kind of contact that applies to all other cases of κινοῦν and κινούμενον. The former is reciprocal; it is a legitimate inference to think that the latter is not.

---

[49] Gill (1989), 195–8, thinks of a sense of 'contact' which does not require that the mover and the moved have their extremities together.

The two passages do not constitute an argument, because points 1 and 2 anticipate a problem which will be discussed again in the following chapter (I. 7), and establish a common feature of κινεῖν and ποιεῖν; on the other hand, points 3 and 4 establish a difference between κινεῖν and ποιεῖν which is not grounded in what is said in 1 and 2, and which will not be discussed again in the following chapters. The attempt of the commentators from Philoponus to Joachim to tie the four passages together in a single argument, by interpreting the distinction of point 1 in the light of point 4 (unmoved mover = a mover unmoved by the object it moves) fails, because it admits a conclusion which is contradicted by the text; namely, the idea that there are no unaffected agents.

Anyway, Aristotle has established that there can be unmoved movers and unaffected agents. He has also distinguished the case of alteration from other motions, and has introduced, in a somewhat oblique way, a new sense of contact, which does not require the reciprocity of motion we find in qualitative change.

6. Cases of non-reciprocal contact (323ᵃ25–34)

In order to be as brief as possible, we will comment on just the main points of the last section. After having said that there is a kind of contact which requires a reciprocal movement, a kind of contact which requires only that something moves another thing, but is not moved in return, Aristotle goes on to describe a different case: that is, when something moves another thing by touching it, but is not touched by it. In the preceding lines there was reciprocal contact but not reciprocal movement; now there is neither reciprocal contact nor reciprocal movement.

Aristotle formulates the question of reciprocal contact in terms of 'touching' (ἅπτεσθαι) and no longer in terms of 'moving' (κινεῖσθαι), as he did in the preceding lines. He distinguishes two cases:

1. On the one hand (ἔστι μὲν οὖν), and in the majority of cases, what touches touches something which touches it. This is proved by the fact that the majority of movers move things with which they are in contact (τὰ ἐμποδών),[50] and in those cases it is evident that the reciprocal contact is necessary (323ᵃ25–8).

2. On the other hand (ἔστι δέ), there are cases in which only the mover touches the thing moved, but not vice versa, as we sometimes say. For instance, we say that the man who grieves us touches us, but we do not touch him. This way of speaking, even if it is present in our ordinary

---

[50] I follow the translation given by Mugler and Migliori. But it would be possible to translate also 'les choses de notre monde' (Joachim, Philoponus, Tricot, Williams).

language, contrasts with the assumption that in general what touches a thing is touched by what it touches. We have this assumption because we see that all the movers, when they are of the same kind as the things moved, move by being moved. The other cases are exceptions: when the mover moves without being moved, it is in contact with the thing moved, but not vice versa (323ª28–33).

What are those objects, which move without being moved, and consequently touch without being touched? It is clear that they do not belong to the same kind as the things moved (they are not ὁμογενῆ), because when they belong to the same kind reciprocal movement and contact are necessary. It is also clear that the exception is a fact of everyday life, and present in common language (ὡς ἐνίοτέ φαμεν, 323ª28).[51] This is confirmed by the example: 'we sometimes say that the man who grieves us touches us' (323ª33).

As in the case of movement, the question is about 'reciprocity': there is reciprocity between A and B when both do and suffer the same thing.

Most commentators think that the example of the offensive man is not well chosen, and only a metaphor. They look for a better case: the final cause, which moves while being unmoved (Philoponus, Tricot, Migliori), but which seems out of place here; or the celestial spheres which move the sublunary world without being moved by it (Zabarella, Joachim); or the unmoved mover of the *Physics*, considered as moving cause and not as final cause (Williams). All those cases are good Aristotelian examples, but Aristotle does not say a word about them. The arguments that Williams, with good reasons, uses against those who see a reference to the celestial spheres could be employed against his proposal as well.[52] But in favour of his interpretation we could quote the last line of the chapter: 'This is the way in which we define the notion of contact which occurs in the things of nature' (323ª33–4). One could say that the case of 'grieving' is not a good example of what occurs in the things of nature. Is that true?

Psychology in Aristotle is a physical science, and psychological processes have a material substrate. There is no doubt that by speaking of 'the man who grieves us' he refers to a common way of speaking, but often Aristotle thinks that common language hides a deeper truth, and provides physical science with many interesting data. Pseudo-Thomas Aquinas gives us a good hint[53] when he glosses τὸν λυποῦντα with 'contristantem' and 'contristantem' with 'qui dicit verbum iniuriosum'; that is

---

[51] Here I think that the reference is to the way of speaking of the common people and not to the jargon of the philosophical schools.

[52] Williams (1982), 115–18.

[53] J. Mansfeld *per litteras* suggests a different case, which works in the same manner: an actor in theatre provokes in us ἔλεος and φόβος without being moved himself. This is perfectly true, and we think it is possible to find many other similar cases.

to say, ὁ ὑβρίζων. Hubris is in fact an asymmetrical relationship which implies both a spiritual factor and a physical factor. In the *Nicomachean Ethics* Aristotle says that the relation between the man who injures and another man who responds to the injury with anger is not symmetrical. The insolent man grieves his victim without feeling any pain (*EN* VII. 6. 1149^{b}20) and he is the originator of the action because he provokes anger in the victim (*EN* V. 8. 1135^{b}26–7). The victim responds to the offence with impetuosity (θυμῷ) and anger: the anger is the principal manifestation of the impetuosity. But, in turn, anger is connected to pain, because 'every one who acts in anger acts with pain' (*EN* VII. 6. 1149^{b}20–1). When 'reason or imagination inform us that we have been insulted' (ὕβρις, *EN* VII. 6. 1149^{a}32) the θυμός is provoked, and this arousing is a process at the same time physical and psychical, because the θυμός provokes an overheating of the blood (θερμότητος γὰρ ποιητικὸν ὁ θυμός, *PA* 650^{b}34) and anger is, at the same time, 'the appetite for returning pain for pain' and 'boiling of blood surrounding the heart' (*de An.* I. 1. 403^{a}30–^{b}1).[54] Consequently the man who grieves us provokes in our body some physical movements connected to anger, and he does not suffer the reaction in himself, because 'the man who commits outrage acts with pleasure' (ὁ δ' ὑβρίζων μεθ' ἡδονῆς, *EN* VII. 6. 1149^{b}21) and without pain.

We can say that there is a sense in which ὁ λυποῦν of line 323^{a}33 provokes a physical movement, the boiling of the blood in his victim, without suffering the same influence in return. He finds pleasure in the action, while the one insulted sees in it the source of his pain and anger. The different interpretation of the same act is the reason for the non-reciprocity of influences, and for the fact that the mover is not touched by the thing moved with the same kind of movement.

7. Summary

In the second part of the chapter we have learned that the term 'contact' is used in many ways and that it has a focal meaning. This focal meaning is ἁφὴ κυρίως and is more complete than the other senses, which derive from it in various ways. To have contact properly speaking three conditions have to be met, in the other cases only two conditions are necessary, or just one.

---

[54] Cf. C. Viano, 'Colère et θυμός dans la rhétorique des passions d'Aristote', in A. Lopez Eire, J. M. Labiano Illundain, and A. M. Seoane Pardo (eds.), *Retorica, politica e ideologia desde la Antiguedad hasta nuestros dias* (Salamanca, 1988), i. 101–6.

Contact properly speaking occurs when something touches some other thing and between them there is a reciprocal movement, so that both things are at the same time mover and moved. It seems strange to call the proper case of contact such a particular case. But Aristotle does not consider the most common case as the most important. He thinks that the most important case of contact is the case in which we have the most complete interaction. From this he distinguishes other cases, which are less complete: a more frequent case, which occurs when A moves B without being moved in return; another particular case, in which A moves B but there is no reciprocal touching, because A touches B but not vice versa; and the case of mathematical entities. In other words we have:

1. Reciprocal contact with reciprocal movement, i.e. alteration (322^b32–323^a12)
2. Reciprocal contact with one-way movement, i.e. movement in general (323^a12–25)
3. One-way contact with one-way movement, i.e. cases like grieving (323^a25–33).
4. Reciprocal contact without any kind of movement, i.e. the mathematical entities (323^a1–2).

This situation is similar to the case of δύναμις described in *Metaphysics* VIII. 1: δύναμις is πολλαχῶς λεγόμενον (1046^a4–5) and, partly, πρὸς τὸ αὐτὸ εἶδος (1046^a9). Also, in the case of δύναμις we have a κυρίως definition and other definitions that derive from the first. In those other definitions some, though not all, parts of the most important definition are present (1046^a15–19). The focal meaning is the most complete and therefore primary.

On the one hand, the analysis of 'contact' precedes the study of the elements because it is a simpler notion and does not require any preliminary knowledge of the four elements and their qualities to be understood. On the other hand, the principal sense of 'contact' is preliminary to the knowledge of the other notions, action/passion and mixing. To understand those relationships we need the idea of a kind of contact in which things, being separate magnitudes, have their extremes together and are able to move, and to be moved by, one another.

8

On Generation and Corruption I. 7: Aristotle on *poiein* and *paschein*

CHRISTIAN WILDBERG

The seventh chapter of the first book of *On Generation and Corruption* opens with a laconic statement. 'Affecting and being affected must be discussed next', Aristotle writes, and the first task is to remind ourselves why he is turning, apparently with a certain amount of urgency, to just this topic. Secondly, we should ask whether the vocabulary of 'action' and 'passion' (so Forster and Williams) appropriately captures the sense of the Aristotelian ποιεῖν and πάσχειν used in this context.

As we turn to the first task, we have to keep in mind that the problem Aristotle attempts to solve in the treatise *On Generation and Corruption* is an almost paradoxical one. What he tries to accomplish is to show how it is possible to understand, and theoretically describe, the processes of coming to be and passing away (and by extension of growth and alteration) in a world that is eternal, and, importantly, to describe these processes in such a way that they do not turn out to be—once again—ontologically secondary 'epiphenomena' of topical rearrangements of some basic stuff. This was the solution typically offered by several Presocratic philosophers of nature. For Aristotle, in contrast, the universe is everlasting in its essential shape, composition, and configuration; yet within this eternally stable system nature undergoes *real* processes of substantial, quantitative, and qualitative change, processes that are as 'real' as they appear to be.

An understanding of such changes taken as real presupposes a sophisticated theory of the precise mechanisms that are involved in these processes, and especially so in the case of processes at the most fundamental ontological level, the level of elementary bodies. The atomists Democritus and Leucippus had famously paved the way with a theory sophisticated enough to offer a potentially very powerful insight into the microcosmic processes that take place beyond the barrier of what is accessible to the senses. In the *Timaeus* Plato had tried to better the atomists' view by investing it with mathematical elegance. With an array of good arguments, Aristotle wholeheartedly rejects both atomism and the Platonic attempt to understand physical bodies as composites of essentially mathematical entities (two-dimensional triangles). But what is needed, clearly, is a rival theory, equally sophisticated, and powerful enough to illuminate with precision the actual mechanisms of elemental interaction, of nature's qualitative and quantitative fluctuations, and importantly, of higher-order substance formation.

An early treatise in which Aristotle lays down the theoretical basis for such a theory is the *de Caelo*. In book III he first determines the total number of the sublunary elements, and then seems to be keenly aware of the fact that he now has to build on these presuppositions a comprehensive theory dealing with the problems just outlined and offering a scientific account of nature's metamorphoses, avoiding above all the paradoxes of both atomism and Platonism. Aristotle makes certain moves to prepare the reader for this narrative and apparently sets out to tackle it at the end of book III of *de Caelo*. In chapter 6 of that treatise he acknowledges, on the strength of empirical evidence, that the elements are not eternal but are observed to be in processes of dissolution (304^b25–7). Moreover, one must suppose, he claims, that they come into being from one another (305^a31–2) because generation out of nothing is impermissible and because there is no other body from which they could originate. Chapter 7 then opens with the statement:

Now again, one must ask what is the manner of this generation out of one another? Is it as Empedocles and Democritus say it is, or as those who analyse bodies into surfaces, or is there some other manner besides these?[1]

Note that here, just as in the treatise on generation and corruption, the dialectical opposition is represented by Democritus and Empedocles on the one hand and by Plato on the other. Chapters 7 and 8 of the third book of *de Caelo* then contain a brief criticism of atomism and a more detailed repudiation of Plato; surprisingly, however, we hear nothing of Aristotle's own theory of the processes of nature. Book III ends with the programmatic statement:

From what has been said it is clear that shapes are not what differentiates the elements. The most essential differences between bodies are differences in properties and functions and powers (for these are what we say pertain to natural objects: properties and functions and powers). Therefore one should speak about

---

[1] 305^a33–<sup>b</>1 πάλιν οὖν ἐπισκεπτέον τίς ὁ τρόπος τῆς ἐξ ἀλλήλων γενέσεως, πότερον ὡς Ἐμπεδοκλῆς λέγει καὶ Δημόκριτος, ἢ ὡς οἱ εἰς τὰ ἐπίπεδα διαλύοντες, ἢ ἔστιν ἄλλος τις τρόπος παρὰ τούτους. Throughout, the translations are my own.

these first, in order that from a consideration of *them* we grasp the differences between element and element.[2]

The fourth book of *de Caelo* (on 'heavy' and 'light'), the treatise on *Generation and Corruption*, and the fourth book of the *Meteorology* are all part of this extensive project: understanding the properties, functions, and powers of the elements.[3] And so, when Aristotle says at the beginning of *GC* I. 7 that he must talk about (λεκτέον) ποιεῖν and πάσχειν, the necessity does not simply arise from the fact that an agenda to this effect was announced in the previous chapter, I. 6. A more fundamental urgency is involved. Since Aristotle has committed himself to the quartet of sublunary elements as being equally primitive *and* to a non-reductive view on quantitative, qualitative, and substantial change, he is now under an obligation to give an account of what *he* takes to be happening when, at a fundamental level, simple bodies interact with one another in terms of ποιεῖν and πάσχειν.

This obligation is all the more intriguing since, by Aristotle's own standards, the account must needs be a physical one, operating with explanatory concepts that are firmly grounded in sense perception. The concepts he thinks are going to help him to theorize *phusikôs* about this topic are announced in chapter 6: touch, ποιεῖν and πάσχειν, and mixture. It is in terms of these basic concepts that Aristotle will suggest elementary interaction has to be understood, and understood in a less problematic way than by the shuffling and reshuffling of atoms or incorporeal triangles.

The upshot of these introductory remarks is that, both on the large scale of the systematic exposition of Aristotle's physical theory (roughly from the *Physics* to *de Anima*) and on the smaller scale of the structural economy of the present treatise on generation and corruption, the discussion of chapters I. 7–9 forms an essential and integral part in the sense that they are building blocks in a sequence of interconnected physical theorems. The considerations offered in this chapter (as in much of the rest of the treatise on generation and corruption) are in a sense foundational for a comprehensive theory of qualitative and quantitative changes in nature. Elsewhere Aristotle himself looks back at these chapters as containing his general account of ποιεῖν and πάσχειν.[4]

---

[2] 307^b18–24: "Ὅτι μὲν οὖν οὐ τοῖς σχήμασι διαφέρει τὰ στοιχεῖα, φανερὸν ἐκ τῶν εἰρημένων· ἐπεὶ δὲ κυριώταται διαφοραὶ τῶν σωνάτων αἵ τε κατὰ τὰ πάθη καὶ τὰ ἔργα καὶ τὰς δυνάμεις (ἑκάστου γὰρ εἶναί φαμεν τῶν φύσει καὶ ἔργα καὶ πάθη καὶ δυνάμεις), πρῶτον ἂν εἴη περὶ τούτων λεκτέον, ὅπως θεωρήσαντες ταῦτα λάβωμεν τὰς ἑκάστου πρὸς ἕκαστον διαφοράς.

[3] I do not wish to suggest that these texts were originally *composed* in that sequence, but they most certainly were intended to be read in that order as a continuous narrative.

It could be instructive to read this ostensibly general account in I. 7 side by side with other passages in the corpus where *poiein* and *paschein* play significant roles. I shall not do this here, for it might result in a mere highlighting of apparent tensions and contradictions.[5] It seems to be more important to turn to the second question asked at the beginning; namely, how the two technical terms ποιεῖν and πάσχειν should best be translated. As is well known, the term πάθος, for example (and by implications its verbal cognate πάσχειν), has many different senses and applies to a broad and diverse semantic field: it can mean the process of being affected, of suffering, physically or mentally; it can mean that which is being suffered, an affliction, injury, or illness; or it can refer to the perfectly harmless affections of the soul, perceptions and feelings; moreover, πάθος in Aristotle can mean the attribute in the widest sense of a ὑποκείμενον; and finally, and more specifically, it can be used synonymously with τὸ ποῖον, a qualitative attribute of a subject. A similar list could be drawn up for ποιεῖν and ποίησις.

The most common translation of ποιεῖν and πάσχειν is 'action' and 'passion'; but these terms, when no context is specified, carry a strong anthropocentric connotation of human activity and emotion. To be sure, Aristotle himself at times slips into a discourse that embraces human activity, for example at the end of chapter 6, when he says that somebody who grieves us touches us without himself being touched by us in turn, or when he speaks of doctors healing their patients. But the purpose of these and other examples is merely to help us better to grasp the mechanisms of qualitative physical processes at levels that lie beyond the domain of what is accessible to the senses. After all, Aristotle is struggling with the problem of how to speak about fundamental microcosmic physical processes *eulogôs, phusikôs,* and above all non-reductively.

'Action' and 'passion' therefore seem to be terms that are in fact too broad and imprecise for the subject matter in hand. 'Agency' and 'patiency', the higher-strung abstract terminology adopted by some commentators, avoids this shortcoming to some extent, but that terminological pair, too, drives an unnecessary and probably unhelpful wedge between our own hermeneutic presuppositions and Aristotle's concern.

---

[4] Aristotle appears to refer to these chapters when he says in *de An.* II. 5. 416[b]35–417[a]2: 'Now some say that like is affected by like; but the sense in which this is possible or impossible we have already stated in our general account of affecting and being affected.'

[5] In *Ph.* III. 1–3 ποιεῖν and πάσχειν are used in a wider sense than here, covering all kinds of changes, not just qualitative changes. In *de An.* II. 5 we get the same distinction as here, that agent and patient are both like and unlike; but in the psychological treatise this is a matter of time: before the change agents and patients are unlike, thereafter like. The text of the *Categories* is unfortunately damaged in ch. 9, where Aristotle begins to discuss ποιεῖν and πάσχειν.

His concern is quite simply that physical substances, and especially the four simple bodies, are capable of *affecting* one another in virtue of their qualitative differences, and that an understanding of the conditions and modes of such processes of interaction (along with touch and mixture) is requisite for an Aristotelian account of natural change.[6] We are looking at a domain of reality in which it is difficult precisely to identify discrete 'agent' and 'patient' bodies, where it seems quite impossible to conceptualize processes in terms of neat chains of A acting on B, B on C, C on D, etc., and, finally, where the 'agents' and 'patients' involved have no awareness of their activity or experience. The dynamics of their mutual interaction is mechanical and blind. Although the language of action (or agency) and passion (or patiency) cannot be avoided completely, I shall, for the reasons indicated, try to turn down the unwanted overtones by speaking simply of (qualitative) 'affection'.

The chapter on qualitative affection, then, can be divided into seven connected sections:[7]

Section I (323ᵇ1–15: περὶ δὲ τοῦ ποιεῖν καὶ πάσχειν λεκτέον ἐφεξῆς ... τοῦτο συμβαίνειν αὐτοῖς). This section functions as the *doxographical opening:* Conflicting and incompatible, indeed contrary, accounts of the mutual affection of natural bodies can be found in the natural philosophy of Aristotle's predecessors. On one view natural affection presupposes similarity, on another it presupposes difference.

Section II (323ᵇ15–29: τὰ μὲν οὖν λεγόμενα ... μήτ' ἐξ ἐναντίων ἐστίν). A *dialectical discussion* of the two received opinions. It seems an important question to ask what exactly Aristotle is doing in this passage, and I shall come back to this question below.

Section III (323ᵇ29–324ᵃ5: ἀλλ' ἐπεὶ οὐ τὸ τυχὸν ... ἕτερα καὶ ἀνόμοια ἀλλήλοις). In this section Aristotle outlines *his own doctrine:* Natural affection occurs among things that either are contraries or have contraries which constitute their specific differences; but agent and patient must also be of the same genus; they are in a sense similar, in a sense different.

---

[6] In fact, we cannot understand Aristotle's view of mixture (I. 10) without it, nor the important Aristotelian tenet that the elements are capable of forming, at a higher level, homoeomeric substances that are not earth, air, fire, and water but in fact wood, flesh, bone, and so on.

[7] As regards the original text, I propose the following readings that are at variance with Joachim's text and largely in agreement with the suggestions made by Verdenius and Waszink (1968). Unfortunately, these readings are of no philosophical consequence:

323ᵇ7: πεφυκέναι with EHJ instead of πέφυκεν
323ᵇ22: τούτων ὄντων οὕτως with FHJG instead of τούτων οὕτως ἐχόντων
324ᵃ15: ὁμοίως with EFHJL instead of ὅμως
324ᵃ35: αὕτη instead of αὐτὴ

Section IV (324^a5–14: ἐπεὶ δὲ τὸ πάσχον καὶ... εἰς τοὐναντίον ἡ γένεσις). A point of *corroboration:* The account just given ties in with (or is indeed explanatory of) the view of generation and corruption expounded earlier.

Section V (324^a14–24: καὶ κατὰ λόγον δὴ... εἰς θάτερα τοὐναντίον). Aristotle's account of natural affection also explains why his predecessors, in holding their views, grasped only the partial truth of the matter and hence created an apparent contradiction.

Section VI (324^a24–^b13: τὸν αὐτὸν δὲ λόγον... τὸ πρῶτον ποιοῦν ἀπαθές). A long section on the analogy between motion and qualitative affection. Just as in the case of motion, we must distinguish between first and proximate causes of affection: as the prime mover is unaffected by anything else, so is the first qualitative agent unaffected by another qualified body. This section is not without difficulties: What role precisely does 'matter' play in these arguments? Is Aristotle introducing the notion of immaterial qualitative agents (Joachim, Williams), or is he operating with the idea of (generically) distinct material substrates (Verdenius, Waszink)? And what is the point of all this?

Section VII (324^b13–22: ἔστι δὲ τὸ ποιητικὸν αἴτιον... ἐπ᾽ ἐκείνων ἂν εἴη τὸ λεγόμενον ἀληθές). Apparently another puzzling passage in which Aristotle relates the theory of natural affection just developed to his theory of causation. Why he does this seems to have a lot to do with what is going on in the previous section.

Chapter I. 7 ends in one of those irritating Aristotelian statements of closure, proclaiming comprehensive clarity precisely at the moment when the various leads, suggestions, and arguments have finally generated maximum obscurity. But at the beginning of the chapter (I. 323^b1–15) the narrative is still unassuming: Aristotle the 'historian' eases his readers into the discussion by a placid piece of doxography.

Section I (323^b1–15)

Affecting and being affected must be discussed next:

We have received conflicting accounts from earlier philosophers. Most hold unanimously at least so much that like is altogether unaffected by like because none of them is more capable of affecting or being affected than the other (since all the same attributes belong to things that are alike in the same way). They claim instead that things that are unlike and different naturally tend to affect, and be affected by, one another. For even when a smaller fire is extinguished by a larger one, it is so affected because of the contrariety involved, they say, for large is contrary to small.

Only Democritus expressed a view peculiarly at variance with that of the others. He says that what affects and is affected is the same and alike, for it is not possible for things that are dissimilar and different to be affected by one another; rather, even if two dissimilar things affect one another in some way, this does not happen to them in so far as they are dissimilar but in so far as some same thing belongs to them.

Aristotle's predecessors offer conflicting views on the question of why things naturally affect one another. The majority of philosophers appeal to the principle of (in-)sufficient reason, arguing that things which are alike can hardly affect one another because there is no reason why one should affect the other rather than vice versa; the things in question possess after all the same attributes in just the same way. Hence, one must embrace the contrary supposition that in fact things that are dissimilar and different are the ones that influence one another.

This latter view, reasonable as it seems, can be challenged by an empirical counterexample of two flames affecting one another. As Philoponus explains, commenting on this passage (*in GC* 140. 14–15), when you hold the flame of an oil lamp near the flame of a bonfire the oil lamp will go out. Prima facie, this seems to be a clear case in which two things that are similar and alike affect one another. The majority, compelled to concede an identity in substance, explains this phenomenon by an appeal to a quantitative difference: a large fire will put out a small one precisely because one is large and the other small.

Although this is not explicitly prompted by the text, it might be instructive to press this majority view a bit further by asking whether dissimilarity and difference were taken to be *sufficient* or merely *necessary* conditions of natural affection? At first sight it seemed as if the claim in 323^{b}6–7 should be read in a strong sense: 'whenever bodies possess dissimilarities and differences they affect one another'. But the example of a lamp being snuffed out by a bonfire should caution one against taking any kind of dissimilarity as sufficient to effect qualitative change. It is certainly not the case that an ice cube is going to melt if it is placed in the vicinity of an iceberg, nor will a deluge dry up a puddle. The only defensible stance seems to be the weaker one, taking dissimilarity as a necessary condition: Whenever there are qualitative affections, they are grounded in some sort of dissimilarity of the bodies involved. At a linguistic level, the cautious construction of φύειν with infinitive in 23^{b}7 (ποιεῖν καὶ πάσχειν ἄλληλα πεφυκέναι) seems to support this reading.[8]

Democritus, whose views are taken very seriously throughout the treatise, is said to disagree with the common view. According to him

---

[8] Cf. LSJ s.v. φύω B II. 2: 'c. inf., to be formed or disposed by nature to do so and so'. The reading of the perfect infinitive πεφυκέναι of the better manuscripts EHJ is well defended by Verdenius and Waszink (1968), 33 f., and seems to be the correct one, though nothing substantive depends on this.

what affects and is affected (taking τό τε ποιοῦν καὶ τὸ πάσχον as the subject of the infinitive) is what is the same and alike, ᵇ11–12.[9] No good grounds are given in support of this view; we get a γάρ clause, but all it contains is a strong denial of the opposite view: 'For it is not possible for things that are dissimilar and different to be affected by one another' (ᵇ12–13).

Again, the Democritean view is best understood as enunciating a necessary, not both a necessary and sufficient, condition for agency and patiency. Whenever there is a process of qualitative affection it occurs in virtue of there being some sort of similarity; *not*: any kind of similarity in bodies invariably initiates qualitative change. To be fair, it needs to be said that the proponents of the two rival explanations of change presumably would not appreciate being asked to parse their causal theory in terms of necessary and sufficient conditions. Similarity and difference are part, so it seems, of a much more fuzzy mode of making sense of the world, in which 'similarity' and 'difference' amount to somewhat more than necessary and somewhat less than sufficient conditions. Precisely how they function as causes or *explanantia* of change would have to be spelled out in much greater detail, and by themselves as set out by Aristotle the two rival theories are much too sketchy to be persuasive. This peculiar way of setting the stage is, as I will suggest below, part and parcel of Aristotle's own rhetorical strategy.

Before going on to the next section I should note that commentators, both ancient and modern, do not normally ask the question why Democritus should wish to hold such a counter-intuitive opinion. The reason that *Aristotle* adduces later on in the chapter (ᵇ24–9), illustrated with the example that 'white' is not affected by 'a line' and vice versa, is neither introduced as Democritus' reasoning nor is it very likely to have been his reasoning. Democritus may have had an independent argument to offer; but it is probably more likely that he took his view to be a corollary of atomism. All atoms are essentially alike, distinguished only in terms of their shape, position, and arrangement. When they interact with one another atoms of the same kind tend to conglomerate, and form more complex substances.

The most important independent evidence, a fragment from Theophrastus' *Phusikai Doxai* preserved by Simplicius, suggests that Aristotle

---

[9] It is an open question whether Democritus is actually alone in holding this view; cf. Joachim's note (1922:130) ad loc: 'It is strange that Aristotle should attribute this view to Demokritos *alone*: for in discussing the theory of Empedokles that "Like perceives Like", he treats it as an application to the relation of Percipient and Perceived of the general principle that "Agent and patient are like". Cf. *de Anima*, e.g. 409ᵇ23 ff., 416ᵇ33 ff., where there is a reference to the present discussion of action–passion.'

is indeed reporting Democritus' view accurately, but here too we hear little about the precise reasoning behind this thesis:

Democritus assumed atoms as matter for the things that exist, and he generated the other things in virtue of their [the atoms'] differences. These are form, position, and arrangement. For *like is naturally disposed to be moved by like*, and kindred bodies are naturally disposed to gather together, and each shape arranged in a different composition produces a different disposition.[10]

Section II (323ᵇ15–29)

Now, these are the things that are said, but those who speak in this way seem to appear to be enunciating contradictory opinions (ὑπεναντία). The dispute arises because each side describes in fact only part of the issue, when it is necessary to look at it as a whole. For it is reasonable that what is alike and in every respect indifferent is not affected at all by what is like it. (For why should one of two things be the cause of affecting rather than the other? In addition, if something could be affected by what is like it, it should also be affected by itself. Yet if this were so, nothing would be imperishable or immovable, if indeed like were able to affect in so far as it is like, since everything would then move itself.)

And the same holds true for what is entirely dissimilar and in no respect the same. For whiteness is presumably not affected by a line, nor a line by whiteness, except somehow by accident, when, say, the line happens to be white or black. For things that neither are contraries nor consist of contraries do not displace one another[11] from their nature.

The doxographical exposition of the problem in the first section seemed clear enough. In the second section (323ᵇ15–29) Aristotle discusses the two received opinions. First he says that those who speak in this way appear to be uttering ὑπεναντία. The not terribly common word ὑπεναντία occurs in *GC* only twice, both times in this chapter (ll. 323ᵇ2 and 16); it is probably best rendered in a loose sense by 'conflicting' or 'contrary' ideas or opinions[12]—tempting as it may be to employ the more technical sense of ὑπεναντία attested in later Greek philosophical literature. There the word has the sense of 'sub-contrary', and in the square of opposites sub-contrary propositions are the kind of (particular) statements that cannot

---

[10] Simp. *in Ph.* 28. 15–21: παραπλησίως δὲ καὶ ὁ ἑταῖρος αὐτοῦ Δημόκριτος ὁ Ἀβδηρίτης ἀρχὰς ἔθετο τὸ πλῆρες καὶ τὸ κενόν, ὧν τὸ μὲν ὄν, τὸ δὲ μὴ ὂν ἐκάλει· ὡς (γὰρ) ὕλην τοῖς οὖσι τὰς ἀτόμους ὑποτιθέντες τὰ λοιπὰ γεννῶσι ταῖς διαφοραῖς αὐτῶν. τρεῖς δέ εἰσιν αὗται ῥυσμὸς τροπὴ διαθιγή, ταὐτὸν δὲ εἰπεῖν σχῆμα καὶ θέσις καὶ τάξις. πεφυκέναι γὰρ τὸ ὅμοιον ὑπὸ τοῦ ὁμοίου κινεῖσθαι καὶ φέρεσθαι τὰ συγγενῆ πρὸς ἄλληλα καὶ τῶν σχημάτων ἕκαστον εἰς ἑτέραν ἑτέραν ἐγκοσμούμενον σύγκρισιν ἄλλην ποιεῖν διάθεσιν.

[11] For ἑαυτά in the sense of ἄλληλα cf. 314ᵃ23, where MS FH reads, no doubt correctly, πρὸς αὐτά (Joachim: πρὸς αὑτά).

[12] According to Bonitz's *Index*, ὑπεναντίον in Aristotle is synonymous with ἐναντίον.

both be false but might well both be true. For example, 'Some diamonds are precious stones' and 'Some diamonds are not precious stones'. Now Aristotle is clearly discussing two universal statements which look like outright contraries:

Natural affection depends on difference.
and
Natural affection depends on similarity.

However, the point is that Aristotle wishes to argue that it is in fact not the case that one is true and the other false (nor of course that both these views are false), but that *both* contain a kernel of the truth (cf. the εὔλογον in ᵇ19). The apparent conflict arises simply because the two sides of the debate failed to grasp the whole matter and therefore enunciated only a partial truth (μέρος τι τυγχάνουσι λέγοντες ἑκάτεροι, ᵇ18).

For an overall interpretation of the chapter it seems extremely important to ask what precisely Aristotle is doing in the next lines (up to ᵇ29); the answer is not at all obvious. At first sight it seems that Aristotle is offering additional arguments; first why it is εὔλογον to agree with the majority, and then why it is εὔλογον to agree with Democritus. This is the way Williams understands the overall strategy of the passage. The problem is that on this reading the arguments Aristotle offers are in fact terribly weak (as we shall see in a moment). Worse than that, they would not have found the backing of the original proponents of the conflicting views.

Let us take the arguments separately; first the one that appears to be supporting *e negativo* the majority (non-Democritean) view that affections depend on differences (ᵇ18–24). It is reasonable to reject the atomists' opinion, Aristotle argues, and deny that things that are similar and wholly undifferentiated affect one another, for (a) why should one of two interacting things be active rather than the other,[13] and (b) if affection by what is similar were possible, affection by the thing itself would be too, because (though this is left unsaid) there is no greater similarity than the identity of one thing with itself.

Presumably none of this would have worried an atomist, who could simply reply to the common reasoning in (a) with (a'): There is indeed no reason why one thing should be more influential than the other; atoms do *interact* with one another on the strength of their similarity, and when they happen to accumulate in some region of space they affect one

---

[13] This repeats the argument of the majority stated in 323ᵇ4–5. Aristotle seems to be adding a consideration of his own to it.

another with atomic forces operating in both directions. And against the specifically Aristotelian attack in (b) the atomists could counter with (b′): Similarity by itself is not a *sufficient* condition for affection; other circumstances such as a critical number of atoms and their proximity have to obtain as well; in consequence, in no case would one have to suppose that a single atom could affect itself.

In this way, an atomist could respond effectively to the first argument and flatly deny the consequence of the second. For in order to make this second argument work Aristotle seems tacitly to have shifted his ground, treating the condition of similarity enunciated by the atomists as a *sufficient* condition; and there is no reason why anyone should concede this move.

Aristotle takes the latter point of self-affection one step further (22–4): 'If this is the case, that is if something can actually affect itself because the similar is capable of acting qua similar, then there wouldn't be anything imperishable or immovable, for everything would move itself.' But this only follows if again one concedes that similarity be treated as a sufficient condition, which is what Aristotle wants the reader to do when he says in 23–4: εἴπερ τὸ ὅμοιον ᾗ ὅμοιον ποιητικόν. It seems clear that an atomist would not have made such a strong claim. And so, if these arguments were set down as a serious attempt to *support* the majority view against Democritus, the attempt is an extraordinarily lame one.

The same is roughly true of the second argument (now supporting Democritus); it amounts to not much more than a counter example *against* the majority view (ᵇ24): 'Likewise it is reasonable to hold (with Democritus) that entirely different things do not affect one another because whiteness is not affected by a line nor a line by whiteness, except somehow by accident.' One cannot imagine that Democritus would have thanked Aristotle for this kind of support, especially when one bears in mind what an atomist has to say about lines and colours. And again, there is no reason to suppose that a proponent of differential affection would have been shaken by this apparently haphazard example.

Philoponus and Joachim both try to make the most of these arguments; only Williams expresses impatient dissatisfaction. To be sure, dissatisfaction must prevail as long as we read this second section of the chapter either as some kind of historical account of the arguments put forward on either side (actually a rather impossible interpretation) or as Aristotle's attempt to support and strengthen the two transmitted opinions respectively in order to highlight the conflict of opinions. It seems to me that Aristotle is neither giving the former nor is he doing the latter. But what is he doing? And is it possible to offer a more charitable reading of the chapter up to this point?

I propose that the two initial sections of this chapter, which have the air of a proper τιθέναι τὰ φαινόμενα approach, are in fact thoroughly dialectical in character, garnished with a modicum of historical gesturing. Aristotle is raising difficulties on either side, but these difficulties are not at all intended to refute one or the other view. (N.B.: Aristotle does not wish to refute them.) Rather, they serve the purpose of furthering understanding of a perplexing issue in a manner that satisfies Aristotle philosophically. To be more precise, the difficulties Aristotle raises are much better understood as difficulties that *he himself* might have to grapple with if he were to adopt either of these views and to attempt to incorporate it into his own body of thought. The absurd consequences that become apparent then help him to articulate the difficulties at a higher level of understanding. One could say that for dialectical and heuristical purposes, that is in order fully to spell out the consequences, Aristotle treats the broad conditions of change enunciated by his predecessors strictly as sufficient conditions. The impossibilities that result then allow him to see what kind of solution he might offer in order to avoid contravening some of his own physical tenets.[14]

The procedure we witness here is the application of a hermeneutical move that Aristotle at times announces and recommends in theoretical terms. In a well-known passage, for example, Aristotle speaks about the usefulness of one of his treatises. The *Topics* is said to be useful (χρήσιμον) πρὸς δὲ τὰς κατὰ φιλοσοφίαν ἐπιστήμας, ὅτι δυνάμενοι πρὸς ἀμφότερα διαπορῆσαι ῥᾷον ἐν ἑκάστοις κατοψόμεθα τἀληθές τε καὶ τὸ ψεῦδος.[15]

Thus, if Aristotle were to follow Democritus and to identify similarity as such and without qualification as a principle of physical affection he might be forced to abandon his belief in imperishable and immobile substances. Likewise, if he followed the majority he might have to concede the possibility of affection across category boundaries. Neither of these consequences is acceptable, but since it is not possible to dismiss one view in favour of the other, nor to dismiss them both, Aristotle offers a solution which acknowledges a partial truth in each of them.[16] One

---

[14] The Aristotelian tenets put in jeopardy by the Democritean view are that motion involves a mover and a moved and that there are things that are imperishable and unmoved (cf. 323^b21–4); the tenet possibly undermined by the majority view is that physical affection does not operate across categories (cf. 323^b25–8).

[15] Cf. *Top.* I. 2. 101^a34–6. Other examples are *EN* VII. 2. 1146^b6–8: αἱ μὲν οὖν ἀπορίαι τοιαῦταί τινες συμβαίνουσιν, τούτων δὲ τὰ μὲν ἀνελεῖν δεῖ τὰ δὲ καταλιπεῖν· ἡ γὰρ λύσις τῆς ἀπορίας εὕρεσίς ἐστιν; or again, at the beginning of *Metaph.* III. 1. 995a27–31: ἔστι δὲ τοῖς εὐπορῆσαι βουλομένοις προὔργου τὸ διαπορῆσαι καλῶς· ἡ γὰρ ὕστερον εὐπορία λύσις τῶν πρότερον ἀπορουμένων ἐστί, λύειν δ' οὐκ ἔστιν ἀγνοοῦντας τὸν δεσμόν, ἀλλ' ἡ τῆς διανοίας ἀπορία δηλοῖ τοῦτο περὶ τοῦ πράγματος.

[16] That Aristotle is debating, as it were, with *himself* receives support from the rather obscure sentence ^b28–9: οὐκ ἐξίστησι γὰρ ἄλληλα τῆς φύσεως ὅσα μήτ' ἐναντία μήτ' ἐξ

cannot overlook the fact that the accomplished *effect* of this entire discourse is to favourably dispose the reader towards the Aristotelian narrative that follows, spelling out the solution to an aporia constructed in Aristotelian terms. Once the dialectical procedure and rhetorical purpose of the text up to this point are understood, there is no reason to be overly dissatisfied with it.[17]

Section III (323^{b}29–324^{a}5)

But since no chance thing is naturally disposed to being affected and to affect but rather those that either have a contrariety or are contraries, that which affects and that which is affected must be similar in genus, in fact identical, yet dissimilar and contrary in species. Body is of a nature to be affected by body, flavour by flavour, and colour by colour; in general, something of a given genus is affected by something of the same genus. The reason for this is that in all instances contraries belong to the same genus, and that it is contraries which mutually affect one another. In consequence, both what affects and what is affected must in some sense be the same, in another sense different and unlike one another.

Section IV (324^{a}5–14)

Since what is affected and what affects are the same in genus and alike, but unlike in species, and since contraries are just like that, it is evident that contraries and their intermediates are capable of mutually affecting one another—and indeed, corruption and generation generally take place among these contraries. Which is why it immediately stands to reason, too, that fire warms and a cold thing cools, and that in general an agent of an affection assimilates the affected thing to itself; for they are contraries, and generation is a process into the contrary. In consequence, what is affected must change into the agent, for only in this way will there be generation into the contrary.

After the dialectical debate stating clearly the difficulties to be avoided, Aristotle is quick to outline his own solution to the quandary (Sect. III: 323^{b}29–324^{a}5). First he reiterates his doctrine that natural affection presupposes not just similarity or difference but in fact contrariety, which is a similarity in difference. Contraries properly understood are never random entities but always related to one another as differences

ἐναντίων ἐστίν. ('For things that neither are contraries nor consist of contraries do not displace each other from their nature.') This thoroughly Aristotelian reason justifies (γάρ) the claim in the first part of the previous sentence that 'line' and 'white' do not affect one another.

[17] This does not mean that I approve of either Philoponus' or Joachim's grasp of these passages.

within a common genus. And so in one sense ($\pi\hat{\omega}s$ $\mu\acute{\epsilon}\nu$) natural affection presupposes similarity between the items involved, namely at a generic level, in another sense ($\pi\hat{\omega}s$ $\delta\acute{\epsilon}$) it presupposes a difference, namely at the level of specific differentiae.

Once the general direction in which the solution has to be sought is clear Aristotle proceeds to tie it in with his earlier account of generation and corruption, Section IV (324^{a}5–14). Agency and patiency take place among things that are contrary to one another, and it is precisely in this same realm of nature's contraries that we find generation and corruption. Fire heats and water cools, and in general each agent causes the affected body to become like the agent, thus initiating a change from one contrary to the other. Hence, the doctrine that agency and patiency occur among contraries dovetails nicely with the theory that generation and destruction too involve contrariety. Aristotle does not explicitly address the question whether he wants the processes of natural affection to be restricted to cases of generation where something becomes something, or whether they are also at play in cases of generation *haplôs*. Lines 7–8 ($\kappa\alpha\grave{\iota}$ $\gamma\grave{\alpha}\rho$ $\ddot{o}\lambda\omega s$ $\varphi\theta o\rho\grave{\alpha}$ $\kappa\alpha\grave{\iota}$ $\gamma\acute{\epsilon}\nu\epsilon\sigma\iota s$ $\grave{\epsilon}\nu$ $\tau o\acute{\upsilon}\tau o\iota s$) appear to be a clear statement pointing in the latter direction. But the language in the following lines insists that generation is a change from one contrary to another, and this tallies better with cases of generation *tis*. The tension disappears if one supposes that Aristotle is focusing on the generation of elements from one another, in which case generation *tis* is generation *haplôs* and vice versa.

Section V (324^{a}14–24)

And it is reasonable, too,[18] that the two sides got a hold of the matter in a similar way,[19] even if they don't say the same things. For sometimes we say that the substrate is being affected (for example, we say that a human being is cured and warmed and cooled and such similar things), but at other instances we say that the cold is being warmed or the ailment is being cured. Both kinds of expression are correct (and similarly in the case of the agent, when we sometimes say that a human being is warming, at other times that what is warm is warming). For in the former case it is affected as matter, in the latter as contrary. Hence, those who inspected the former case believed that what affects and is affected must have some same thing in common, whereas those who inspected the latter case believed that they had to have a contrary.

Section V diverts the readers' attention briefly away from Aristotle's exposition of his own doctrine and reopens the perspective on the

---

[18] The $\kappa\alpha\grave{\iota}$ $\kappa\alpha\tau\grave{\alpha}$ $\lambda\acute{o}\gamma o\nu$ in 324^{a}14 picks up the $\delta\iota\grave{o}$ $\kappa\alpha\grave{\iota}$ $\epsilon\ddot{\upsilon}\lambda o\gamma o\nu$ in ^{a}9.

[19] Reading $\acute{o}\mu o\acute{\iota}\omega s$ with EFHJL instead of $\ddot{o}\mu\omega s$ (the reading of a second hand in J and probably Philoponus' text) adopted by Joachim. See Verdenius and Waszink (1968), 36.

dialectical discussion earlier in the chapter. If Aristotle's solution has received corroboration from its seamless congruency with his account of generation and corruption, it can be given an additional boost by the fact that it allows him to offer a persuasive explanation of the origin of doctrinal conflict among his predecessors. What Aristotle offers is a meta-theory: a theory about a theory.

First he makes a comment about the way we speak (λέγομεν, 324^{a}15 ff.). In some cases we say that a human being is being cured and warmed and refreshed and so on; in other cases we say that the cold is warmed or an affliction cured. Both of these modes of speaking are valid (and there is in fact a corresponding usage with active verbs: a human being warms/the temperature warms). In one case the language picks out the fact that an underlying material substrate is being affected, in the other case it is the contrary quality itself. The reason why his predecessors had gone astray was that each side exclusively inspected (εἰς ἐκεῖνο βλέψαντες, ^{a}22) one aspect while ignoring the other.

This seems to be roughly right: The majority presumably concluded from the observation that identical qualities do not interact with one another that qualitative changes in nature presuppose, as a necessary condition, some kind of contrariety and difference in the qualities. The atomists, who looked at change in their idiosyncratic way, concluded that the interaction of material atoms at the higher level of emergent properties presupposes some kind of basic similarity, since one atom alone is neither hot nor cold and so on. What his predecessors should have done, Aristotle seems to imply, is to pay attention to the way we speak and to use the analysis of language as a tool to discover scientific truths. For Aristotle, this type of analysis had become second nature, as it were, based on the belief in the essential congruence of words, concepts, and things that underlies the *Categories*.

We must now turn to a discussion of the substantial sixth section, which offers numerous hermeneutic difficulties that are aggravated by sloppy penmanship; the text is both unpolished and philosophically dense.

Section VI (324^{a}24–^{b}13)

One must assume that the same account applies to affecting and being affected as it applied to being moved and moving. For we speak of a 'mover', too, in two different senses, since both of the following seem to move: that in which the principle of motion resides (a principle is primary among causes) and again that which is last in relation to what is moved, and to generation. The same is true in the case of the agent of an affection, since we say that both a doctor and wine procure health.

Now in the case of motion nothing prevents the first mover from being unmoved (in some cases this is even necessary), but the last mover always moves while being moved. In the case of affection, the first is unaffected, but the last is also affected itself. For all those things that do not have the same matter, what brings about the affection is unaffected (for example the art of medicine: although this (αὔτη) is what procures health, it is not at all affected by what is being healed); however, the food affects and is itself affected somehow, be it that it is warmed or cooled or subject to some other change just when it affects the body. The art of medicine functions as principle, whereas the food functions as the last thing, which is also in contact with what it affects.

So, all affecting agents that do not have their form in matter are unaffected, those that do have their form in matter *can* be affected, for according to us the matter of either one of the opposite qualities is the same in a similar way, so to speak, as the genus is the same, and something that can be warm is necessarily warmed if the source of heat is present and draws near. Which is why, as has just been said, some of the affecting agents are unaffected, others are liable to be affected, and the same mode applies to affection as it does to the case of motion. For there the first mover is unmoved, and in the case of affection the first agent is unaffected.

It is best to begin by taking stock of what has been established so far. First, qualitative affection in nature depends on contrariety, that is to say differences which share some generic similarity: qualitative affection occurs among contrary qualities, flavours, colours, etc.

Second, the way we speak allows us to enunciate agents and patients in two different ways: we can either refer to the carriers of the quality, the *hypokeimenon*, or we can refer to the quality proper, whether it affects or is affected. Both modes of speaking are admissible. We also take away from the previous chapter, I. 6, that qualitative affection presupposes a touching of the bodies whenever they affect one another.

That previous chapter, in its discussion of touch, also pointed out that change (κίνησις) and qualitative affection (ποίησις) are closely related, except that the latter is a narrower concept than the former (I. 6. 323ᵃ12–20): Every ποίησις is a κίνησις, but not every κίνησις is a ποίησις. Now that in chapter 7 qualitative affection has been further specified, and specified in a way that would not readily apply to the general notion of change (namely, as involving generic similarity and specific difference), the question arises how this is going to affect the conceptual relationship between change in general and qualitative affection? Aristotle focuses on the issue of whether or not one must suppose that there is, in the case of qualitative affection, just as there was in change in general, a first unaffected agent of qualitative change. This seems to be one of the central issues problematized in the present section.

Ammonius and Philoponus (*in GC* 150. 3 ff) think that the issue at stake in lines 324ᵃ24 ff. is rather the phenomenon of reciprocal affection:

when A heats B, B in turn cools A. I don't think that this is correct; reciprocal affection was an issue that appeared dimly on the horizon of the previous chapter, but it is never turned into a central issue, nor is it thought to be problematic.[20] Nevertheless, as we shall see, the direction in which Ammonius and Philoponus point us is a helpful one.

Aristotle opens section VI of chapter I. 7 with the remark that his discussion of qualitative change has in fact not driven a wedge between it and change in general (τὸν αὐτὸν δὲ λόγον ὑποληπτέον εἶναι κτλ.). One of Aristotle's central concerns in the *Physics* was to argue that (a) everything that moves (intransitively) is moved by something, and that (b) there must necessarily be at least one instance of such a (transitive) mover which is not moved by anything—a first unmoved mover—for otherwise one would arrive at an inscrutable and infinite chain of moved movers. And so the question arises quite naturally: Does the distinction between unmoved and moved movers carry over into the realm of qualitative affection?

Why should Aristotle be concerned about this? One reason is, I suppose, that he might be worried that his discussion of qualitative affection could jeopardize his more general notion of change. In *Physics* III. 3 Aristotle spelled out his conception of κίνησις in terms of ποιεῖν and πάσχειν, using these two terms in a very loose sense to cover all sorts of change. Evidently, that chapter committed Aristotle to regarding the processes that take place between ποιοῦντα and πάσχοντα as types of κίνησις, and this commitment is borne out in *GC* I. 6. But if ποιεῖν and πάσχειν are more specifically understood as qualitative affections that presuppose contrariety, and if contraries cannot exist separately but always require a substrate which, qua matter, is itself susceptible to qualitative change, and if moreover qualitative change is therefore just the kind of process that is so clearly *reciprocal*, it does not seem at all obvious that one is obliged to postulate a first cause of qualitative change in order to avoid an infinite regress. One way for Aristotle to tackle the issue might have been to admit that processes of qualitative change, just like the endless chain of generation and decay, do indeed have no first member but constitute an infinite *cyclical* process of a finite set of qualified natural substances. He could have defended this move by pointing out that locomotion is in fact prior to qualitative change[21] (just as it is prior to generation and corruption; cf. *GC* II. 10), and that although we have to postulate a first unmoved local mover, there is no reason also to postulate a first unaffected source of qualitative change.

---

[20] The notion of reciprocal affection plays a role later, in 10. 328^{a}19 ff., when Aristotle begins to offer his own solution to the problem of mixture. Other instances of the notion of reciprocal affection are *Ph.* VIII. 5. 257^{b}21–4; *Mem.* 453^{a}26–8.

[21] Cf. *Ph.* VIII. 7. 261^{a}18–23.

Aristotle resists a move such as this presumably because he wants the analogy between κίνησις and ποίησις to hold, and because he evidently entertains a different view of the global scenario of qualitative affection. So, what does Aristotle have in mind?

In order to get a better handle on the passage before us, it is helpful to return to the suggestion made by Ammonius and Philoponus; that is, that this passage involves the notion of reciprocal affection. In the *Physics* Aristotle canvassed the distinction between moved and unmoved movers using the chain model as paradigm: A moves B, B moves C, C moves D, and so on. D is a moved mover because it is moved by C, C is a moved mover because it is moved by B, and B in turn by A, but A is the initiator of the whole sequence. In the present chapter, when Aristotle wants to distinguish between the unaffected first initiator and the last agent of qualitative change (324^a32-4), the criterion he uses to draw a line between them is that the former is not *reciprocally* affected by the object it affects whereas the latter is so affected (cf. e.g. what he says about food in 324^b1-3).

Adopting this reciprocal model of change instead of the chain model of the *Physics* leads Aristotle to explain the difference between first and last qualitative agent by the puzzling distinction between things that have the same matter and those that do not have the same matter.[22]

What does Aristotle mean by qualities that have matter in common? He cannot mean numerical *identity* of the material substrate. For example, red, hot, and solid are all properties of a piece of metal being forged and share the numerically same matter; but these qualities do not interact with one another, as they are supposed to do in this context. For qualities to be able to interact with one another they have to be of the same genus, like hot/cold, wet/dry. But he cannot possibly mean that *these* latter qualities can share the numerically same matter, because they can't. The processes of interaction are precisely the physical expression of this impossibility. Hence, there seems to be a fundamental difference between genus and matter: If two contraries are of the same genus (and thus form a pair), they will never share the numerically same matter at the same time; if two contraries do share the same matter at the same time, they are not going to be of the same genus.

So perhaps when Aristotle speaks of the same matter he means 'the same matter in kind'. But in that case we run the danger of losing the distinction, because, as Ammonius and Philoponus point out (146. 1 ff.),

---

[22] This latter distinction is not just a slip of the pen, for it recurs in 10. 328^a19-22: τὰ μὲν οὖν ἀντιστρέφει, ὅσων ἡ αὐτὴ ὕλη ἐστί, καὶ ποιητικὰ ἀλλήλων καὶ παθητικὰ ὑπ' ἀλλήλων· τὰ δὲ ποιεῖ ἀπαθῆ ὄντα, ὅσων μὴ ἡ αὐτὴ ὕλη.

all things in the sublunary realm of qualitative change ultimately share the same kind of matter and should therefore in principle be able to affect one another reciprocally. But the worry should not deter us from further pursuing this line of interpretation. There are three indications both that Aristotle meant by identity here identity-in-kind and that he was aware of the difficulty that arises from this sense.

The first indication is that he fine-tunes his example in lines 29–30. The 'doctor' was good enough as an instance of a first and presumably unaffected agent; yet in line 35 he finds it safer to speak of the art of medicine as that which initiates health. The reader might swallow more readily that medicine qua λόγος of health does not share a common kind of matter with the patient,[23] whereas the doctor certainly does.

Next, as he continues to labour over the distinction, Aristotle drops the specification αὐτή and speaks simply about matter (324ᵃ34, with ᵇ4 and ᵇ5): agents that are not in matter are impassive, agents that are in matter are susceptible to affection.[24] Aristotle could have written ἐν τῇ αὐτῇ ὕλῃ;[25] the sense would have been the same, given that αὐτός here means 'the same in kind'.

The third indication occurs in the sentence immediately following in which the specification of identity, which had dropped out of sight, is brought to the fore again. Unfortunately, that sentence (τὴν μὲν γὰρ ὕλην λέγομεν ὁμοίως ὡς εἰπεῖν τὴν αὐτὴν εἶναι τῶν ἀντικειμένων ὁποτερουοῦν, ὥσπερ γένος ὄν) is one of the more puzzling clauses of the whole treatise, and it is not immediately obvious how it should be translated. I tentatively offer the following: 'For we enunciate matter in the same way, that is to say that it is the same of either one of two opposite qualities, as if it were a genus.'[26]

Now what this means, I take it, is that for the purpose of the present argument one could look at the matter of black and white as the same in

---

[23] Cf. e.g. *PA* I. 1. 640ᵃ31–2: ἡ δὲ τέχνη λόγος τοῦ ἔργου ὁ ἄνευ τῆς ὕλης ἐστίν.

[24] To spell the short sentences out completely: 'All those things capable of influencing that do not have their form in matter are unaffected, but those things capable of influencing that do have their form in matter are susceptible to affection.'

[25] The suggestion of Verdenius and Waszink (1968), 38.

[26] There is a possibility that the phrase ὡς εἰπεῖν τὴν αὐτὴν εἶναι τῶν ἀντικειμένων ὁποτερουοῦν originated as a marginal gloss that intended to explain what it means to treat matter, for the purpose of the argument, as a genus: τὴν μὲν γὰρ ὕλην λέγομεν ὁμοίως ὥσπερ γένος ὄν. The participle ὄν, which should really be οὖσαν, has presumably been changed to the neuter by attraction. In addition, I take ὁμοίως as looking forward to ὥσπερ; Joachim (1922) and Forster (1955) take it to qualify ὁποτερουοῦν, though they can't be doing this for any grammatical reason; Williams (1982) leaves the word untranslated. He writes: 'For we say that each of a pair of opposites has more or less the same matter, which is like the genus'. Verdenius and Waszink (1968) do not translate this clause but take it to imply that it 'does not mean matter in general but a distinct matter, viz. which two things have in common'. My own translation agrees perhaps best with Forster's: '(F)or we say that the matter of either of the two opposed things alike is the same, so to speak, being, as it were, a kind.'

kind, and likewise the matter of hot and cold, or soft and brittle, sweet and sour, etc. Although each of these properties does not exist in the same bit of matter at the same time as its contrary, the matter that carries the opposite quality is in fact the same in kind. This accounts for the fact that some pairs of contraries are only found in particular kinds of matter: sweet and sour are not properties of the elementary bodies, for example. And so, just as two contraries always fall under the same genus, they also always presuppose and involve the same kind of matter.

And now, going back to line 324^b5-6 and the phrase ὅσα δ᾽ ἐν ὕλῃ παθητικά, what Aristotle is suggesting on the basis of this conception of matter as a kind of genus for contraries is that whenever we have a quality embedded in matter we also have a receptivity and possibility for qualitative affection by its contrary. Matter qua potentially qualified substrate ensures this, and qualitative change will necessarily take place if only one further condition is realized; namely, proximity: πλησιάζοντος ἀνάγκη θερμαίνεσθαι (324^b8-9).

So what is the overall train of thought in this section? In the *Physics* the necessity to avoid an infinite regress led to the postulate of a prime mover which was then further specified as an incorporeal entity on the strength of the argument that it must have infinite capacity to cause motion and no finite body can have such an infinite capacity (cf. *Ph.* VIII. 10. 266^a10 ff.). Here, in the treatise on generation and corruption, Aristotle distinguishes right away between corporeal and incorporeal agents of qualitative change. The former, which are always in matter, are invariably going to be reciprocally affected by their own action *in some way* precisely because matter is like an extremely broad genus receptive of any kind of contrariety (324^b6-7; cf. 324^b18). The latter are not so affected, and the upshot of section VI is, then, that ποίησις parallels κίνησις in the sense that in both cases we will have affected and unaffected agents.

And so, wholly in agreement with the discussion in the *Physics*, Aristotle further insists in the last sentence of the section (324^b12-13) that there is some first thing which is entirely unsusceptible to qualitative affection: τὸ πρῶτον ποιοῦν ἀπαθές. What in the world could this be? Although this is not explicitly stated, it seems best to understand, with Williams, the last section of the chapter (section VII: 324^b13-24) as a preliminary enquiry into the nature of this unaffected agent of qualitative change.

Section VII (324^b13-24)

The affecting cause has to be understood as the principle from which the change arises. But the 'for the sake of which' is not causing an affection (which is why health does not cause an affection, except in a metaphorical sense). Moreover, when an agent is present something becomes affected, but when certain dispositions are present nothing is affected any longer but it already is; forms and ends are kinds of dispositions.

Matter qua matter is receptive of affection. But now, fire has heat in its matter, and if there were something that is warm separately, that indeed would not be affected at all. Now, perhaps it is impossible that there be such a thing, separately, but if there are such things, what we have said would be true of them.

In this way, then, let it have been determined what affecting and being affected is, and to what things it belongs and why and how.

Reading this final section of the chapter, it seems obvious that Aristotle has *something* quite concrete in mind here, but it is equally obvious that he is not giving it away easily. Key words in the passage are $αἴτιον$, $ἀρχή$, $τὸ οὗ ἕνεκα$, $ἕξις$, $εἶδος$, $τέλος$, $ὕλη$, and above all it seems that Aristotle is going through his list of causes, eliminating possible suggestions of what kind of cause the $πρῶτον ποιοῦν ἀπαθές$ might be. One such suggestion, surely informed by what we know of the prime mover, is that the first qualitative agent be a final cause. That however, Aristotle points out, must be ruled out because the $ποιητικὸν αἴτιον$ has to be understood as that *from which* the change originates. Final causes do not function as causes 'from which' (324^b13-15), and so the primary cause of affections cannot be conceptualized as a final cause. Some scholars think that this passage is irreconcilably at variance with *Metaphysics* book XII. But this is only so if we suppose in advance that the $πρῶτον ποιοῦν$ better coincide with the supreme prime mover specified in *Metaphysics* book XII as a final cause.[27]

The $πρῶτον ποιοῦν$ is also not going to turn out to be a disposition ($ἕξις$), because dispositions are as such not productive of anything; a form ($εἶδος$) or a form in completion ($τέλος$) are dispositions ($^b15-18$), and they must therefore be ruled out as candidates for the first cause of qualitative change.

The $πρῶτον ποιοῦν$ is also not going to be a material cause because matter is precisely the kind of thing that is per se passive and susceptible to affection ($^b18$).

Heracliteans might think that fire is actually the entity we are looking for, but the heat of fire subsists in matter, and in virtue of that fact, as the previous argumentation has shown, even fire will be susceptible to change and therefore not be $ἀπαθές$ ($^b18-19$).[28]

---

[27] On the question of whether or not the prime mover in Aristotle is ambiguously invested with final and efficient causality cf. Broadie (1993), Judson (1994), 165, and Laks (2000).

[28] Cf. also the explicit statement in *GC* II. 9. 336^a6ff.: $φαίνεται δὲ καὶ τὸ πῦρ αὐτὸ κινούμενον καὶ πάσχον$.

At first sight, the final suggestion (that there might be some θερμὸν χωριστόν) seems to be targeted, in a familiar vein, at the Platonists; they might propose that Aristotle's πρῶτον ποιοῦν is in fact the immaterial form of fire, existing separately. Aristotle concedes that this indeed would not be affected (τοῦτο οὐθὲν ἂν πάσχοι), and goes on to remark that it is of course an open question whether some such separate forms actually exist (ᵇ21–2). But the anti-Platonist reading of these lines cannot be right. Material, formal, and final causes have been excluded from consideration, and Aristotle is evidently looking for a primary *efficient* cause of qualitative change, and even for Plato forms are not efficient causes. Rather than taking this as a rejection of a Platonic way of answering the question, we should regard these last lines as indicating the only possible direction in which a first cause of affection in nature might be sought.

The chapter concludes with a profession of comprehensive clarity: τί μὲν οὖν τὸ ποιεῖν καὶ πάσχειν ἐστὶ καὶ τίσιν ὑπάρχει καὶ διὰ τί καὶ πῶς, διωρίσθω τοῦτον τὸν τρόπον. The ancient commentators were very good at spelling out summary statements such as this. Ammonius and Philoponus explain concisely, 153. 12–16:[29]

Ποιεῖν means to incur a πάθος; πάσχειν means to be subjected to a πάθος; in the course of the process, the affected body is assimilated to the agent body; the process belongs to contraries and is grounded in the fact that matter is common and capable of receiving these contraries; the manner in which it takes place is that the agent has to approach the patient.

Aristotle's final sentence, even if it is fleshed out in this way by the commentators, provides only a closure of sorts, for it in no way satisfies his readers' curiosity, left as they are to ponder the tantalizing question: What is the πρῶτον ποιοῦν ἀπαθές?

In the terse and laconic Section VII (324ᵇ13–24) we learn a lot about what the first agent of qualitative change is not, but Aristotle refuses, here as elsewhere (if I am not mistaken) positively to specify what the πρῶτον ποιοῦν is, and how exactly it is going to be related to the prime mover of the *Physics* or *Metaphysics*.

Since Aristotle does not tell us here what he has in mind, we have to resort to speculation and rely on other passages from the *Corpus Aristotelicum*. One thing that the chapter does make clear is that whenever we wish fully to understand and explain some particular and perhaps even

---

[29] Phlp. *in GC*, 153. 12–16: ῞Οτι π ο ι ε ῖ ν ἐστι τὸ εἰς πάθος ἄγειν, π ά σ χ ε ι ν δὲ τὸ εἰς πάθος ἄγεσθαι · καὶ ὅτι ποιεῖν ἐστι τὸ ὁμοιοῦν ἑαυτῷ τὸ πάσχον, πάσχειν δὲ τὸ ὁμοιοῦθαι τῷ ποιοῦντι. κ α ὶ τ ί σ ι ν ὑ π ά ρ χ ε ι. ὅτι τοῖς ἐναντίοις. κ α ὶ δ ι ὰ τ ί. διὰ τὸ κοινὴν ὕλην ἔχειν δεκτικὴν τῶν ἐναντίων παθῶν. κ α ὶ π ῶ ς. ὅτι προσιόντος τοῦ ποιοῦντος καὶ πλησιάζοντος τῷ πάσχοντι.

quite complex process of bodies affecting one another, we need to look
for some agent that has initiated that process but is itself not reciprocally
involved in it. The first cause of some particular instance of an affection
is itself not affected, and Aristotle explained in this chapter that the way
in which this can be so is when and if the first cause is immaterial. The
example he mentions is the art of medicine (324^{a}35), and we can safely
infer from this that, in general, whenever a process of affection is initiated by a rational agent we can point to an intention, a plan, skill, or
expertise which ultimately explains that this process is going on. On this
reading, the first cause need not be some one thing in the strict sense, but
it could be a number of different items for different changes, all of which
share the characteristic feature that they do not rely on some material
substrate for their being.

  Yet, this view of the matter is not wholly satisfactory, for two reasons.
There are, in Aristotle's view presumably, many affections which are not
so caused. For want of a better example: when a maggot affects in an
adverse way the piece of ham it happens to live in, it seems quite impossible to invoke an immaterial art or design as first and unaffected cause
of *that* particular affection. Moreover, if the analogy between κίνησις and
ποίησις is as close as Aristotle claims it to be, there ought to be, just as
there is in the case of κίνησις, a first and primary cause of *all* affections in
the material world. One possibility would be to argue that the πρῶτον
ποιοῦν is in fact identical with the prime mover we are already familiar
with from the *Physics* and *Metaphysics*. This hypothesis would harmon-
ize well with the requirement that the πρῶτον ποιοῦν has to be immaterial.
However, the passage already mentioned, where Aristotle points out that
the primary cause of (all) affections cannot be a final cause (324^{b}13–15)
forcefully militates against this suggestion. What we are looking for is
a universal, immaterial, efficient first cause of qualitative changes
in matter.

  One way to move forward could be to remind ourselves that it
was possible to understand Aristotle's specification in 324^{b}4 ὅσα μὲν οὖν
μὴ ἐν ὕλῃ κτλ., as shorthand for ὅσα μὴ ἔχει τὴν αὐτὴν ὕλην (see 324^{a}34)
and to mean that the first causes of such changes are required
not to be in the same kind of matter. In other words, we may wish
to resist Williams's suggestion that Aristotle is actually committed to
the strict requirement of immateriality.[30] The most evident cause of
qualitative change in nature is of course the sun, and if we relax
the requirement of immateriality it is possible to see what Aristotle
may be hinting at. The sun is a material body, but its matter (ether) is
of such superior character that it is wholly unaffected by the changes in

---

[30] Cf. Williams (1982), 123: 'The possibility of immaterial agents must not be ruled out'.

the sublunary world.[31] According to Aristotle, too, the sun is itself not hot; rather, it causes heat through the friction its movement generates in the lower spheres:

> But the upper bodies are carried each on its sphere; hence, they do not catch fire themselves, but the air which lies beneath the sphere of the revolving element is necessarily heated by its revolution, and especially in that part where the sun is fixed.[32] (Guthrie)

If we wish to tighten the requirement of immateriality again, we could say that, strictly speaking, the god responsible for the movement of the sun along the ecliptic is ultimately the cause of the sublunary bodies mutually affecting each other.[33] Aristotle can say, for example, that the movement along the ecliptic is responsible for coming to be and passing away: 'Which is why the cause of coming to be and passing away is not the first movement, but the movement along the ecliptic' (GC II. 10. 336ª31–2).

It is moreover not entirely surprising that here, in the discussion of *poiein* and *paschein*, Aristotle does not simply dogmatically state that the sun is the primary cause of the ubiquitous mutations, changes, and alterations in the physical world. For in order for this to be palatable he would have to give a rather complex account of what the sun is (an ether-body), how it transmits heat to the lower regions (through friction), and how precisely it generates the seasons (through the variation of its distance from us when it travels along the ecliptic). This account would have to show, above all, that the sun is entirely unaffected by the qualitative changes of the sublunary world. What we get instead is little more than vague and suggestive hints. Admittedly, a certain amount of puzzlement remains, for in other contexts Aristotle was perfectly happy to surprise his readers with startling and uncorroborated statements such as ἄνθρωπος γὰρ ἄνθρωπον γεννᾷ–καὶ ἥλιος (*Ph.* II. 2. 194ᵇ13).

---

[31] The matter of the celestial bodies is wholly distinct from the matter of the sublunary world and not subject to any kind of change, except locomotion, cf. *Cael.* I. 2–3, esp. 270ᵇ1–4.

[32] See *Cael.* II. 7. 289ª28–34: τῶν δὲ ἄνω ἕκαστον ἐν τῇ σφαίρᾳ φέρεται, ὥστ᾽ αὐτὰ μὲν μὴ ἐκπυροῦσθαι, τοῦ δ᾽ ἀέρος ὑπὸ τὴν τοῦ κυκλικοῦ σώματος σφαῖραν ὄντος ἀνάγκη φερομένης ἐκείνης ἐκθερμαίνεσθαι, καὶ ταύτῃ μάλιστα ᾗ ὁ ἥλιος τετύχηκεν ἐνδεδεμένος· διὸ δὴ πλησιάζοντός τε αὐτοῦ καὶ ἀνίσχοντος καὶ ὑπὲρ ἡμῶν ὄντος γίγνεται ἡ θερμότης. See also *Mete.* I. 3. 341ª19–27: τὸ μὲν οὖν γίγνεσθαι τὴν ἀλέαν καὶ τὴν θερμότητα ἱκανή ἐστιν παρασκευάζειν καὶ ἡ τοῦ ἡλίου φορὰ μόνον· ταχεῖάν τε γὰρ δεῖ καὶ μὴ πόρρω εἶναι. ἡ μὲν οὖν τῶν ἄστρων ταχεῖα μὲν πόρρω δέ, ἡ δὲ τῆς σελήνης κάτω μὲν βραδεῖα δέ. ἡ δὲ τοῦ ἡλίου ἄμφω ταῦτα ἔχει ἱκανῶς. τὸ δὲ μᾶλλον γίγνεσθαι ἅμα τῷ ἡλίῳ αὐτῷ τὴν θερμότητα εὔλογον, λαμβάνοντας τὸ ὅμοιον ἐκ τῶν παρ᾽ ἡμῖν γιγνομένων· καὶ γὰρ ἐνταῦθα τῶν βίᾳ φερομένων ὁ πλησιάζων ἀὴρ μάλιστα γίγνεται θερμός. The same view is enunciated in *GC* II. 10. 336ᵇ5–18, except that here the sun's drawing near is said to cause coming to be, its receding passing away.

[33] Cf. the reference to a god in *GC* II. 10. 336ᵇ32.

9

On Generation and Corruption I. 8

EDWARD HUSSEY

Introduction

1. Having discussed the general nature of acting on and being acted on ('action–passion'; ποιεῖν καὶ πάσχειν) in I. 7, Aristotle turns in I. 8 and 9 to the question of 'how it is possible for this [action–passion] to come about' (324ᵇ25, cf. 326ᵇ29–30, 327ᵃ27–8). This question seems to mean: What possibilities are there for what actually happens, in terms of natural bodies and their interactions, in any case of action–passion? A similar demand for an account of the physical realities involved in natural processes appears earlier at 315ᵃ32–ᵇ6, where Democritus is praised for being the only previous theorist to have given a well-worked-out account of this kind for growth, mixture, and action–passion, and in general for being good at giving such accounts.[1] In I. 7 this question of the physical mechanism has been answered, if at all, only in the broadest outline, though 324ᵇ23 seems to imply that it has had some sort of answer. I. 8 begins with the proposal to reconsider the question (324ᵇ25), and proceeds to give a review of previous theories (Aristotle's own substantive account being reserved for I. 9).

2. As usual, Aristotle first sets out then critically discusses the opinions of his predecessors. The division between the two stages is marked by the formulaic sentence at 325ᵇ12–13.

The menu of previous theories is meagre. As just mentioned, Aristotle has previously complained (315ᵃ29–ᵇ6) of the poverty of earlier theorizing on the subject, with the shining exception of Democritus. Just two types of theory are considered: action–passion 'through pores' (324ᵇ26, 325ᵇ2: Empedocles and others), and 'through the void' (325ᵇ3: the

---

[1] See David Sedley's paper on *GC* I. 2 in Ch. 2 of this volume, pp. 65 ff. Compare also *GC* II. 7.334ᵃ15–27, where Aristotle turns from the rejection (II. 6), on general grounds, of Empedocles' theory of non-convertible elements, to the demand for an account of the physical structure of homoeomerous compounds (πῶς ᵃ20, 26; τίς...τρόπος ᵃ27; τίνα τρόπον ᵃ22). Here too Empedocles stands accused of failing to meet the demand adequately.

atomists). Though he mentions, at 325^b24–34, Plato's account (*Ti.* 53c4–55c4) of the transformations of the simple bodies, it would seem either that Aristotle does not regard it as constituting a substantive theory of action–passion, or that he treats it as an inferior version of the atomist theory.

The arrangement of the chapter is not straightforward. In the first place, some general and radical criticism of the earlier theories is reserved for I. 9 (327^a6–25). Within I. 8 itself it is only Empedocles' theory of pores that gets straightforward exposition and refutation. The two parts of the discussion of Empedocles begin and end the chapter, like the outsides of a sandwich. Inside the sandwich is a long discussion (324^b35–326^b6) of atomism as a physical theory, which goes well beyond the topic of 'action–passion'. All this has the effect of throwing the spotlight on the atomists, and of metaphorically, as well as literally, marginalizing Empedocles.

Empedocles and pores

1. The theory of action–passion 'through pores' or 'by the movement through the pores' held by Empedocles and unnamed others[2] is expounded at 324^b25–35, and criticized at 326^b6–28. We are told that the hypothesis of pores was supposed to explain not only (i) how action–passion comes about, with sense perception taken to be an important special case, but also (ii) why and how some things are transparent, and (iii) the phenomena of mixture.

Poros ($\pi\acute{o}\rho o\varsigma$) is a very general word for a means of transit, a way or means of getting through or across something. A *poros* through a solid body need not necessarily be a passageway 'cut out' through that body. It could be a 'vein' along which the solid body is less resistant to penetration, like a vein of metal in rock, as at 326^b33–327^a1. In that place Aristotle is suggesting an alternative to Empedocles' theory; 'vein' is *not* the sense of *poros* in I. 8. In I. 8 itself, in fact, it is clear that the *poroi* are passageways, or gateways, 'cut out' through the surrounding

---

[2] For Empedocles' theory of pores, the principal source (besides the present passage) is Thphr. *Sens.* 1–2, 7–24, on the role of pores in sense perception. For other testimony see Emp. frs. A 88–94 DK. It has been suggested that the pores theorists include Alcmaeon of Croton. But the 'pores' mentioned by Theophrastus in his report on Alcmaeon (*Sens.* 25–6) are clearly not minute passageways in the sense-organs, enabling them to receive input from the outside world, but sensory pathways from the sense-organs to the brain. There is no other evidence that Alcmaeon had a pores theory of sense perception, let alone of action–passion generally.

body, which themselves contain none of that body (esp. 326^{b}9–10), and *poros* is given as Empedocles' own word (325^{b}10).[3]

Aristotle mentions in passing (324^{b}30–1) that the pores were supposed to be 'so small as to be invisible'. He understands them as minute passageways through material bodies, whether elements or compounds, which were part of the ultimate microstructure of those bodies. They are not like the *poroi* recognized in Aristotle's own biological writings, which are macroscopic pathways, visible to the anatomist.

2. At 324^{b}35 the word *summetroi* must mean, not 'proportionate' nor just 'of the same size' but 'of the same dimensions'; that is, 'of the same size *and shape*': so as to fit something else exactly. This is not a standard Aristotelian usage (possibly it occurs at *HA* 612^{b}26, *GA* 739^{b}3), but Aristotle is here drawing on Empedocles or some report about him.[4]

Next, 'the pores are of the same size and shape, in relation to one another' implies not that, for mixture to occur, the pores have to fit *into* one another (which would naturally be absurd), but just that they have to fit *on to* one another. Given that their corresponding pores *match* one another in shape and size, two adjacent bodies will possess continuous passageways, each of the same cross-section throughout, by means of which they can exchange materials in some minute form ('effluences').

That is apparently the main point of the pores, in Aristotle's account of Empedocles: (a) they make possible the transfer of materials and/or effluences, and (b) they do so selectively, acting as filters to prevent certain transferences from taking place while permitting others. (In the case of transparency, it seems they serve simply as holes that light or vision can pass through.) There are then two kinds of questions to be asked. One kind is about the nature of the pores themselves, what they are supposed to contain at any given time, and what kind of material can pass through them and how. The other kind is about how such transferences could possibly bring about, or constitute, action–passion. Aristotle's

---

[3] Cf. διά τινων πόρων, 'through some sort of "pores" '(324^{b}26), where τινων has the effect of putting πόρων in quotation marks). The word occurs three times in the extant fragments of Empedocles, but not in the sense indicated here. Pl. *Men.* 76c7–d2, implies that Gorgias took over both the theory and the term πόρος from Empedocles. See further n. 4 below. Aristotle's own usage of πόρος mostly reserves it for the manifest passageways in animal and plant bodies. (On *Mete.* IV. 8–9 see n. 9 below.)

[4] The word σύμμετρος and its derivates are used, in the context of Empedocles' pores theory, by Pl. *Men.* 76c4–d5 (on Gorgias' theory of vision, derived from Empedocles), and by Thphr. *Sens.* 12, 14, 15, 35, 91. It is noteworthy that both the noun πόρος and the verb ἁρμόττειν (or ἐναρμόττειν) are also present in all these contexts. There is a similar usage of σύμμετρος, in connection with the theory of vision in the *Timaeus*, at Pl. *Ti.* 67c4–7, Thphr. *Sens.* 5, 86, 91. For this sense of σύμμετρος outside philosophy or physics, but again in connection with the notion of an exact fit, see E. *El.* 532–3.

criticism begins with the first kind of question (326^b6–20) and passes to the second (326^b21–4).

3. Given pores of this kind, the first problem Aristotle poses for Empedocles is: What do they contain at any given time? It seems more or less necessary, as Aristotle remarks in anticipation at 325^b5–10, for the pores theory to postulate *empty* regions within the bodies. (For instance, if air has pores accounting for its transparency and for its mixture-capacities etc., what are these pores filled with? It is conceivable, but physically implausible, that the pores might automatically collapse when not 'in use'.) If 'empty' has to mean 'not containing any body at all', then the theory becomes, as Aristotle remarks, practically the same as the atomist one. It requires a void, either an all-pervasive atomist void, or at least isolated empty regions, trapped inside bodies, like air bubbles in water. Aristotle claims that Empedocles rejected the first and accepted the second; that is the basis of his final argument (326^b16–20), although other testimony suggests that Empedocles rejected any kind of void, on general grounds.[5]

4. The criticism of the pores theory, 326^b6–28, not surprisingly, features this aporia.

The first argument ($^b8$–20) sets up a dilemma.[6]

(*a*) Suppose, first, that at the material time (when the agent is penetrating via the pores) the pores contain some 'filler' (326^b8). Then the agent will have to make its way *through* this filler. So, as regards the actual physical situation, one might as well count the 'filler' as part of the original body, and say that it is 'continuous' (i.e. not containing pores). The 'pores', considered as *interruptions* to the continuity of the affected body, make it no easier in this case to understand how it is permeated. So they are superfluous (326^b8–10).

(*b*) If the pores do not at the material time contain 'filler' then they can be described as 'empty regions'; that is, they do not contain anything, *apart from possibly the transient bodies at the time of transit*. (The exception is necessary to make sense of the argument.) There are again two possibilities:

(*b*(i): $^b15$–16) There are no actual voids; that is, no empty spaces containing no body. Hence the pores contain *only* the transient bodies, at the time of transit; either there are always such transiting bodies or previously the pores must either have contained 'filler' or have been 'collapsed'. Whichever solution one adopts, this case is not materially different from supposing that the transient body tunnels through (and

---

[5] Emped. frs. 13 and 14 DK; also Thphr. *Sens.* 13, which poses the same dilemma as Aristotle here.

[6] The parenthesis ἔτι ($^b10$) ... πλῆρες ($^b14$) is a sideswipe at the use of pores to explain transparency (324^b29–32); it too argues that pores add nothing to any possible explanation.

expels parts of) the original body. 'The same consequence will follow' (326^b16); that is, the postulation of pores will still be superfluous, for the same reasons as in case (*a*).

(*b*(ii): $^b16$–20) So if pores are not to be superfluous one must postulate actual empty spaces within the pores (cf. 325^b10). 'So small as not to receive any body' must mean that these spaces are too small to admit any *ordinary* material body.[7] They *must*, of course, be able to admit the postulated transient things (effluences, or whatever they may be), which are supposed to explain the phenomena in question, otherwise it would be futile to postulate them. (This point also serves to confirm that 'voids' (κενά: $^b15$) is meant to carry a tacit exception for the transient things.)

Hence, as Aristotle adumbrated earlier (325^b5–10), the only way out for Empedocles is a theory very close to atomism. (It does not seem to require absolutely indivisible bodies, though at 325^b7 that requirement is stated[8]). Interestingly, he does *not* attack the last possibility (*b*(ii) above) on its merits, as an account of the physical mechanism. He seems thereby to concede tacitly that, like its atomist cousin, from a purely physical point of view it *could* do the work required of it.[9]

An *ad hominem* refutation follows ($^b17$–20). It is absurd for Empedocles to postulate small voids not admitting ordinary bodies but to reject larger ones. For we must understand 'void' as meaning 'space for body' (i.e. empty space which can be occupied by body, as at *Ph.* IV. 6. 213^a27–9, 7. 213^b31). Hence if there are voids at all there can be a void large enough to contain any given body. So any pores theorist is forced in the atomist direction, which Empedocles has rejected.

---

[7] Why does Aristotle omit the possibility that the voids are capable of containing bodies but are not forced to contain any? Is he assuming the principle of *horror vacui*: that any void capable of containing bodies would be filled immediately by the inrush of bodies from outside? This principle was invoked not long afterwards by Strato of Lampsacus, who probably held a theory much like the one envisaged here (see Simp. *in Ph.* 693. 1–18, and Furley (1985)).

[8] Phlp. *in GC* 159. 18–24 is probably right in taking the argument implied at *GC* 325^b5–10 to rely on the threat of an infinite regress: if the solids surrounding the pores are not impassive and indivisible they must themselves contain pores, and so on.

[9] From the way Aristotle writes, it looks as though he thought that Empedocles actually accepted option (Bb). That would imply that he thought Empedocles made a physical difference between ordinary bodies and the 'effluences' or other minute particles passing through the minute pores in bodies. The point is of interest for the interpretation of Empedocles. Aristotle himself argues against inseparable voids as well as separable ones in *Ph.* IV. 6–9 (see esp. IV. 9. 216^b34–217^a10). There are 'voids' and 'pores' inside various kinds of bodies at *Mete.* IV. 8.385^a28–31; 9.385^b19–26, 386^a15–18, 386^b2–7, 387^a2–4. These pores, however, are used to explain only certain special physical properties of particular kinds of body; and the 'voids' are, as the context makes clear, regions 'void of the same kind of body' (386^b2–3).

The essential step in the argument is compressed, but may be expanded as follows. It has been shown in *Physics* IV. 213^{a}19–214^{a}17 that the concept of *void* must be dependent on that of *place*, so that the only theory of void with a prospect of being coherent is one that postulates an occupied 'space' wherever there is a natural body. But natural bodies can always change position, and so if there can be voids at all there must be a possibility of unoccupied spaces; that is, voids of the size of any natural body. The emphasis on the possible meaning of the word 'void' echoes *Physics* IV. (213^{a}22–31, 213^{b}30–214^{a}15).

5. After the refutation of Empedocles on his own terms Aristotle adds two remarks. These outline general arguments, based on obviously Aristotelian principles. Their aim is not so much to convince an opponent as to reveal the real reasons (from an Aristotelian standpoint) for the inadequacy of any theory of pores. The use of 'in general' (ὅλως: 326^{b}21) is characteristic for this kind of move to a higher Aristotelian vantage point in criticism of an opposed view (cf. e.g. 327^{a}14, *Ph.* II. 8.199^{b}14). It here also signals the move from the questions about the nature of pores to the deeper questions about the nature of action–passion in such theories.

First (326^{b}21–4), either simple contact of two suitable bodies is sufficient for action–passion to take place or it is not. If it is sufficient then pores are not needed to bring about action–passion, since contact occurs at the surfaces anyway. If it is not sufficient, then there is no reason why the more intimate kind of contact brought about by pores should be sufficient either. So either way pores contribute nothing.

This argument requires the assumption that contact *at the surface* is sufficient for action–passion (or at least 'passion') to occur *throughout* the body affected. That would hardly be accepted by an atomist, or by an Empedoclean pores theorist, whose aim is precisely to find a mechanism for there to be contact *within* the body affected.

The second remark (326^{b}26–8) removes the need for this assumption, but introduces another, and equally Aristotelian, assumption. It is ridiculous, because needless, to postulate pores, once we admit that bodies are divisible everywhere. For then division of bodies will do any explanatory work that can be done by passage through pores.

6. Aristotle's overall conclusion (326^{b}24–6) is that the Empedoclean theory of pores is 'either false or useless'. Given the Aristotelian view, that bodies are everywhere divisible, there is no need for pores at all. But, even apart from that view, which the atomists in particular emphatically did not share, Aristotle's claim is that the pores theory cannot be made to work without the atomist void. So there is no 'third way'; one must take either an atomist or an Aristotelian view of the matter.

C. Eleatics and Atomists

1. Aristotle introduces the atomists, and explains their methodological superiority, by means of a flashback (325^a2–17) to the Eleatic theories.

The common argumentative structure of Eleaticism is given thus ($^a3$–6 with two steps supplied): (1) Void is not 'what-is'; [hence (2) there is no void;[10]] but (3) movement requires separated void;[11] [hence (4) what is does not move;] and (5) there is no plurality without void to separate things; hence (6) what is is one. A possible objection to (5) is then considered ($^a6$–13): there might be no void, and yet many things all in contact. Aristotle makes the Eleatics counter this objection by claiming that it either (i) reduces to that of void; or (ii) is inexplicably arbitrary; and (iii) in any case still bars motion.

Two striking points about this account of the Eleatics are (a) the central role assigned to the non-existence of void (on which more later); and (b) the thorough assimilation of Parmenides to Melissus. Elsewhere Aristotle stresses differences between them, both in content and in quality of thought (and to the detriment of Melissus: *Ph.* I. 2. 185^a10–12; III. 6. 207^a15; *Metaph.* A 5. 986^b26–7). Here, no differences are mentioned, except for the question of whether what is is finite or infinite.

2. So the Eleatics represent not a physical theory but a preliminary challenge, which must be answered if natural science is ever to stand on good foundations. The Eleatics, convinced by their arguments, 'passed over' (or 'went beyond') and 'disregarded' sense perception ($^a13$–14); that is, they paid no attention to its justifiable claims. The implicit moral is that one should never rest content with a position involving a radical conflict between sense perception and reasoning. That is already a sign that something has gone badly wrong, even when no mistake is apparent in the reasoning.[12] The Eleatics' approach was one-sided. The superiority of the atomists to all other previous natural scientists lies for Aristotle in the facts that (a) they did not accept the intolerable conflict, yet (b) they took the Eleatic arguments seriously, and began by seeking to accommodate them within the framework of sense-experience.

---

[10] τὸ ... κενὸν οὐκ ὄν, with εἶναι idiomatically omitted, cannot simply mean 'there is no void', as Philoponus takes it (*in GC* 156. 20–157. 1).

[11] 'Separated' emphasizes that the void in question here is 'free-standing' void, not void permanently enclosed within bodies; cf. *Ph.* IV. 8. 214^b12 for this use (and perhaps 'separable' (χωριστόν) at *GC* I. 5. 320^b27, 321^a6).

[12] That the phenomena of sense experience exercise a kind of non-rational pressure on the theorist is implied also at *Metaph.* 986^b31–3 (on Parmenides): ἀναγκαζόμενος δ' ἀκολουθεῖν τοῖς φαινομένοις.

3. The thought that theorizing in the Eleatics has ceased to respond to, and interact with, the evidence of the senses, in the way that ought to happen, is surely what underlies the remarks about *mania* (325ª17–23: see app. below for some points of text and language in ª17–25). To hold wildly incorrect beliefs can be seen, by an unprejudiced ordinary observer, as 'closely similar to *mania*', if the beliefs are ones generally resembling the delusions of *mania*. The next point adds a turn of the screw: the beliefs of the Eleatics actually seem to be *more* completely wrong than those of the person suffering from ordinary *mania*. For such a person, usually, does *not* think that 'fire and ice are the same thing', but can correctly identify and discriminate ordinary objects, at least. So far, this is an intelligible account of a 'healthy common-sense' reaction to the Eleatic position. 'Since' (ª17) identifies that reaction as the basis, in some sense, of Leucippus' response.

The problematic point is the meaning of the parenthesis at ª21–3. There is a syntactical ambiguity, to begin with. Is the dative ἐνίοις (ª22) to be understood as governed by δοκεῖ (ª22) or by διαφέρειν (ª23)?

In the first case we have: 'to some people, because of *mania*, there appears to be no difference between those things which are fine, and those that appear [fine] through habit'. The indicative (δοκεῖ: ª22) shows this to be a remark made by Aristotle in his own person. It can hardly be his intention to ascribe *mania* to just anyone who, through habituation, wrongly sees something as 'fine' (*kalon*) when it is not. It must, therefore, be directed against people who think that the *meaning* of the word '*kalon*' just is 'whatever people see as fine, through habituation'. That might be a conventionalist theory of some sophist.[13] Yet it is surprising to find Aristotle condemning any philosophical theory, even a sophistic one, as 'mad', and therefore, presumably, beyond the reach of reasonable discussion. The closest parallel in his writings (not all that close) would seem to be *Topics* 105ª3–7, which claims that anyone who really doubts whether one should honour the gods and support one's parents is in need of punishment, not reasoning.[14]

The alternative construction gives the less interesting but more probable sense. Here δοκεῖ is 'it seems [to unprejudiced common sense]', just as at ª18 above; the parallel tells in favour of taking it this way. Though madmen can usually tell the difference between fire and ice, 'some people do seem to be unable, on account of madness, to distinguish between things that are fine and things that seem fine to them because of their habituation'. The increasingly eccentric and offensive acts of chronic

---

[13] As suggested in discussion by Michel Crubellier.
[14] The language and thought are slightly reminiscent of Xenophon, *Mem.* I. 1. 11–16, III. 9. 6–7.

mania are explained if the sufferers are genuinely convinced, because of their habitual and ingrained misunderstanding of how things are, that what they are doing is fine. In this respect they are like the Eleatics, in being chronically alienated from common-sense perceptions.[15]

4. Eleatic thinking is implied to contribute to the genesis of atomism, in Leucippus' version, as follows.

Leucippus refused to reject the features of the world that sense perception forces upon us: real *genesis* (coming to be) and *phthora* (passing away), change generally, and plurality. But he is also said ([a]26–8) to have accepted in some sense three Eleatic claims that on this reading are fundamental: (A) that void is 'what-is-not' ($\mu\grave{\eta}\ \check{o}\nu$); (B) that 'what-is-not' is no part of 'what-is'; (C) that change requires the existence of void. (On the problems of text and language at [a]26–9 see app.) Comparison with 325[a]3–13 (see Sect. 1 above) clarifies this list: (A) and (C) are the same as (1) and (3) above, while (B) is the step used by the Eleatics to get from (1) to (2). How did Aristotle think Leucippus proposed to circumvent the Eleatic argument that there is no void, while accepting these three claims?[16]

If Leucippus accepted both (A) and (B), and the consequence that the void is 'no part of what-is', he yet refused, in Aristotle's account, to draw the further conclusion that 'there is no such thing as void'. For Leucippus said that there *is* a void ([a]31); so he must have held, as Aristotle saw it, that to be (unqualifiedly) is not necessarily to be part of 'what-is'. On this account, Leucippus, starting from the Eleatic argument, uses 'what-is' to denote not the sum of all that there is but a particular kind of existent, with the characteristic properties attributed to it by the Eleatics: immutability, impassivity, completeness, internal unity. The Eleatic theory follows only if 'what-is' is supposed to be all that there is, and this is what Leucippus denies. When this is denied, not only does the possibility of the void and hence of motion and plurality follow, but something such as the void is positively necessary, in order to explain why 'what-is' is *not* all there is.

---

[15] This interpretation is substantially that of Philoponus (*in GC* 158. 4–11). The understanding of *mania* is close to that of [Hippocrates] *Morb.Sacr.*, where it is the brain by which (*inter alia*) 'we discriminate between shameful and fine things' (VI. 386. 18–19 Littré), and *mania* is caused by disease of the brain. In particular, chronic *mania* caused by corruption of the brain by bile makes the sufferers 'doers of evil acts ... always doing something unsuitable' (VI. 387. 14–16 Littré). (Myles Burnyeat has suggested a chiastic analogy here: the Eleatics stick to reason and are impervious to sense-experience, while *mania* makes one stick to customary values and reject reasoning that runs contrary to them.)

[16] What follows is indebted to several members of the Symposium who raised objections to my original reading of this passage, though I may not have succeeded in meeting those objections to their satisfaction.

How then is Leucippus supposed by Aristotle to have justified the claim that 'what-is-not' is something that is? The clue is supplied by the description of 'what-is' as 'that which is in the principal or decisive sense' (κυρίως: 325ª29). Aristotle need not be implying that Leucippus' account of uses of the verb *einai* ('be') was similar to his (Aristotle's) own.[17] But Leucippus at least is seen as resolving the difficulty in an Aristotelian way. He avoids an apparently irreconcilable conflict by invoking the complexity of the usage of *einai*. He is thereby enabled to accept the physically plausible part of each opposing view.

What results from this solution, however it was arrived at, is the atomist void. In this chapter it is noticeable that the atomist void, as such, is never attacked. In some sense it is almost the hero of the story. It is, rather, the indivisibility of the atoms that here underlies almost all of Aristotle's criticisms of the atomists.

5. Given the existence of void, the way is open for Leucippus to redeem his pledges to the acknowledged truths of sense-experience. He promised (ª24–5) to deliver (a) *genesis* and *phthora*; (b) change (or at least movement); (c) a plurality of things. Movement and plurality being made possible by the void, in the obvious way,[18] and the atoms being postulated as below the limit of visibility (continuing the refusal to contradict sense perception), it remained to account for *genesis* and *phthora*, which he did by explaining them in terms of 'aggregation and disaggregation' of atoms (ª31–2).

6. At 325ª32 Aristotle at last returns to the starting-point (325ª2) of his long excursus on Eleatics and atomists. The atomists' account of the mechanisms of action–passion, promised at 324ᵇ35–325ª2, is expounded in 325ª32–ᵇ11, together with those of qualitative change (ᵇ2), of growth (ᵇ4), and of 'begetting' (γεννᾶν: ª34). (On some problems of language and interpretation in ª32–4 see app.)

The atomist starting point, derived from the existence of the ultimate entities, is given at ª34–6. A general principle is stated: What is truly one can never become many, nor can what is truly many become one. This too (though Aristotle does not mention the point) is a piece of Eleatic heritage, adapted by Leucippus to his own ends.[19] The principle has the

---

[17] The need to distinguish senses of εἶναι in order to answer the Eleatics is asserted at *Ph.* I. 8. 191ª24–ᵇ34, but in the context of a different analysis of their reasoning. For distinguishing senses of εἶναι as a good way in general of resolving an aporia cf. esp. *Ph.* III. 6. 206ª12–14.

[18] Why the particles of 'what-is' were supposed collectively infinite in number and individually invisible because of their smallness (ª30) is left unexplained.

[19] Though the connection is not made explicitly by Aristotle, it is natural to suppose that here too he sees Leucippus as adapting Eleatic arguments to his own purpose. This time it would be the arguments of Parmenides (fr. B8. 26–33 DK) and Melissus (fr. B7. (2)–(6) DK) to show that what-is, because of its unity and completeness, cannot undergo

consequence that all the compounds and aggregates commonly seen as unities are not really unities, nor is their dissolution really a coming to be of many out of one. It follows that action–passion, and other observed phenomena of the same kind, are (according to Leucippus) commonly misconceived; the underlying processes must be ones of rearrangement of individual atoms within aggregates. This is the underlying point of the sentence [a]32–4. Aggregates of atoms are capable of acting and being acted upon, but only because they are not true unities. They are unities only 'by contact', and hence the points at which the *individual* atoms make contact are the points at which rearrangements can begin and hence action–passion can be brought about.[20] Rearrangement also requires void spaces, of course (325^b3–5, cf. 325^b31); such processes must take place 'through the void' ([b]3). The preposition διά ('through') with the genitive appears here, as sometimes elsewhere in Aristotle,[21] to bear both a spatial and an instrumental sense: the processes can take place only *by means of* the void, and only by the motion of atoms *through* the void.

7. The account of atomist foundations was originally introduced to explain the judgement (324^b35–325^a2) that it was Leucippus and Democritus who were the best of the earlier physical theorists (not just on the question of action–passion, but generally).

First, they 'took as their principle (ἀρχή) in accordance with nature just that which *is* [the principle]' (325^a1–2). The syntax is ambiguous, but the point is in any case the same: the atomists' starting point was the one that is 'in accordance with nature', the one needed for a proper understanding of the natural world.[22] Since they chose the correct starting point for their theorizing, it is not surprising that they, more than others, proceed 'most of all in correct method' and that they are able to derive a treatment of all subjects in a single rational account. They can give a single, methodical, coherent, and universal discussion of *all* relevant matters. As a result their system is, at least, internally coherent, unlike that of Empedocles (325^b14–16).

---

any change. The principle is attributed to Democritus at *Metaph.* 1039^a9–10 and fr. 208 Rose[3], and to Leucippus and Democritus at *Cael.* 303^a3–8.

[20] Hence also καὶ συντιθέμενα ... γεννᾶν is not mere pointless repetition of [b]31–2; it places what has been said in its atomistic explanatory setting. The focus is now on the contact points between *individual* atoms—which may be why Aristotle writes τυγχάνουσιν rather than τυγχάνει at [a]33.

[21] Besides 325^b31 and 326^b7 below, see e.g. *de An.* III. 13. 435^a16.

[22] κατὰ φύσιν may be taken with any or all of ποιησάμενοι, ἀρχήν, and ἐστίν. For κατὰ φύσιν in similar contexts compare *Ph.* 189^b31, *Metaph.* 986^b12. But to take φύσιν rather than ἀρχήν as antecedent of ἥπερ is unsatisfactory: 'according to (that kind of) nature that really is' is not an Aristotelian way of speaking.

But what is this correct starting point? It must be the examination of the Eleatic arguments, or some question (the existence of void?) that arises directly therefrom. We are probably meant to recall the praise of Democritus in chapter 2, for being an habitué of natural science, and so being able to choose the right kind of principles, and using the appropriate ('natural-scientific') kind of reasonings (316^a5–14). The moral of Leucippus' procedure is that it is appropriate to start, in natural science, from arguments that appear to show that the natural world does not exist: for the answering of those arguments will show on what foundation a coherent natural science can be built up. On this reading there is a discrepancy between the praise of Leucippus here and the claim at *Physics* I. 2. 184^b25–185^a20, that it is no business of the natural scientist, even when establishing first principles, to concern himself with the Eleatic arguments.[23]

Both Leucippus and Democritus thus get their separate moments in the spotlight in *GC* I, in chapters 8 and 2 respectively. Several points are common to these chapters. (1) The atomists are given unusually explicit praise. (2) They are said to throw other earlier natural philosophers into the shade, for consistent and effective coverage in the right kind of way. They alone have a notion of the right kind of method, and the right kind of principle, in natural science. (3) By contrast, there is a pointed downgrading of the Eleatics (here) and Plato (in chapter 2), who are seen as having resorted to purely abstract reasonings taking no account of the actual world. (4) The basis of the atomists' theory is revealed as a train of reasoning which is 'proper to natural science' (though it is actually, in Aristotle's opinion, ultimately mistaken), on a question which is a proper starting point for natural science.[24]

---

[23] Admittedly, even in *Ph.* I. 2–3 Aristotle thinks it right to include a discussion of the Eleatic *thesis*, on the grounds that it incidentally contains difficulties belonging to the province of natural science (περὶ φύσεως μὲν οὔ, φυσικὰς δὲ ἀπορίας συμβαίνει λέγειν αὐτοῖς, 185^a18–19). But that discussion produces no positive guidelines for the search for the principles of natural science. The discrepancy between *Ph.* I. 2–3 and *GC* I. 8 is even clearer from the remark at 187^a1–3: the atomists' two great mistakes in natural science, void and indivisible atoms, were a direct consequence of taking the Eleatic arguments seriously. *Top.* I. 11. 104^b19–105^a9 and *Cael.* III. 1. 298^b14–25 also imply that Eleatic monism is a *thesis* worth considering, but (according to *Cael.*) *not* by the student of natural science, but as part of an investigation which is prior to natural science. Aristotle's variations, on the question of the Eleatics' relevance to natural science, may well be the result of understandable fluctuations about how to interpret them: was their theory a strangely mistaken account of the world of experience, as this chapter seems to assume, or was it concerned with some other order of being?

[24] Two interesting questions: How far Aristotle's reconstructions of the reasonings of Democritus (in ch. 2) and of Leucippus (in ch. 8) were, and were intended to be, historically correct. On the historicity of the Democritus of chapter 2 see David Sedley's contribution to this volume (Ch. 2 above). In presenting his reconstruction of Leucippus,

Unlike other passages, where the atomists constitute part of the problem (in Aristotle's view of the history of natural philosophy), here the atomists are a part of the solution. The positive side of their achievement is brought out.

The criticism of atomism

1. At 325^b13 the expository part of the chapter is declared complete. What follows, 325^b13-36, seems to be meant as a transition to the criticisms of atomism. It is an awkward passage, and suggests that at the least some rearrangement of material has occurred. (1) 'Concerning these people' ($^b13$) must refer to the early atomists generally, even though from 325^a23 onwards Leucippus alone has been mentioned, and he will be mentioned alone again at 325^b26 and 30. (2) The subject is widened without warning: it is no longer action–passion alone, but the ability of the theorists to account consistently for various natural phenomena, principally coming to be and ceasing to be ($^b16$, 20–4, 29–32) and qualitative change ($^b16$); and this in spite of the fact that these subjects have already been discussed in earlier chapters.[25] (3) At 325^b24 the transition to the theory of the *Timaeus* is abrupt in itself, and all the more surprising since the theory has hitherto gone completely unmentioned in this chapter.

2. 325^b33-6 introduces the criticisms. The criticisms of Plato's *Timaeus* theory 'in the previous discussions' may be the ones found in *de Caelo* III and IV (especially *Cael.* III. 1. 299^a2-300^a19). The criticisms of atomism are presented not as a full, detailed examination but as the result of 'digressing slightly' (325^b36). From what implied agenda is Aristotle here claiming to be 'slightly digressing'? From the stated overall plan of the chapter? If so, then instead of simply criticizing the accounts of the physical basis of action–passion in the atomists he is turning aside slightly to consider briefly a wider subject: the nature of atomistic physical theory generally. (The digression may be also called 'slight' by contrast with the larger, postponed, task of making a systematic and thorough examination of atomism.)

The criticism divides naturally into two parts. $325^b34-326^a24$ look at the relation or lack of relation between (the shapes of) individual atoms and

---

Aristotle writes confidently and expresses no uncertainty, by contrast with the tentative tone of Δημόκριτος δ' ἂν φανείη οἰκείοις καὶ φυσικοῖς λόγοις πεπεῖσθαι (316^a13).

[25] Possibly the explanation for the illogicalities is that Aristotle wishes above all to drive home the contrast between the consistency of the atomists (strongly reasserted here, 325^b13-15) and the inconsistencies of 'the others' and notably Empedocles (325^b15-23; cf. 315^a3-4, and on Anaxagoras 314^a13-16).

sense-perceptible qualities. 326ᵃ24–ᵇ6 then add some miscellaneous but fundamental problems on the physical foundations of atomism.

3. The first section (325ᵇ36–326ᵃ24). For a start I divide the text into five chunks of unequal size: (I) 325ᵇ36–326ᵃ3 (πάθους); (II) 326ᵃ3 (οὔτε γὰρ... εἶναι); (III) 326ᵃ3 (καίτοι)–14 (μαλακόν); (IV) 326ᵃ14 (ἀλλὰ μὴν)–21 (παθημάτων); (V) 326ᵃ21 (τοῦτο γὰρ)–4 (ἀδιαιρέτοις). These chunks are, in themselves, reasonably coherent; the question is how they are related to one another. I interweave paraphrase and commentary for all except (II).

4. (I). 325ᵇ36–326ᵃ3:
The atomists have to say that individual atoms are incapable of acting or being acted upon, in relation to the affections. They can't be acted on—for that requires void—and they can't act on anything either.

This is presented as what they *should* say, to be consistent; 326ᵃ3 ff. then notes a divergence in what they *did* say. The atomists have to say that being acted on requires void, as at 325ᵃ32–ᵇ5, since it consists in rearrangement of aggregates of atoms. If the indivisibles singly cannot be acted on, then they should also be unable singly to act on anything, both on Aristotelian principles and by Democritus' own principle of similarity (323ᵇ10–15).

5. (III). 326ᵃ3–8:
Two absurd consequences of a departure from the general principle by the atomists. They said only that spherical atoms were hot. Not only does this arbitrarily contravene the principle, but (even if we still suppose there's no action–passion) (a) if spherical atoms are hot then there must be a shape opposite to spherical which is cold; and (b) if there are hot atoms and cold atoms, why not also heavy atoms, light atoms, hard atoms, and soft atoms?

With arguments (a) and (b), compare *de Caelo* III. 8. 307ᵇ5–10 (part of a much more thorough critique of Plato's and the atomists' attempts to associate sensible qualities with shapes).

326ᵃ9–12:
In fact Democritus does say that atoms are 'heavier in respect of the "excess"'. But though this exception may palliate the earlier one, it implies that intensity of any pathos in the atom is linked to its volume. So atoms will, if hot, be hotter in proportion to their volume. So there will be degrees of heat, and so there must be action–passion between atoms with different degrees of heat.

Two interlinked problems: (a) what is meant by 'in respect of their "excess"'; (b) what sense can be given to ᵃ9–10: 'that each of the indivisibles is heavier in respect of the excess'?

To start with (b). The root problem is that the point of comparison implied by 'heavier' is unclear. There seem to be two types of solution possible, involving two different uses of ἕκαστον ('each'). (1) The standard of comparison is the 'average atom', or some particular standard atom specified by Democritus. Then ἕκαστον just means 'each', but we must understand 'or lighter, as the case may be'. (2) There is no fixed standard of comparison involved; 'heavier' means 'heavier than some other one that one might consider'. Here again we should understand 'or lighter, as the case may be'. ἕκαστον here would be functioning in a 'telescoped' way (see app. on 325ᵇ28); it is in effect standing in for the phrase ἄλλο ἄλλου ('one than another'), emphasizing that what we are doing is comparing individual atoms with individual atoms. It focuses on the range of possibilities available for an arbitrary individual atom: as we might say, 'any atom is heavier or lighter, as the case may be, according as etc.'.

Either way, the result is much the same, and 'excess' must be understood as abbreviated (as often) for 'excess or deficiency': atoms are heavier or lighter, as the case may be, according as they have an excess or deficiency... of what? With no specific indication in the context, we must suppose that the 'amount' of the atom is meant, that is its volume, since there is no other quantity directly attributable to it (cf. *Cael*. IV. 2. 309ᵃ1–2; Thphr. *Sens*. 61 and 68).

326ᵃ13–14:
Besides, if there are hard atoms, there are soft ones too; and softness implies a capacity to be acted upon. So, either way, not merely is the atomist theory arbitrary, it also implies a contradiction.

The implied moral is that to be consistent they should have denied both hotness and heaviness to individual atoms. There is here both homology of thought and verbal similarity with arguments against the supposition that points can be heavy, at *de Caelo* III. 1. 299ᵇ7–14, where Aristotle claims (a) that what is heavy must be hard or soft; (b) that what is heavy must be dense, and what is light, rare. But softness is inconsistent with indivisibility, just as here it is inconsistent with impassibility; and so is density. (For softness as implying yieldingness and passivity cf. *GC* II. 2. 329ᵇ22–6, 330ᵃ8–10).

6. (IV). 326ᵃ14–17:
If (i) the atoms have as properties only shape (but none of the action–passion properties), that is odd. It is also odd if (ii) they have but one extra each (say, hard for some, cold for others). There would not then even be one nature of all of them (as claimed by the atomists).

On (i). The absurdity is that if atoms have only shape and none of the action–passion properties then they can't be subject to action–passion and will not interact at all.

On (ii). If we read ψυχρόν ('cold') at ᵃ16 (see app.), the argument goes as follows. If each atom has just one *pathos*-property, but not all atoms have the same one (or not all such properties are chosen from the same spectrum or pair of opposites), then there will be different natures of atoms: those that are just hard (and incapable of being either hot or cold) will behave in quite different ways from those that are just hot (and incapable of being either hard or soft). That contradicts the atomists' claim that there is one single nature for all atoms, so it is not an option for them. It would also, by Democritus' principle (cited in the previous chapter, 323ᵇ10–15) that action–passion implies *sameness*, make all action–passion impossible.

326ᵃ17–21:

But if (iii) each atom has many different pathê *then that too is impossible; for each atom will be subject to action–passion but will have the passions and the actions in the same thing.*

The way of reading this is dictated by the way of reading the previous part. Namely, 'if the one [atom] has more [*pathê*]' must mean: two or more *pathê* on different spectra. What is meant is then clear: to parry the last objection, we must suppose that every atom is in principle capable of action–passion on the same set of spectra as *all* the other atoms. (This is confirmed by the explicit mention of action–passion at ᵃ19–20.)

The objection here is at first sight obscure, but can be understood by reference to *de Caelo* III and Physics VI. I suggest that the thought is that change along any *one pathos*-spectrum requires that the changing thing be divisible (whether or not the spectrum itself is *continuous*). At *de Caelo* III. 1. 299ᵃ17–24 Aristotle claims that *pathê* themselves are necessarily divisible, either in kind or accidentally, that is by being in a divisible; and so the *simple pathê* (which aren't divisible in kind) must be in divisibles. Why must they be divisible? It is *Physics* VI that supplies arguments to this effect (*Ph*. VI. 4. 234ᵇ10–20 and VI. 10. 240ᵇ8–241ᵃ26). The idea of the principal proof is that if X changes from A to B (without intermediates) then when it is all in A it is not yet changing, when it is all in B it is no longer changing (234ᵇ10–15); hence during the change some of X must be in A and some in B.

The argument here can be taken as the same, but turned around so as to make a *reductio ad absurdum*: an indivisible, in changing from *pathos* A to *pathos* B, has to have both A and B simultaneously 'in the same thing', that is in itself as a whole, since it has no parts. Hence it will be (e.g.) both cold and warm all over at once, which is a contradiction. (See also app.)

7. (V). 326ᵃ21–4:

All theories of indivisible elementary constituents suffer the same consequence, since they cannot become denser or rarer, there being no void in the indivisibles.

The problem about (V) is how it is supposed to fit its context. As an addition to, or explication of, (IV) it is unintelligible. Yet the 'for' (γάρ: ᵃ21) indicates a close attachment to what immediately precedes. Hence (V) must be misplaced. One place where it would fit very well is after ὑπάρξει (ᵃ8). For in *de Caelo* III. 1 Aristotle claims to show that (i) indivisibles cannot be dense or rare (299ᵇ10–11); (ii) hence they cannot be heavy or light (299ᵇ7–10). And the parallel argument from soft to rare is suggested at 299ᵇ13–14: what is soft is what retreats into itself. Hence the *de Caelo* III. 1 context, while arguing (in connection with the *Timaeus*) about indivisibles generally and divisible lines in particular, claims that the possession of density/rarity is implied by the possession of heaviness/lightness and by that of hardness/softness. This is just the connection needed to make sense of (V) when placed after ᵃ8.

8. This whole section, 325ᵇ36–326ᵃ24, can thus be reduced to something like order and good sense, without any too drastic measures. Admittedly, the placing and point of (II) ('for [it] cannot be either hard or cold': 326ᵃ3) remain obscure. It might perhaps stand in its present position, as an illustration of Aristotle's implicit reasoning, though it would be one of those illustrations that is no help to the reader who has not already seen the general point that is being illustrated. It might have stood more usefully (e.g.) at 326ᵃ18. Also the placing of (V) after ᵃ8, though attractive, is at best conjectural. But apart from these two small bits, we have a sequence of coherent and intelligible arguments, focusing on the problems caused by the absolute indivisibility of the atoms, in connection with their possession or lack of sense–perceptible *pathê*. As has been noted, there is a close affinity with *de Caelo* III. 1. 299ᵃ2–300ᵃ19 (arguments on the same theme, but ostensibly directed against Plato's *Timaeus*) and with *de Caelo* III. 8.

9. The second section (326ᵃ24–ᵇ6) offers some more general problems with atomism as a physical theory.

(A) (ᵃ24–29). Absolute indivisibility should not require small size (as it did for Leucippus at least, 325ᵃ30):[26] the association of indivisibility and smallness is inexplicable, since indivisibility is not caused by smallness.

(B) (ᵃ29–ᵇ2: see app. on some points of language). A dilemma on the question of 'one nature' for atoms. (a) If all atoms have the same nature, what keeps them apart when they touch; why don't they just merge like raindrops? There can't be anything to differentiate and keep them apart, when the void doesn't. (b) But if they have different natures (i) what are these different natures? (ii) The principles will then have to be these particular natures, not just atoms and void. And (iii) they will in this case individually act and be acted upon, when in contact (this assumes Aristotle's own view of what is sufficient for action–passion).

(C) Finally (ᵇ2–6) on the source of motion for atoms. (a) If the source of their motion isn't in the atoms themselves, then something outside will

---

[26] The upper limit on the size of atoms is affirmed for Democritus as well at fr. 208 Rose³.

cause them to move. But how are they caused to move? If by being struck or pushed by another atom, this implies resistance, and they must be hard (cf. above); in which case they can have *pathê* (hard/soft). (b) If they move themselves, they will be divisible; otherwise, being indivisible, they will violate the principle of non-contradiction, and opposites will be true of the very same thing simultaneously. The analysis of self-movers in *Physics* book VIII is invoked here, and the thought is just that of *Physics* VIII. 5. 257^b2–12. If in a self-mover the part that moves and the part that is moved are identical, then two absurd consequences follow: (i) the very same part, 'one and indivisible in form', will be causing and undergoing motion simultaneously; (ii) if the change is from not-X to X, the same part will be both already X (as the mover) and not yet X (as that which is being moved).

'Their matter will be not only one in number but also one in potentiality'. This too is immediately intelligible in the light of the *Physics* VIII passage: it corresponds exactly to 'one and indivisible in form' (257^b3–4). What is indivisible in form is not even potentially divisible.[27]

10. Two Aristotelian criticisms of atomism are here notable by their absence: the impossibility of void (which is not dependent on the nature of indivisibles); and the impossibility of indivisibles on *mathematical* grounds. Aristotle here concentrates on the purely physical arguments against indivisibles, as being the appropriate ones for natural science. This differs strikingly from *de Caelo* III. 1. 299^a12–17, where it is said that the mathematical impossibility entails a physical one (and so is directly relevant to natural science).

11. Aristotle's basic disagreement with the atomists, as well as his admiration for their methods, goes much deeper than the question of the physics of action–passion. He does indeed make some very general criticisms on this question in chapter 9, 327^a14–25. These, it might be said, are the real counterpart for the atomists to the criticism of Empedocles' pores. But, at 2. 315^b24–8, he insists that the really crucial question for all physical theory is whether or not to take the primary magnitudes to be *indivisible*. In agreement with that, the examination of the atomists in I. 8 focuses on what the assumption of indivisibles means for physical theory generally. (This examination is oddly placed in I. 8, it may fairly be said; it would be more logical to locate it earlier in the book.) It makes use of, or is at least closely related to, the relevant parts of *de Caelo* III and IV, and of *Physics* VI and VIII. Aristotle's unusually positive attitude to the atomists' achievement overall does not extend to the postulation of indivisibility, to which he maintains his opposition.

---

[27] So too 'one in potentiality' at *Ph.* I. 9. 192^a2 has to be understood as 'one in form': see Ross (1936) ad loc.

The atomist void, and the mechanisms for action–passion that go with it, are another matter. In I. 9, as mentioned, there are some criticisms of these in general terms. But that Aristotle has no real problems in *GC* I with the atomists' *mechanisms*, in themselves, or even with *void*, is perhaps suggested in I. 8 by the fact that he assimilates Empedocles' theory to theirs (325^b5–11). Now Empedocles' theory is destroyed on its own terms, for Aristotle, by the problem of what fills the 'pores'; for Empedocles cannot allow void to do that. But the atomists can; so their mechanism is implied by Aristotle to be unassailable on its own terms; that is, granted their presuppositions. (Aristotle himself seems willing to accept the analogous possibility of 'veins' (φλέβες: 326^b35).)

The chapter as a whole: some remarks

1. The notable 'sandwich-like' structure of the chapter has already been mentioned. So have the awkward and abrupt transitions at 325^b12–24. Similar structural features can, of course, be found in many other places in the works of Aristotle, and are no doubt in some way a consequence of his methods of work.[28] But the detailed 'geological' history of the evolution of Aristotle's writings inevitably escapes us. It would be foolhardy to try to reach, on the evidence available, firm conclusions about the genesis of the chapter as we read it.

Nevertheless, a commentator is bound, when faced with such 'geological' features, not merely to point them out, but also, if possible, to indicate what *kind* of hypothesis might plausibly account for them. In the present case it is not difficult to construct a simple hypothesis. Examination of the text shows that the passages in which the atomists are the centre of attention hang together well internally and with one another: these are 324^b35–325^b11, and 325^b24 (from ὥσπερ) to 326^b6. If these are removed, what remains is the skeletal framework of the discussion, plus the exposition and criticism of Empedocles' theory (324^b25–35; 325^b12–24 (ἁπάντων); 326^b6–28). It looks very much as though the original exposition of the atomist and other theories of action–passion (presupposed by 325^b12–15), and the original criticisms of these theories, were at some point excised, to be replaced by the present material on the atomists, which had originally been written for some other work.

It may be objected that there is no obvious reason why Aristotle should have intruded this more general material on the atomists into his discussion of the theories of action–passion. That is true, but all that can sensibly be hoped for is a reasonably plausible motivation.

---

[28] See Myles Burnyeat's introduction to this volume, pp. 7 ff. above.

A possible scenario, for instance, is the following. Aristotle, after a rereading of atomist writings, wished to revise *GC* I, so as to make it much more of a direct and detailed confrontation with atomism on the really fundamental questions at issue in natural science.[29] The first step, for I. 8, was to take the relevant material from some other piece of work and splice it into the original discussion in an approximately satisfactory way. This was done; but the chapter was never properly reworked thereafter.

2. A connected but independent question about I. 8 is the general nature of its criticisms of the atomists, and in particular its treatment of the atomistic void.

We have seen that in the criticism of atomism Aristotle draws upon certain abstract analyses in *Physics* books VI and VIII; and that there is a general affinity with the criticisms of atomism in *de Caelo* books III and IV. What perhaps distinguishes the criticism in *GC* I. 8 from all of these is the determination to bring abstract analysis into contact with the physical realities that natural science has to confront.

As for void, it is clear in the criticism of Empedocles (326^b16–20) that Aristotle is there just as much opposed to any form of actual void, whether 'separated' or not, as he is in *Physics* IV. 5–9. But in the treatment of the atomists he notably does *not* make their void a target for criticism, though he perhaps hints at his non-acceptance of it at 325^a27 (see app. on 325^b25–9). One possible explanation is that he has come to see the question of the void as a secondary one for natural science. His thinking would then be as follows: If one operates with indivisible bodies as the atomists did then some sort of void is a necessity; but if not, not. It is the question of indivisibility that is primary, and closer to the physical realities with which natural science deals, and therefore the natural scientist should take it first.[30]

[29] Naturally, I am not suggesting that such a hypothesis is sufficient to account for all the structural problems of *GC* I. For example, it will not by itself account for the problems raised by *GC* I. 1 and 2, on which see the papers by Jacques Brunschwig and David Sedley in this volume. Still, there are enough parallels and homologies between I. 1–2 and I. 8 to make a further hypothesis worth airing. We might try out, as a variant of Brunschwig's hypothesis (I. 2 as a rewriting of I. 1), and as a parallel to the hypothesis about I. 8, the suggestion that *GC* I. 1 and I. 2 likewise contain material belonging to two different versions ('original' and 'intruded'), and, in particular, that the passages in I. 2, praising the atomists at Plato's expense and examining the Democritean argument for indivisibles (315^a29–$^b15$, 315^b24–317^a17), belong to the 'intruded' material. (There is further point of contact between I. 8 and I. 1–2 (as Jaap Mansfeld remarks): 325^b13–24 on Empedocles echoes the harsh treatment of Empedocles in I. 1, as being inconsistent both with the *phainomena* and with himself (315^a3–4).)

[30] For criticisms, suggestions, encouragement, and the invaluable atmosphere of co-operative discussion at Deurne, I am indebted to all the members of the 1999 Symposium, whether mentioned by name above or not.

Appendix: some points of text and language

325ᵃ17. There is no need to suppose a lacuna after ἀληθείας (ᵃ17), as Joachim does. It is true that ἔτι hardly gives an apt connection. But Marvan Rashed has shown that the manuscript tradition is here divided between ἔτι and ἐπεί (hitherto reported as an isolated reading of one manuscript (L) only). Hence we not only can but must read ἐπεί. This yields a long sentence, ending only at ὄντων (ᵃ25), in which the ἐπεί clause goes right on down to διαφέρειν (ᵃ23); then follows a 'resumptive' or 'apodotic' δ' to pull the unwieldy structure together again ('well, so then Leucippus...'). Such apparently colloquial sentence structure is found occasionally in Aristotle, though attempts have sometimes been made to remove it by 'emendation': e.g. GC II. 10. 337ᵃ17–22, de An. 433ᵇ13–18, Pol. 1278ᵃ32, Rh. 1355ᵃ10 (other examples in Bonitz (1870) s.v. Anacoluthia, 47ᵃ4–18; on apodotic and resumptive δέ see Denniston (1934) 177–81 and 182–3).

325ᵃ26–9. The textual tradition has until now been thought to be (with minor variations): τοῖς δὲ τὸ ἓν κατασκευάζουσιν ὡς οὐκ ἂν κίνησιν οὖσαν ἄνευ κενοῦ, τό τε κενὸν μὴ ὄν, καὶ τοῦ ὄντος οὐθὲν μὴ ὂν φησιν εἶναι. τὸ γὰρ κυρίως ὂν παμπλῆρες ὄν. Here, on a superficial view, all seems acceptable. The researches of Marvan Rashed on the textual tradition have transformed the situation. He shows that at ᵃ28–9 one branch of the tradition has no γάρ; further, the tradition is split between ὄν and ἕν for the word after κυρίως.

Removing the γάρ gives a much more logical structure, in which the three Eleatic theses accepted by Leucippus are joined together as coordinate (by οὔτε, τε, καί), and are all governed by ὁμολογήσας and separated syntactically from Leucippus' own contribution, which is introduced by φησιν, thus: τοῖς δὲ τὸ ἓν κατασκευάζουσιν ὡς οὐκ ἂν κίνησιν οὖσαν ἄνευ κενοῦ, τό τε κενὸν μὴ ὄν, καὶ τοῦ ὄντος οὐθὲν μὴ ὄν, φησίν εἶναι τὸ κυρίως ὂν [or: ἕν] παμπλῆρες ὄν.

Some care is needed with the syntax. ὡς οὐκ ἂν κίνησιν οὖσαν ἄνευ κενοῦ, after ὁμολογήσας, is 'accusative absolute' with ὡς after a verb of saying: there is a close parallel at Pl. Cri. ἃ ἄν τις ὁμολογήσῃ τῳ δίκαια ὄντα (49e6: for the construction see Kühner-Blass II. 2, sects. 482. 2; 484. 18; 488. 1d). The coordinated clauses τό τε κενὸν μὴ ὄν, καὶ τοῦ ὄντος οὐθὲν μὴ ὄν, should, therefore, continue the same construction. It should be noted that, since negation in such clauses is regularly expressed by οὐ and not by μή, the expression μὴ ὄν is here twice functioning not as a negated participle parallel to οὖσαν but as an indivisible whole in the special sense of 'what-is-not'. (The ὄν which would have been parallel to οὖσαν has been twice, idiomatically, omitted: Kühner-Blass II. 2, sect. 491.) The ὡς in this construction seems here, as sometimes elsewhere, to have the effect of distancing the speaker or writer from the propositions stated: Aristotle is indicating that Leucippus was not (necessarily) right to accept these Eleatic principles.

The second question raised by Rashed's researches here is whether ὄν or ἕν is the preferable reading after κυρίως. The tradition is evenly split, the two readings are palaeographically very close, and the types of error involved (assimilation of ἕν to ὄν, or dissimilation of ὄν to ἕν) seem equally possible. A decision can be founded only on the relevance of either reading to the context. On that ground ὄν is to be preferred, since it makes it easier to understand Aristotle's account of how Leucippus succeeded in reconciling the Eleatic premises with the world of experience.

Finally, in φησίν εἶναι τὸ κυρίως ὄν παμπλῆρες ὄν the second ὄν must be functioning not as an ordinary participle but as a substantive (just as in the two previous instances of μὴ ὄν), and παμπλῆρες is attributive: 'that which is, in the principal sense, is absolutely-full-being'.

325ᵇ28. τῶν ἀδιαιρέτων στερεῶν ἕκαστον, excised by Joachim as illogical, can perhaps be defended as a concise conflation of two thoughts: (a) there are infinitely many possible shapes for the indivisibles collectively; (b) a shape is something that necessarily belongs to (one or more) particular indivisibles.

325ᵇ29–31. The objections of Joachim and of Verdenius and Waszink to the transmitted text have force; it can hardly stand. The 'two manners' should be those of the atomists and of Plato (as at ᵇ25–6). The least radical remedy would be to read ἐκ δὴ ... διακρίσεις, <καὶ> (or <ἂν>) δύο τρόποι ἂν εἶεν, Λευκίππῳ μὲν.

326ᵃ3. We should (following Verdenius and Waszink) take καίτοι (ᵃ3) as progressive.

326ᵃ6. On κᾶν εἰ here see Bonitz (1870) s.v. ἄν, 41ᵃ4–47, who gives many parallels.

326ᵃ12. There is a split in the textual tradition: θερμόν and ψυχρόν both have support. Not much seems to hang on the choice, but θερμόν is perhaps preferable as a little less obvious.

326ᵃ16. The textual tradition is divided between σκληρόν and ψυχρόν. The latter is preferable on grounds of sense.

326ᵃ19. The textual tradition is split between ἧπερ and εἴπερ. On the interpretation here proposed, either gives adequate sense, provided ἧπερ is taken in its local meaning. We must also understand ταύτῃ as local.

326ᵃ34. 'The one in front' and 'the one behind' are puzzling expressions, but may refer to atoms drawn diagrammatically. This may also be the explanation of the similarly puzzling τοῦ προύχοντος and προέξει in Zeno fr. B1 DK. To take τὸ ὕστερον as 'the latter example [of raindrops]' and τοῦ προτέρου as 'the former case [of atoms]' is not in accord with Aristotelian usage.

326ᵃ34–5. We should probably write εἰ δ' ἕτερα (rather than εἰ δ' ἔτερα), since it is a difference in the *nature* of different atoms that is being supposed. But ποῖα ταῦτα and the second ταῦτα in ᵃ35 then need explanation. The simplest view would be that they refer to the different natures, but are switched into the neuter in a *constructio ad sensum*.

326ᵇ2–6. On the interpretation given above, one should place a strong stop after ὑπάρξει. Also, the καί of καὶ ἡ ὕλη is then best taken not as progressive but as 'reminiscent', almost equivalent to καίτοι (for this use see Denniston (1934), 292). The sentence it introduces is not a statement of the absurd consequence, but reminds the reader of a relevant feature of the hypothetical situation, a feature which helps to generate the absurdity.

326ᵇ6–8. The textual tradition is διὰ τῆς τῶν πόρων κινήσεως, but attempts to justify it are not convincing. One should accept Mugler's simple suggestion, διὰ τῆς ⟨διὰ⟩ τῶν πόρων κινήσεως, as by far the most probable remedy (the second διά being lost by haplography). The word διά, as at 325ᵇ3, 325ᵇ31, may well be deliberately double-sensed (see Sect. 6, 243–4 and n.21).

326ᵇ18. Take ἤ (ᵇ18) as epexegetic.

10

On Generation and Corruption I. 9

MICHEL CRUBELLIER

Chapter 9 of *On Generation and Corruption* I is comparatively short, but neither its topic nor its structure is fully clear on a first reading. Modern commentators have followed the interpretation of Philoponus, who distinguished chapter 9 from the preceding discussions because he considered that Aristotle, 'having refuted the hypotheses by which the ancients accounted for affecting and being affected, sets out the remaining conception; that is the true one'.[1] The opening sentence supports this description of the chapter. Aristotle says: 'Let us explain the way in which things possess generation and action and passion, and let us start from the principle we have often enunciated' (326^b29–30). Since this 'starting point' ($\dot{a}\rho\chi\acute{\eta}$) turns out to be the eminently Aristotelian doctrine of actuality and potentiality, it may seem that Philoponus' interpretation must be valid. Unfortunately, the remainder of the chapter does not read like a straightforward development of such a programme. Its main part (327^a6–25, 20 lines out of the 36 of the whole chapter) returns to the criticism of rival theories already developed in the second part of chapter 8 (325^b13–326^b26). Only eleven lines of the first part (326^b31–327^a6) contain a piece of positive doctrine—two distinct theses, expressed in a very brief and compressed manner. Thus we have to ask whether this chapter, as individuated by modern editors, does have a literary or argumentative unity, or whether it should not rather be seen as an appendix, or loose series of additional notes, to the main discussion of chapters 7 and 8.

The text is made up of five main sections, each of which shows syntactical and logical continuity, although the transitions between them are far from clear. This division into five sections coincides with the demarcations marked out by Philoponus, and it is followed by Williams in his commentary, though neither of them examines the unity and continuity of the chapter as a whole.

---

[1] Phlp. *in GC* 182. 10–11.

(a) 326^b29–327^a1: The title sentence ($^b29$–30), followed by the statement of the thesis that a body affected by the agency of another body is affected, or rather susceptible of being affected, throughout ($^b31$–2). This statement is governed by a conditional which indicates the 'principle' or 'starting point' on which it rests, and followed by a qualification ($^b32$–4) which leads Aristotle to what appears to be a concession to the theory of pores.

(b) 327^a1–6: Two conditions for one body to affect another: the bodies must be distinct from each other ($^a1$), but also in contact, either immediately or through another body susceptible of the same affection, just as air works as an intermediary between the sun and some particular body (e.g. a stone or the sea) which the sun warms ($^a1$–6).

(c) 327^a6–14: This section is particularly obscure. It presents itself as a critical examination of the contradictory thesis; that is, the claim that the affected body is susceptible 'in some of its parts, but not in others', introducing two alternatives which recall the dialectical arguments of chapter 2: either there are indivisible bodies, or all bodies are divisible. One is tempted to see these as two horns of a refutative dilemma, but the discussion does not result in any explicit conclusion. In fact, even the outcome of the second horn of the dilemma (if such it is) appears obscure, enunciated as it is in the cryptic sentence: οὐδὲν διαφέρει διῃρῆσθαι μὲν ἅπτεσθαι δέ, ἢ διαιρετὸν εἶναι (327^a10–11). The following section begins with an ὅλως ('More generally speaking...') which strongly suggests progress in the same line of argumentation; and since this section is clearly polemical, it seems reasonable to accept that the preceding section was too. But one must be careful here, since it is not clear whether both passages do discuss the same thesis or theses.

(d) 327^a14–25: Here Aristotle develops two independent, but parallel, arguments against a rival conception. The first (ll. 15–22) is that (on this conception) alteration in the strict sense of the word would be impossible, and the second (ll. 22–5) is that growth and diminution would become impossible as well. But notice that we are given here a quite different account of what I elusively called the 'rival conception': 'nothing can be generated except in this way, that is, by a splitting of the <affected> body'. This phrase is more comprehensive and less precise than those Aristotle used in (a) and (c), and might well have been devised to cover the whole range of the theses examined in chapter 8: Democritean atoms and Empedoclean pores, as well as Plato's elemental triangles. So it might also refer (as I think it does) to the discussions of that chapter.

(e) 327^a25–9: This is a general conclusion which recapitulates the preceding discussions by means of three related questions.

Let us consider first this last section, keeping in mind that we will have to determine which part of the text is meant to be summarized here. (Is it our chapter alone, or the whole of chapters 7–9, or something else?) The three questions which Aristotle raises indicate three distinct goals:

(e₁) to establish that generating and acting on, being generated and being acted upon, really occur;
(e₂) to show in which way such processes are possible;
(e₃) to examine critically some rival answers to question (e₂), and to show that the explanations offered by these theories are 'impossible' (οὐκ ἐνδέχεται).

The object of this investigation is described in (e₁) by the complex formula τὸ γεννᾶν καὶ τὸ ποιεῖν καὶ τὸ γιγνέσθαί τε καὶ πάσχειν ὑπ' ἀλλήλων (ᵃ26–7)—Nearly the same list, with the omission of γιγνέσθαι, as is to be found in the title sentence of the chapter (ᵇ29–30). The conjunction τὸ γιγνέσθαί τε καὶ πάσχειν suggests a grouping by pairs (generating and acting, on the one hand, being generated and being acted upon, on the other), in which the second term explains or specifies the first one. If this is so, 'generating' and 'being generated' cannot mean only (and maybe not at all) absolute generation but will rather apply to cases in which some feature is brought about in one thing by the influence or agency of another one. This 'feature' may be a qualitative or quantitative property, as well as the specific form which characterizes some substance, so that the only kind of change which is left aside is local motion. On the other hand, it is important to note that the 'things' here are bodies. It is true that the words ὑπ' ἀλλήλων do not refer explicitly to any specific class of objects. Similarly, the title sentence mentions only 'beings', so that it might include, for instance, the process of heat producing heat. Nevertheless, the discussions in chapter 9 constantly refer to *bodies*, and this qualification seems essential, since Aristotle's arguments (or at least some of them) bear on the divisibility or dividedness of the 'things' in question. Furthermore, it appears that Aristotle refers not only (as he did in ch. 7) to qualitative influence but also to other types of change, since he mentions growth and diminution (that is, a change of quantity predicated in the thing affected) in section (d).

While it is clear enough that the three questions just introduced do encompass the contents of chapters 7–9 as a whole, it is not so easy to determine exactly where each of them receives its proper and specific answer. Perhaps this is obvious in the case of (e₃), the critical examination of Aristotle's predecessors' theories which has been carried out in chapter 8 and in a large part of chapter 9. But where has Aristotle demonstrated (e₁) that acting on and being acted upon are real processes? Although one might think this was done in chapter 7, the last lines of that chapter (324ᵇ22–4) do not mention ὅτι ἔστι ('that it is'), but only τί ἐστι ('what it is'). In fact, this latter phrase seems to fit in better with the general topic of the chapter. For, although it does not contain an explicit definition or description of acting and being acted upon, Aristotle seems, while establishing in chapter 7 the conditions for one body to act on another, to show what acting and being acted upon really are. Perhaps the absence of a formal demonstration of the existence of these processes should not surprise us. For who would seriously doubt that they actually exist? Their case seems different from that of blending, which might plausibly be considered as a mere appearance and reduced to some other phenomenon, as emerges in chapter 10. However, we know that there were, in ancient Greece, some thinkers who did deny the existence of action and passion: the Eleatics. And, indeed, Aristotle set out (in the first part of chapter 8) a line of argument intended to dismiss their paradoxical theses. But this line of argument was not his, but Leucippus' and Democritus', and immediately Aristotle proceeded to show that the hypotheses on which their argument rests had to be discarded. So he still needs an explanation of the possibility of action and passion to replace the atomist one which he has rejected. His problem might be stated thus: 'How is it possible to maintain, against the Eleatics, the reality of acting and being acted upon, without being committed to the atomist assumption of the discontinuity of matter?' We will see that this question is a clue to the unity of chapter 9.

The remaining question, (e_1), 'In which way can these processes occur?', coheres well with our title sentence ('Let us explain the way in which things possess generation and action and passion'). But we should notice that there is a very similar formula at the beginning of chapter 8: πῶς δὲ ἐνδέχεται τοῦτο συμβαίνειν, πάλιν λέγωμεν, and that a 'How?' question occurs in the final summary of chapter 7. In this last passage, admittedly, the issue turns precisely on a sort of general and formal condition which must exist between agent and patient: they must be different from one another but belong to the same genus. At this point Aristotle's question is: 'What kind of beings are able to come into an agent-to-patient relationship?', while in chapters 8 and 9 his question concerns the physical conditions of the process itself. This is clear in chapter 8, which sets out and discusses some models of the inner structure of physical bodies which are supposed to explain how one body can be affected through the agency of another. Thus, chapters 8 and 9 are closely interrelated, in the same way as questions (e_2) and (e_3) are. In fact, chapter 8 gives the doxographical background for the main philosophical question (e_3). So far, Philoponus is certainly right. But we are left with the problem of the strange or seemingly awkward composition of our chapter. For since Aristotle gives only a terse answer to his question, namely that the affected body must be affected 'through and through', and then seems to turn back to the refutation of Empedocles and the atomists, lines 26^{b}29–27^{a}6 read like a very short positive parenthesis buried in a copious polemical diatribe.

Still, Philoponus' interpretation might be defended in the face of these difficulties, since the question 'How are acting and being acted upon possible?', even though it remains substantially the same throughout, undergoes an important change in chapter 9. Aristotle rephrases it as a closed question, that is, as an alternative between two contradictory theses concerning the body which undergoes the change: either it is affected 'in some parts but not in others' (τῇ μὲν τῇ δ' οὔ), or it is affected 'through and through' (πάντῃ, 26^{b}31–2) (it is certainly significant that the first sentence of the chapter, which is also the first statement of Aristotle's own solution, explicitly contrasts it with its contradictory). Further, chapter 9 is dialectical, while chapter 8 was mainly doxographical. It is true that an important preparatory move was carried out in chapter 8, when Aristotle showed that Empedocles' theory (and Plato's as well) may be considered as a sort of variant of the atomistic model. But chapter 9 operates at a still higher level of abstraction, as it brings out a conceptual feature common to a set of theories, rather than focusing on one particular theory considered as the type of the set as a whole. The common feature in question is the notion that the process must be located in some places of the affected body and not in others. Indeed, once we appreciate that Aristotle was introducing examples to set up the basic conceptual structure for the whole discussion, we can more easily understand his apparently rash assimilation of Empedocle's pores, and the surfaces of contact between Plato's polyhedra, to the void of the atomists. All these theories involve the existence of 'places' in a physical body which are in a way 'parts' of it, without possessing the real nature or essential identity of this body. It does not matter whether these places are conceived as three-dimensional items with a definite and permanent form (as in the case of the channel-like πόροι), or changing and indefinite (the void between the atoms) or even, as in Plato, the two-dimensional *loci* of the contact surfaces. Naturally, this general and abstract account implies some schematization which may seem an oversimplification. Only Empedocles' theory of pores clearly involves partial affection. In the case of the atomists one cannot say without qualification that the internal void inside a body is 'affected', or that it is the path through which an affection penetrates the body. These complexities result in an equivocation in Aristotle's tactics: for although he says on several occasions that the atomistic model is the most consistent version of the position he attacks (since it proposes a clear model for the discontinuity of physical bodies), he takes most of his examples from the pore theory.

These reflections suggest that chapter 9 may be taken as an independent and comparatively continuous stretch of argument. Further, they can account for its inner unity, since Aristotle's own position is stated as one of a pair of alternatives. Thus, the negative aspect of the chapter provides strong corroboration for its affirmative one; indeed, it amounts to an indirect demonstration of its positive thesis.

1. The first thesis: a body is susceptible of being affected 'through and through'

This thesis is stated in lines [b]31–2: 'it is the nature of <the affected body> not merely to be susceptible of suffering action in some parts while insusceptible in others, but through and through'. The verb πέφυκε occurs with the same meaning in 323[b]30 and 33: it indicates a particular disposition of a body, which makes it capable of being affected by some agent. This sentence implies some narrowing of the topic, since it concerns only one member of the pair, the passive one. Such a restriction is certainly convenient for a dialectical treatment of the problem, since it allows for its presentation in a clear-cut way. Further, it can be justified on the basis of the results of the general analysis of change at the beginning of book III of the *Physics*, and particularly by the claim that the actualization of an agent and of the correlated patient is one and the same, and that it is located in the patient. From a doxographical point of view, it shows that Aristotle sees the explanations proposed by his predecessors as setting conditions which concern mainly or exclusively the affected body. As I said before, this is clearly so in the case of pores, which render the body capable of being invested with some quality (or of working as a medium in a physical process), but this is less clear within atomist theory. However, Aristotle does not stick to this restriction, since the conditions of possibility of the affection which he recalls in the second section include some aspects of its relation to the agent. To complete this literal explanation of the thesis, let me mention the obvious fact that the adverbs πῇ and πάντῃ in this context must have a strictly local meaning, in keeping with the use of πάντῃ in chapter 2 in the general discussion of the divisibility of bodies.

The thesis itself is accompanied by a conditional: εἰ γάρ ἐστι τὸ μὲν δυνάμει τὸ δ' ἐντελεχείᾳ τοιοῦτον, which Aristotle calls the 'starting point' or 'principle' of his account. Although the doctrine of potentiality and actuality is certainly 'well known' (πολλάκις εἰρημένην), less obvious is its relevance as a premiss for the conclusion that a body is affected through and through. First, one must determine the exact reference of τοιοῦτον. This is revealed in the following sentence, where it occurs twice and unequivocally means the quality or predicate that the agent produces in the affected body and which the affected body must 'have' or 'be' potentially by its very nature. Second, we must decide whether 'that which is *actually* such-and-such' refers to the agent's intrinsic possession of the feature designated by the predicate 'such-and-such' (this is Philoponus' interpretation) or to the actual presence of this property in the patient at the end of the process of being affected (as modern commentators, following Joachim, seem to understand it) or to both. It is to be noted that the conditional can have two different meanings, depending on whether one puts the stress on the opposition (τὸ μὲν . . . τὸ δέ . . .) or on the identity of the predicate 'such-and-such'. In the first case it means that 'to be potentially such-and-such' and 'to be actually such-and-such' are two distinct states, while in the second case it means that although these are different states, the meaning of the phrase ' . . . is such-and-such' is the same, and both states are just different phases of one and the same feature. Both interpretations are doctrinally and grammatically acceptable. Translators are divided, with a small majority in favour of the first solution (preferred by Forster, Gohlke, Joachim, Migliori, and Williams, while Mugler, Russo, and Tricot opt for the second solution). However, I cannot see how, on this interpretation, the intended conclusion follows from such a premiss, since the premiss would be strictly negative, saying only that being x in potentiality is not, or is not like, being x in actuality. The alternative interpretation, on the contrary, expresses a positive relation between these states. If taken in its full strength it must mean that 'being such-and-such' will be identical, in all, or in its most important, aspects when something is potentially, and when it is actually, such-and-such. One could compare this claim with Kant's remark that there is nothing more in the notion of twenty existing thalers than in the notion of twenty possible thalers; or, to take an example from our chapter, if a mass of ice is solid through and through, the same mass of water, when liquid (i.e. potentially-congealed), must be potentially-solid through and through. So we could obtain our conclusion in a plausible way by adding one supplementary premiss:

'to be x' is basically the same thing, be it in potentiality or in actuality;
<qualitative states of a physical body, when actualized, are present in all its parts>;
therefore, the possibility of such states, when it exists in some physical body, must be present in all its parts.

One might question the second premiss. It seems very close—maybe too close—to the desired conclusion. But the claim expressed in the conclusion is weaker than that. It does not demand that the quality x could not be actualized in some parts and not in others, but only that it can be actualized in any part. Suppose you are able to test in some way or other the presence or absence of '*x*-susceptibility' in an unaffected body. Then wherever you investigate, and however small the test zone, the thesis says that you will find that it is susceptible of becoming *x*. But, if this is so, is it justified to assume as a general rule that if a body is actually *x*, then it must be *x* πάντῃ, 'through and through'? There are cases of change where the body seems to be affected in this way, but these cases are comparatively rare, and everyday experience shows many examples of partial or non-uniform affection. Aristotle could answer that if a body is not actually *x* in all its parts then there remains in it some amount of potentiality, or alternatively if these parts cannot be, and will never be, *x* in actuality, then they are not, properly speaking, parts of the affected body. Still, one might ask why he seems to consider 'through-and-through affection' as the rule, and the latter cases as degenerate forms.

I will return shortly to this question, which bears upon the abstract and, so to speak, metaphysical significance of the thesis. However, for the time being, let us follow Aristotle, who meets the objection at a more empirical level in the second part of section (a), where he introduces a restriction or qualification of the main thesis. I assume that this second part begins right after πάντῃ, although there is no punctuation at this place in Joachim's text: καθ' ὅσον ἐστὶ τοιοῦτον, ἧττον δὲ καὶ μᾶλλον ᾗ τοιοῦτον μᾶλλόν ἐστι καὶ ἧττον· καὶ ταύτῃ πόρους ἄν τις λέγοι μᾶλλον, καθάπερ ἐν τοῖς μεταλλευομένοις διατείνουσι τοῦ παθητικοῦ φλέβες συνεχεῖς (26ᵇ32–27ᵃ1): [a body is susceptible through and through] 'precisely in so far as it is such-and-such. Its susceptibility varies in degree according as it is more or less such-and-such, and in that regard one would be more justified in speaking of "pores", that is veins of <greater> susceptibility, just like <the veins of ores> stretching continuously in the mines'. It is important to realize that the phrase καθ' ὅσον ἐστὶ τοιοῦτον cannot belong to the statement of the main thesis, for it would turn it into a mere tautology: a body would be 'susceptible of being affected', that is of receiving the property of being *x*, in so far as it is (potentially, it must be assumed) *x*. Indeed, that would amount, as Williams says,[2] to the old story of the dormitive virtue of opium. Thus, it is better to stress the καθ' ὅσον and view this phrase as introducing a qualification of the thesis. The aim of such a qualification is easy to understand. Aristotle probably thinks he has to make his thesis cohere with empirical data which suggest that susceptibility, like physical qualities in general, is not always uniform in physical bodies, and that he must do so without departing from the strict phrasing demanded by the 'either/or' form he has followed in

---

[2] Williams (1982), 138.

his discussion. Thus, he admits, it is true that many bodies do not seem to behave in a strictly homogeneous manner when involved in reciprocal change and affection, but he contends that this does not jeopardize the thesis itself, as long as those inner differences can be considered as variations in the degree of susceptibility, so that the body be seen as susceptible in all its parts, but not to the same degree in every part. In a gesture of equity of a type not uncommon from him, although seldom devoid of ulterior motive, Aristotle declares he is ready to acknowledge a certain validity in the pore theory, but (1) only in some particular cases, (2) only at a macroscopic level (since in his version the so-called 'pores' are made of a stuff which itself is already capable of being affected, with the result that these alleged pores do not account for the susceptibility, but rather presuppose it), and (3) in a way which depends on relative differences between more receptive and less receptive zones in a continuous mass. In sum, his gesture amounts to a rejection of the pore model as a universal explanation of acting and being acted upon. Let me insist on the second point (the scale of the phenomenon under consideration), because it is crucial for the subsequent argument, as it implies a distinction between a physical level and another one which might be called (anachronistically) 'microphysical', but in fact is rather metaphysical. The formula $\tau\hat{\eta}$ $\mu\grave{\epsilon}\nu$ $\tau\hat{\eta}$ δ' $o\mathring{v}$ does not refer to any spatial repartition of the susceptibility or of the process of affection, but must apply to the ultimate parts of a body. That is why Aristotle will affirm later that this thesis can only be upheld within a discontinuist conception of matter (27ᵃ7–9).

The text of this section raises a small but interesting archaeological problem: To what does the comparison $\kappa\alpha\theta\acute{\alpha}\pi\epsilon\rho$ $\grave{\epsilon}\nu$ $\tauo\hat{\imath}\varsigma$ $\mu\epsilon\tau\alpha\lambda\lambda\epsilon\upsilon o\mu\acute{\epsilon}\nuo\iota\varsigma$ etc. refer? Some translators speak of 'veins of susceptible stuff stretching continuously through the substance' of metals (Joachim and the Revised Oxford Translation, Migliori and Tricot. Gohlke, Mugler, and Russo prefer to translate $\tau\grave{\alpha}$ $\mu\epsilon\tau\alpha\lambda\lambda\epsilon\upsilon\acute{o}\mu\epsilon\nu\alpha$ as 'the mines'; Forster and Williams are more evasive). But after a short survey of ancient texts on that topic, and some conversations with metallurgists, I have not been able to find any phenomenon which plausibly matches this description. On the contrary, metals appear to be models of physical homogeneity. And although it is probable that metals produced by the ancient smiths were not as homogeneous as ours, it is very unlikely that the irregularities caused by their primitive techniques could have brought out effects that they could have noticed with their—equally rudimentary—methods of measurement. Moreover, what kind of irregularities might they have observed? Certainly not differences of conductivity of heat or electricity. One might think only of mechanical properties, such as differences of solidity. However, the 'flaws' in a metal piece are caused by its structure rather than qualitative differences in the metal itself. Of course, there is

one passage in Alexander of Aphrodisias' *Questions* which deals with the
magnetic properties of the 'stone of Heraclea' and mentions some explanations of these facts by means of 'pores'.[3] But these explanations
(which Alexander unsurprisingly attributes to Empedocles and Democritus) are precisely of the kind Aristotle is trying to rule out in our chapter.
For such pores appear to be ad hoc fictions, while Aristotle, when he
speaks of the μεταλλευόμενα, obviously has particular empirical facts in
mind. So that it seems more plausible that μεταλλευόμενα here are the
mines or deposits of ores or native metals. This meaning, though less
frequent in the Aristotelian corpus than that of 'metals', is well attested
in Greek texts of the same period. If this is correct, the mention of 'veins'
here would only provide a model for the spatial structure of the 'more
susceptible' parts of a body (so that their form could resemble the
Empedoclean pores), but should not be considered as a real example of
such a difference of susceptibility in nature. I assume that as a result of a
compressed syntax (as often in Aristotle's prose) the genitive τοῦ
παθητικοῦ does not belong to the term of comparison (i.e. the veins of
metal in the rock), but to the term compared (the unspecified bodies in
which the zones of greater susceptibility are supposedly distributed in
'veins'). Be that as it may, this is certainly a case in which one may safely
avail oneself of the old adage: 'This does not affect the general meaning
of the argument, which is quite clear.'

2. The two conditions of the agent-to-patient relation

The second section (327^a1-6) sets out two conditions for one body to act
upon another: (b_1) they must be distinct, that is they must not form
together some object 'naturally coherent and one', but (b_2) they must be
in contact, either directly or through another which would be able both
to be affected and to affect with respect to the same feature.

What is the exact meaning of the first condition? It might mean (a
claim important in Aristotle's discussion of atomism) that what is one
and absolutely simple cannot be affected in any way whatever. If the
sentence is understood in that way it will be another concession (and a
more real one) to the rival theories, which all presuppose that the affected
body is made of really distinct parts. However, it should be noted that the
words συμφυές and σύμφυσις are used in the *Physics* to denote the relation
between the parts of the continuous body. Indeed, one may read a strictly
parallel sentence in *Physics* book IV: 'Things which are one by nature
(συμπεφυκότα) are not affected by one another, but if they are in contact

---

[3] Alex. Aphrod. *Quaest.* 72–4.

they can act and be acted upon' (*Ph.* IV. 5. 212ᵇ31–3).[4] Thus, I assume that the phrase συμφυὲς καὶ ἕν ὄν applies to two objects, although it states that they are συμφυές and in this way one. Under this assumption, the two conditions will seem quite clear. The first is well attested in Aristotle, and the second was generally accepted as an analytical truth until the time of Newton, and maybe that of Kant. Moreover, they are nicely symmetrical, since the first one expresses the necessity of a real distinction between the bodies involved in a process of physical influence, while the second warns us that this distinction must not be turned into an absolute separation.

So far, so good, but there are two further difficulties. One concerns the role of this section in the chapter, since it seems to interrupt the discussion of integral or partial susceptibility, which starts up again at line 327ᵇ6. The other concerns the obviousness of these conditions: what is the point of introducing them here? To begin with the second question, let us observe that the two conditions do not boil down to an insignificant truism. Although they could be admitted without difficulty by a supporter of a discontinuist theory of matter, and even by an atomist, they are carefully phrased in the vocabulary of *Physics* book V, which suggests an alternative picture: a world without any void, in which well-individuated and continuous bodies may act upon one another through contact, provided that one of them be potentially what the other is actually. The phrase ἃ ποιεῖν πέφυκε καὶ πάσχειν, at lines 327ᵃ2–3, would be redundant in an atomistic perspective, but has its full meaning in Aristotle's world, where it leads to a distinction between pairs of objects (or chains, on the model of sun, air, and stone) which are liable to start a process of action and passion and others which are not. So this section is an important part of Aristotle's development of his own conception of action and passion.

It is not so easy to account for its position in the chapter. Indeed, I must admit that I have not reached a satisfactory answer to this question, partly because its resolution would require a satisfactory explanation of the next section, which is particularly obscure. That said, it is worth noting how this section is connected with the preceding and the following one. It is introduced by μὲν οὖν, which itself is ambiguous, since it can be interpreted as a collocation (μέν + οὖν) or as a combination. The first reading seems natural, given that μέν is answered by a δέ in the following line ('*On the one hand*, the two bodies involved in the process must be distinct, but *on the other hand* they must not be separate'). But this would make οὖν an independent particle, which must then be either conclusive

---

[4] See also *Ph.* VIII. 4. 255ᵃ12–18, where the point is the elimination of the hypothesis of a self-mover.

or resumptive. Most translators understand it in this way. Joachim alone[5] writes 'indeed', which captures the use of μὲν οὖν to express an undisputable fact. This is more plausible in this context, since one cannot find in the preceding lines anything which could be summarized or brought to a conclusion by the words συμφυὲς μὲν οὖν ἕκαστον καὶ ἓν ὂν ἀπαθές. Further, 'indeed' fits well with the fact that these conditions, as I have already remarked, could be accepted even by Aristotle's most radical opponents.

As to the transition to the next section, we must notice that its first sentence (327^a6–7) is particularly obscure, a situation which led Joachim to suspect a lacuna in the text at line 6. For these two lines, if construed according to ordinary syntax, would mean: 'Having distinguished at the beginning <various versions of> the claim that a body can be affected in some parts and not in others, we now have to say this: ...'. The 'beginning' would then be the enumeration of the discontinuist models in the previous chapter. But Joachim rightly observes that the following lines do not allude at all to differences between the doctrines of the predecessors, but do have striking resemblances with the dialectical discussions of chapter 2 about continuous or indivisible magnitudes. So he assumes that there must be a lacuna in the text and proposes the following restitution: 'The supposition of partial susceptibility <*is possible only for those who hold an erroneous view concerning the divisibility of magnitudes. For us*> the following account results from the distinctions established at the beginning <of our treatise >'.[6] In fact, as Verdenius and Waszink rightly remarked, one can avoid such a heavy modification of the transmitted text, while keeping Joachim's general meaning, if one admits an anacoluthon.[7] As a result of their reasonable suggestion, the transition between sections (b) and (c) appears dry and even abrupt, since it is reduced to a mere δέ. But this is not at all impossible. In fact, such a use of δέ is common in Aristotle to mark a fresh start (this is the kind of δέ that one can often find at the beginning of a 'chapter'). Thus, it is possible to explain the order of the sequence 326^b29–327^a14 by saying that sections (a) and (b) go together to state the two parts of Aristotle's positive thesis, while (c) occurs as an appendix, where the negation of (a) is discussed and rejected. The reason why there is no such counterpart for (b) is apparently that, in Aristotle's view, these two conditions cannot be reasonably denied.

(Another possibility, and a very attractive one, would be to look for a premiss for the refutation developed in section (c) in the two conditions

---

[5] But not absolutely alone, for Marwan Rashed has taken a similar view in an unpublished translation.
[6] Joachim (1922), 173.   [7] Verdenius and Waszink (1968), 53–5.

of section (b). This is appealing because the model of parts in contact plays a prominent role in the discussion of the second horn of the dilemma at lines 327ᵃ10–14. I think that nevertheless this suggestion[8] must be resisted. The crucial point, in my opinion, is that the two conditions concern the relations between distinct bodies, while the following argument is about the inner structure of one single body. It is true that Aristotle sometimes proceeds in this way when he has to determine, within a phenomenon generally taken, without further analysis, as a unity, the exact conditions and the precise limits of its realization: he picks out the proper ($\pi\rho\hat{\omega}\tau os$) process, and what belongs properly ($\pi\rho\acute{\omega}\tau\omega s$) to it. He uses this tactic for instance in the *Physics*, when he defines the 'proper place' of a body (IV. 2) or the 'proper instant' of a change (VI. 2), and in the criticism of the notion of a self-mover in book VIII. In this discussion he claims that the proposed self-mover, although it apparently forms a unity, is a complex made of a moving part and a mover, each of which must be considered as a physical object distinct from the other. But the point, in our chapter, is not the distinction between active and passive parts of a compound thing but the distinction between parts susceptible or insusceptible of being affected. The two conditions of section (b) do not bear on that point.)

3. The dilemma at lines 327ᵃ7–14

This section is particularly obscure, mainly because it seems oddly curtailed or unfinished. The opening sentence ($\tau\grave{o}$ $\delta\grave{e}$ $\tau\hat{\eta}$ $\mu\grave{e}\nu$ $o\ddot{\iota}e\sigma\theta\alpha\iota$ $\pi\acute{a}\sigma\chi\epsilon\iota\nu$ $\tau\hat{\eta}$ $\delta\grave{e}$ $\mu\acute{\eta}$, $\delta\iota o\rho\acute{\iota}\sigma\alpha\nu\tau\alpha s$ $\grave{e}\nu$ $\grave{a}\rho\chi\hat{\eta}$ $\tau o\hat{\upsilon}\tau o$ $\lambda\epsilon\kappa\tau\acute{e}o\nu$), besides the syntactical difficulty discussed above, raises problems of reference. We have already dealt with $\delta\iota o\rho\acute{\iota}\sigma\alpha\nu\tau\alpha s$ $\grave{e}\nu$ $\grave{a}\rho\chi\hat{\eta}$, but $\tau o\hat{\upsilon}\tau o$, at line 7, is also problematic. It may refer to what precedes (according to the regular usage), but also to what follows. The latter solution has been preferred by the great majority of translators, indeed by all except Mugler and perhaps Gohlke (Mugler refers $\tau o\hat{\upsilon}\tau o$ to the opponents' thesis, but he gives no reasons for this choice; besides, he adopts an implausible interpretation of $\delta\iota o\rho\acute{\iota}\sigma\alpha\nu\tau\alpha s$ $\grave{e}\nu$ $\grave{a}\rho\chi\hat{\eta}$[9]). Grammar is not enough to decide this point, since there are examples of $\tau o\hat{\upsilon}\tau o$ used to indicate what follows, but the possibility of a reference to what precedes must also be considered. In this case the

---

[8] I explored and defended an interpretation of that kind in former versions of this paper, in Padua and at the Symposium, but the remarks and objections of my audience served to convince me that this was, to say the least, a somewhat risky enterprise.

[9] 'Quand on pense qu'une chose peut être affectée dans telle de ses parties sans pouvoir être affectée dans telle autre, *il faut faire précéder ses affirmations d'une définition*' (Mugler (1966), 39, my emphasis).

sentence will mean: 'As to the claim that a body is susceptible in some parts but not in others, it must be taken with reference to the distinctions we established at the beginning', giving λέγειν (in λεκτέον 327^{a}7) its full sense of 'to mean' rather than 'to tell'. This is a regular, even if a somewhat rhetorical, way of introducing a refutation: Aristotle intends in fact to show the impossibility of the contrary thesis, but prefers to introduce his refutation as a question about the exact meaning of that thesis. I suppose this could be paraphrased thus: 'since we have already made (in chapter 2) some important distinctions about the ways in which a body may be said to be "divided", he who says that a body is affected "in some parts and not in others" must say which kind of "parts" he means'. Then he proceeds, using these distinctions, to show that none of the possible interpretations of this phrase stands up to critical examination.

This argument rests on a distinction between two conceptions of the divisibility of matter—or rather of bodies, geometrical as well as physical, since Aristotle speaks of the divisibility of magnitude (τὸ μέγεθος, ^{a}8) and mentions indivisible plane figures, obviously with an eye on the *Timaeus* doctrine of elemental solids. This distinction is a familiar one, at least to readers who have already met it twice in *On Generation and Corruption* I: first in chapter 2 (316^{a}14–^{b}18 and 316^{b}21–317^{a}1), where it is used by the atomists as the framework of an argument 'to establish the necessity of atomic magnitudes' (316^{b}34–317^{a}1), and later on, in chapter 8 (325^{a}5–12), where it is used to support the Eleatic claim that being cannot be many. In both places, as in our passage, two possibilities are offered: either there are indivisible bodies, or a body must be divisible everywhere. Even the treatment of each of these hypotheses is similar in all three passages. Aristotle never dwells on the atomist thesis, while the thesis of total divisibility is always introduced by means of a thought-experiment: although the integral division of any magnitude, however small, would in this account require an infinite number of cuts, let us put ourselves at the end of such a process and see what could be the result (316^{a}14–^{b}14, 316^{b}21–7, 325^{a}6–9). This move relies on a standard Aristotelian definition of 'possible' as what could be realized without entailing impossibilities; and in chapter 2 (the atomist argument) as well as in chapter 8 (the Eleatic argument) it leads to the rejection of integral division, since its realization leads to contradictions or paradoxes. Thus, it would seem that we are compelled either to adopt the atomist thesis or, if we choose to reject it, to forsake plurality and change altogether. Aristotle's own way out of this dilemma has been developed in chapter 2, and consists in introducing a weaker interpretation of the phrase 'divisible everywhere'; namely, that there is no point at which a magnitude could not be divided. Let us call this 'potential' (vs. 'actual') integral division. It rests on the geometrical assumption that there cannot be a point consecutive to another, and this implies that one must give up the conception of generation as a process of composition (σύγκρισις), since this conception requires that the first elementary components are attainable by a process of physical analysis.

But although the general outline of the argument is clear enough, the detail is often difficult and sometimes obscure. In the first horn of the dilemma (327^a7–9) Aristotle considers the hypothesis of the discontinuity of matter, but he dismisses it by saying that in this case, 'nothing at all would be continuous'. The claim that the discontinuity thesis can provide some support for partial susceptibility seems intuitively correct, but what exactly is its basis? Aristotle certainly considers that the conjectured susceptible and insusceptible parts must exist actually as such in the physical body, and that this can be secured only by the existence of actual discontinuities. Moreover, the optative οὐκ ἂν εἴη suggests that in any case this is not a sufficient condition; that is, that the existence of indivisible magnitudes does not by itself entail partial susceptibility. It would still need the existence of contacts, which may be conceived either as events (the temporary contact of some indivisible bodies) or as permanent structures such as the pores.

It is worth noticing that in this first horn the refutation does not rest on inner contradictions in the thesis under consideration, but rather on its excessive theoretical cost: denying continuity would ruin physics, which cannot do without it. The discussion of atomism in chapter 8 (325^b34–326^b6) stresses some of the 'strange' (ἄτοπον) implications of the theory, but never mentions an outright impossibility. In chapter 2 Aristotle's strategy is clearly defensive: he only intends to show that the atomists' arguments are not unanswerable; that is, that one is never forced to stop the process of division. In that chapter he mentions en passant 'impossibilities' (ἀδύνατα, 316^b16–18). But, since he refers to these in an imprecise way, saying only that he has dealt with them 'somewhere else' (ἐν ἑτέροις), it is impossible to determine whether he has in mind mathematical contradictions, conflict with empirical data, or internal contradictions within the theory itself. In any case, the idea that physics demands continuity is apparent everywhere in books III–VI of the *Physics*. At the beginning of book VI we read something which sounds like a demonstration of this thesis, although it is phrased in a slightly different manner: 'a continuous object cannot be made of indivisible parts', while elsewhere it is taken for granted that natural objects and natural phenomena must be continuous (in book III, at 1. 200^b16–17, Aristotle notes that 'it is admitted that motion, [or "change" in general] is among continuous things').

The difficulties of the second horn ($^a9$–14) arise from the fact that it is incomplete. What Aristotle says, at least, is clear enough. As I have suggested above, he relies on the standard definition of possibility to state and to consider the hypothesis of actual integral division. This interpretation requires, first, that the future ἔσται διῃρημένον, at 327ᵃ13, be taken (despite Williams' reference to Hintikka's 'principle of plenitude'[10]) as the mere statement of an implausible implication, and, second, that the sentence δυνατὸν γὰρ διαιρεθῆναι, γίνεται γὰρ οὐθὲν ἀδύνατον, at lines 13–14, be definitely ironical, since it is put forward to draw a conclusion which Aristotle himself considers untenable. Of course, since the argument breaks off at that point, it is impossible to render this interpretation absolutely certain, but it is supported by a possible parallel with chapter 2, and it seems easy and natural (Williams eventually remarks that 'the reason for his [Aristotle's] apparent appeal to the principle of plenitude is not clear').

A more important problem is to determine the (presumably negative) conclusion of this second horn. There seem to be two possibilities. Either Aristotle meant only to refer back to the rejection of actual integral division mentioned in chapters 2 and 8, or he intended to develop a specific refutation of the thesis of partial susceptibility, based on this representation of integral division but appropriate to the specific problem of qualitative influence of a body upon another. One might prefer the second possibility, since the argument of chapters 2 and 8 is neither specifically Aristotelian nor even properly physical; but one cannot find in this context the slightest trace of such a physical argument. So it is safer to admit that Aristotle was content with the claim that his opponents' thesis rests on an inconsistent concept of the division of bodies (i.e. actual integral division, which was refuted in chapter 2), unless they accept the hypothesis of indivisible magnitudes, which in Aristotle's view is epistemologically inferior, since it makes physics impossible.

So much for the dilemma's second horn. But there is a more general problem: the dilemma as a whole lacks an explicit conclusion and, still worse, rests on a dichotomy (between atoms and actual integral division) which is not exhaustive, since it does not mention potential division, Aristotle's own hypothesis. It is natural to find such an incomplete statement of the alternatives in chapter 8, where Aristotle only means to report an Eleatic argument against change and plurality, or in the first part of chapter 2, where he sets out an argument for the existence of indivisible elementary objects. In both places potential integral division is put forward as a way of escaping the unpleasant implications of the two rival theses. However, since Aristotle's point is precisely to question the exact meaning (if there is one) of the thesis of partial susceptibility, he

---

[10] Williams (1982), 140–1.

may have considered that this thesis, in any case, presupposes the actual existence of parts within the affected body. In this case, the section would be aptly described as a dilemma in the technical sense of the term; that is, a forced choice between two equally untenable options. In the first horn (327ᵃ7–9) he says that the thesis of partial susceptibility can be maintained if one assumes the conception of indivisible magnitudes, which he himself considers mistaken, while in the second he seems to develop an argument to the effect that if one accepts the continuity of physical bodies one must reject partial susceptibility. But perhaps we may credit Aristotle with a more positive intention: to indicate the correct solution of the problem, leaving its detailed elaboration to the sagacity of his readers, who would have to work out for themselves how the doctrine of the continuity of physical bodies entails the thesis of through-and-through susceptibility.

This is not an easy task, although Aristotle gives an important indication as to how it could be achieved at the beginning of the chapter, where he mentions as his ἀρχή the fact that something may be 'potentially *x*' or '*x* in actuality'. Indeed, it is only natural to wonder about the meaning of his conception of 'through-and-through susceptibility', about which he is particularly sparing of words. He merely opposes to the abstract schema of partial susceptibility the still more abstract formula that a body must be affected—and consequently must be capable of being affected— 'through and through'. I shall venture a little further than Aristotle himself and offer some suggestions as to how this formula might be interpreted, with the specific aim of showing how such a claim might enable Aristotle to meet the Eleatic paradoxes after his rejection of the atomist answer to them.

For him, a natural process basically consists in some object taking some form; that is, in a process of information. I take the word 'form' in its broadest sense, as there are processes which lead to the loss of a form but which can be understood by analogy with the information model, if the state of privation is thought of as a form of a kind. More precisely, what I mean by 'information' here is the communication of the form by an agent to the affected thing. To take a plausible parallel from our physics, one may think of the diffusion of a sound in classical acoustics. Here we have the spreading and conservation of a form (the physical structure of the initial vibration) through a medium which must be conceived to be as full and elastic as possible. In a similar way, Aristotle's physics has no need of void or interstices, although these are indispensable to philosophers who depict physical influence as the circulation of some material substances, or as the communication of a certain amount of mechanical energy, from one body to another.

This comparison between Aristotelian physical influence and acoustical phenomena must be qualified in one essential regard: the sound (in the latter account) has a given and definite origin, from which it spreads out in an unlimited space, until it becomes faint and confused and finally vanishes. In the Aristotelian conception, by contrast, the process of influence is essentially directed towards a definite and well-individuated body, of which the form takes hold entirely. In the case of generation properly speaking, this hold of the form over matter gives a body the individuality it lacked before, and which will thereafter define it. The form, Aristotle says, 'envelops' or 'contains' (*Ph.* III. 7. 207^b1), and 'entelechy separates' (*Metaph.* Z 13.1039^a6–7). Thus, if one considers physical change in its perfect form it becomes clear why a body must be affected 'through and through', in its totality. Indeed, it is simply impossible to imagine that it could be otherwise. For if it were, it would not be really one body, or its name would be equivocal. It is, of course, true that most processes of change take some time, and that some of them advance, as one might say, through the affected body. For example, (1) a whole black surface lightens gradually overall, going through all the shades of grey to become entirely white, and (2) a whole black surface becomes white at one edge and the whiteness spreads gradually to the whole surface. In the second case it is clear that if the process were to stop at some time only some parts would be white. But, even so, the standpoint of perfect form and completed process is primary and basic for the understanding of what is going on and how it can be explained. In *Physics* V Aristotle describes all processes of change as whole items, in which you can only virtually, or mentally, make cuts and distinguish steps. If a process has been interrupted you will not be able to account for what has happened unless you refer it to its natural term. This is trivial in the case of teleological explanations. But there are also more refined and complex applications of this rule: we have seen how, in chapter 5, he rules out the conception of growth as an accretion of new material parts, by distinguishing between the standpoint of form and the standpoint of matter. Material parts of the nutriment may be said to go 'here' or 'there' in the animal's flesh, but the real phenomenon is the growth of the form taken as a whole. In the genus of alteration there are paradigm cases of 'instantaneous change' (ἀθρόα μεταβολή), such as freezing, where there is no intermediate state between liquid and solid, and even changes that seem to affect instantaneously a large quantity of matter, such as the illumination of air. Thus, in *de Anima* II. 7 Aristotle criticizes Empedocles for having said that light 'travels' and takes some time to cross the interval between east and west (418^b20–6).

The distinction between progressive and instantaneous changes is crucial, because instantaneous changes may be correctly described as 'the maintenance of what is potentially by the agency of what is actually'. This phrase is used at *de Anima* II. 5. 417^{b}3–4 to bring out the distinctive nature of phenomena such as sense perception, and perhaps intellection, and a similar criterion occurs in *Metaphysics* Θ 6.1048^{b}18–36 to distinguish some actions (πράξεις), which may properly be called 'acts' (ἐνεργείαι) from 'motions' (κινήσεις), since 'every motion is imperfect'. All these examples are cases of animal, and for some of them exclusively human, activities. But we need not restrict this formula to such cases. We have seen that there is at least one example of a physical process which falls under this description: illumination. In fact, a change takes some time when it involves the destruction of a pre-existing state of affairs. For instance, a person becomes ill when the balance of elementary qualities such as warmth and coldness etc., which constitutes health, has been altered. This means that when the state of affairs which is contrary to the form *x* rests on a complex system of relations within a body, this body's becoming *x* will take a certain length of time. But in the cases of instantaneous changes the body which is susceptible to such a change needs nothing more to become *x* than the actual presence of the form *x* (embodied in some particular object, that is the agent) in its immediate proximity. This type of change, although it is very rare, indeed exceptional, in the physical world (for reasons which stem from the ontological structure of this world), may be taken as a paradigm of susceptibility considered strictly in itself, which is present within all natural processes, but is mostly hindered and slackened by the complexity of natural states of affairs (the distinction I have in mind here is of the same kind as the one between strict necessity and ὡς ἐπὶ τὸ πολύ determinations). In other words, I think that the 'susceptibility' (τὸ παθητικόν) in our chapter is nothing other than this pure ability to receive the form. This is not exactly the same thing as the matter of the body in the ordinary sense of the word 'matter'. Rather it is an example of this more abstract and refined kind of 'matter' which is mentioned in *Metaphysics* N 2. 1089^{b}28–9: a matter which is 'proper to each kind' (for instance, a matter for colour, for size, or even for grammar[11]) and 'inseparable from substances', while it is distinct from them. The 'transparent' which is the medium of vision,[12] which is neither air nor water, but a quality common to both, is a physical example of such a matter.

We can now see why Aristotle, when he first states his own thesis at the beginning of our chapter, emphatically indicates that the distinction between potentiality and actuality is the basis of his solution. He is

---

[11] For the matter of grammar (or rather of the art of writing and reading) see *de An.* II. 5. 417^{a}22–8, esp. 26. The matter for size has been aptly described by Plot. *Enn.* II. 4 [12] 9–10.

[12] *de An.* II. 7, *Sens.* 3.

advocating a dialectical way of accounting for action and passion by fixing a priori conditions of its possibility, which can supplant the earlier physical theories which used patterns of material adaptation (such as interstices proportionate to the alleged active substances). As he said in chapter 7, agent and patient must belong to the same genus, and so the patient qua patient is characterized by the fact that (1) it is deprived of the form that the agent possesses, and (2) it is fully ready to receive it. This latter combination of 'not being *x*' and 'being *x*' enables him to answer the Eleatic paradoxes more satisfactorily than the atomists (or Empedocles) did when they understood not-being simply as empty space.

4. Two additional arguments

Section (e) is introduced by ὅλως ('more generally speaking'). This word indicates a broader perspective, for the last two arguments of the chapter are not directed specifically against the discontinuist conceptions of qualitative influence, but rather concern all kinds of change, including growth and diminution. In fact, Aristotle wants to stress that the discontinuist theories cannot account for the specific nature of the various kinds of physical change: generation *stricto sensu*, growth, and alteration.

The target of both objections seems to be Democritus. Here Aristotle severely reduces the good marks he had awarded the atomist at the beginning of chapter 2. While it is true that Democritus considered all forms of γένεσις, he neglected the particular nature of each of them. Aristotle's objections at that point are not part of his argument about partial or complete susceptibility, but are nonetheless more or less closely connected with his overall discussion of discontinuist theses in chapter 8. The first objection, about alteration, is complicated and might even seem awkward, while the second one (about growth and diminution) is straightforward and fits without difficulty into its context. So it may be simpler to discuss the latter briefly before turning to the former.

'This theory, it must be added, makes growth and diminution impossible also. For it is impossible that any and every part should have become greater, if there is to be an addition, instead of the growing thing having changed as a whole, either by the admixture of something or by its own transformation' (327^a22–5). The point appears to be mainly semantical. If growth and diminution are to be defined precisely, and thus strictly distinguished from addition and substraction, one can see at once that they must affect every part of the growing or diminishing thing, and so imply that its matter be continuous. Aristotle does not need to dwell on that point, since it has been set out at some length in chapter 5, nearly in the same terms. In fact, it is equivalent to the third of the five conditions specified in lines 321^{b}10–16: 'Every perceptible particle (ὁτιοῦν σημεῖον αἰσθητόν) of <the growing thing> has become larger or smaller'. It is to be noticed that neither there nor here does Aristotle refer to any empirical data to vindicate his claim, but merely appeals to the abstract notion of growth and diminution and to the conditions of their possibility. He does not even ask whether there are in nature such phenomena as growth and diminution so defined, a claim that a stubborn, or rather any consistent, atomist would certainly reject.

The first objection, in contrast, rests mainly or exclusively on empirical evidence:

we see the same body as liquid at one time and as solid at another, without losing its continuity. It has suffered this change not by division and composition, nor yet by 'turning' and 'intercontact', as Democritus asserts; for it has passed from the liquid to the solid state without any change of order or position in its nature. Nor are there contained within it those 'hard' particles 'indivisible in their bulk'; on the contrary, it is liquid—and again, solid and congealed—uniformly all through (327^{a}16–25).

Joachim and Williams rightly question the relevance of this appeal to perception, since atoms are supposed to be imperceptible.[13] Nevertheless, I think that one could accept an empirical argument of this kind against the claim that the absence or presence of some 'hard particles' could cause the liquid or solid state of a body. 'It is liquid—and again, solid and congealed—uniformly all through': this may mean that one could make sure, by an appropriate experimental device, that the body has changed from a solid to a liquid state, and conversely, without any kind of matter emanating from it or being fixed during the process. Of course, it would be more difficult, not to say impossible, to establish that no modification of the microscopic structure had taken place in the affected thing. But since Aristotle mentions freezing, he may have chosen this example precisely because this is, in his view, a case of instantaneous change, a fact which (he thinks) can occur only with alteration.[14] And he may have considered that such a sudden transformation of a body through all of its mass would not be really explained by the many elementary motions implied by the atomistic account. An atomist might suppose, in order to account for crystallization, that all the particles which constitute one particular body can be arranged simultaneously into one and the same pattern (as they are in fact, in a process which strikingly recalls the Democritean notions of τροπή and διαθιγή). But Aristotle could have answered, first, that such a great number of elementary changes would take some time, no matter how short. Second,

---

[13] Joachim (1922), 175; Williams (1982), 141.
[14] *Ph.* VI. 5. 236^{b}17–18 ; see also VIII. 3. 253^{b}23–6 and I. 3. 186^{a}15–16.

that even if it were granted that all these changes happened instantly and simultaneously, this fact itself, according to Aristotle, would not be sufficiently explained unless one also accepted an instant modification of the mass as a whole, which would be the real change to him.

But all this is only a tentative suggestion about a difficult text. The main interest of this last section is that here Aristotle claims for his continuist conception of bodies the advantage of explaining all forms of change with due consideration of their diversity, maintaining both the conceptual distinctiveness and the phenomenal reality of growth and alteration as opposed to absolute generation.[15]

[15] Enrico Berti kindly invited me to read a first version of this paper at his seminar in Padua in April 1999. The discussions there, and later in Deurne, greatly helped me to find my way through the puzzles of this chapter. And I owe many thanks to David Charles, who once again, while correcting my English, greatly helped me to clarify the content as well.

On Generation and Corruption I. 10: On Mixture and Mixables

Dorothea Frede

Prologue

Mixture is a kind of process that does not receive much attention in Aristotle's natural philosophy. Thus *mixis* or *krasis* does not form part of his canonical catalogue of change alongside generation and destruction, alteration, locomotion, growth, and shrinking. If he dedicates a chapter to the question of the nature of *mixis* and how it differs from other kinds of processes in *De generatione et corruptione*, it at first sight appears like a *paralipomenon* in his discussion of the *Grundbegriffe* of all kinds of generation and destruction—both simple and with qualification.[1] That Aristotle is not overly preoccupied with this concept even here seems to be suggested by the fact that its elucidation is tucked away at the end of book I, at the close of the discussion of all the basic processes and their constitutive factors, before the investigation of the elements and elemental change in book II.[2] But, as a closer look at the text will show, this impression of mixture's relative unimportance is quite wrong. *Mixis* has an important role to play in the analysis of homogeneous stuffs and is therefore an essential concept in Aristotle's elementary physics and chemistry. Nor is it treated as a mere addendum in the distinction of the different kinds of physical processes in *GC* I. Aristotle first refers to *mixis* in his general complaint about the unclear state of the basic concepts concerning change among his predecessors in

---

[1] As Bonitz's *Index* shows, Aristotle refers to both κρᾶσις (s.v. 407^a–408^b) and μίξις (s.v. 469^b–470^a) in various meanings and contexts throughout the corpus. Μίξις has a very wide extension; it refers to sexual intercourse as well as to the connections between different classes in a πόλις. Why the distinction between μίξις as a composite of dry ingredients and κρᾶσις as the fusion of liquids of *Top.* 122^{b}26–31 plays no role in *GC* I. 10 will emerge later.

[2] The division of books and chapter is, of course, not Aristotelian. But the ancient editor clearly saw a natural caesura here.

chapter 2.[3] He refers to *mixis* again in his clarification of the exact nature of growth in chapter 5: food might mistakenly be treated as the junior partner in a mixture with a dominant partner. And in his preliminary summary of all kinds of change in chapter 6, Aristotle again mentions mixture as one of the basic processes that must be clarified if the origin and nature of the first elements is to be explained (322^b6-8): 'All philosophers, both those who make the elements come to be and those who make things come from the elements, make use of aggregation (σύγκρισις) and segregation (διάκρισις), action and passion. Now, aggregation is mixing; but what we mean by mixing is not clearly determined.'[4]

Since this survey of the earlier occurrences of mixture in *De generatione et corruptione* suggests that Aristotle assigns to it an important role in the explanation of basic change, it seems strange that it does not appear to be a major player in the 'league of change' elsewhere. A preliminary explanation is not difficult to find: *mixis* is not easily classified as a kind of change within one of the ten categories. As we will see, it is a change that involves different substances and their properties in a complex way. It is neither the result of simple substantial change in the sense of generation proper, nor a straightforward case of alteration, nor a change in quantity, nor is it locomotion. The fact that it cannot easily be classified may indeed be one of the reasons why Aristotle usually leaves it out of his standard list of change. But, as will become clear, its omission elsewhere is not just a matter of taxonomy and convenience. While *mixis* plays an important role in the explanation of the processes that take place at the most elementary level and that are the topic of *De generatione et corruptione*, mixtures of a higher complexity present special problems which may account for Aristotle's avoidance of that topic elsewhere.

Procedure and argument in chapter 10

That Aristotle indeed regards the exact determination of the nature of mixture as a matter of importance in *De generatione et corruptione* is

---

[3] *GC* I. 2. 315^b2-4: 'There was still no discussion of how this is effected (sc. growth), nor of mixing, nor, practically speaking, of any of the other topics such as action and passion.' All translations are taken from C. J. F. Williams (1982). For brevity's sake I shall not here distinguish between *mixing*, the process, and *mixture*, its product.

[4] For the need to disentangle generation and destruction from association and dissociation as well as from alteration cf. *GC* I. 2. 315^b16-24. Recognition of the importance of *mixis* in the Aristotelian philosophy of nature has inspired Kit Fine (1995) to an extensive analysis of both Aristotle's text and its importance for contemporary discussion. I owe this reference to Alan Code, whose reply to Fine in the same volume is also worth consulting. If I refrain from an explicit discussion of Fine's 100-page article and Code's comments it is because a proper comparison and contrast would far exceed the limits of this article.

shown by the fact that he promises a thorough and methodical treatment of this concept at the beginning of chapter 10 (327^a30–4). First there is to be a definition of its essence (τi $\dot{\epsilon}\sigma\tau\iota\nu$). Next is to follow a determination of what is mixable (τi $\tau\dot{o}$ $\mu\iota\kappa\tau\dot{o}\nu$), as well as of the kinds of things to which mixture applies ($\tau i\sigma\iota\nu$ $\dot{v}\pi\dot{\alpha}\rho\chi\epsilon\iota$). Then the mode ($\pi\hat{\omega}s$) of mixing is to be determined. In addition, Aristotle promises to refute an argument that purports to show that mixture is impossible. But his subsequent treatment of *mixis* in chapter 10 does not follow the promised order; in fact, it reverses it in a way that makes the discussion hard to follow. (1) The first part refutes the argument against mixture (327^a34–$^b22$). (2) Next comes a brief indication of Aristotle's own conception of mixture (327^b22–31). (3) This indication is not immediately followed by fuller elucidations. Instead, Aristotle raises a further difficulty ($\dot{\alpha}\pi\dot{o}\rho\eta\mu\alpha$) against the possibility of mixture (327^b31–328^a17). (4) Only the last part contains the promised explanation of mixture, its ingredients, and its preconditions, concluding with a formal definition (328^a17–$^b22$). Since Aristotle's own conception of mixture and the nature of mixables unfolds only gradually, it will be best to follow the text to get a proper understanding of the rationale for this procedure.

(1) The argument against mixture consists of the following trilemma: either (a) the ingredients of the mixture remain intact, in which case there is no mixture at all because nothing actually happens to its components; or (b) one of the ingredients perishes, in which case there will also be no mixture, because it no longer contains both ingredients; or (c) if on coming together both ingredients perish, there will once again be no mixture because there cannot be a mixture that is not *of* its mixables.[5] To deal with the trilemma Aristotle first of all shows that mixture must be a process *sui generis* and not identical with generation and corruption, nor with any of the other kinds of change that he had described in the previous chapters (327^b6–22). To prove his point he first appeals to common sense and ordinary language to show that none of the combinations that fulfil the trilemma's conditions (a), (b), or (c) could be mixtures. Mixture is neither generation nor destruction *simpliciter*: wood and fire are not said to 'mix' when wood burns. The wood is destroyed while fire comes to be. Nor is mixture the same as growth: food is not said to 'mix' with the body.[6] Nor is it alteration: no one would say that the shape 'mixes' with the wax when a lump of wax is

---

[5] As Zabarella (1602) suggests (862–5), the fact that Aristotle starts with the trilemma may show that he thereby intends to clarify the meaning of the term $\mu i\xi\iota s$, not to refute an actual opponent.

[6] The examples of burning and food illustrate case (b) where one of the ingredients disappears; perhaps the cryptic remark at 327^b12 that the parts of burning wood don't mix with each other is supposed to rule out case (c).

formed—just as qualities, affections, or dispositions are not said to 'mix' with their respective carriers. Nor are accidental unities mixtures: white mixes as little with knowledge when they coincide in a subject as do any other of the items that depend on a substrate.[7] Failure to realize this fact vitiates theories that assume that 'all things used to be together and mixed'.[8] For every mixable must be able to exist separately, a condition which *pathê* clearly do not fulfil. This *reductio* indicates why mixables neither come to be and perish in mixtures nor grow and wane like substances nor stay intact in the way that properties or accidentals do.

The successful elimination of inapplicable accounts is, of course, not yet a sufficient refutation of the trilemma. For it does not show that the trilemma does not apply to proper cases of mixtures. But the elimination gives Aristotle occasion to point to his own solution.

(2) The distinction of *dunamis* and *energeia* will show that mixables continue to exist in a mixture in a modified way, so that neither condition (b) nor (c) applies. For though they do not remain in actuality what they were before they entered the mixture, each of them still possesses its nature potentially: in the mixture they retain but do not display their own nature. Hence condition (a) is not fulfilled in mixtures either; namely, that the two ingredients simply remain the same after entering the mixture. A mixture consists of elements that were separate before and that remain potentially separable. Though they do not retain their actual identity, as do combinations of accidental properties in a body, their separability proves that they have not perished. The trilemma can therefore be dismissed ($327^{b}31$).[9] This appeal to the familiar distinction between *dunamis* and *energeia* is, of course, at best a *formal* solution to the trilemma. It does not explain in what way the ingredients subsist in mixtures nor does it indicate what actual 'existent' results from their conjunction.

(3) The fact that Aristotle raises yet another difficulty against mixture shows that he is aware of the insufficiency of his postulate.[10] The *aporêma* concerns the question whether mixture may not actually be just relative to perception ($αἴσθησις$). Would it not be sufficient for a mixture if the ingredients were so small, and commingled in such a way, that they could no longer be discerned ($327^{b}34$–6)? Aristotle rejects this suggestion

---

[7] The shaping of the wax and the coincidence of accidentals apparently is meant to rule out combinations of type (a) as mixtures.

[8] The critique seems to apply to both Empedocles and Anaxagoras, Aristotle's main opponents in the *De generatione et corruptione* apart from the atomists.

[9] That is, (a) applies only with the qualification that the ingredients are potentially there, while (b) and (c) do not apply at all: neither one of the ingredients nor both perish. For a fuller discussion of the trilemma cf. Joachim (1922), 179–81; Williams (1982), 143–4.

[10] For an alternative interpretation of this section of *GC* I. 10 see John Cooper, in Chapter 12 of this volume.

by pointing out why mixture cannot be a matter of being perceptible or imperceptible. A conglomerate of imperceptibles would not even fulfil the common-sense expectations of what it is to be a proper mixture; namely, that each particle of the first ingredient must be next to a particle of the second ingredient, as in a thorough mixture of wheat and barley. But Aristotle clearly is not just concerned with common sense. He intends to show that no kind of juxtaposition of parts can count as a mixture, no matter how fine the particles. Since matter is not infinitely divisible in actuality, there will always be parts preserved intact and hence not every (unseparated) particle of the first ingredient will be adjacent to a particle of the second sort. Hence at every level of division there will always be a mere aggregation of different particles and no true mixture because such a conglomerate cannot attain real homogeneity. The smallness of the particles makes no difference, for a Lynceus would still be able to tell them apart.[11] But mixture properly so called presupposes that all its parts share the definition of the whole,[12] just as every particle of water is water. Hence mixture is not relative to perceptibility, and perception turns out to be useless as a criterion.[13]

Though Aristotle's reasons for disposing of the *aporêma* are fairly clear, it is not at all easy to say why he raises it in the first place. It cannot be meant to present a difficulty for his own solution via the distinction between *dunamis* and *energeia* since it precludes the elements of a mixture from staying intact anyway. It is also not likely that Aristotle merely wants to address a naive everyday objection that mixture obtains once the mixables have become indistinguishable to the human eye. The argument is much too elaborate to meet such naivety. The reference to the eyes of a Lynceus would have sufficed to show that such a mêlée is only a conglomerate. Nor can the argument be intended as a further refutation of the atomists. Not only has Aristotle proved the impossibility of indivisible particles earlier in our treatise;[14] his objection to the *aporêma* applies equally to the continuum theory of matter (328^a5-6). Hence if there were an embarrassment accounting for mixture, both atomists and continuum-physicists would share in it.

---

[11] The eyes of Lynceus are a substitute for the microscope in Aristotle's discussion: the non-homogenous structure of a mere conglomerate would be obvious to his penetrating vision (328^a15). On Lynceus and the microscope cf. also Solmsen (1960), 370 with n. 8.

[12] I therefore take τὸν αὐτὸν λόγον in 328^a9 to refer to a difference in the definition of the parts and the whole, and not to a difference in proportion, as in Joachim's and Williams's translations.

[13] On the distinction between the two positions, i.e. the assumption of an ordinary conglomerate vs. the one based on minimal particles, cf. the discussion in Williams (1982), 145–8.

[14] Cf. *GC* I. 2, esp. $316^a14-317^a12$, with David Sedley's contribution in this volume (ch. 2).

A better explanation for the inclusion of the *aporêma* is, then, that
Aristotle wants to rule out the confusion of mixture with all sorts of
combinations that do not result in homogeneous stuff. This is all the
more plausible as similar objections have been raised earlier in connection with generation, growth, and alteration: none of them is to be
accounted for by processes that represent mere *aggregation*.[15] Since
those objections were addressed to the atomists, to Empedocles, and to
Anaxagoras, their theories are, at least implicitly, his target here once
again. Since they do assume minimal particles, they cannot justify the
existence of mixtures except as conglomerates of particles that are beneath the level of perception.

But though all these considerations may be of some importance,
Aristotle's overall aim here seems to be a different one. So far we have
left out his remark that the *aporêma* of visibility is συνεχὲς τούτοις
(327ᵇ32); namely, connected with the alternatives of the trilemma,
which have already been dismissed.[16] He would feel the need to add yet
another refutation only if he regarded the 'argument from invisibility' as
a last-ditch defence of condition (a) of the trilemma against his own
solution: invisibility is a way of accounting for mixtures that do retain
their ingredients intact. Though the *aporêma* clearly does not present a
serious difficulty in Aristotle's eyes, it serves an important *rhetorical*
purpose: it gives him the occasion to announce the need for a fresh
start in the search for mixture. This is indicated by the assessment of
the situation that concludes his discussion of the *aporêma*: either there
are no proper mixtures at all or the problem has to be treated in a
completely different way (328ᵃ17–18: πάλιν). The 'different way' will
then bring an analysis of mixture *more Aristotelico*. Such a fresh start
has, of course, already been adumbrated by his reference to *dunamis* and
energeia. The *aporêma* is then an additional argument to show that
Aristotle's solution is the only way to go.

(4) What then *is* the Aristotelian way? We would now expect a proper
explanation of what mixture is and how mixables interact on the basis of
the distinction between *dunamis* and *energeia* as indicated in (2). But
Aristotle does not proceed that way. Instead of providing a full explanation, he merely refers back to the specifications of action and passion in
the previous chapters as the basic conditions for mixtures: if there is to be
reciprocity between active and passive factors in mixture, the partners
must have the same matter (ὕλη). Only then can they engage in mutual
action and reaction. If an agent cannot be acted on in return, it does not

---

[15] That both γένεσις and ἀλλοίωσις presuppose continuous matter is explained in 2.
317ᵃ17–27; cf. also 6. 322ᵇ8, 9. 327ᵃ17–18).

[16] The τούτοις in l. 327ᵇ32 must refer to the ταῦτα in the line before, while ταῦτα refers
back to the three options of the trilemma.

have the same matter. In that case there is no question of a mixture.[17] But even where there is reciprocity a further condition must be fulfilled: the power of the ingredients must be equal. If one ingredient overpowers the other, there will be no mixture, but only an increase in the bulk of the predominant element. Thus a drop of wine does not mix with ten thousand pints of water but loses its form and merges entirely with the water.[18] Only if the ingredients are somehow equal in power can there be mixture. In that case there is change in both constituents, but neither will turn into the other. Instead, the mutual change will result in a dominant state (κρατοῦν) that is 'in between and common' (μεταξὺ καὶ κοινόν) to both. Given that mixables must be able to affect each other, there must be a basic opposition (ἐναντίωσις) between them.[19] This means, then, that only objects of the same genus can form real mixtures. Mixtures therefore depend on three conditions: sameness of genus, opposition of qualities, and overall equality in their respective powers.

In the rest of the chapter Aristotle settles some finer points concerning the conditions under which things mix more or less easily (328ᵃ33–ᵇ14). Small quantities of ingredients mix faster and more thoroughly, while large quantities take a long time to mix.[20] Mixtures also come about more easily if the ingredients are easy to divide and 'shapable' (εὐόριστον). Liquids therefore turn out to be the most mixable bodies, unless they happen to be viscous. In that case there will be no real mixture but merely an increase in the bulk of the compound, as in the case of water and oil. If only one of the ingredients is ready to react as recipient while the other ingredient resists, their combination will either lead to no increase in bulk or to a small one: there will a 'takeover' rather than a joint product. In that case the one partner acts as a receptacle, the other 'as if it were the form'. Aristotle refers to the mixture of tin and bronze as a case of such an unequal combination: the tin supposedly disappears in the mixture, modifying only the colour of the bronze, as if it was a mere affection and had no matter of its own.

---

[17] Aristotle here cites the medical art and health as examples: if they produce health, they do not do so by mixing with the body (328ᵃ22–3).

[18] The reason for this total loss of identity must be that there is no specifiable ratio between water and wine in this case. How Aristotle would deal with a sorites argument concerning such ratios is unclear.

[19] Contrariety as such does not yet determine what mixture is, for in the *De generatione et corruptione* all kinds of changes including generation and destruction involve contrariety (320ᵃ2–5). The difference lies in the kinds of opposites and in their relation to the substrate in question.

[20] The 'finer points' seem to answer to the question whether there is a true distinction between 'τί τὸ μικτόν' and 'τίσιν ὑπάρχει' that disappears in Williams' translation but that divided commentators from Philoponus (189. 5) to Zabarella (861). On Philoponus and the later tradition cf. De Haas (1999). That division in smaller quantities speeds up processes of change of all sorts is mentioned already in *GC* I. 2. 317ᵃ27–9.

Aristotle obviously regards these specifications as a satisfactory conclusion to his treatment of mixture. In the final paragraph he sums up the solutions to the questions raised in the introduction: that there is mixture, what it is, what mixables there are, and how mixtures come about and under what conditions (328^{b}14–22). The ingredients of a mixture must be mutually affectable (παθητικὰ ὑπ᾿ ἀλλήλων); they must possess a flexible shape (εὐόριστα) and divisibility (εὐδιαίρετα). Given these conditions the initial trilemma does not apply: the ingredients neither perish nor stay the same. Mixture is neither a mere aggregation nor is it relative to sense perception. Instead, mixables engage in active and passive interaction with each other. This summary finally leads to the formal definition of *mixis* that concludes the chapter (328^{b}22): 'Mixing is the union of the things mixed after they have been altered.'

All's well that ends well. The brief survey of the chapter and of its results might in fact suggest that all *is* well.[21] Deeper problems with Aristotle's conception of mixture emerge only when we reflect on the kinds of questions that he does *not* raise in this chapter and on the information he does not give. To those 'untouched' questions we shall now have to turn.

Problems with mixture

A closer look at the injunctions concerning *mixis* reveals that matters are not as clear as Aristotle pretends in his summary at the end of the chapter. Apart from the refutation of the trilemma, what have we actually learned about mixtures and their nature? We can leave aside the specifications of the preconditions of mixture, such as that the ingredients should be largely equal in quantity,[22] that liquids are more easily mixable than solids (328^{b}3),[23] and that in general the mixables mix more easily if they are divided up in small quantities. All these conditions seem straightforward enough. But in fact they teach us nothing about the process that is actually supposed to take place in mixture. We are not told what it means to say that the ingredients must 'interact' with each

[21] Problems with details in the text have consciously been passed over here since they do not affect the overall line of argument presented. Cf. John Cooper's contribution to this volume (ch. 12).

[22] As it will turn out this postulate of equality is to be taken with more than just one grain of salt.

[23] Aristotle does not exclude the possibility that two kinds of solid bodies can mix, though he recommends liquidity especially for the role of the παθητικόν (328^{b}1). The reasons why he neither limits mixture to liquids nor introduces a distinction between μίξις and κρᾶσις will become clear when he explains the kinds of mixtures he is really concerned with, i.e. the ὁμοιομερῆ.

other in such a way that they are both 'acting and affected'. Nor do we learn to what extent they both retain their nature only 'potentially and not actually'. We are not informed what kind of change Aristotle has in mind when he says they change 'from their own nature into something *dominant*, though not into each other'. Is *mixis* really a kind of mutual alteration of *qualities*, as the final definition suggests, and, if so, of what qualities? Finally, what kind of *unity* of opposites is a mixture supposed to bring about?

The chapters on acting and being acted upon, *GC* I. 7–9, which precede our discussion prima facie do not shed any light on the kind of *reciprocity* between mixables that Aristotle has in mind. For in that discussion he seems to adhere to the position that in all interaction there is always *one* thing that acts and *another* that is acted upon. Nor is that impression limited to *De generatione et corruptione*. For in *Metaphysics* IX. 5 Aristotle insists on a clear separation of the function of the active and the passive partner (1048^{a}5–8): 'As regards potentialities of the latter kind (sc. non-rational *dunamis*), when the agent and the patient meet in the way appropriate to the potentiality in question, the one must act and the other be acted on... For the non-rational potentialities are all pro-ductive of *one* effect each'. A further difficulty consists in the fact that Aristotle seems to presuppose that in all interaction the actual process of change takes place in the patient only. In the case of teaching and learning, for instance, though both teacher and student actualize their potential, the change occurs only in the student/patient.[24] How, then, can there be *reciprocal* action and affection in which neither agent remains the same as before? Unfortunately the two examples that Aristotle gives in *GC* I. 10 are quite uninformative as to the kind of mutual interaction he has in mind. For the mixture of water and wine purports to show that the quantitatively inferior ingredient may lose its form entirely (328^{a}26–8).[25] There is no indication of what the proper middle state would be like in this case, an equilibrium in which the watery and the winey character would exist only potentially and constitute a joint new quality. Since the example of tin and bronze (328^{b}12–14) also refers to an untypical mixture, it does not explain the kind of equilibrium that is characteristic of proper mixtures either.

In spite of the fact that the conception of mutual modification of agents is unusual in Aristotle, he does not seem to see a problem in his departure from the standard schema 'one-agent-one-patient'.

[24] See *Ph.* 201^{a}18; 202^{a}12–^{b}22; *de An.* 426^{a}9–10.
[25] Aristotle has discussed their mixture already in connection with growth at 321^{a}32–^{b}2. As he explains there, 'the mixture remains wine as long as it does the work (ἔργον) of wine, not that of water'. Only when the mixture gets too thin does wine lose its power (cf. *GC* I. 4. 322^{a}31–3). But no median between them is mentioned here.

Reciprocity of action and passion in fact need not present any difficulty for his explanatory scheme as long as there is the requisite active *and* passive *dunamis* in each of the agents/patients. This, at any rate, seems to be the assumption on which his final definition of mixture is based; mixture is a union ($\H{\epsilon}\nu\omega\sigma\iota\varsigma$) of two partners that have both undergone an alteration ($\dot{\alpha}\lambda\lambda o\acute{\iota}\omega\sigma\iota\varsigma$) through their mutual interaction (328^b22). The question of *alloiôsis* takes us to our next point, however. If Aristotle is serious that mixture presupposes a mutual *alloiôsis*, the change in question must be the emergence of a third quality that is somehow between the two opposed qualities. But if *mixis* consists in a mutual quality-change in two substances, the question is whether the qualities in question are *essential* qualities.[26] Aristotle can hardly be thinking of accidental qualities. Otherwise the joint product would not be sufficiently different from the original state of each of the ingredients. Such a combination could hardly fulfil the condition that 'some other thing (*heteron*) which comes to be from them is actually, while each of the things which were, before they were mixed, still is, but potentially' (327^b24–6). This injunction raises a host of further questions. First of all, how *heteron* is the *heteron* to be if it constitutes a different compound? And of what kind is the *dominant* state that is to supervene on the original state of each of the participants (328^a30)? What does it mean that the partners must be equal in power (328^a29)? If there is to be equality, is there only *one* mean between two opposed qualities that is sufficient to constitute a mixture?[27] Finally, how, precisely, are we to interpret the condition that only things that have the same kind of *matter* can mix (328^a20)? If only items in the same genus fulfil the condition of *opposition* of the ingredients, it would seem that Aristotle is left with quite a narrow field of mixables.

Since none of these questions can be answered on the basis of what Aristotle says in our chapter itself, we will have to turn elsewhere for further information. To obtain sufficient clarification it is necessary to take a look backwards at what precedes the discussion of mixture in *De generatione et corruptione*, and a look forwards at what happens to mixture later in book II, in the discussion of the elements and elemental change. Additional information on the scope and importance of *mixis* in Aristotle's philosophy of nature will be provided by a review of certain evidence outside *De generatione et corruptione*.

---

[26] That some $\pi\acute{\alpha}\theta\eta$ are per se is stated explicitly in *GC* I. 5. 321^b3–4. Though Aristotle speaks as if the *qualities* could act alone this must be a mere *façon de parler*. Qualities do not fly around unattached; hence there must be two different substances involved. Equally misleading is the impression that the mutual 'tempering' of the opposites is just a matter of degree (more or less hot). Joachim's (1922: 179–81) suggestion that there are different degrees of being is itself too unclear to solve the problem.

[27] Since Aristotle later stipulates that mixtures must contain all four elements, the concentration in *GC* I. 10 on two ingredients must be merely a matter of convenience.

Preliminary clarification: looking backwards

While the discussion of generation, alteration, and growth in book I, chapters 1–5 provides a clarification of the meaning of those concepts themselves, the second half of the book contains an investigation of the material basis and of the mechanisms of these different kinds of processes (chs. 6–10). As Aristotle complains, there is particular confusion on the basic conditions of change among the philosophers of nature no matter what their provenance. To make up for that deficiency he proposes to provide an analysis of action, passion, and mixture to account for all kinds of combination, starting with 'contact' as their fundamental condition (I. 6. 322^{b}21–6). Aristotle treats contact as the basis of all change because in *De generatione et corruptione* the focus is on corporeal interaction at the *elementary level* only. This fact also explains the peculiar distinction between action (*poiêsis*) and change (*kinêsis*) that significantly narrows down the use of *poiêsis*. Here it does not mean 'making' in the broad sense of acting or producing, but is confined to an active physical impact that produces an alteration in *quality* in its passive counterpart (I. 6. 323^{a}19).[28] This specification allows Aristotle to fine-tune the relation between acting, being acted on, and contact: it is an interaction of physical bodies in mutual contact that share the same substrate, and which results in alteration only. Though Aristotle cites only whiteness and heat as examples (I. 6. 323^{a}19–20), there seems to be no limit to the kind of quality changes to which his analysis applies.

That Aristotle means to keep acting and being affected within the narrow scope of qualitative change in the subsequent chapters 7–9 is not always conspicuous because the argument often turns into a quite general controversy with his predecessors about matters of principle that he wants to correct. So a good deal of chapter 7 is occupied by a discussion of the general question whether 'like acts on like' or 'unlike on unlike', while chapter 8 is to a large extent preoccupied with the refutation of his predecessors' erroneous assumptions about action and affection. Aristotle's critique is directed against Empedocles, the atomists, and the Eleatics, as well as against the explanation of interaction in Plato's *Timaeus*. Given this polemical tendency, the discussion of Aristotle's own presuppositions concerning the kind of interaction remains fairly general (I. 7. 323^{b}29–323^{a}14): the objects in question must share the same genus, but belong to different and opposite species.

---

[28] Its use here certainly differs from the wide sense suggested in *Cat.* 4. 2^{a}3–4 and 9. 11^{b}1–8, which includes both physical and non-physical influences (cutting and burning, heating and cooling, as well as giving pleasure and pain) and the special sense of human production referred to in *EN* VI. 4. 1140^{a}1–3.

There is a great variety of examples: bodies act on bodies, flavour on flavour (χυμός), colour on colour.

Aristotle is a little more explicit about the result of the interactions he has in mind: they concern contrary or at least contradictory *qualities* only (I. 7. 323ᵇ28–9): 'Nothing dislodges another from its nature unless both are either contraries or from contraries.' What happens in all such cases is that the agent imposes its own quality on the originally contrary or intermediary patient (324ᵃ8: μεταξύ), such as in heating or cooling, but also in curing and illness. Aristotle is here quite careful to explain why the proper mode of interaction is not always obvious in these cases. Some-times the so-called agent is only the first link in a long causal chain, where only the last link is the actual agent (ποιοῦν): it is not the doctor who passes on his own health to the patient; rather, the medication—the 'immediate agent' (ἔσχατον ποιοῦν)—is the agent that directly affects the patient's constitution, as when wine is administered as a drug (324ᵃ30).²⁹ Only the 'immediate agent' will pass on its own quality to the patient. And in that case there is change into the opposite state (324ᵃ12–14): 'So it is necessary that the patient change into the agent, because this is the way in which coming into being will be to the contrary.'

Given this explanatory scheme of acting and being affected, it comes as no surprise that Aristotle dismisses the theories of all his predecessors as besides the point in chapter 8. For in the case of indivisible and unalter-able elements there can be no mutual affection in the Aristotelian sense at all; in that case alteration can mean no more than aggregation and segregation of a particular kind.³⁰ The final summary in chapter 9 confirms that Aristotle is not willing to meet his opponents on their own terms. As he points out there, interaction presupposes continuous and overall homogeneous bodies. All seemingly irregular cases can be accounted for on the basis of the distinction between *dunamis* and *energeia* (I. 9. 326ᵇ31–327ᵃ14): difference in degree of potentiality ex-plains the difference in the impact achieved; impassivity is the sign of the object's strict inner unity; action at a distance works through an affec-table medium; where there is no continuity there is no homogeneous effect. The atomists' theory cannot explain, as Aristotle's theory can, changes of quality (ἀλλοίωσις) in the same bodies, nor growth or shrink-ing, since they can resort only to aggregation, separation, and change of place or position (327ᵃ14–25). Such an explanation by mechanical accre-

---

²⁹ In curing a sick patient the 'first agent' (the doctor or the art of medicine) is not affected in return, but the 'last agent', the medication, must be engaged in a direct physical interaction (324ᵃ32–ᵇ4). Aristotle makes it quite clear here that this applies to all kinds of ποιεῖν: the actual interaction presupposes contact and direct mutual affection (324ᵇ3–4).

³⁰ Cf. especially his complaint that atoms have no qualities of their own and can also not get into 'contact' in his sense (326ᵃ34–ᵇ2).

tion is not sufficient to explain quality change (23–5)—'rather than the whole having changed either through the admixture of something (μιχθέντος) or because it changes in itself (μεταβάλλοντος)'.

Change of quality is then the result of all kinds of action and affection, including that of mixture. What distinguishes mixture from the other kinds of alteration is that in *mixis* there is a *two-way* rather than just a *one-way* change: both constituents in a mixture act as agent in one sense and as patient in another, for each actively modifies the opposite quality in the other without eradicating it. Otherwise the change in question will be generation and destruction instead of mixture. Does this review provide us with answers to the catalogue of questions on *mixis* that are left open in chapter 10? Some of the problems on our list have indeed disappeared. It is clear from the account of acting and being affected that Aristotle is not speaking loosely when he specifies the result of a mixture as a new *quality*, but does indeed have a special kind of mutual alteration in mind. In addition, the fact that Aristotle carefully analyses the conditions of *poiein* and *paschein* indicates that he wants to prepare for the reciprocal interaction that constitutes *mixis*, precisely because such reciprocity through mutual action and affection is unusual in his normal scheme of things.

But most of our questions still remain open and give rise to further problems. First of all there is the general question why Aristotle does not consider mixture as a subclass of substantial change, but instead regards it as a kind of quality change. Then there is the question of what kinds of qualities constitute mixtures and what equilibrium between the ingredients Aristotle has in mind. Then there is the question in what way the constituents of mixtures must possess the same kind of *matter*. Though the discussion of acting and being acted upon emphasizes this last condition it leaves open what, precisely, the sameness of matter is supposed to consist in. The discussion in chapter I. 7 emphasizes that for action and affection to occur the two factors must be 'alike or the same in genus', but, as stated before, Aristotle's examples suggest that 'genus' may be taken in a wider or in a narrower sense: 'It is natural for body to be affected by body, flavour by flavour, colour by colour, and generally things that are of a given genus by other such things' (323ᵃ33–5). This explanation seems to be rather vague on the appropriate substratum of mixtures.

The result of this review of the preceding chapters in *De generatione et corruptione* concerning the nature of mixture and its preconditions is limited. It amounts to little more than a confirmation that the discussion of contact, as well as that of action and passion, is designed to prepare the account of mixture, and that mixture consists in the mutual 'tuning' of the characteristic qualities of its ingredients. It does not tell us what kinds of qualities are at stake, nor does it tell us anything about the kind of equilibrium that is to be attained.

Further clarification: looking forwards

The complaint that Aristotle leaves open the kinds of qualities he has in mind in *GC* I. 10 is actually not quite justified. In the course of the chapter he does give one important clue about the overall aim he is pursuing in his discussion of mixture. That clue is contained in the postulate that the product of mixture should be *homogeneous* and therefore also 'homonymous' (328^{b}21).[31] Though Aristotle does not make much of the condition of homogeneity here, it can hardly be an accident that he uses the expression *homoiomeres* at this point (328^{a}4, 10). If the structure of *homoiomerê* is the ultimate aim of his analysis of mixture then it is clear why he is so circumspect in his clarification of mixture and mixables. He is not concerned with just any sort of combination of what is fusible in some way or other, but intends to investigate the formation of the 'basic stuff' by a mixture of the simple bodies (ἁπλᾶ σώματα).

If that assumption is correct, then Aristotle is here concerned with the netherworld of inorganic and organic chemistry.[32] I call it a 'netherworld' because he normally takes the four elements and the simple compounds as basic and sees no need for further analysis. The *De generatione et corruptione*'s purpose is, *inter alia*, to make up for this important omission. The adjective 'homoeomerous' applies, however, not only to the different kinds of uniform chemicals but also to the organic tissues that form the basic physiological constituents of all live organisms. That Aristotle means to account for both kinds in *De generatione et corruptione* actually comes to the fore already in the discussion of growth. Not only does he refer to homogeneous tissue like flesh and bone as the proper subject of growth, but he also points out that such growth is at the same time the cause of the non-homogeneous parts of the body.[33] The reference to 'basic stuff' in book I shows that *De generatione et corruptione* was conceived from the start as a study of the conditions of generation and corruption at the elementary level. The focus accounts for

[31] This use of homonymy does, of course, not agree with the definition of homonymy in *Cat.* 1. 1^{a}1–6.
[32] The label is Joachim's (1904). Though Williams (1982), 142, rightly objects that modern chemistry presupposes an atomic theory while Aristotle rejects it, there are some important similarities; for, like molecules, the compounds have analysably different constituents. This may explain in what sense Aristotle insists on their separability (327^{b}27–9). Should the mixture dissolve, its ingredients would return to their former state.
[33] *GC* I. 5. 321^{b}18; 322^{a}19.

the fact that Aristotle hardly mentions the conditions of generation and change of living things at a higher level.[34] But while the first book largely leaves open the kinds of 'agents' and 'patients' Aristotle is concerned with, the second book of *De generatione et corruptione* turns to that very question. We will therefore take a brief look at that further development to see what light it sheds on the remaining questions concerning mixture.

The beginning of the second book of *De generatione et corruptione* makes it explicit that Aristotle deliberately confined the first book to a clarification of basic processes and their conditions. His analysis now turns to the elements themselves. Since a proper discussion of this intriguing subject would take us too far afield, I will mention only what is necessary for the explanation of homoeomerous mixtures. It is significant that the term 'element' (στοιχεῖον) does not, as one might expect, refer to the four simple bodies (ἁπλᾶ σώματα), earth, water, air, and fire, but rather to the four basic *qualities* that determine the nature of the simple bodies, namely the hot and the cold, the wet and the dry. Their exchange is what makes transformation between the 'simple bodies' possible. Genesis or substantial change at the most elementary level is nothing but the exchange of one of the four basic qualities for another. If, for instance, the dry in fire is replaced by its opposite, the wet, then fire changes into air. Though Aristotle in that connection occasionally speaks of 'mixing' of elemental properties to explain elemental change,[35] this cannot be the sense of mixture that is discussed in *GC* I. 10. For though it remains somewhat unclear by what mechanism elemental change comes about, the product is in each case a different 'simple body', and not a fusion of two different kinds of substances: 'The elements (στοιχεῖα), however, have to be capable of acting upon and being acted upon by one another, since they mix and change into one another (II. 2. 329^{b}22–4).' The 'elements' that act and are acted upon here are clearly the single basic qualities, not the different simple bodies.[36] Hence the mixing in question is of a different kind than the one presupposed in the discussion of *mixis* proper: A different simple body does not result

---

[34] This explains why remarkably little use is made of the otherwise ubiquitous opposition between matter and form, ὕλη and εἶδος, in this discussion. Aristotle only once obliquely refers to that fact: in the case of simple substances (ὁμοιομερῆ) such as flesh and bone, form and matter are difficult to separate, while they are much more easily recognizable in higher-order objects like a hand (5. 321^{b}19–32). It is only in the last chapters, 9–11, of book II that the four causes are reinstalled in their usual function because Aristotle discusses generation and destruction at a cosmic level.

[35] *GC* II. 1. 329^{a}34; II. 2. 329^{b}11 and *passim*.

[36] Since only the contrary *qualities*, the dry, liquid, hot, and cold, are elements (στοιχεῖα), the *simple bodies* are here not treated as 'elementary' but as *composites* of different qualities. Aristotle in fact sticks quite faithfully to the terminological distinction between the στοιχεῖα, the elementary qualities, and the ἁπλᾶ σώματα, the simple *bodies*. It is as bodies that they are simple.

from an equilibrium of opposed qualities (e.g. of hot and cold) but from a new *combination* of qualities, where one opposed quality is replaced by the other; for instance, when the hot and dry (fire) changes into the hot and moist (air).[37] If Aristotle uses the term mixture in a misleading way, it must be because of the lack of a better term to designate the relation between the elementary qualities.[38] The reason why Aristotle resorts to such a misleading use of 'mixture' to explain the combination of *stoicheia* that determine the nature of the simple bodies is not hard to see once the peculiarity of their nature is noted (II. 2. 330[a]24–6). There is no apt term to explain the strange configuration that constitutes the simple bodies and makes possible their interchange. This explains why in his accounts of both substantial change and mixture Aristotle resorts to *quality* rather than to *form* as one might expect him to do, given the prominent role of form ($\epsilon \hat{\iota} \delta o s$) in his physics and metaphysics.[39] That Aristotle avoids the distinction between matter and form at the elementary level is because the 'forms' of the simple bodies consist in nothing but the combination of two qualities that (somehow) jointly constitute its essence. Aristotle calls both qualities *differentiae* (II. 4. 331[a]15–16) and leaves no room for any kind of underlying 'matter' in the case of the four simple bodies.[40] There are no more basic entities in his scheme than the *stoicheia*; that is, the hot, the cold, the wet, and the dry. The simple bodies *are* therefore strange entities: they consist of two *differentiae* with no underlying matter ($\ddot{\upsilon}\lambda\eta$). Not only is there nothing *neutral* at the most elementary level that could function as a substratum for elemental change, as prime matter was notoriously supposed to do according to some interpretations, Aristotle unequivocally rules out the possibility that there is a state in which a simple body consists of only *one* quality, as a kind of molecular 'radical' ready to link to another quality. 'Prime matter' is nothing but the *potential* of the simple bodies to engage in different basic combinations.[41]

---

[37] Cf. II. 2. 329[b]23. A little later Aristotle states explicitly that the 'simple' bodies are themselves compounds of a kind (II. 3. 330[b]22): 'Neither fire nor air nor any of those we have mentioned is in fact simple but mixed ($\mu\iota\kappa\tau\acute{a}$).'

[38] Cf. *GC* II. 4. On the 'combativeness' of elemental interaction in Aristotle's account in comparison with Plato and the Presocratics cf. Solmsen (1960), 357–67: 'In Aristotle the imagery of warfare somewhat pales, yet there is the same readiness to conquer and destroy' (p. 359).

[39] Cf. n. 32 above. Philoponus speaks of 'forms in a restrained state' ($\epsilon \ddot{\iota} \delta \eta$ $\kappa \epsilon \kappa o \lambda a \sigma \mu \acute{\epsilon} \nu a$) in the case of the mixable (192. 12).

[40] The question of the nature of the $\ddot{\upsilon}\lambda\eta$ of the elementary composites cannot be addressed here; cf. *GC* II. 1. 329[a]24–35.

[41] Though the qualities are called contraries, they are at the same time contradictory opposites, for one member of the pair is the privation of the other, cf. *GC* II. 5. 332[a]23–5. On Aristotle's tendency to associate not only the differentia but also genus and species with qualities cf. *Cat.* 5. 3[b]15–21: 'they signify substance of a certain qualification ($\pi o \iota \acute{a} \nu$ $\tau \iota \nu a$ $o \dot{\upsilon} \sigma \acute{\iota} a \nu$)'. The 'adjectival character' of *mixis* has already been noted by Joachim (1922), 177.

Since there is no further substrate (ὑποκείμενον) that underlies the elementary compound, the characteristic combination of two of the basic qualities is all there is to each of them. Change among the simple bodies comes about when one quality is exchanged for its opposite, the hot instead of the cold or the dry instead of the wet or vice versa.[42]

Though the use of *mixis* and *mikton* in the first chapters of book II is at first rather confusing, it is not the result of carelessness. Aristotle seems intent to point up the similarity and difference between the basic exchange that generates the simple bodies and the process of mixture, properly so called: both kinds of processes involve change of the *stoicheia*, albeit in a different way. In the one case there is exchange between opposite qualities, in the other there is a mutual tuning between them. But here the comparison ends and Aristotle does little to avoid confusion.[43]

On the nature of mixture properly so called there is valuable further information to be drawn from chapters 7 and 8 of book II, where Aristotle turns to an explanation of the formation of homoeomerous composites. This discussion, once again, is not as extensive as one might wish because he introduces the topic not for its own sake but as part of a *reductio ad absurdum* of theories that deny the possibility of interchange between the simple bodies. To refute those views, Aristotle points out that such a theory also rules out the possibility that tissues like flesh, bone, and marrow are homogeneous materials. Tissue would then consist of heterogeneous conglomerates, with particles joined together like bricks and stones in a wall. In spite of the fact that the discussion is (sometimes overly) encumbered by such polemical attacks against his opponents, we do get some information about Aristotle's own explanation of homoeomerous tissue on the basis of his *mixis* theory. Flesh, for instance, originates from fire and earth but is identical with neither (334^b5). Though the exact components that actually constitute flesh remain somewhat vague, the main point is clear: the mixture in question results from a mutual modification of the elementary *qualities*; the hot-cold or cold-hot that characterizes the mixture is a moderation of the two extremes that continue to exist potentially in the mixture.[44] The upshot of this clarification is as follows: if one of the basic qualities or

[42] This answers Williams's (1982, 144) query about the difference between mixing and corruption.

[43] Plato is not mentioned here, but Aristotle no doubt also has the various combinations of the elements in the *Timaeus* in mind when he points out that atomic theories cannot account for homogenous matter.

[44] As Aristotle states in 334^b11-12 the mixture destroys not the compound but the *extremity* of the contraries. Code's (1995) query how mixture differs from generation can be answered by reference to mutual modification: the potency in question is not the mere possibility of eventual regeneration. It is a modified but *active* power that re-emerges in its

differentiae succeeds in replacing its opponent, there is generation of a different substance. If the respective *differentiae* manage to balance each other out, the result is a homoeomerous mixture. Thus mixtures are the result of *incomplete substantial change*. That the elementary qualities allow for mutual moderation has not been explicitly stated in the discussion of mixture in *GC* I. 10. But since Aristotle does assume equilibrium and an in-between state for them, he must have had such a mutual 'tuning' in mind.[45]

However the mechanism of the interaction between the simple bodies may be explained, we are on safer ground concerning the mixture of homoeomerous stuffs. As Aristotle says, mixture is not just a mutual modification of the opposed qualities that leads to a certain equilibrium between those properties; the modification in quality is at the same time a modification of matter, resulting in a joint product that is neither pure fire nor pure earth (II. 7. $334^{b}10-16$):

when it is not completely so, but as it were hot-cold or cold-hot, because in being mixed things will destroy each other's excesses, then what will exist is neither their matter nor either of the contraries existing *simpliciter* in actuality, but something intermediate, which, in so far as it is in potentiality more hot than cold or vice versa, is proportionately twice as hot in potentiality as cold, or three times, or in some other similar way.

Thus Aristotle here spells out the material conditions of mixtures that he has left largely open in *GC* I. 10, though the review of the preceding chapters has actually provided sufficient evidence that mixture must consist in a mutual 'toning down' of the opposed qualities. For obvious reasons Aristotle does not want to commit himself to a precise ratio between hot and cold in his account of flesh. He is not thinking of an arithmetically precise mean. Nor does he want to limit the mixture to two ingredients, though for convenience's sake he usually mentions only two. Occasionally he does indicate that a certain mixture contains more than one pair of opposites, as for instance in the mixture that constitutes flesh and bone (II. 7. $334^{b}28-30$): 'Similarly dry and wet and suchlike produce flesh and bone and the rest in the middle range'. He clearly is not trying to give a proper account of the actual consistency of flesh and bone, but wants to explain in general terms the *principle* that is responsible for entities of a higher order of complexity. For this is how he continues (II. 7. $334^{b}16-20$):

original form once its interaction with the second agent ends. That is why Aristotle insists on the co-presence of two active forces that influence each other.

[45] Cf. $328^{a}31$. Williams's (1982), 175–6 complaint of an inconsistency in Aristotle's theory on this issue is therefore unfounded.

It is as a result of the contraries, or the elements (στοιχεῖα), having been mixed that the other things will exist, and the elements from these latter, which in potentiality, in some way, are the elements, not in the same way as matter but in the way we have explained. In this way what comes to be is a mixture, in that way it is matter.

What this somewhat cryptic sentence means to tell us is that the mixtures themselves can in turn serve as the ingredients of more complex composites. For the modified contraries that characterize the resulting mixture may again become part of a *further* mixture that will display different qualities. It is only in their extreme form that opposite qualities cannot do so. That is why Aristotle mentions that nothing comes from an excess of the extreme contraries like ice or burning fire: because of the extremity of their qualities they do not, or do not easily, enter a mixture (II. 3. 330^b25–30).

Mixtures presuppose a certain equilibrium between the elements, otherwise the contraries will destroy each other and there will be complete substantial change. So whether or not a mixture results depends on the ratio of the available elements. If there is an appropriate mean a mixture of a certain kind will result (II. 7. 334^b25–8): 'But flesh and bones and suchlike come from these, the hot becoming cold and the cold hot when they approach the mean, for they are neither one thing nor the other.' It emerges, then, that mixtures are not necessarily precarious states that easily dissolve when the balance between their qualities is disturbed. As Aristotle asserts, the mean is not a fine point that is easy to miss, but actually constitutes a broad middle field (II. 7. 334^b28–30): 'And the mean is large and not an indivisible point. Similarly dry and wet and suchlike produce flesh and bone and the rest in the middle range.' Proper mixtures are therefore conceived as stable affairs; they are not precarious products of chance circumstances. Concerning the ingredients that constitute mixtures Aristotle makes it quite clear in what follows that there are no limitations in complexity above the basic level.

Given this account, it should be clear by now why Aristotle does not distinguish between *mixis* and *krasis* in *GC* I. 10. Since mixture is accounted for by the combination of the *stoicheia* only, there is no point in working out an opposition between overall dry and overall liquid ingredients and end-products. As combinations of the basic *stoicheia*, all mixtures are on a par, regardless of what the phenotype of the product is like. It would therefore have been an impediment to Aristotle's task to separate 'fusibles' from other kinds of mixables. If the properties of dry stuff, for instance, could not engage in action and reaction at all, there would be neither incomplete nor complete substantial transformation.

As Aristotle emphasizes, in all stable mixtures the extremes must be counterbalanced by their opposites, for otherwise no elemental change would occur at all (II. 8. 335ᵃ6–9): 'Since, therefore, comings to be are from contraries, and one member of each pair of contraries exists in these things, the other members must also exist in them; so that all the simple bodies are present in every composite body.' This applies in particular to earth, the driest and most inert of the simple bodies, which Aristotle treats as a necessary ingredient in every mixture (II. 8. 334ᵇ32–4). Without earth no composite would stay near the centre. Though Aristotle occasionally gives other reasons for the need of the co-presence of all four elements, the principle of a balance between contraries seems to be his most basic concern. [46]

This leaves us with one further question; namely, what kind of sameness of *matter* it is that Aristotle presupposes for mixtures. This may seem to present a particular problem in the case of mixtures of the simple bodies since they do not share a common matter, since prime matter, for the reasons stated above, is not available to fulfil this function. The problem disappears if one remembers that the condition of sameness of genus is quite liberal, as the examples are supposed to show (I. 7. 323ᵇ33–324ᵃ1): 'bodies act on bodies, flavour on flavour, colour on colour'. The liberality of the condition indicates that Aristotle must have had the simple bodies and their mixtures already in mind. In their case it must suffice that they are all bodies (σώματα) of one sort or another; there is no further genus or matter. In the case of more complex mixtures the sameness of matter or genus becomes more complex as well. The question arises then of what kinds of 'opposites' Aristotle has in mind to account for their mixtures. In *De generatione et corruptione* the analysis concentrates almost entirely on an explanation at the elementary level; there are only occasional hints that the account applies to higher-order mixtures, as in the case of organic matter such as flesh and bone. If we want to know more about the mixing that constitutes organic tissue of a higher complexity, other texts have to be consulted. Since no thorough treatment of this topic is possible here, we shall just take a brief glance at one such discussion of *homoiomerê*.

---

[46] He mentions that all four elements are necessary for the nourishment of living things, including plants, but this is cited merely as a piece of evidence and not as his main concern (cf. 335ᵃ9–13). Joachim (1904), 78 ff., assumes that mixture proper is limited to the four simple bodies in various proportions and therefore regards blends such as those of wine and honey as *mixeis* only in an extended sense. But no such restriction seems indicated, provided that the constituents of mixtures possess the elementary qualities that act on each other.

Further clarification: looking elsewhere

A fairly extensive discussion of homoeomerous bodies is contained in *Meteorologica* IV. 8–12.[47] That the question whether this book is genuine or not is still a matter of controversy need not overly concern us here.[48] Though 'mixture' in this work is not used in the technical sense specified in *GC* I. 10, there are no major disagreements between its explanation of homogeneous matter, including organic tissue, and the account of mixture in *De generatione et corruptione*. In both works homoeomerous tissue is explained as a compound of the four simple bodies and their properties. What divergence there is between *Meteorologica* IV and *De generatione et corruptione* stems from the fact that the former investigation is geared to material components of a higher complexity. Thus the explanation does not start with the combination of the four *stoicheia* as such, but it employs them as active (hot and cold) and passive (wet and dry) *powers*. These powers are responsible for the formation of all that is homogeneous (IV. 6. 384^{b}31–2): 'vegetable and animal and also the metals under the ground'. The author's main concern is with the properties and behaviour characteristic of complex homogeneous bodies (IV. 8. 385^{a}5–10): 'I mean solubility, solidification, flexibility, and the like, all of which, like wet and dry, are passive qualities. It is by these passive qualities that bone, flesh, sinew, wood, bark, stone, and all the other natural homoeomerous bodies are differentiated.'

We shall leave aside the long discussion of the 'passive qualities' in chapters 8 and 9 in order to turn to chapters 10 and 11, where the author discusses the proportions of water and earth that he takes to be characteristic of different kinds of homogeneous stuff, and elucidates the *powers* that are necessary for their generation; that is, the hot and the cold. There is, to begin with, a long list of homoeomerous bodies, both inorganic and organic (IV. 10. 388^{a}13–18): 'By homogeneous bodies I mean, for example, metallic substances (e.g. bronze, gold, silver, tin, iron, stone, and similar material and their by-products) and animal and vegetable

---

[47] As Lee observes (1952), 336, from *Meteor.* IV. 8 on the text is concerned mainly with the properties and behaviour of homoeomerous stuff even where this is not explicitly stated.

[48] For a defence cf. the introduction in Lee (1952), pp. xiii–xxi. Because of the book's poor style one feels somewhat reluctant to attribute it to Aristotle himself; it may be a compilation by a student who followed the master's instructions. As even Solmsen, in a review of *Meteorologica* by Lee, *Gnomon*, 29 (1957), 132–3—one of the main opponents of its *Echtheit*—admits, there were good reasons for the members of the Peripatos to compile such a book. His objections against *Mete.* IV (1960: 402–3) largely rest on an alleged agreement between the author and Plato's *Timaeus* that 'in a study of this kind the λόγος and the teleological cause have little scope'. But Solmsen seems to ignore the fact that *De generatione et corruptione* is not concerned with teleology either.

tissues (e.g. flesh, bone, sinew, skin, intestine, hair, fibre, veins) from which in turn the non-homogeneous bodies, face, hand, foot, and the like are composed'.[49] In what follows the author does not explicitly take up the question of what mixture, precisely, underlies the different substances. Nor does he try to explain what kind of *median* state there is between the contraries in each case. Instead of a battle between opposed qualities we find an account in terms of Aristotle's canonical causal scheme. The author explains the difference among homogeneous bodies as the product of the interaction by the two different active or *efficient* causes, the hot and the cold, and the *material* causes, the dry and the wet 'which produce concrete homoeomerous bodies out of water and earth'. The basic material cause for all homogeneous bodies is therefore water and earth, not, as in *De generatione et corruptione*, their *stoicheia*.

Such a division of labour among the four simple bodies, the assignment of an active and a passive role to them and the identification of the passive elementary stuff with 'matter', may, of course, represent a certain change of mind on the author's part. But it is not necessary to draw that conclusion. For the division between active and passive forces, with the hot and the cold as active powers, the dry and the wet as passive ones, is also supported in *De generatione et corruptione*.[50] The reason for the difference in the explanatory scheme in *Meteorologica* IV seems to lie in the great *range* of homogeneous bodies whose chemical consistency and behaviour its author needs to explain; the separation of 'passive matter' as the basic stock clearly is meant to facilitate that task. The text will suffice to confirm this claim (IV. 10. 388ᵃ29–ᵇ10):

Liquids which evaporate are made of water; those which do not are made of earth or are a mixture of earth and water, like milk, or of earth and air, like wood, or of water and air, like oil. Liquids whose density heat increases are a combination (κοινά). . . . Liquids whose density cold increases are earthy: bodies whose density is increased both by heat and cold are compounded of more than one element (κοινά πλειόνων), like oil and honey and sweet wine.

We cannot now engage in a survey of the different kinds of materials that are treated under the general heading of *homoiomerê*, nor should we be concerned with the specifications that supposedly explain the whole variety of characteristic behaviour he seems to have come across in his empirical research. If the author was not Aristotle himself then he at least displays a genuinely Aristotelian love of detail, as his long list of classifications shows (IV. 10. 389ᵃ7–23):

---

[49] I am following Lee's translation. Cf. his remarks on the somewhat loose enumeration, 358 n. *b*.

[50] This distinction is mentioned in *GC* I. 3. 318ᵇ14–18; II. 2. 329ᵇ21–32, but plays a subordinate role, since the ability of heat to move and to weld together and that of cold to arrest and to compress are not employed there.

'The following are therefore composed of water: gold, silver, bronze, tin, lead, glass...for all of these are melted by heat...Earth preponderates in the following: iron, horn, nail, bone, sinew, wood, hair, leaves and bark...Blood and semen, on the other hand, are composed of earth, water, and air, blood which contains fibres having a preponderance of earth, blood which contains no fibres having a preponderance of water; semen is solidified by cooling when its moisture leaves it at the same time as its heat.'

The special importance that is attributed to two of the simple bodies, namely earth and water, clearly comes from the need to keep simple the basic principles that underlie the wide variety of phenomena. This need also explains why 'Aristotle' does not apply the principles of differentiation that he uses in De generatione et corruptione here. It would be impossible to account for all those different stuffs on the basis of the four *stoicheia* only. Aristotle would soon have run out of specifications for the stable 'mean states' between contraries had he tried to do so.[51] His concern here is not to explain how mixtures come about at all, as it is in De generatione et corruptione, but to account for the different structure of complex material. The combinations, κοινά, he speaks of here are in fact mixtures of mixtures rather than the elementary kinds discussed in De generatione et corruptione. The difficulties that emerge in the classification of certain combinations indicate that the author is conscious of the fact that even the derivation of all substances from earth and water as basic materials can only be taken as a quite rough indication. As he maintains in the case of wine, it is a compound of several elements, and different sorts of wine may differ in their consistency.[52]

The impression that the complexity of homoeomerous stuff strains the explanatory scheme on the basis of the four simple bodies and their basic properties is confirmed in the final chapter, where the author attempts to work out the components of flesh, bone, and other such organic tissue. He there abandons simple chemical explanation and resorts instead to considerations about the compounds' final causes. An account of their nature necessarily must refer to the *end* (τέλος) they serve in the live organism (IV. 12. 389^{b}26–8): 'for the homoeomerous bodies are

[51] Not just any ratio can constitute a proper mixture. Fine (1995) manages to work out algorithms for the computation of an unlimited continuum in the quantities of the ingredients (esp. pp. 301–21), but thereby provides only *ex post facto* reconstructions of the presumptive ratios in question. He does not explain what kind of ratio would constitute the 'form' of a stable homoeomerous kind (pp. 328–32), but rather admits that there must be different 'bonds' that account for the different products. What accounts for such 'molecules' remains an open question (pp. 340–7). Even in seemingly promising disciplines like metallurgy where the ingredients are easily quantifiable we would be hard pressed to determine the quantities of the *stoicheia* that characterize each kind of metal.

[52] New wine supposedly contains more earth than old wine because its solidity increases under the influence of heat and lessens under the influence of cold.

composed of the elements (στοιχεῖα), and serve in turn as material (ὕλη) for all the works of nature (ἔργα τῆς φύσεως)'. The author admits, however, that while the requisite τέλος does not present much of a difficulty in the case of *non-homogeneous* parts of living things, at the more elementary level a purpose is hard to find (IV. 12. 390ᵃ2). 'The distinction [sc. between matter and form] is less clear in the case of flesh and bone, and less clear again in the case of fire and water. For the final cause is least obvious where matter predominates.'

This agrees with our earlier diagnosis that in the discussion of elementary composites Aristotle avoids the distinction between matter and form.[53] If this distinction is hard to apply at the elementary level, the specification of a τέλος is totally out of place. The simple bodies and their properties supply the matter for every corporeal being and therefore cannot serve specifiable ends. In an account of the most basic constituents of matter the kinds of considerations that emerge at the end of the *Meteorologica* are therefore quite remote. The concern with the *telos* of homoeomerous tissue signals, then, an important change of aspect. It prepares for a step up on the *scala naturae*; namely, the transition to an analysis of the function of homoeomerous stuff in biology. But that step definitely exceeds the concerns of *De generatione et corruptione*, a treatise that does not purport to investigate the role of homoeomerous tissue in live organisms.

That there is no real incompatibility in Aristotle's theory in *De generatione et corruptione* and *Meteorologica* book IV should have become clear by now. That there is agreement about the basic principles is also confirmed by the conclusion of the *Meteorologica* (IV. 12. 390ᵇ2–10):

Heat and cold and the motions set up by them are therefore, since solidification is caused by heat and cold, sufficient to produce all parts of this sort, that is to say all homoeomerous parts like flesh, bone, hair, sinew, and all the like. For these are all distinguished by the *differentiae* we have already described . . . which are produced by heat and cold and the combination of their motions.

It is only when it comes to the higher formations—the non-homogeneous parts of organisms—that nature needs different and more sophisticated means of production.

If the explanation of 'chemical' interaction as we find it in *De generatione et corruptione* may seem un-Aristotelian at first sight because it ignores both form and τέλος, closer analysis shows that this disregard is a strength rather than a weakness on Aristotle's part. For it indicates that he is quite capable of adjusting his explanatory principles when they turn

---

[53] He has acknowledged the difficulty of distinguishing matter and form in homogenous stuff like flesh and bone already in *GC* I. 5. 321ᵇ20–3.

out to be useless for the subject matter, as he does in his explanation of the material components at the most elementary level.

Epilogue

It is not just Aristotle's flexibility in the application of his principles to account for the basic elements and processes that calls for admiration. Equally admirable is his concern with economy in that field. In his attempt to account for the composition of the material universe he assumes as few kinds of 'building blocks' and as uniform a 'cement' as possible. In the last analysis, everything comes to be from the four *stoicheia* and their specific powers. This applies to generation and destruction as well as to alteration, growth, and mixture, as we have seen. A proper assessment of the rationale of Aristotle's procedure in the analysis of the most basic materials and the processes of their combinations explains at the same time, however, why he was not predestined to become the 'father of chemistry', as he became the father of so many other disciplines. If his study of the elements and their properties did not encourage the development of chemistry in antiquity, this is because of the constraints imposed by his principles. As indicated above, his basic schema does not explain how there can be sufficient diversification to account for the great variety of natural materials. The combinations resulting from the four basic *stoicheia*, the hot and the cold, the dry and the wet, are soon exhausted. Therefore the construction of all else out of their basic opposition in terms of different 'means' is confined to rough indications of the different ratios that may obtain in each case. Aristotle must have realized that the combinations of the *stoicheia* would soon sound embarrassingly monotonous and implausible if carried to a higher level of complexity. Apart from some very general remarks about the possibility of diversification, Aristotle wisely refrains from speculating about the mathematics in question. Instead, he contents himself with phenomenological descriptions of the behaviour and properties of the homoeomerous bodies. The confinement to four basic contrary principles that supposedly constitute the nature of all physical bodies has the consequence that there is a desperate shortage of differentiae at a higher level of complexity. We may, then, find even Solmsen's diagnosis overly generous: 'Beyond the formation of the tissues, the concept of mixture offers little help.'[54] Instead, our less optimistic assessment must be: 'The concept of mixture offers little help when it comes to the actual

---

[54] Solmsen (1960), 374. Cf. his remarks on the fact that Aristotle made no attempt at quantification (p. 377).

explanation of the *consistency* of tissue.' Admirable as Aristotle's self-restraint and the economy of his construction of material compounds may appear, it undeniably imposed a severe restraint on the development of natural science at its most basic, chemical level, for centuries. It discouraged further chemical research among the Aristotelians, most of all the kind that would search for quantifiable results. But this aspect of the *Nachleben* of *De generatione et corruptione* is a story for the historian of science to tell.

A Note on Aristotle on Mixture

JOHN M. COOPER

For Aristotle mixtures are homoeomerous or 'like-parted' stuffs, and their ingredients are physically more basic like-parted stuffs. According to his account of the nature and composition of flesh, for example, any quantity of flesh is divisible indefinitely into parts that have the same nature as each other and as any expanse of flesh of which they are parts. Further, flesh and all the other naturally occurring mixtures are composed of all the simple bodies (fire, air, water, and earth), and each of these ingredients is similarly like-parted. When the right proportions of some quantities of fire, air, water, and earth are combined to form some flesh, he tells us, each of these acts on and is acted upon by the others so that their differences in terms of what are for him the basic elements, namely the fundamental opposed material qualities of hot and cold, wet and dry, are brought into a specific unity characteristic of flesh, in particular.[1] Flesh has a particular, uniform, range of temperatures and locations on the scale of wetness-dryness, together with a consequent range of thickness or consistency, colour, hardness-softness, weight, and so on. And similarly, *mutatis mutandis*, for all the other like-parted materials to which in the course of nature the simple bodies give rise.

Does Aristotle also hold that each and every part into which a 'chemical compound' like flesh might be divided has the same ingredients as the wholes to which it belongs? On his view, is every part of such a stuff (however small) like every other part not only in its actual properties of wetness-dryness, hotness-coldness, colour, consistency, etc., but also in the types of ingredients from which it originated? Does each part of flesh (and of all the other compounds) have inside it (in 'potential' form) some earth, some air, some fire, and some water, in the same proportions as are in the whole of which it is a part, which could at least in principle be

---

[1] See *GC* II. 3. 330^{a}30, 33; Aristotle goes on to contrast his view with that of 'those who make the simple bodies elements' (330^{b}7). Cf. also Aristotle's frequent reference to the simple bodies as 'the so-called elements' (I. 6. 322^{b}1–2; II. 1. 328^{b}31, 329^{a}16, 26), and the argument of II. 1.

reconstituted by separation out from it? Commentators often attribute to Aristotle this view (more on this below). But it is important to see that, if that is Aristotle's opinion, this is a further thesis, not one already implied by the two claims set out in the previous paragraph. Flesh, for example, would still be perfectly homogeneous in all its actual qualities of temperature, texture, colour etc., all the way down into its parts—however small a particle of flesh you might imagine—even if at some stage in the division leading to those parts one reached particles whose materials were from not all four of the simple bodies but from three, or two, or even a single one. That is because, as we have seen, the key process involved in mixture, according to Aristotle, is certain quantities of the simple bodies interacting so as to 'destroy one another's excesses' and to produce *in each body as it enters the compound* a common, shared set of specific intermediate properties. Even if each largish mass of flesh requires to have all four of the simple bodies as its ingredients (I discuss this requirement below), it does not follow that each tiny particle of flesh must likewise come from proportionate quantities of all four simple bodies. So long as each particle has the same relevant intermediate properties as each other particle and as the whole, flesh will remain a like-parted stuff. In order to sustain that result a particle does not have to have its material origin in some quantities of all four of the simple bodies. Since each entering quantity, considered separately, has been altered so that it comes to possess the same set of qualities as each other entering quantity, nothing rules out the derivation of *some* very small portions of the material mass of the compound simply from one, or two, or three, and not all four, of the entering ingredient bodies. In fact, careful attention to Aristotle's account, in the second part of *GC* I. 10, of the processes by which mixtures are formed will reveal that his account exploits this possibility. Indeed, as we will see, the alternative view that commentators attribute to him is incompatible with his own (very reasonable) understanding of these processes. (On what grounds the commentators nonetheless attribute this view to him is a question to which I return below.)

Aristotle develops his account of mixtures in I. 10 in four principal phases.[2] Before beginning to argue for his own theory, he first sets out an argument alleging that mixture is impossible (327^a34-^b10). To dissolve this aporia or difficulty one must obviously argue that a coherent account can be provided which satisfies two conditions: (1) none of the ingredients of any mixture is destroyed when they are combined to form the mixture, but all retain their identities and can in principle be

---

[2] Compare Dorothea Frede in Chapter 11 of this volume, pp. 291–6.

retrieved, while (2) in being combined they undergo alterations so that while combined in the mixture they are not in every way the same as they are in their separated and uncombined state. In effect (see ^{b}6–9), these conditions, which Aristotle ultimately says his own account can satisfy, are the ones that together define mixture, as against other sorts of relationships among bodies from which other bodies or masses are derived. In the second phase Aristotle presents the first part of his theory and disposes of one element in this aporia (327^{b}22–31). Here he explains that, thanks to the Aristotelian distinction between what a thing is actually (ἐνεργείᾳ) and what it is potentially (δυνάμει), we can say that a compound stuff can perfectly well be actually (e.g.) flesh while potentially earth, air, fire and water, the ingredients that were mixed together to form it: thus earth, air, fire, and water, flesh's ingredients, have not been destroyed when being combined in the flesh, since the flesh, though actually flesh and not actually any of these, is nonetheless potentially all of them. In the fourth and final phase Aristotle explains the second part of his theory, in the last section of the chapter (328^{a}17–^{b}22). Here he takes up the question 'how it is possible for this [i.e. mixing so under-stood] to take place' (328^{a}17–18). In doing so he adds the remaining condition which, from the aporia, we can see his account needs to satisfy: he shows how, though not actually destroyed in the mixture, the ingredients are in fact altered, so that they are not in all respects the same as they were before being combined together in the mixture. This is the passage I want to focus on.

But, third, before presenting this second part of his theory, Aristotle first deals (327^{b}31–328^{a}17) with a second *aporêma* or difficult point, connected to or following on from (συνεχές, 327^{b}32) the preceding one. The preceding one concerned the non-destruction of the ingredients. The point of this second difficulty is, it seems, to propose an alternative response to the one Aristotle has just offered (via the distinction between being something actually and being it potentially) to the demand that in a mixture the ingredients not be destroyed. So, before proceeding to the second part of his own theory, Aristotle wishes to show that this alterna-tive is unacceptable. Thus, he can say, only his theory can acceptably satisfy this demand. We ourselves need to consider closely what Aristotle says against this alternative, before proceeding to examine the second part of his theory.

On the alternative suggestion the ingredients remain fully actual in the mixture (and are not, after all, altered in any way from what they were when separate): what constitutes their being *mixed* is the additional fact that the ingredients, having been divided into small bits (and not des-troyed), have then been distributed so that the bits of the one are among the bits of the other in such a way that neither of the ingredients is

John M. Cooper

perceptible. The model here is grains of barley and wheat distributed among one another in some pile so that the pile doesn't look or taste like a pile of either barley or wheat.[3] The stuff looks, tastes, etc. throughout like a single, new, and different kind of stuff, neither barley nor wheat. Or rather, Aristotle adds, we must impose as a further condition that the distribution of the bits should be made in such a way that any bit ($\mu \acute{o} \rho \iota o \nu$, 328[a]1, 9–10) of the one ingredient should actually be alongside a bit of the other ($\acute{o} \tau \iota o \hat{\upsilon} \nu \ \pi \alpha \rho' \ \acute{o} \tau \iota o \hat{\upsilon} \nu$, 328[a]4–5).[4] The motivation for this further requirement is clear enough. The simpler initial suggestion could be satisfied even if there were some bunching of bits (grains) of one or other of the ingredients, provided only that this did not produce a visible or otherwise perceptible irregularity in the overall expanse; yet it is counter-intuitive to count such a case as one of thorough mixture, when, as would be so on that suggestion, a more thoroughly even distribution of the bits could be achieved. As Aristotle indeed immediately reminds us (328[a]2–3), appealing to what we would ordinarily say was really a mixture of barley grains and wheat grains, we do intuitively

---

[3] See 328[a]2–3. I take $\check{\epsilon} \kappa \alpha \sigma \tau o \nu$ at 327[b]35 to mean not 'each of the bits' (so Williams in his translation, and also Joachim in his note to 327[b]33–5 (1922:183)), but 'each of the ingredients', i.e. each of the $\mu \iota \gamma \nu \acute{\upsilon} \mu \epsilon \nu \alpha$ just referred to ([b]34). This is not only the more natural way of taking the Greek, it is also the only way of taking it that really makes sense of the proposal. No one would think you had a *mixture* of, say, water and wine, if upon surveying the putative mixture you could see or otherwise perceive (for example in different parts of it) any of the water or the wine in it—i.e. if what you were presented with had the full perceived character, in at least some parts of it, of one or the other of the separate ingredients. The relevant point is not that you must not see any bits that it has, but that you must not see the ingredient stuffs themselves. It's all right, according to this proposal, and reasonable enough in itself, that you should see that the stuff you are presented with is grainy and consists of assembled bits, just so long as the physical appearance is nowhere that of a lot of bits of the one ingredient or a lot of the other, as opposed to that of a uniform mass however grainy and however composed of bits.

[4] Following Christian Wildberg's suggestion in his Princeton seminar, April 1999, I read the MS text at 328[a]1 without Joachim's addition of $<\acute{o} \tau \epsilon>$, and interpret as follows, drawing the elliptical material in the interposed bracket from 327[b]33–5, immediately preceding: $\mathring{\eta} \ o \mathring{\upsilon}, \ \mathring{\alpha} \lambda \lambda' \ \check{\epsilon} \sigma \tau \iota \nu \ (\mu \acute{\iota} \xi \iota \varsigma \ \acute{o} \tau \alpha \nu \ o \mathring{\upsilon} \tau \omega \varsigma \ \epsilon \mathring{\iota} \varsigma \ \mu \iota \kappa \rho \grave{\alpha} \ \delta \iota \alpha \iota \rho \epsilon \theta \hat{\eta} \ldots \tau \hat{\eta} \ \alpha \mathring{\iota} \sigma \theta \acute{\eta} \sigma \epsilon \iota) \ \mathring{\omega} \sigma \tau \epsilon \ \acute{o} \tau \iota o \hat{\upsilon} \nu \ldots$ ('Or, rather, there is mixture if the ingredients being mixed together have been so divided into small bits and placed among one another in this way, so that each ingredient is not obvious to perception, [and] so that any bit you like of [one of] the things that have been mixed is alongside a bit [of the other].'). This makes good sense of the connection between the first and the second, corrected, suggestion, and it is acceptable in Aristotelian elliptical Greek for the ellipsis to be the whole of the relevant preceding text, as I propose. An alternative way of filling the ellipsis would be to take only the text from $\acute{o} \tau \alpha \nu$ to $\tau \rho \acute{o} \pi o \nu$, thus treating $\mathring{\omega} \sigma \tau \epsilon \ \acute{o} \tau \iota o \hat{\upsilon} \nu \ldots$ as a *substitute* for the previous $\mathring{\omega} \sigma \tau \epsilon$ clause. But in that case the second suggestion would not include the thought that it is crucial to mixture that the result should not allow us to perceive the separate ingredients anywhere across its extent; and in introducing this whole 'difficulty' at 327[b]32–3 Aristotle seems clearly to envisage that all the suggestions to be considered will be ones according to which 'mixture is something relative to perception'.

require, if something is to count as a mixture of bits of two sorts, that the bits be perfectly evenly distributed.[5]

Before considering Aristotle's response to this suggestion (or these two suggestions, one weaker, the other stronger), I should point out that the interpretation I have proposed avoids the premature and confusing introduction into Aristotle's discussion here of ideas drawn from ancient atomism about how mixtures might be understood, which commentators beginning with Philoponus have regularly indulged in.[6] The suggestion Aristotle introduces here, in either of its versions, owes nothing to the idea of a division of apparently uniform, continuous stuffs into tiny indivisible and invisible corpuscles not possessed of any perceptible qualities whatsoever (apart from solidity, if that would count as perceptible in the relevant sense). On the contrary, his concern is with much more commonsensical ideas. His central thought is that in a mixture one ought not to be able to see or otherwise perceive the ingredients, but the whole should have its own distinct, uniform character. Ordinary division into ordinary bits is what he has in mind—not theoretical division into atoms.[7]

What, then, does Aristotle have to say against this alternative? The sponsors of the suggestion are depicted as accepting (328^a4) that the ingredients that go into a mixture must be like-parted. In his reply Aristotle introduces the further claim ('but *we* say', $328^a10–11$) that the same is true of the resultant mixture: in both cases, all the parts must be like the parts of water, on the common-sense view of the latter and on Aristotle's own conception of it as a uniform material continuum. So the

---

[5] Thus I take ἐκείνως in 328^a2 to refer back (as would be normal in contexts like this) to the simpler proposal (at $327^b33–5$): Aristotle is saying that we *do* say that barley and wheat grains have been mixed when the bits of the two sorts have been distributed among one another so that you cannot see wheat or barley anywhere (it nowhere looks like a pile of wheat or of barley grains, but has the uniform look of a different sort of pile altogether), but only provided that the grains are perfectly evenly distributed (i.e. when everywhere one grain of barley is next to one grain of wheat). (It is no obstacle to this interpretation that on Aristotle's own view of what counts as a mixture solids like grains of wheat and barley cannot mix at all. He is speaking here simply of how we ordinarily speak; and we do speak of a mixture of grains under the conditions and with the restrictions he specifies.)

[6] See Philoponus, *in GC* 193. 1–9. See also Joachim and Williams ad loc. Philoponus' commentary is available in English translation by C.J.F. Williams (1999). For Philoponus' interpretation of mixture see de Haas (1999).

[7] Here I have learned from Wildberg's account in his seminar (see n. 4 above). Wildberg pointed out that if, as Joachim thinks, Aristotle in the stronger of the two proposals is discussing atomist division into bits, he must be very confused when he introduces as part of his exposition of the proposal (328^a4) the assumption that when bodies are mixed with one another each is like-parted: obviously, the atoms of any body, which are its ultimate parts on atomic theory, are not of the same character as the whole, nor as parts of the whole that are themselves conglomerates of atoms.

parts into which a mixture could be divided could not include any bits
consisting simply of one of the ingredients, since such a part would differ
in its qualities from at least some other parts of the same mixture (ones
coming from the other ingredient): because a mixture is a like-parted
stuff, each part has to be like every other part of that mixture, Aristotle
insists. You could certainly have a combination or collection of such
differing parts (a σύνθεσις, 328ª6, 8), which could give rise to a mass with
perceptual characteristics of its own, different from those of either ingredient, but that would not be a mixture or blend. This response applies
equally well to both the weaker and the stronger of the two versions of
the current suggestion, since it addresses the aspect of the overall view
that both have in common: that non-perceptibility of the ingredients is
sufficient to make a collection of intermingled bits of the ingredients into
a mixture of the ingredients.

Aristotle adds an independent objection specially tailored for the
stronger version alone. On that suggestion we were imagining any bit
of the one ingredient as being alongside a corresponding bit of the other.
He now points out (328ª15–17) that in fact that is in any case strictly
impossible, since (as he has argued elsewhere) matter is indefinitely
divisible: the smallest bit, however small, of an ingredient stuff is divisible
into further parts, and such parts of an undivided bit, when in the
mixture, are adjacent to (alongside) not any parts of another ingredient
but ones of the same ingredient of which they too are parts. You will in
principle never reach a point in the analysis of an ingredient into its parts
where *all* its parts ever could be aligned in the proposed way with the
parts of another ingredient. Some parts will still remain inside undivided
bits and so alongside their congeners, not alongside bits of another
ingredient.

So much, then, for a summary of Aristotle's response to this alternative suggestion about how to understand the survival of the ingredients
within a mixture. Against both versions he has insisted that any mixture,
properly and narrowly speaking, is itself a like-parted stuff (so that the
model of the ingredients as like grains of barley shuffled through grains
of wheat does not apply, even if that were effected in such a way that the
whole had new and distinctive perceptual properties of its own: such
parts could not be parts *of a mixture*). And he has added that the stronger
version's idea that the parts of the ingredients are aligned alongside each
other on a one-to-one basis is an impossibility. Now in both versions we
are presented with stuffs which as ingredients retain their original natures
as separated stuffs, fully realized: the 'bits' are like grains of wheat and
barley which all have the full nature of those kinds of material. But notice
that the objection added against the stronger version clearly carries over
also to stuffs formed from ingredients that in the new substance do not

retain their full natures, but only, as on Aristotle's theory, some diminished or 'restrained' version of those. In that case, too, it cannot be that in the mixture all the bits of the materials coming from any one of the ingredients are aligned alongside bits coming from the others. Because of indefinite divisibility and like-partedness, there will always be parts of the new substance that came not from a different source ingredient from that of their immediate neighbours but from the same ingredient.

Let us turn now to the second part of Aristotle's own theory of mixture ($328^a17^{-b}22$). Here, as I have said, he explains how it is that in being combined in the mixture the ingredients come to be altered in their perceptible properties (while somehow retaining their identities as distinct ingredients). Aristotle's central idea is the following. Sometimes, of two materials which are each easily divisible into their constituent parts, one overpowers the other through the action of its larger number of larger parts, so that, by acting on the fewer and smaller parts of the latter, it converts the other to its own nature (328^a23–8). Thus a large fire converts a smaller quantity of wood to fire—the overpowering fire consumes the wood, growing larger through the addition to itself of the wood's substance (328^a23–6).[8] This is a case not of the alteration of materials that continue to exist but rather of the destruction of one material, the wood, so as to increase the other by generating additional amounts of the latter. However, when two such materials are more or less equalized in their powers (ὅταν δὲ ταῖς δυνάμεσιν ἰσάζῃ πως, 328^a28–9), then each makes the other shift in its qualities *toward* the one acting on it,[9] but neither converts the other to its own condition; instead, they jointly come to an intermediate state in common that differs from that of each of the agents themselves, as they were when the process began (328^a28–31). Thus each of the ingredients comes to possess exactly the same perceptible qualities as the other then possesses, as a result of the mutual and equal action-on and being-acted-upon-by each other, a process which brings them into a common equilibrium state.[10] Thus,

---

[8] Aristotle's own example is a drop of wine poured into thousands of measures of water. On fire and wood see 327^b10–13.

[9] See 328^a29–30; I accept the MS reading εἰς τὸ κρατοῦν in $^a30$, and interpret it as meaning not the resulting stuff (= what 'predominates' precisely by being the result), but rather the one ingredient that is acting upon the other. In this case it is true that the acting ingredient does not completely 'overpower' the other one and so convert it into the same kind of stuff as itself (which is the sense of the verb κρατεῖν e.g. at $^a26$), but it does force the latter to lose its 'extremeness' and move towards the agent's own quality.

[10] Aristotle points out that this happens mostly with liquid stuffs, or stuffs in a liquefied state, because they are in fact the ones that can be most easily divided into small parts and thus can act and be acted upon in the way indicated (328^a35–$^b4$). I leave aside such further details of his account.

allegedly, as we have seen, the ingredients survive in the mixture while nonetheless having been altered in their perceptible characteristics of colour, temperature, consistency, etc.—and having been altered in such a way that each of them then shares exactly the same such characteristics as the others. The effect is that what was earth, say, now comes to have just the same perceptible characteristics as the fire, and/or the air or the water, that it has been mixed with also come to have. These characteristics are in fact the distinctive characteristics of the specific mixture—flesh, say, or sugar-water—that has resulted from this particular interaction.

As I have indicated, Aristotle speaks here of the materials that can undergo this joint mixture as ones that are easily divided into their parts while the parts remain marked off as separate bits, and that can therefore, by the many contacts with one another that such division makes possible, easily act on and be acted upon by one another (328^a35–$^b4$). His implication is that large and undivided quantities of stuffs cannot mix with one another, or not easily, whereas such easily divided ones can. With many places of contact, the necessary pervasive mutual action and affection, leading to the common and intermediate qualitative characterization that constitutes the mixture, is made possible.[11]

Notice that Aristotle maintains that for a mixture to take place the ingredients must first divide each other into bits—small coherent masses of the same nature as the wholes. Then the small bits act on one another, each causing the other to shift in its perceptual characteristics of hotness-coldness and wetness-dryness so that they reach a new, common position on those scales. So his theory involves the inclusion in the mixture of bits of the ingredients, just as was the case on the rejected alternatives discussed in 327^b32–328^a17. The important difference is that on his theory, but not on the alternatives, the bits do not remain possessed in full actuality of the defining perceptual qualities of the ingredients from which they came: they *each* shift, in the way we have seen, so that they lose those qualities which mark them off from one another and *each* gets in replacement a *common* new set of qualities that constitute the nature of the new substance itself. Hence the new substance comes out like-parted, as Aristotle insisted against the alternatives it had to do. Each of its parts comes to be characterized by the same set of new perceptual properties, those belonging to the whole as well. This applies to each of the interacting bits of the different ingredients from which it was constituted. For Aristotle's argument against the stronger version of the alternative view applies also to his own bits: it cannot be that *every* bit of the new substance that comes from one ingredient is alongside a set of bits

---

[11] See *GC* I. 6. 322^b25–9, on the necessity of contact for action and passion.

coming from the others. And it is easy to see from his description of how the process of mutual 'assimilation' of the bits of the ingredients works that his theory respects this requirement. Aristotle requires each finitely small bit of one ingredient to act on an adjacent finitely small bit of another ingredient *throughout* each of the small bits in question. By acting at the points of contact along the common border, each of the two contacting bits is assumed to be able to have its effects not just there, along that surface, but (given the unified condition of each of the bits) back into and all the way through the bit that it is acting upon.

Thus Aristotle's theory denies, and his basic ideas are incompatible with, a complete interfusion of *all* the potentially infinitely many bits of the two ingredients as they engage in this process of mutual action and passion. And Aristotle's theory of how mixture comes about not only does not imply but in fact denies that the ingredients interpenetrate one another in such a way that any quantity of the resultant mixture has the same composition, in terms of the ingredients and their ratios to one another, as the whole mixture. Some parts (those deriving from the interacting bits of the ingredients) come from only a single ingredient and do not consist of some of each of the ingredients in potential form. Aristotle asserts that all the expanses of the resulting mixture have the same perceptible characteristics, but, since he also claims that this results from the mutual interaction of finitely small bits of the separate ingredients acting on one another and converting each other into the same set of common characteristics, he implies that some expanses (small ones, no doubt, corresponding to the small size of the interacting bits) will come to have those common characteristics because they began as bits of one ingredient, others will similarly come to have the same characteristics because they began as bits of another. In that case, although the whole resultant mixture will be completely uniform in its perceptual characteristics, this would be the result of a lot of separate bits of distinct ingredients coming to have those characteristics—and many parts of the like-parted mixture would not have in them, even in potential form, anything but the one ingredient from which they were produced by the mutual alteration that Aristotle's theory describes.

Thus Aristotle's theory in *GC* I. 10 of how mixtures are created denies that each expanse within a mixture (however small, and all the way down through its potentially infinite divisions) must have originated from, and so preserve within it in potential form, a proportion of each of the ingredients of the mixture of which it is a part, equal to the proportion within the total mixture of those ingredients. His theory denies that when a mixture takes place the ingredients are totally interfused with one another.

Nonetheless, as I began this note by saying, commentators at least since Philoponus often attribute to Aristotle this 'total interfusion' view of the ingredients in mixtures. Now in II. 8 Aristotle states and argues at length for the thesis ($334^{b}31$–2) that 'all the mixed bodies are put together from all the simple ones'—that is, that every compound material (animal flesh and blood, tree bark, plant stems, rocks, veins of copper, etc. etc.) is made of all four of the simple bodies. Each compound has in it (of course, in merely potential form) some earth, some air, some fire, and some water (in differing proportions, of course). In beginning his commentary on II. 8 Philoponus paraphrases this thesis as follows: 'from every part of compounds, such as flesh, every element is [i.e. can be] separated out'.[12] That is, Philoponus interprets Aristotle as holding here that every part of flesh, however small, comes from and has in it some of *each* of the simple bodies. But is that in fact Aristotle's thesis in this chapter? Aristotle seems to be envisaging whole, self-contained masses of these bodies—the flesh of my arm, the wood of a given tree, and so on. As we have seen, in his theory in I. 10 of how mixtures take place Aristotle does of course assume that each of the ingredients will be preserved in certain proportions in the whole mass of any such self-contained mixture. But how about very small quantities within such self-contained mixtures? Does Aristotle's thesis here maintain about them too that they all have to have all four ingredients within them in Aristotle's potential way? If not, then what Aristotle says here would not contradict his theory in I. 10. So when he says 'all the mixed bodies are put together from all the simple ones' perhaps he only means to refer to

---

[12] *In GC* 278. 7–8. Philoponus claims that Aristotle has assumed this thesis, so paraphrased, in his refutations of the views of 'those who hold that the elements don't change into one another' (i.e. Empedocles), so that he is now, quite reasonably, going to give his arguments to establish something on which he has relied previously. I find no place where this is in fact so; certainly the argument of I. 10. $328^{a}5$–17 (discussed above), which seems to be one of the places Philoponus must be referring to (even though in his comments there he does not mention Empedocles as one of Aristotle's opponents), does not rely on any such assumption. Indeed, as I have shown, it directly contradicts it. In his commentary on I. 10 Joachim slips quite casually into describing Aristotle's theory in these terms, without ever formally addressing the issue. Commenting on $328^{a}9$–10 he says: 'since the compound is ὁμοιομερές, the constituents must be present in the same proportions in every part of it as in the whole'. (Compare Williams in his comment at $327^{b}31$, offering to explicate what it means to say that a mixture is a like-parted stuff: 'If the mixture as a whole is 55% B and 45% C each part must similarly be 55% B and 45% C: i.e., however small the parts into which you divide and subdivide A (the mixture), they will all be mixtures of B and C in this same ratio.' I have shown above, pp. 315–16, that this is a mistake; the like-partedness of compounds definitely does not have this implication.) And at $327^{b}33$–$328^{a}17$, explaining Aristotle's objections to the alternative views on mixture he there discusses, Joachim says: 'According to both of them, μίξις is a mechanical mixing or shuffle, and not an interpenetration or a fusion, of the constituents'—as, he implies, with suitable qualifications, Aristotle makes it.

such self-contained instances—without specifically thinking of all their parts. On a strict interpretation, of course, the smallest bit of my flesh, on Aristotle's theory, *is* flesh, just as much as is all the flesh in my arm, taken together; so, strictly interpreted, as Philoponus interprets it, the thesis that 'all the mixed bodies are put together from all the simple ones' would imply or state that the smallest bit of my flesh is put together from all the simple bodies. But does Aristotle wish to be interpreted in that strict way when he states this thesis?

One of Aristotle's arguments for his thesis in II. 8 might be thought to imply the stricter application. Aristotle claims (335^a1–2) that without water in it something made from earth, as all the compounds including flesh must be, would crumble and fall apart. It may seem that this ought to apply equally to any and every quantity of flesh—whether or not it is large enough to stand on its own as a self-contained expanse of flesh. You can't have your flesh crumbling apart even in very small volumes inside your arm or leg. So if, in general, flesh has to be composed of both earth and water in order not to crumble apart, then any bit of flesh, however small, must likewise be composed of both these ingredients— and, by extension, of all four. But perhaps we shouldn't fear that a small bit of flesh that did not derive from any water, but only from some earth, and was deeply imbedded in an expanse of flesh where there *was* lots of water, would fall apart. Maybe this fear would only be justified in relation to large quantities. So it is not so clear, after all, that this argument does require us to put the stricter construal on the thesis. The same applies, I think, to the other arguments, too. It seems to me, therefore, an open question whether Aristotle's thesis in II. 8 ought to be taken in the strict or the looser way. Only if it is taken in the strict way will a contradiction arise between II. 8 and I. 10, and only if it is so taken will Aristotle be committed in II. 8 to a theory of total interfusion of the earth, air, fire, and water that make up any compound body. The charitable interpretation, therefore, will take the thesis of II. 8 in the looser way.

Despite the tenuous evidence, I suspect that commentators are so quick to attribute the total-interfusion view to Aristotle because in interpreting him they have their eye surreptitiously on the Stoic doctrine of mixture of Chrysippus. According to the Stoics a mixture contains within itself in fully actualized form all of its ingredients.[13] The ingredients are spread through one another so that everywhere in the mixture we would find, on analysis, each of them fully present. In a water-wine mixture both water and wine are everywhere to be found. On this theory

---

[13] See the texts collected in A. A. Long and D. N. Sedley, *The Hellenistic Philosophers* (Cambridge, 1987), ch. 48.

there is a total interfusion of the ingredients, while they retain their full actualities. Now this theory obviously faces the formidable difficulty of explaining how two or more ingredient bodies can be in all the same places at the same time. Aristotle's theory can seem to suggest the possibility of finessing this difficulty in a subtle and satisfying way: on his view, the distinct bodies (the ingredients) are not present in their full and actual condition, but only in some submerged or diminished, potential form. On that view, it would be possible to maintain, with the Stoics, that everywhere within wine-water there is both wine and water—so there is total interfusion—but these ingredients are present not in their actualities but only in some sort of potential form. The objections against the Stoic view thus fall by the wayside. It is perhaps this thought that has led commentators to find it so natural to understand Aristotle's theory in this way. However, it is well worth noting that this is not how Alexander of Aphrodisias seems to have interpreted it. So far as I can see, in the exposition of Aristotle's view in his *On Mixture* XIII–XV Alexander nowhere supposes that Aristotle's theory does involve total interfusion. Since his treatise is aimed at criticizing and rejecting the Stoic theory, in favour of the Aristotelian one, he could hardly have failed to emphasize clearly the salutary difference between interfusion of potentially existing and actually existing ingredients, if he had thought of Aristotle's theory in those terms. Alexander's exposition coheres with my own interpretation, according to which interfusion, in whatever form or condition, is no part of Aristotle's view.[14]

Still, as I have granted, it may be that Aristotle does in the end (in II. 8) commit himself to the total interfusion view of the composition of mixtures. If so, however, it is important to see that he does not show at all how to reconcile this idea with his account in I. 10 of how the ingredients of a mixture can act on one another so as to produce the uniform stuff that results and that constitutes the given mixture. There, as we saw, he envisages a resultant that would as a whole have all of both or all of the ingredients within it somehow potentially, but in such a way that small volumes of its total mass would not.

---

[14] See esp. *Mixt.* 231. 12–22, where Alexander discusses the role of small bits of the ingredients in effectuating their mixing. He says nothing at all there to suggest that he thinks the ingredients become totally interfused.

REFERENCES

ARISTOTLE: EDITIONS, TRANSLATIONS, AND COMMENTARIES

ACKRILL, J. L. (1963), *Aristotle, Categories and De Interpretation* (Oxford).

ALEXANDER OF APHRODISIAS (1892), *De Mixtione et Augmentatione*, ed. I. Bruns *Scripta Minora*, Suppl. Aristotelicum, II/ii, ed. I. Bruns (Berlin).

BARNES, J. (1984) (ed.), *The Complete Works of Aristotle* (Princeton, NJ).

BEKKER, J. (1831), *Aristotelis Opera* (Berlin).

BONITZ, H., (1849), *Aristotelis Metaphysica: Commentarius* (Bonn, repr. Hildesheim 1960).

CHARLTON, W. (1970), *Aristotle: Physics Books I and II* (Oxford).

DORION, L. A. (1995), *Aristote: Les réfutations sophistiques* (Paris, Quebec).

FORSTER, E. S. (1955), *Aristotle: On Sophistical Refutations, On Coming-To-Be and Passing Away,* LCL (London, Cambridge, Mass.).

FREDE, M., and PATZIG, G. (1988), *Aristoteles: 'Metaphysik Z', Text Übersetzung und Kommentar*, 2 vols. (München).

GOHLKE, P. (1958), *Aristoteles: Die Lehrschriften, iv. Vom Werden und Vergehen* (Paderborn).

HUSSEY, E. L. (1983), *Aristotle's Physics Books III and IV* (Oxford).

GUTHRIE, W. K. C. (1939), *Aristotle: On the Heavens*, LCL (London, Cambridge, Mass.).

JAEGER, W. (1957), *Aristotelis Metaphysica* recognovit brevique adnotatione critica instruxit, OCT (Oxford).

JOACHIM, H. H. (1922), *Aristotle: On Coming-To-Be and Passing-Away (De Generatione et Corruptione)*: A Revised Text with Introduction and Commentary (Oxford, repr. Hildesheim, New York, 1970; special edn. for Sandpiper Books, 1999).

LEE, H. D. P. (1952), *Aristotle: Meteorologica*, LCL (London, Cambridge, Mass.).

LOUIS, P. (1982), *Aristote: Météorologiques*, Coll. Budé (Paris).

MIGLIORI, M. (1976), *Aristotele: La generazione e la corruzione*: traduzione, introduzione e commento (Naples).

MUGLER, CH. (1966), *Aristote: De la génération et de la corruption*, Coll. Budé (Paris).

PELLEGRIN, P. (2000), *Aristote: Physique, traduction et présentation* (Paris).

PEPE, L. (1982) *Aristotele: Meteorologica* (Naples).

PHILOPONUS (1897), *In Aristotelis libros De generatione et corruptione commentaria,* ed. H. Vitelli (Berlin). (For a translation see Williams (1999).)

PRANTL, C. (1857), *Aristoteles: Vier Bücher über das Himmelsgebaüde und zwei Bücher über Entstehen und Vergehen* (Leipzig).

Ross, W. D. (1936), *Aristotle's Physics*: A Revised Text with Introduction and Commentary (Oxford).

——(1953), *Aristotle's Metaphysics*: *A Revised Text with Introduction and Commentary*, 2 vols. (Oxford 1924; 2nd edn. 1953).

Spiazzi, R. M. (1952), *Thomas Aquinas: In Aristotelis Libros De Caelo et Mundo, De Generatione et Corruptione, Meteorologicorum Expositio* (Torino).

Thomas Aquinas *see* Spiazzi

Tricot, J. (1951), *Aristote: De la génération et de la corruption* (Paris).

——(1955), *Aristote: Les Météorologiques*, 2nd edn. (Paris).

Verdenius, W. J., and Waszink, J. H. (1968), *Aristotle On Coming-to-be and Passing-away*, 2nd edn. (Leiden).

Williams, C. J. F. (1982), *Aristotle's De Generatione et Corruptione*, trans. with notes (Oxford).

——(1999), *Philoponus: On Aristotle On Coming-to-Be and Perishing*, 2 vols.; vol. 1: 1. 1–5, vol. 2: 1. 6–2.4 (London).

Zanatta, M. (1999), *Fisica di Aristotele* (Torino).

Zabarella, Iacobus (1602), *Commentarii in . . . Aristotelis libros Physicorum, item in libros De generatione et corruptione, item in Meteora . . . De Augmentatione et Putrefactione . . .* (Frankfurt).

SECONDARY LITERATURE

Algra, K. A. (1995), *Concepts of Space in Greek Thought* (Leiden).

Barbone, S. (1992), 'Are there Discrepancies between Aristotle's *Generation and Corruption II* and *Meteorology IV*', *Dialogue* 35, 7–13.

Barnes, J. (1979), *The Presocratic Philosophers*, 2 vols. (London).

——(1997), 'Roman Aristotle', in J. Barnes and M. Griffin (eds.), *Philosophia Togata II* (Oxford), 1–69.

Bemelmans, R. (1995), *Materia prima in Aristoteles: een hardnekkig misverstand*, Ph.D. diss. (University of Leiden).

Bogen, J. (1995), 'Fire in the Belly: Aristotelian Elements, Organisms, and Chemical Compounds', *Pacific Philosophical Quarterly*, 76, 370–404.

Bonitz, H. (1870), *Index Aristotelicus* (Berlin).

Bos, A. P. (1973), *On the Elements. Aristotle's Early Cosmology* (Assen).

Bostock, D. (1988), 'Time and the continuum: A Discussion of Richard Sorabji, *Time, Creation and the Continuum*', *OSAP* 6: 255–70.

——(1995), 'Aristotle on the Transmutation of Elements in *De generatione et corruptione* 1.1–4', *OSAP* 13: 217–29.

Broadie, S. (1993), 'Que fait le premier moteur d'Aristote? (Sur la théologie du livre Lambda de la "Metaphysique")', *Revue philosophique de la France et d'etranger* 183: 375–411.

Brunschwig, J. (1991), 'Qu'est-ce que la *Physique* d'Aristote?', in F. De Gandt and P. Souffrin (eds.), *La Physique d'Aristote et les conditions d'une science de la nature* (Paris), 11–40.

BURNET, J. (1930), *Early Greek Philosophy*, 4th edn. (London).

BURNYEAT, M. F. (2001), *A Map of Metaphysics Zeta* (Pittsburg).

——(2002), 'De Anima II 5', *Phronesis*, 47: 28–90.

CAPELLE, W. (1912), 'Das Proömium der Meteorologie', *Hermes*, 47: 514–35.

CHARLTON, W. (1991), 'Aristotle's Potential Infinites', in L. Judson (ed.), *Aristotle's Physics* (Oxford), 129–49.

CODE, A. (1976), 'The Persistence of Aristotelian Matter', *Philosophical Studies*, 29: 357–67.

——(1995), 'Potentiality in Aristotle's Science and Metaphysics', *Pacific Philosophical Quarterly* 76, 405–18.

COOPER, J. M. (1988), 'Metaphysics in Aristotle's Embryology', *Proceedings of the Cambridge Philological Society*, 34: 14–41.

DE HAAS, F. A. J. (1999), 'Mixture in Philoponus: An Encounter with a Third Kind of Potentiality', in J. M. M. H. Thijssen and H. A. G. Braakhuis (eds.), *The Commentary Tradition on De generatione et corruptione: Ancient, Medieval and Early Modern* (Turnhout), 21–46.

DENNISTON, J. D. (1934), *The Greek Particles* (Oxford).

FINE, K. (1995), 'The Problem of Mixture', *Pacific Philosophical Quarterly*, 76: 266–369.

——(1996), 'The Problem of Mixture', in Lewis and Bolton (1996), 82–182.

FURLEY, D. J. (1967), *Two Studies in the Greek Atomists* (Princeton, NJ).

——(1985), 'Strato's Theory of the Void', in J. Wiesner (ed.), *Aristoteles: Werk und Wirkung*, i (Berlin), 595–609.

GERMAIN, P. (1954), 'L'Étude des éléments dans le *De caelo* et dans le *De generatione et corruptione*', *LThPh* 10: 67–78.

GERSHENSON, D. E. and GREENBERG, D. A. (1964), *Anaxagoras and the Birth of Physics* (New York, London, Toronto).

GILL, M. L. (1989), *Aristotle on Substance: The Paradox of Unity* (Princeton, NJ).

GRAHAM, D. W. (1987), 'The Paradox of Prime Matter', *JHPh* 25: 475–90.

JOACHIM, H. H. (1904), 'Aristotle's Conception of Chemical Combination', *Journal of Philology* 29, 72–86.

JUDSON, L. (1994), 'Heavenly Motion and the Unmoved Mover', in M. L. Gill and J. G. Lennox (eds.), *Self-Motion* (Princeton, NJ), 155–71.

KING, H. R. (1956), 'Aristotle without *prima materia*', *JHI* 17: 370–89.

LAKS, A. (2000), '*Metaphysics Λ 7*', in M. Frede and D. Charles (eds.), *Aristotle's* Metaphysics *Lambda* (Oxford), 238–43.

LEWIS, F. and BOLTON, R. (1996), *Form, Matter, and Mixture in Aristotle* (Oxford, Malden).

LURIA, S. (1933), 'Die Infinitesimallehre der antiken Atomisten', *Quellen und Studien zur Geschichte der Mathematik, Astronomie und Physik*, 2: 106–85.

MAKIN, S. (1989), 'The Indivisibility of the Atom', *AGPh* 71: 125–49.

——(1993), *Indifference Arguments* (Oxford).

MANSFELD, J. (2002), 'Aëtius, Aristotle and Others on Coming to Be and Passing Away', in V. Caston and D. W. Graham (eds.), *Presocratic Philosophy: Essays in Honour of Alexander Mourelatos* (Aldershot), 273–92.

MARTIN, A., and PRIMAVESI, O. (1998), *L'Empédocle de Strasbourg* (Strasbourg, Berlin, New York).

MAU, J. (1954), *Zum Problem des Infinitesimalen bei den antiken Atomisten* (Berlin).

MORAUX, P. (1951), *Les Listes anciennes des ouvrages d'Aristote* (Louvain).

NETZ, R. (1999), *The Shaping of Deduction in Greek Mathematics* (Cambridge).

ROBINSON, H. M. (1974), 'Prime matter in Aristotle', *Phronesis*, 19: 168–88.

SCHOFIELD, M. (1972), '*Metaph. Z* 3: Some Suggestions', *Phronesis*, 17: 97–101.

SEDLEY, D. J. (2002), 'The Origins of Stoic god', in D. Frede and A. Laks (eds.), *Traditions of Theology* (Leiden), 41–83.

SOLMSEN, F. (1958), 'Aristotle and Prime Matter: A Reply to Hugh R. King', *Journal of the History of Ideas*, 19: 243–52, repr. in *Kleine Schriften* (Hildesheim, 1968), i. 397–406.

——(1960), *Aristotle's System of the Physical World* (Ithaca, NY).

SORABJI, R. (1972), 'Aristotle, Mathematics, and Colour', *CQ* 22: 293–308.

——(1983), *Time, Creation and the Continuum* (London).

——(1988), *Matter, Space and Motion* (London).

TAYLOR, C. C. W. (1999), *The Atomists: Leucippus and Democritus* (Toronto).

VAN DER BEN, N. (1978), 'Empedocles Fragments 8, 9, 10 DK', *Phronesis*, 23: 197–215.

VUILLEMIN-DIEM, G., and RASHED, M. (1997), 'Burgundio de Pise et ses manuscrits grecs d'Aristote: Laur. 87. 7 et 81. 18', *Recherches de Théologie et Philosophie médiévales* 64: 136–98.

WEST, M. L. (1969), 'An atomist illustration in Aristotle', *Philologus*, 113: 150–1.

WIELAND, W. (1962), *Die aristotelische Physik* (Göttingen).

ZELLER, E., and MONDOLFO, R. (1969), *La filosofia dei Greci nel suo sviluppo storico* I 5, con nuovi aggiornamenti a cura di A. Capizzi (Firenze).

INDEX LOCORUM POTIORUM

INDEX NOMINUM ET RERUM*

* The editors are grateful to Anne van Zilfhout (Leiden) for her assistance in compiling this index.

Moderni